PRISONS around the world

Studies in International Penology

Michael K. Carlie and Kevin I. Minor

Southwest Missouri State University

WCB Wm. C. Brown Publishers

This book is dedicated to my parents, Milton and Bess Carlie, who ultimately and with great generosity made this endeavor possible.
Michael Kaye Carlie

This book is dedicated to Marsha, Kevin Nicholas, and my parents.
Kevin I. Minor

Book Team

Editor *Ed Laube*
Developmental Editor *Sue Pulvermacher-Alt*
Production Coordinator *Deborah Donner*

WCB Wm. C. Brown Publishers

President *G. Franklin Lewis*
Vice President, Publisher *Thomas E. Doran*
Vice President, Operations and Production *Beverly Kolz*
National Sales Manager *Virginia S. Moffat*
Group Sales Manager *John Finn*
Executive Editor *Edgar J. Laube*
Senior Marketing Manager *Kathy Law Laube*
Managing Editor, Production *Colleen A. Yonda*
Manager of Visuals and Design *Faye M. Schilling*
Production Editorial Manager *Julie A. Kennedy*
Production Editorial Manager *Ann Fuerste*
Publishing Services Manager *Karen J. Slaught*

WCB Group

President and Chief Executive Officer *Mark C. Falb*
Chairman of the Board *Wm. C. Brown*

Cover design by Jeanne M. Stephens
Copyedited by Kathryn McKay

Library of Congress Catalog Card Number: 91–71537

ISBN 0–697–14310–4

Printed in the United States of America by Wm. C. Brown Publishers, 2460 Kerper Boulevard, Dubuque, IA 52001

10 9 8 7 6 5 4 3 2 1

Contents

Section IV PRISONERS' RIGHTS AND PROTESTS 261

Foreword

When Professors Carlie and Minor approached me about writing this introduction, it happened that I was taking a year's sabbatical, living in the Wimbledon Village section of London. This fortuitous circumstance left me with a profound recognition of the importance of comparative studies in corrections, for living in England and learning about its correctional system has been an eye-opening professional experience. Although *Prisons Around the World* is addressed to an international audience, I want to introduce it by writing as a U.S. citizen.

We Americans are a parochial people. Sometimes, in fact, it is astonishing how little we know about other countries. How many of us can name the leaders of four other nations? Or of our neighbors, Canada and Mexico, for that matter? How many can describe the workings of the government of Japan, or even of the United Kingdom?

There are reasons for our self-centeredness. The United States is a geographical giant, especially compared to Europe, and it contains many major cities of the world: Washington, D.C., New York, Los Angeles, Houston, Atlanta, Miami, Seattle and more, all of which are international cities of multinational importance. Some of our states are larger than many nations, and in some sections of the country, two languages are spoken on the streets. Perhaps it takes a special concentration simply to keep track of our own affairs. We are, after all, a nation that stretches across six time zones and runs from the Arctic Circle nearly to the Equator. There is a lot to know just about our country.

But we lose something by our ignorance of the rest of the world; we become self-absorbed and miss out on opportunities to learn from others. Most significantly, by our insulation, we suffer a diminished capacity to understand ourselves, to see the ways in which our fates are similar to that of others—and to learn of our uniqueness, as well. To use a type of cultural symbolic-interactionism, how else can we really know about ourselves except by knowing about others?

There is much about American corrections that strikes us as important and special. Our massive prison system is composed for the most part of aged and decrepit facilities, and almost all of our institutions seem paralyzed with overcrowding. Volatile race-relations and entrenched urban poverty, the social inheritance of past slavery, produce dominating policy problems of ethnicity in the selection and management of prisoners. Our prisons face ever increasing rates of AIDS-infected inmates.

But on closer inspection, are we so different? From the articles contained in this volume, the reader will recognize that our "unique" difficulties are reproduced, with variations, in other settings. Elsewhere, the correctional physical plant is as outmoded as it is here. We are not the only Anglo nation facing problems of incarcerated ethnic minorities. Our prisons are not the only, or even the most, overcrowded in the world. As our prisoners become ever more persistent in attempts to exercise and expand their rights, they make invisible bonds with their fellow incarcerates who, in other societies and under other laws, strain toward the same basic humanitarian justice. Even AIDS recognizes no national boundaries.

Yet it would be facile to conclude that "corrections is corrections, no matter where you go." Other nations face less difficulty than we in sustaining an ethic of humane correctional methods. Correctional experimentation and reform observed elsewhere are curiously less prevalent in the United States. The law as the foundation for the prison system, and the culture that surrounds it, differs from nation to nation, with important results. Social tolerance for deviance even varies.

We need to study other societies' correctional systems, but we need to do so carefully and with a critical eye. The general body of literature on comparative corrections is thin, both in quality and *quantity*. *If* we are to make effective use of what exists, we must read carefully, with an eye toward the best examples of what is known and what may be learned about corrections.

Professors Carlie and Minor have done the rest of us a tremendous service, for they have assembled a remarkable collection of articles from a broad spectrum of disciplines. Their selections represent an impressive gleaning of the very best studies available. The compilation ably represents the numerous issues and problems of comparative corrections and provides a rich body of lessons to be learned.

Dr. Todd R. Clear
Wimbledon Village
February, 1991

Preface

The world is rapidly becoming a global community and, for this reason, an international perspective is needed in nearly every academic field. The field of institutional corrections is no exception. However, we could not imagine how one author or a small group of authors could gain all the detailed knowledge required to cover more than a few nations' prison systems in a single article, monograph, or standard text. It is for this reason that we decided to create a reader on the subject, wherein the writings of diverse penologists, from diverse nations, are brought together. *Prisons Around the World* is such a reader.

Prisons Around the World has been created to acquaint students and researchers with key issues and problems facing prison systems in select nations throughout the world. By adding an international perspective, the book complements and expands upon existing institutional corrections texts. As of this writing, there is no single source of cross-cultural information on prison systems which is as current, wide-ranging, concise, or, we believe, as exciting as *Prisons Around the World.*

From the over 150 articles published in English that we found during a two-year long search of the literature on international penology, we carefully selected 24 of the most current and outstanding. These readings were chosen and organized to match and enhance the contents of leading introductory corrections texts. Major section headings include an overview of various nations' prison systems, offender rehabilitation and prison problems, issues of policy and management, as well as prisoners' rights and protests.

We have included information on a wide variety of countries and have selected readings which accurately represent the current state of research and knowledge on international penology. The readings and their accompanying discussion questions are designed to stimulate comparison, spark critical thinking and debate, further the search for solutions to penal problems, and highlight exemplary comparative research methodology. Our introductory comments preceding each section are meant to make the readings cohesive and to link the articles to concepts and developments in the broader field of institutional corrections. A glossary of potentially unfamiliar terms (bolded in the text) appears at the end of the book.

In his 1895 book, *The Rules of the Sociological Method,* the famous French scholar Emile Durkheim suggested that comparative, cross-cultural sociology should not be viewed as a specialized area within the field but, instead, should be considered sociology itself. It is with this ideal in mind that *Prisons*

Around the World is offered. We believe that an international perspective can enrich understanding of a given country's prisons and, in particular, can do much to provoke solution-oriented thought about prison problems.

We are indebted to many people for assisting us in the preparation of this book. Special thanks go to the contributors, journal editors, and publishers who allowed us to include their works. We are grateful to the staff of Meyer Library at Southwest Missouri State University, particularly Lynn Freeman, Frances Rottmann, Willa Garrett, and Jeanne Stephens, for their efforts in helping us obtain the necessary literature and for assistance in preparing tables and figures. Financial assistance was graciously provided by the Southwest Missouri State University Office of Graduate Studies and Research. Special thanks are in order for Sharon Walter whose word processing and clerical skills proved invaluable. We express our appreciation to the reviewers whose insights improved our book and also to the staff at Wm. C. Brown Publishing, especially Dorian Ring, Sue Pulvermacher-Alt, and Deborah Donner, for their fine work throughout the project. Finally, the ordering of our names following the title of this book is purely alphabetical. That is, the editors shared equally in the task and joy of creating this reader.

Michael Kaye Carlie and Kevin I. Minor
Springfield, Missouri
August, 1991

AN OVERVIEW OF PRISONS AROUND THE WORLD

section I

Introduction

The five articles comprising this section and the discussion questions that follow the articles are meant to establish the tone for the rest of this volume by encouraging cross-national or comparative thinking about prisons and imprisonment. The articles provide a sampling of the prison policies and issues found in a wide variety of nations. Included is information about imprisonment in Israel, Western Australia, China, Cuba, Finland, Norway, Sweden and, by way of comparison, imprisonment in the U.S. Collectively, the articles provide a diversified and insightful overview of select country's penal systems and philosophies.

In "Corrections in Israel and the United States: A Comparative Analysis," Gad J. Bensinger skillfully highlights the similarities between Israeli and U.S. prisons. These similarities include overcrowding, the lack of a meaningful rehabilitative orientation, and the generally poor state of occupational and educational opportunities for inmates. As might be expected in view of the comparable prison problems, the recidivism rates of the two nations, although difficult to accurately calculate, seem to be quite similar.

"Imprisonment: The Aboriginal Experience in Western Australia," by Richard Midford, provides a fascinating account of what incarceration means for a minority native people whose social system and culture is radically different from the majority Australian culture. The comparative value of this article arises from the interesting parallel which may be drawn from the meaning of imprisonment for members of the "underclass" in the U.S. The link between imprisonment and class oppression becomes abundantly clear.

In the third selection, Lee-Jan Jan examines the prison system of Taiwan. The author describes the types and operations of Taiwanese institutions and provides up-to-date prison statistics. The manner in which Taiwan attempts to promote offender rehabilitation is a focal point of the article, with attention drawn to the unique "Progressive Grade System." The relatively calm atmosphere of the crowded Taiwanese system might strike some Americans as odd, since crowding is so often associated with disruption in U.S. prisons. Lee-Jan Jan offers insights as to why the calm atmosphere prevails, such as the effect of establishing self-discipline programs. He also outlines the future direction of Taiwan's penal policy.

Cuban prisons have, for many years, been unavailable for scientific study. In "Cuban Prisons: A Preliminary Report," researchers from the Institute for Policy Studies located in Washington, D.C. reveal the findings of their on-site visitations to four Cuban prisons and interviews with 120 prisoners. The philosophy of Cuban penology is discussed. Perhaps the most enlightening part of the article is the objective assessment of the positive and negative features of Cuban institutions.

The last article in this section, "Conditions of Confinement Within Security Prisons: Scandinavia and California," by John R. Snortum and Kåre Bødal, gives a rich descriptive comparison between the conditions found in certain Californian prisons and conditions found in Norway, Finland, and Sweden. Although known for their progressive and humane prison systems, these Scandinavian countries have a number of rather traditional prisons. However, there are also important differences between prisons in Scandinavia and California. The research conducted by Snortum and Bødal addresses such things as living conditions, staffing ratios, and the nature of prison programs. The investigators conclude that, in general, the most favorable conditions of confinement are exhibited in Sweden and Norway followed by Finland; California seems to rank a distant last. When considering these rankings, it is imperative to realize, as Snortum and Bødal contend, that the better prison conditions in Norway and Sweden cannot be fully explained by the observations that these countries are smaller, more homogeneous, and blessed with lower crime rates than the U.S. Officials of Norway and Sweden have engaged in the political struggles that are necessary to promote a more humane system of imprisonment. These struggles, coupled with less punitive public attitudes toward offenders in Scandinavia, should be kept in mind when considering the problematic conditions of U.S. prisons.

1. Corrections in Israel and the United States: A Comparative Analysis*

Gad J. Bensinger
Loyola University of Chicago

Abstract: The general underlying philosophical intent of corrections in both Israel and the United States is the restoration of the offender to a productive role in the community. Since the correctional intent is essentially the same, it is not surprising that the systems established to implement this aspiration are rather similar and exhibit many of the same ambiguities, weaknesses, and frustrations. The focus of the paper is on two correctional alternatives: incarceration and probation.

As in America, Israel's prisons are overcrowded; most of the correctional facilities are unfit for human habitation; sanitary conditions are poor; occupational, vocational, and educational opportunities are virtually non-existent; and rehabilitation exists in name only. The recidivist rate of criminal offenders is as high in Israel as in the U.S. Various Israeli commissions in recent years have decried the prison conditions and have called for reform but, again as in the U.S., the problem has defied an acceptable solution.

Israel's probation services are part of the country's social services delivery system rather than the penal or judicial systems. That is the case because, unlike the U.S. conception, probation in Israel is not considered a punishment. Probation services are utilized by the Criminal Justice System, but organizationally they are not part of it. Still, the functions carried out by the Israeli probation officers very much resemble those of their counterparts in the U.S. Probation services in Israel have not expanded in recent years, even though the number of incarcerated offenders has increased.

Corrections has never been a priority in Israel and will not be so long as the country remains preoccupied with security matters. On the other hand, the crime rate continues to increase and so does the prison population. Consequently, the country's correctional problems and policies, in all their dimensions, should be reexamined, and the sooner the better.

Introduction

Corrections—the community's official reaction to the criminal offender, whether adult or juvenile, in Israel and in the U.S.—is guided by social philosophies and values that are common to Western democracies. Consequently, the general underlying philosophical intent of corrections in both countries is the restoration of the offender to a productive role in the community and

---

*Prepared for presentation at the 35th Annual Meeting of the American Society of Criminology, November 9–13, 1983.

From Gad J. Bensinger, "Corrections in Israel and the United States: A Comparative Analysis" in *International Journal of Comparative and Applied Criminal Justice* (8 (1): 55–62, Spring, 1984).

his/her reintegration into society. Since the correctional intent is essentially the same, it is not surprising that the systems established to implement these aspirations are rather similar and exhibit many of the same ambiguities, weaknesses, and frustrations. Differences and distinctions are, of course, present, too, as is pointed out below.

Courts in America and in Israel have a number of options for dealing with an offender. They may order a person to serve a prison term; impose a suspended sentence, probation, or fine; or decide on a combination of these as provided for by law. The focus of this paper is on two of these options: incarceration and probation.

The Prison System

Prisons in Israel manifest many of the same problems that plague American prisons and jails: they are repeatedly characterized as inhumane and in need of reform. Violence, pervasive homosexuality, and the existence of a "barn boss" system in Israeli prisons were first revealed by the Shimron Commission[1] in 1978 (Shimron et al., 1978). A later report, issued in August 1981 by the prison Service Investigation Commission appointed by the president of the Israeli Supreme Court, warned that "the conditions of the prisons are so serious, subhuman and on the verge of explosion, that it calls for a revolutionary change in the way prisons are run" (*Maariv,* 1981).

The prison population in Israel includes approximately 3,000 convicted criminals, both Jews and Arabs, and 3,000 Palestinian security prisoners held for security breaches and terrorist activity. (The rate of incarcerated criminal offenders per 100,000 citizens in Israel is 75. This figure approximates the "prison rate" in Europe and is much smaller than in the United States.) Like American correctional institutions, Israeli prisons are rated as maximum-, medium-, and minimum-security. While the Israeli prisons are relatively new, most of the correctional facilities were not designed for the purpose for which they are being used.

The Israeli prison system has its roots in the Palestinian mandate, namely, during the period between World War I and the establishment of the State of Israel in 1948. For most of that period, the prison system was part of the Palestine Police Administration established by the British in 1926. When the State of Israel was created, little attention was paid to crime and punishment. The crime rate of the Jewish population at that time was very low and there were many other priorities. Many of the Jewish inmates held in the British prisons were serving sentences for illegal acts carried out against the British and were, therefore, released as soon as the British exited the country in 1948. In February 1949, a general amnesty was declared leaving only 29 inmates in prison. They were housed in the Tel Mond prison, a converted British police fortress with a capacity of 120. Not long after, it was realized that the State's prison capacity

1. The Shimron Commission was appointed in 1977 by the Government of Israel to examine the causes of crime and the administration of justice in Israel. Although much smaller in scope, it emulated the President's Commission on Law Enforcement and the Administration of Justice.

of 120 was insufficient; other police fortresses, originally built by the British in the 1930s, were converted into prisons.

In Israel as in the U.S., Parkinson's Law applies to prison construction; prison populations grow to fill expanding capacity and so, in Israel the growth in prison population has consistently outstripped all official estimates. The Beer-Sheva maximum-security prison, the first modern facility built in Israel specifically as a prison, was completed in the late 1960s for 300–400 inmates and heralded as *the* answer for Israel's prison problem. This same prison now houses over 1,000 inmates. It has been characterized by the Prison Service Investigation Commission as the largest and most overcrowded prison in Israel, exhibiting all the ills that the Commission decried. The second largest prison in Israel is the Ramle prison, a converted police fortress with a capacity of 450, now housing approximately 650 inmates. The Prison Service Investigation Commission reported that 500 of these inmates were being held in subhuman, overcrowded living conditions, and it recommended that several of the prison buildings be demolished because they are unfit for human habitation.

As recent incidents at the Beer-Sheva and Ramle prisons suggest, prison overcrowding in Israel continues to breed violence:

- On July 25, 1983, ten inmates were injured when a home-made grenade exploded in the Beer-Sheva prison.
- During the week of August 15, 1983, two Ramle prison inmates committed suicide and a third tried, but failed.
- On September 9, 1983, two inmates at Beer-Sheva prison were caught stabbing a man, and the day after another prisoner was assaulted while watching television.

Israel's other correctional institutions are smaller, but physical assaults, sexual attacks, invasion of privacy, and theft from inmates are quite common there too.

Israeli prison inmates charge that the codes for inmate behavior are ambiguous and that punishment is arbitrary and unfair. There also have been allegations of brutality against inmates, which, considering the country's correctional personnel practices, are hardly surprising.

Though there seems to be no shortage of correctional manpower in Israel (in 1981, 2,710 employees were budgeted, indicating a favorable officer-inmate ratio), there exists a dire need to hire better qualified officers. The Prison Service Investigation Commission in 1981 found that "there is very little difference between the backward social background of the prisoners and that of the jailers" and recommended that better qualified personnel be recruited and hired (*Haaretkz*, 1981). More recently, the Chief Warden of Ramle prison, David Peri, briefed the Knesset (Parliament) Interior Committee and related that about 70 percent of the correctional staff in Israel cannot read or write (*Jerusalem Post*, 1982). Prison work in Israel is even less attractive than in the U.S. Low pay is a common complaint, turnover rates are high, and the work itself is unrewarding, frustrating and dangerous. While there have been no major prison riots reported in Israel, there are occasional riots and other "troubles." In the most recent such incident, two correctional officers were taken hostage in the Ramle prison in June 1983. Reminiscent of similar incidents in the U.S., the Israeli prisoners demanded to speak with the prison's Commissioner, a lawyer, and a representative of the news media. Following negotiations the two hostages were released. More alarming, and perhaps unique to Israel, has been the recent assassination of the Ramle Detention Center Warden, Roni Nitzan, and the attempted assassination of a correctional officer in charge of security at the Ramle prison. In the first incident, the warden was ambushed and killed by an inmate while on furlough from a 15-year term for bank robbery to visit his ailing father. In the second incident, the correctional officer, his wife and one-year-old son escaped injury when a bomb exploded outside their apartment.

In an effort to upgrade correctional work in Israel, it was recently decided that the term "warden" would be changed to "attendant." The reason for the change, according to the prisons' Commissioner, was to "better define the function of prison as a center of rehabilitation rather than punishment" (*Jerusalem Post,* 1982). This development, of course, brings to mind the change in terms in the U.S. from prison guard to correctional officer and suggests that much more is needed than a change of job title or image to bring about meaningful prison reform.

As the statement by the prisons' Commissioner suggests, the goal of the prison system in Israel is directed toward the rehabilitation of the convicted offender. But for the time being, rehabilitation in the Israeli prison system exists in name only. The recidivist rate in Israel is about as high as that in the U.S. Sixty percent of released convicts return to prison within three to five years, often for committing even worse crimes. To make the goal of rehabilitation meaningful, preparations have begun for the opening of additional educational courses in the prisons. The need for this initiative was documented by a survey of prisoners which showed that over 40 percent of the Jewish prisoners are illiterate, even though they have graduated from elementary schools in Israel. Educational and vocational opportunities have, of course, existed in the Israeli prisons for many years, but most courses have been poorly attended. Current plans call for inmates to study four hours a day, six days a week in prison schools supervised by the Israel Education Ministry (*Jerusalem Post,* 1983). Also some new initiatives have been taken to stimulate prison industries. Israeli industry is being encouraged to invest in factories situated within prison grounds to instill in prisoners "a positive attitude" for work. Despite such efforts, however, work opportunities for inmates are few and most prisoners still remain idle most of the time. Several halfway houses are planned for the near future, but none have yet opened.

In Israel, not only is there little rehabilitation occurring before the prisoner's release, but like the U.S., there is hardly any rehabilitation effort after the prisoner's release. There is no state agency that deals with released offenders. There are voluntary organizations, but they are unable to provide needed services. Also, there are no parole officers under the jurisdiction of the prison system. All parole responsibilities are carried out by probation officers, as is explained on the following page.

Probation Services

In Israel, probation can be ordered by a court either before or after the conviction of an offender. If probation is granted without a conviction, the court must advise the defendant that, should he/she commit another offense while on probation, the original charges could be reinstated. When an Israeli court imposes a penalty involving imprisonment, it may direct that all or part of this penalty be suspended. If the court suspends imprisonment, it may authorize a probation order. (A probation order cannot be made for a period less than six months nor more than three years.)

Probation as a legitimate alternative to imprisonment received worldwide attention only after the creation of the first juvenile court in Chicago in 1899. The concept of probation was introduced into Palestine by the British and was maintained and expanded after the creation of the State of Israel. In Palestine, the first legislation dealing with probation was the Young Offenders Ordinance of 1922 which made it possible for offenders under age 20 to be placed on probation. However, not until 1937 was an official governmental agency for probation services established. That agency was created within the British Mandatory Government's Department of Social Work, and it carried out responsibilities associated with pre-sentence reports and the supervision of juvenile offenders. The system established in 1937 remained in force (with only minor changes) until 1971. Since that time, the Youth Law of 1971 has served as the legal basis for juvenile probation in Israel. The British-enacted Probation of Offenders Ordinance of 1944 made it possible to place adult offenders on probation. This ordinance served as the legal basis for adult probation in Israel (again, with minor changes) until 1969, when it was rewritten as the Probation Order of 1969.

At the present time, administrative responsibility for all probation services in Israel lies with Israel's Ministry of Labor and Social Affairs. Separate adult and juvenile probation departments exist within the Ministry's Division of Youth Development and Corrections. Both departments are organized nationally into six geographic districts. The structure of each includes a director, a deputy director, district chief probation officers and deputies, and probation officers. In 1980 there were 92 adult and 150 juvenile probation officers employed.

It is important to note that Israel's probation services are part of the country's social services delivery system rather than the penal or judicial system, because, unlike the U.S. conception, probation in Israel is not considered a punishment. Probation services are utilized by the criminal justice system, but organizationally they are not part of it. Moreover, the system is organized on a national rather than a local basis. On the other hand, the functions carried out by Israeli probation officers very much resemble those of their counterparts in the U.S. For example, adult probation officers in Israel make pre-sentence investigations and provide the courts with evaluations and recommendations regarding treatment methods and prospects for offenders to be rehabilitated. At the present time, pre-sentence investigation reports are required in all criminal cases involving offenders under age 22. (The adult probation department has responsibility for offenders 18 years and over.) The courts, however, have discretionary power to demand that pre-sentence investigation reports be submitted for all offenders 22 or older. Likewise, juvenile probation officers in Israel conduct socio-psychological investigations which are submitted to the juvenile courts. As in the U.S., such reports generally include information on the offender's criminal record, the offender's cultural background and home conditions, a physical and psychological profile, educational achievements and whatever circumstances may have contributed to the criminal offense. Juvenile probation officers must include in their reports to the court a recommendation concerning the nature of the sentence that ought to be imposed by the judge. Such recommendations are not binding on the court.

Another responsibility juvenile probation officers in Israel have is screening young offenders out of the juvenile justice process. In carrying out this function, they seem to possess greater discretion than American probation officers. Although the legal authority to charge a minor with a criminal offense rests with the Israeli Police (there are no status offenses in Israel), every minor thus charged must be referred to the juvenile probation department. Once a police referral is received, a juvenile probation officer must recommend to the police whether or not to file a petition with the court. In most instances the police abide by the recommendation, though they need not. About one-half of all the juvenile cases opened by the police are closed after the probation officer's initial screening (Bensinger, 1983:72).

Probation officers in Israel also provide treatment and counseling services to probationers within the context of the probationary periods decided upon by the courts. In this respect the Israeli system is much more oriented toward using the social work model than are most current probation systems in the U.S. The treatment objectives in Israel are based primarily on theory and practice in the fields of social work and psychology. Consequently, social work education is specified as the preferred background for probation, and the terms ''diagnosis'' and ''treatment,'' so prevalent at one time in the American corrections literature, are emphasized. Although a probation order can be revoked by the court if its conditions are violated, the task of the Israeli probation officer is not one of the surveillance of probationers.

Israeli courts cannot impose indeterminate sentences on adults. However, the law provides for the early release of offenders and establishes parole services.[2] Like Federal probation officers in the U.S., Israeli probation officers function as parole agents. They submit written reports to the prison parole boards and provide services to released offenders who have been ordered to be, or who on their own volition want to be, engaged with a parole officer.

2. An adult sentenced to prison for more than six months (except when imprisoned for life) is eligible for parole after serving two-thirds of the sentence. This authority resides in a parole board which recommends whether a prisoner should or should not be released. Good conduct in prison does not automatically entitle an inmate to a reduction in the sentence. Neither does an inmate's past criminal record lead to a denial of parole. Since the powers of the Parole Board are very discretionary, the Israel Supreme Court in a judgment rendered on May 22, 1983, recommended that specific guidelines be adopted and issued, as was done recently in England in the Parole Commission and Reorganization Act of 1976.

Israeli probation officers must be university graduates in social work, education, or psychology, or be qualified social workers who are graduates of the Institute of Social Work Training. Since caseloads are quite small (according to Israel's Central Bureau of Statistics, there were 1,653 adults and 1,780 juveniles on probation in 1979), probation officers seem to be able to provide the treatment services they are required to perform and for which they have been and continue to be trained.

Conclusion

As in America, Israel's prisons are overcrowded; most of the correctional facilities are unfit for human habitation; sanitary conditions are poor; occupational, vocational and educational opportunities are virtually nonexistent; and rehabilitation exists in name only. Not surprisingly, the recidivist rate of criminal offenders is as high in Israel as in the U.S. Various Israeli commissions in recent years have decried the prison conditions and have called for reform but, again as in the U.S., the problem has defied an acceptable solution.

Probation services, the most legitimate alternative to incarceration, exist in both countries, but remain underutilized—in Israel more so than in the U.S. In the U.S. three-fourths of all adult offenders under correctional supervision are supervised in the community, through probation and parole. In Israel, on the other hand, only one-third of the Israeli adult offenders under correctional supervision are on probation. Probation services in Israel have not expanded at all in recent years, even though the number of incarcerated offenders has increased. Lagging probation services in Israel are the result of limited government spending policies on social services. A recent study has shown that spending on social services in Israel has hardly changed since 1975,[3] and, now, in the aftermath of the June 1982 invasion of Lebanon and the current economic crisis, probation services may even be reduced. Moreover, corrections in general has never been a priority in Israel and will not be so long as the country remains preoccupied with security matters. On the other hand, the crime rate continues to increase and so does the prison population. Consequently, the country's correctional problems and policies, in all their dimensions, should be re-examined, and the sooner the better.

Discussion Questions

1. What factors may be undermining Israeli prisons in their effort to achieve the goal of restoring offenders to a "productive role in the community"?
2. In your opinion, what steps should be taken to increase the likelihood that persons released from Israeli prisons (or any prison, for that matter) will not recidivate?
3. What similarities between Israeli and U.S. societies might account for Bensinger's observation that the prison problems faced by these two nations are comparable?

3. This study was conducted by the Israel Center for Policy Studies, which is modeled on the Brookings Institute in Washington, D.C.

References

Bensinger, Gad J. 1983. *A survey of criminal justice in Israel.* Chicago: Center for Urban Policy, Loyola University of Chicago.

Haaretz. August 2, 1981.

Israel Central Bureau of Statistics. 1981. *Statistical abstract of Israel 1980.* Jerusalem: Kiryat Arba Press.

Jerusalem Post, June 17, 1982; September 8, 1982; August 7, 1983; September 26, 1983.

Maariv. August 3, 1981.

Shimron, Erwin, et al. 1978. *Report of the commission to examine the topic of crime in Israel (in Hebrew).* Jerusalem: Segal Press.

2. Imprisonment: The Aboriginal Experience in Western Australia*

Richard Midford, BA, B Psych (WA) M Psych (Tas),
Clinical Psychologist
Department for Community Services, WA

Historical Factors in Establishing the Status of Aborigines

Since White colonization, the underlying assumption in relations between the Aboriginal population and the Australian legal system has been that Aborigines are bound by the same law as the general community. Aborigines were officially recognized as British subjects from 1837 onwards (Little, 1972) with the intention of affording them the protection and rights that went with such status. However, this assumption of equality has tended to overlook the fact that Aborigines were not able to perform equally in a White defined culture. They were bound by laws and rules of behavior derived from their own cultural tradition, many of which ran counter to concepts in English derived law. A sentiment dating back to Aristotle pinpoints the inherent problems in such an attitude. "It is as unjust to treat unequals equally as it is to treat equals unequally" (Aborigines Welfare Board, 1967).

Even if the ideal of equal treatment is accepted, the reality of justice administration in the case of Aborigines since colonization has often been discriminatory. Eggleston (1976a) states that several factors are responsible for this discrimination. First, discriminatory legislation, some of which still exists today, has contributed to consigning Aborigines to the bottom rung of the socioeconomic ladder. Secondly, some administrators of the legal system are prejudiced against Aborigines, and because the law allows some discretion in administration, they have had the opportunity to translate their prejudicial attitudes into overt action. These factors specifically affect Aborigines, but like other groups with low community standing, they also experience more general economic and social discrimination. The geographic distribution of Aborigines has also contributed to their disadvantaged position. Eggleston (1976a) states that their present day concentration in outback areas is an historical consequence of White invasion and culture conflict. This remoteness means that they share with other rural dwellers disadvantages related to poor legal representation and jurisdiction of courts more likely to be administered by untrained justices dispensing harsher sentences.

---

*This article was written while the author was employed by the Department for Corrective Services, Western Australia.

From Richard Midford, "Imprisonment: The Aboriginal Experience in Western Australia" in *Australian and New Zealand Journal of Criminology* (21 (3): 168–178, September, 1988).

The Aboriginal Response to Dispossession

In the early years of settlement, Aborigines were dispossessed of their land and thus denied access to their traditional food gathering and hunting sources. As a result, for many Aborigines, initial contact with the Australian legal system was through police expeditions formed to seek out and punish Aborigines for offenses perpetrated against the White community. In Victoria these offenses typically involved animal killing and stealing (Corris, 1968). In Western Australia flour, sheep and cattle stealing, assault, wounding and murder were considered common Aboriginal offenses (Robinson, 1969). In 1837 Governor Stirling commented that the local Aborigines "steal whenever they can, and they will take life rather than be balked in their desires" (Fall, 1978: 26). The colonial newspapers of the day attributed this behavior to an excess of alcohol and the degenerative nature of the race (Martin, 1973). Biskup (1973) has suggested, however, that this behavior, which was most common during the early years of settlement, was a reaction against the European invaders who had occupied their traditional territory.

Aboriginal Imprisonment in the Early Years of the Colony

One consequence of the imposition of English derived law on local Aborigines was that when they transgressed they were liable to the associated forms of punishment, one of which was imprisonment. Few Aboriginal perceptions of this process were recorded, and so it is difficult to know how they adapted to and survived such an alien style of existence. Certainly there was an abiding lack of comprehension or sense of justice about the whole process. This is exemplified by a report in the *Western Australian Government Gazette* of 1842 of a conversation between the Superintendent of Public Works and Wenar, an Aborigine convicted of murdering a fellow Aborigine and imprisoned for life. Wenar could not understand why the Governor was punishing him so severely: "If a White man kills a White man, we never interfere—some time back, the White men killed many of the natives and the Governor took no notice, now why should the Governor take any notice of me, if I kill a fellow native, that steals my wife, or kills my brother, when it is according to our law" (*Western Australian Government Gazette,* 1842, p. 1).

Aborigines of the time seem to have afforded little legitimacy to imprisonment as an appropriate form of punishment and the escape rate was extremely high. Fall (1978) reports that in the early days of the Swan River Colony, Aboriginal prisoners often escaped four or five times during one term of imprisonment. Charles Symmons was appointed as a Protector of the Aborigines in the 1840s. He stated that some of the natives saw their escapes as triumphs over the White men, and that others presumed that having stayed in the bush for a period, their past misdemeanors would be forgotten or overlooked when they returned to settled areas (*Western Australian Government Gazette,* 1841a).

The colonists' solution to an increasing Aboriginal prison population, the high rate of escape and the difficulty of recapture was to establish a native prison on Rottnest Island, offshore from Perth. There was recognition in the Act establishing the prison that imprisonment was especially unpleasant for Aborigines because it severely curtailed their normal mode of living. A native prison on Rottnest allowed a greater degree of personal freedom combined with far greater difficulty of escape. It was also intended to serve as a deterrent to transgression. The island had strong mythic associations for local tribes and many Aborigines viewed the island with terror (Fall, 1978). Charles Symmons in the *Western Australian Government Gazette* (1841b, p. 1) stated that he considered "the prison on Rottnest as one of the most powerful engines which the Colonial Government wields (rather *in terrorem* than in point of fact) over the Aborigines of Western Australia." There may also have been more tangible reasons for the dread of Rottnest felt by many Aborigines. Thomas and Stewart (1978) report that during the 1840s there were repeated charges that Aboriginal prisoners were being ill treated by the Superintendent, Vincent. No charges were, however, proven. Notwithstanding the treatment meted out to Aboriginal prisoners, ill health and death were a recurring theme because of the inappropriate prison diet and diseases introduced by the settlers, to which the Aborigines had no immunity.

In the late 1840s Aboriginal prisoners on Rottnest were transferred to road gangs as an economy measure. However, in 1855 the arrival of convicts in Western Australia made their labor superfluous and they were transferred back to Rottnest.

Imprisonment of Aborigines continued in much the same vein until the end of the century. The elected representatives of the colony showed only occasional interest in Rottnest, and the main concern was the cost of the institution which increased every year. There was little recognition of the needs of traditional Aboriginal prisoners, and while the more enlightened officials had some appreciation of the differing physical needs of Aboriginal prisoners, a paternalistic, culturally superior attitude prevailed at best. The Colonial Surgeon criticized the Rottnest prison diet as being insufficient in quantity and variety for Aborigines used to living in the bush. He believed that much of the sickness on the island was due to the inadequate diet of meat and rice, and the absence of amusements and exercise. He suggested that the Aboriginal prisoners would respond to a system of incentives such as the privilege of wearing "an old hat with a feather in it" for good behavior (Thomas and Stewart, 1978).

Imprisonment of Aborigines in the Northwest at the Time of the Frontier

The crude brutality of the early years of Rottnest was in time replaced by classic colonial paternalism and disregard. In the 1870s and 1880s the frontier moved to the northern areas of the State as vast tracts of land were appropriated by pastoralists. The resultant displacement of northern Aboriginal groups produced cultural conflict similar to that experienced in the first decades of the Swan River Colony. The offenses against White property and possessions took on a similar character and the response of the white settlers was to seek to cow the local Aborigines through control and fear. Prisons for Aborigines were established in the north of the colony, and almost immediately similar problems to those which occurred with the imprisonment of Aborigines in Perth surfaced in the Kimberley and Pilbara regions.

A newspaper report of the time (*Western Mail,* 1897, p. 9) condemned Derby **gaol** as a "tumble down white ant eaten collection of wooden sheds." Gill (1977) reports that the prisons at both Derby and Wyndham were grossly overcrowded and insecure. As a consequence Aboriginal prisoners escaped from these northern prisons in droves. The local White population's perception of prison conditions was completely different: as altogether too convivial. One newspaper (*Nor-West Times,* 1894, p. 2) talked of Derby prison as a place where "the nigger is both happy and comfortable." The newspaper condemned the practice of "bringing niggers into Derby and feeding them on beef (and our local medical officer will have it all fresh for them), good bread and a small supply of tobacco." Biskup (1973) more recently reports that the diet of all prisoners was generous, consisting of rice, vegetables, bread, tea and 12 ounces of meat per day. He says it was little wonder that discharged cattle killers thought nothing of repeating their offence and spending a further period in prison. There seems no acknowledgment in these reports of the paradox of why Aboriginal prisoners should wish to escape in such large numbers from places where they were supposedly well fed and content.

The picture of the well-fed, content Aboriginal prisoner cannot be taken as remotely accurate, according to Gill (1977). Diet was inadequate in many instances and quite alien to Aborigines used to a hunter/gatherer lifestyle. There were even reports of deaths due to "a kind of scurvy" in Wyndham prison (*Western Mail,* 1893, p. 6), which seemed linked to the practice of not requiring the contracting provider to supply fresh meat or vegetables. Deaths in custody were still prevalent two years later when the *Western Mail* (1895) reported nine Aborigines dying in Wyndham prison in less than a two-month period. Generally the rate of sickness and death was of similar proportion to that experienced at Rottnest, half a century earlier. The reasons were similar: inadequate recognition of the different physical needs of Aborigines, overcrowding of prisoners in unhealthy conditions, and poor immunity on the part of local Aborigines to White introduced diseases.

Post Frontier Changes to the Treatment of Aborigines in the Northwest

By the early 1900s pastoral expansion in the north of the State was virtually complete, and while the settlers were less in need of protection, the killing of cattle by Aborigines continued unabated. Mass imprisonment was fast losing its deterrent value, and the cost of imprisoning ever larger numbers of Aborigines was electorally unpopular. In 1906–07 the cost of imprisoning Aborigines was $13,682. Two years later the cost had risen to $18,256 (Biskup, 1973). As there seemed little to gain from this ever increasing expenditure, the idea of feeding Aborigines to preempt their need to kill cattle gained support.

In 1910, as a result of the Colonial Secretary approving the establishment of a self supporting station for the relief of local Aborigines, the government resumed 28 well stocked pastoral leases near the Wyndham-Hall's Creek road. This area was designated an Aboriginal reserve with the intention of getting the Aborigines to "sit down" on the new "blackfellow" station and stop killing the cattle on neighboring properties.

At about the same time, police were instructed to only arrest the leaders of cattle killing groups, and only if the cattle owner could produce evidence that would withstand scrutiny in court.

The practice of paying local police reimbursement for meals supplied to prisoners or witnesses was also discontinued at this time, very much as a result of the findings of Royal Commissioner, Dr. Roth. He stated that the financial advantage to be gained by the police through this practice contributed to large numbers of Aborigines being arrested for cattle killing (Eggleston, 1976a).

These new measures had great impact on the numbers of Aborigines being imprisoned for cattle killing. After a high point in 1908–09, when 219 Aborigines were convicted of cattle killing, the rate dropped dramatically. In 1909–10 only 22 Aborigines were imprisoned and none the following year (Biskup, 1973).

The Development of a More Liberal View Towards the Imprisonment of Aborigines

During the same period there was increasing awareness among the legislators of the cultural conflict between Aborigines and Whites. The 1899 Royal Commission on Native Welfare acknowledged that situations could arise where an act regarded as acceptable or even mandatory by Aborigines would often be deemed illegal by Whites. Elaborating on this theme, the Commission stated that it was unjust for a man to be punished for an offence against tribal law, and then a second time by the laws of the race that dispossessed him. The Commission also believed that there was little to be gained by imprisoning Aborigines. Imprisonment did not deter others because all that his group could comprehend was that "a man had disappeared" (Thomas and Stewart, 1978).

As a result of the Commission's findings that Rottnest possessed none of the conditions needed for proper treatment, it was closed as a native prison in 1903. This, however, did not mean that conditions improved for all Aboriginal prisoners. Prisoners in the north of the State were insecure, and Aborigines imprisoned there generally wore neck chains throughout their sentence (Thomas and Stewart, 1978). There was no legal authority for chains, but their use continued with little adverse comment until the late 1930s. Aborigines were also segregated from Whites in Western Australian prisons, a procedure which only officially ceased at Fremantle Prison in 1966 (Thomas and Stewart, 1978).

The Modern Period-Increasing Rates of Aboriginal Imprisonment

Ostensibly, these days Aboriginal and White prisoners are treated similarly, although in most cases the prison experience is different for Aborigines. After the time of the frontier had passed, the Aboriginal population stabilized at a relatively low percentage of the total. In June 1949, 30 out of 333 men in prison were Aborigines (9%); of the 35 women in prison at this time 5 (12%) were Aborigines (Thomas and Stewart, 1978). In comparison to their percentage of the general Western Australian population, this was gross over-representation; but much worse was to come in future years.

It is difficult to know precisely why the Aboriginal prison population reached its historical low point during this period, but a number of particular influences which operated after the passing of the frontier period changed significantly in the 1960s and 1970s.

A number of missions were established around the State, particularly in the north. These acted to concentrate the local Aboriginal population in centers away from the White townships and the White legal system. The Missionary

Christian philosophy also militated against the sort of drinking behavior that more recently has been such an important factor in the incidence of Aboriginal crime. Alcohol was not even legally available to Aborigines in certain proclaimed areas of Western Australia until 1964 (Newton, 1977).

Aboriginal males in remote areas were frequently employed as stockmen, on cattle stations. However, in 1968, because of a change to the Federal Pastoral Industry Award, Aboriginal stockmen were granted the same pay rates as Whites. Station owners until this time had been prepared to tolerate large family groups of Aborigines on their properties in return for cheap or even free labor. They were not generally prepared to pay award wages, however, and as a consequence of Aborigines being denied station employment, there was a large drift of these people into northern towns (Dixon, 1981). Here there were few opportunities for employment, particularly work that could be accommodated within their traditional lifestyle.

In the 1950s and early 1960s, the percentage of Aboriginal prisoners in Western Australian prisons slowly rose to the point where in 1964, 16.7% of the average daily muster of 818.5 male prisoners were Aborigines. The percentage of Aboriginal prisoners increased rapidly from then on, and a high point of 37% of the average daily male muster was reached in 1981 (Broadhurst, 1986). This compares with an Aboriginal percentage of the general population of approximately 3% (Dixon, 1981).

The Western Australian Aboriginal imprisonment rate also compares unfavorably with other States, according to Dixon (1981). It is two to three times higher than New South Wales and 25% greater than that of South Australia.

Broadhurst (1986) also examines the question of recidivism amongst Aborigines and conservatively estimates that approximately one-third of Aboriginal males over 16 years of age have been imprisoned at some point in time. Recidivism among Aboriginal prisoners is estimated by Broadhurst at around 80%, while for Whites it is about 50%.

Modern researchers in the correctional field (Cohen, 1985; Greenberg, 1977; Tomasic and Dobinson, 1979; Walker, 1983) have found that imprisonment has little effect on reducing recidivism of prison populations. Given these findings, Broadhurst (1986) states it is unlikely that the different treatment of Aborigines and Whites accounts for the substantial difference in their recidivist behavior. He does mention, however, that Aboriginal prisoners differ substantially from Whites in their access to a broad range of correctional programs. Broadhurst (1986) and Duckworth, Foley-Jones, Lowe and Maller (1982) also mention the generally subordinate positions Aborigines occupy within the prison social structure and the unskilled, menial jobs they tend to be allocated.

Broadhurst (1986) argues that high rates of imprisonment and recidivism make it difficult to sustain defensive arguments such as incapacitation and punishment, or the reductionist aims of correction and deterrence. These utilitarian aims of prison have even less face validity as to their impact on Aboriginal prisoners than for Whites. Broadhurst (1986) suggests that imprisonment as a method of control applied out of cultural context is largely ineffective, and certainly the patterns of events and statistical evidence presented in this paper support an argument that imprisonment of Aborigines in Western Australia has never been effective in any of its intended aims. Despite this demonstrated ineffectiveness and the growing availability of alternatives, it remains the most commonly applied sanction for Aboriginal offenders (Broadhurst, 1986).

Aboriginal Attitudes to Imprisonment

Eggleston (1976a) reports that in her experience there are two contrary beliefs as to the subjective effect of imprisonment on Aborigines and as to the question of whether the experience is different for them as compared to White prisoners. One school of thought asserts that Aborigines like prison, or at least do not mind it. Certainly, Lowe (1984) reports that shorter sentences of three to six months are often welcome among Aborigines in the Northwest of Western Australia as time away from the "rough and tumble" of fringe dwelling. The belief that Aborigines do not mind prison is usually associated with the assertion that Aboriginal prisoners and their families see nothing particularly shameful in being imprisoned. Duckworth and Hartz-Karp (1979) found in their survey of Aboriginal attitudes to imprisonment that most of their respondents did not regard their status as prisoners in a particularly negative way. In some cases this may have been because they only considered the really serious infringements as those within the ambit of their own customary law. Lowe (1984) tends to support this proposition. She reports that among the Northwest Aborigines a person punished by White law may not be considered to have committed a crime, in which case imprisonment is irrelevant or unjust. Duckworth, Foley-Jones, Lowe and Maller(1982) report that because of the strong possibility of imprisonment, many young male Aborigines regard the experience fatalistically as an accepted rite of passage to manhood. Nevertheless, there is a strong body of evidence that suggests that many Aborigines regard imprisonment as bad or shameful. Duckworth and Hartz-Karp (1979) report one young man as saying that his relatives would not have anything to do with him upon release because they considered him bad for being in prison. Some prisoners in the Duckworth and Hartz-Karp study report negative feelings on the part of relatives because of the effect of imprisonment on traditional life. Lowe (1984) also talks about young men missing important traditional initiation ceremonies through imprisonment. This not only frustrates tribal elders who want to "make a man of him" but may also lead to sexual problems and social ostracism, since uninitiated men in traditional Aboriginal society are not permitted to take a wife or engage in sexual activity. The strain on family life is also mentioned as being important, particularly by female Aboriginal prisoners. Several female respondents in Duckworth and Hartz-Karp's (1979) study express concern about their children, who are being fostered or cared for by relatives. Eggleston (1976a) considers the view of Aborigines as not minding imprisonment to be generally untrue. She supports her assertion by reference to interviews with small numbers of Aboriginal prisoners, all of whom did not wish to be in prison. She also supports her assertion by personal observation of how an Aboriginal girl reacted to a sentence of imprisonment when she had expected a fine.

Eggleston (1976a) comments that it is sad to consider so many Aborigines not concerned by imprisonment, because this gives an indication of their impoverished living standards within the wider community. Additionally, the fact that so many associate no stigma with a prison term may indicate the legal system has sent such a large proportion of the Aboriginal population to prison that the collective experience is not unusual and thus less ominous.

Despite the strong folklore belief among Whites that Aborigines at least do not mind imprisonment, courts have considered imprisonment a particularly harsh punishment for tribal Aborigines because confinement is so alien to their normal mode of living (Eggleston, 1976a). Ligertwood (1984) specifically reports that magistrates hearing charges in Pitjantatjara settlements are very aware that imprisonment has to be served hundreds of kilometers away from tribal communities and tend to resort to this sanction sparingly. The validity of such a judicial attitude in Western Australia is brought into question, however, by statistical evidence reported by Eggleston (1976b) herself. This evidence shows that in Western Australia proportionately more Aborigines are sentenced to imprisonment than Whites. In 1965 the imbalance was particularly marked, as Aborigines made up almost a quarter of the daily average prison population, although they were only responsible for 11% of the total convictions.

Wilson (1982) also reports equivocal findings. He states that studies show police, because they have wide powers of arrest for minor offenses, are much more likely to arrest an Aborigine than a White person. He also suggests that the judiciary is more likely to fine a White person for minor offenses, while imprisoning Aborigines. He speculates that the opposite result prevails in the case of major offenses. As an example he cites the legal system's response to offenses leading to death on Aboriginal Reserves. Most of these result in convictions of manslaughter rather than murder and the sentences given are lenient.

Cultural Factors Affecting Aborigines' Experiences of Imprisonment

The research literature would suggest that Aborigines hold a range of attitudes to imprisonment, many of which differ from those expressed within mainstream White society. Accordingly, it would be useful to examine the substance of Aboriginal experience of prison, particularly the influence of traditional cultural beliefs and practices.

A factor that impacts on Aborigines even before they face criminal proceedings in court is their degree of adherence to the rules and principles contained in traditional law. Lowe (1984) reports the tribal communities in the Northwest often only recognize their own traditional system of crime and punishment as valid. Australian law, however, grants no formal recognition to Traditional Aboriginal law. The stage is thus set for conflict between the two legal systems. Australian law enforcement agencies assert jurisdiction over actions by Aborigines which constitute crimes under Australian law, but which may not be considered as such by Traditional Law. In some cases these actions represent legitimate punishment of offenders against Aboriginal Traditional Law. Conversely, where a person is considered guilty under Aboriginal law, a punishment imposed by Australian law may not be considered relevant, and pay-back is always a possibility. Lowe (1986) reports that a man or woman may serve a lengthy prison sentence with the knowledge that they still face tribal punishment upon release.

Lowe (1984) states that in court White officials tend to assume that all Aboriginal people speak English. While most Aborigines have some command of the language, for many it remains a second language which they use infrequently. Duckworth and Hartz-Karp (1979) found that many of the Aborigines they interviewed did not understand much of the court language or procedures, and there were few occasions when it was explained in simpler terms. This language barrier, coupled with the tendency of traditional Aborigines to be polite and shy with Whites, means that when faced with a barrage of incomprehensible questions they either say nothing, or if pressed offer the response which they think is expected. This behavior has implications for their treatment by the police and court. In prison it creates many false impressions about Aboriginal prisoners, particularly that they are stupid or hard of hearing (Lowe, 1984). It also means that there is considerable lack of understanding on the part of Aborigines of expectations, options and facilities (Duckworth and Hartz-Karp, 1979).

Time concepts are particularly different among Aborigines by comparison to White people. Tribal Aborigines seldom refer to clocks or calendars, and they are unlikely to know their dates of birth (Lowe, 1984). Neither do the dates of their prison term have much meaning to them, although they are as anxious as any other prisoner to know when they get out. Lowe (1984) reports the case of one old man, serving several years for manslaughter, who comprehended the length of his sentence only in terms of the seasons. He was content when it was communicated to him that he would be released "not this dry season, but after the next one" (Lowe, 1984: 331).

Aboriginal use of different names in different circumstances is often difficult to comprehend by Whites and can confuse bureaucratic transactions in the prison setting. Aborigines can have several personal names, including nicknames and ritual names. They may also be referred to by their section, or subsection name, or their totemic name depending on the circumstances. In addition, they may have a "white-fellow" name, which they use when dealing with White society (Lowe, 1984).

The taboo placed on use of names of recently deceased relatives means that a living person with the same name is obliged to use an alternative. This means that an Aborigine can change his name from one term of imprisonment to another. Quite inappropriately, he may be recorded as using an alias (Duckworth and Hartz-Karp, 1979).

Kinship is the most important single factor in determining the way Aboriginal society functions and very obviously has great impact on the Aboriginal experience of imprisonment. Kinship rules affect prisoners in various ways. Avoidance relationships apply between certain kin, usually in-laws. Prisoners having this sort of relationship may be forced to work together or to live in the same cell or dormitory. Duckworth and Hartz-Karp (1979) report an example of several prisoners claiming avoidance relationships with other prisoners in the same institution. They did not explain their plight to the prison authorities for fear of ridicule. As one expressed it, "If I asked to be moved away from another prisoner in the dormitory the prison officers would think I was very silly and they would probably laugh at me" (Duckworth and Hartz-Karp, 1979, p. 5).

Obligation relationships may cause problems if an Aboriginal prisoner is given supervisory responsibilities over other Aborigines. The bestowal of this formal authority does not override kinship obligations and the two lines of loyalty may cause conflict. It has often been said that this is the most important reason behind the low level of recruitment of Aboriginal Prison Officers.

The meaning of the term family is generally very different for Aborigines than for Whites. It usually takes a wider range of kin than the nuclear group commonly conceptualized as family by Whites. Family kin terms may also be used in a classificatory sense, where no blood ties exist, as in this way behavior towards significant newcomers can be prescribed. The breadth of Aboriginal family relationships makes it difficult for Prison Administrators to judge equivalence when decisions are being made about extra visits, transfers, or leave on compassionate family grounds.

The great benefit of the extended family to the Aborigine in prison is that newcomers almost invariably have kin already in the prison and are accepted into a social group, whereas Whites suffer considerable loss of identity and have to establish new relationships (Robinson, 1969). Midford (1985), in a survey of observation cell placement within Fremantle Prison, found that Aborigines are less likely to require placement in observation. This is possibly due to the availability of such a supportive kin group within the prison. This ready-made social network could act as a mechanism through which Aboriginal prisoners deal with their stress before it reaches the point where the intrusive intervention of observation placement is required.

Consequences of Imprisonment for Aborigines

Irrespective of how Aboriginal imprisonment is examined, the differences between the imprisonment rates of Aborigines and Whites are so great and have such an historical tradition that, according to Broadhurst (1986), they have an unreal Third World quality to them. While this may mean that the issues involved have little impact on the consciousness of the general community, the consequences for individual Aborigines, and the community in which they live, are very real.

Sykes (1958) contends that the inmate's personality and sense of worth are eventually destroyed by confinement within what Goffman (1961) terms a "total institution." Goffman (1961) describes the process as "role dispossession" in which the inmate is stripped of his identity and experiences civil death. Part of this institutionalization is an increase in dependency and reduction in decision-making capacity and self-esteem. These deprivations occur on top of the plethora of disadvantages experienced by Aborigines within the wider community. Ultimately, the repercussions spread beyond the individual.

Patterns of imprisonment tend to be repeated because one generation provides a role model for the next. Many juveniles offend repeatedly and by the time they are in their mid-twenties they have a long record of convictions and have spent a large part of their adult lives in prison. The result, according to Wilson (1982), is that these Aboriginal men have no stable marriage or family relationships. They have little experience of a lifestyle apart from prison and almost inevitably offend again and go back to prison.

Men who are regularly in prison for prolonged periods find it increasingly difficult to readjust to an autonomous life in the community. Broadhurst (1986) estimates that between one-third and one-quarter of Aboriginal males experience imprisonment. They are also faced with erosion of their traditional authority, particularly in urban settings. This forces severe dislocation on Aboriginal families as they accommodate the repeated imprisonment of fathers and husbands. Families may have to move away from traditional communities if they want to regularly visit their men in prison, or they are faced with the large cost of travelling long distances to visit irregularly. Some Aboriginal families become more matrifocal as women of necessity take the initiative in all aspects of household management.

Theories of Causation

Many researchers, when looking at causes for the excessive rate of Aboriginal imprisonment, stress deprivation in areas of health, education, employment and the application of law. Broadhurst (1986) states that because of this emphasis, criminological explanations have tended to rely on strain and labeling theories to account for over-representation of Aborigines in the prison system. Other recent analyses (Stannage, 1981; Reynolds, 1981; Wilson, 1982) have offered theories of cultural conflict, which emphasize a lack of consensus of values and processes between the two cultures, to explain the underlying cause of the greater rate of Aboriginal imprisonment. Irrespective of theoretical explanations of cause, however, the continued high incidence of imprisonment in the post-colonial context constitutes an index of the symptoms of change forced upon traditional Aboriginal society by the all-prevailing power and influence of European culture.

The Scope for Reform

There are various measures which could go some way towards redressing the cultural disadvantage experienced by Aborigines. Offenses for public drunkenness and disorderly behavior could be decriminalized. Fines could be related to the offenders' capacity to pay. Arrangements for bail could be made that do not depend upon the financial resources of the offender or his associates. The use of the summons rather than arrest could be increased. Interpreters could be provided when Aborigines for whom English is a second language are involved in legal proceedings. Greater recognition could be afforded to customary Aboriginal law within the Australian legal system. Affirmative action could be increased to get greater involvement by Aborigines in law enforcement. Greater support could be given to self-administering Aboriginal communities to increase the effectiveness of their own authority and social control mechanisms. Finally, as Broadhurst (1986) suggests, expansion of prison capacity should be resisted to ensure that it is indeed utilized as the institution of last resort.

Discussion Questions

1. How does the phrase "it is as unjust to treat unequals equally as it is to treat equals unequally" apply to this article?
2. Compare and contrast the imprisonment experiences of Aborigines in Western Australia with the imprisonment experiences of such U.S. racial/ethnic minority groups as Blacks, Hispanics, and Native Americans.
3. Midford proposes several reforms in the final section of the article. What political and economic barriers may impede implementation of these policies?
4. What is the value of the type of historical research method used in the article for advancing our knowledge of penology?

Bibliography

Aborigines Welfare Board. (1967) "Aboriginal Policies of the Aborigines Welfare Board" *Report of the Aborigine Welfare Board for the Year ended 30 June 1767*. Government Printer: Melbourne. 12.

Biskup, P. (1973) *Not Slaves, Not Citizens*. Queensland University Press: St. Lucia.

Broadhurst, R. G. (1986) "Imprisonment of the Aborigine in Western Australia: 1957–1985." Unpublished Manuscript.

Cohen, S. (1985) *Visions of Social Control*. Polity Press: London.

Corris, P. R. (1968) "Aborigines and Europeans in Western Victoria" *Occasional Papers in Aboriginal Studies*. Australian Institute of Aboriginal Studies: Canberra. No. 12, Ethnohistory Series No. 1.

Dixon, O. (1981) *Committee of Inquiry into the Rate of Imprisonment*. WA Government Printer: Perth.

Duckworth, A., Foley-Jones, C., Lowe, P., and Maller, M. (1982) "Imprisonment of Aborigines in North Western Australia" 15 *ANZJ Crim*. 26–46.

Duckworth, A. and Hartz-Karp, J. (1979) "Aboriginal Attitudes to Imprisonment: A Preliminary Appraisal of Issues" Internal Research Paper, Western Australian Department of Corrections.

Eggleston, E. (1976a) *Fear, Favour and Affection*. ANU Press: Canberra.

Eggleston, E. (1976b) "Urban Indians in Criminal Courts" *University of Western Australia Law Review* 12(3): 368–404.

Fall, J. (1978) "Crime and Criminal Records in Western Australia, 1830–1955" *Studies in Western Australian History*, November: 18–29.

Gill, A. (1977) "Aborigines, Settlers and Police in the Kimberleys, 1887–1905" *Studies in Western Australian History*, June: 1–28.

Goffman, E. (1961) *Asylums*. Penguin: Harmondsworth.

Greenberg, D. (1977) "The Correctional Effects of Corrections," Greenberg, D. (ed) *Corrections and Punishment*. Sage: Beverly Hills.

Ligertwood, A. (1984) "Aborigines in the Criminal Courts," Hanks, P. and Keon-Cohen, B. (eds) *Aborigines and the Law*. Allen and Unwin: Sydney.

Little, J. (1972) "Legal Status of Aboriginal People: Slaves or Citizens?" Stevens, F. S. (ed) *Racism* 2: 77–87.

Lowe, P. (1984) "Aboriginal Culture and Prison," Swanton, B. (ed) *Aborigines and Criminal Justice*. Australian Institute of Criminology: Phillip.

Lowe, P. (1986) "Guilt, Blame and Sorcery in Aboriginal Murder" Internal Research Paper, Western Australian Prisons Department.

Martin, M. A. (1973) "Aborigines and the Criminal Justice System. A Review of the Literature" Research and Information Series No. 2. Western Australian Department of Corrections, Perth, unpublished.

Midford, R. G. (1985) "Fremantle Prison Observation Cell Survey" Internal Research Paper, Western Australian Prisons Department.

Newton, J. (1977) "Aborigines and the Criminal Justice System," Biles, D. (ed) *Crime and Justice in Australia*. Sun Books: Melbourne.

Nor-West Times. (1894) 10 February.

Reynolds, H. (1981) *The Other Side of the Frontier*. Penguin: Ringwood.

Robinson, M. V. (1969) "Imprisonment of Aborigines and Part Aborigines in Western Australia," Berndt, R. M. (ed) *Thinking about Australian Aboriginal Welfare*. UWA Press: Perth.

Stannage, T. (1981) (ed) *A New History of Western Australia.* UWA Press: Nedlands.
Sykes, G. (1958) *The Society of Captives: A Study of a Maximum Security Institution.* Princeton University Press: Princeton.
Thomas, J. E. and Stewart, A. (1978) *Imprisonment in Western Australia: Evolution, Theory and Practice.* UWA Press: Nedlands.
Tomasic, R. and Dobinson, I. (1979) *The Failure of Imprisonment: An Australian Perspective.* Allen and Unwin: Sydney.
Walker, N. (1983) "Side Effects of Incarceration." *British Journal of Criminology* 23: 61–71.
Western Australian Government Gazette (1841) "No. 235: Symmons's annual report for 1840" 8 August 1841.
Western Australian Government Gazette (1841) "No. 261: Symmons's quarterly report" 9 July 1841.
Western Australian Government Gazette (1842) "No. 291: Trigg's report" 11 February 1842.
Western Mail (1893) 21 October.
Western Mail (1895) 23 March.
Western Mail (1897) 8 October.
Wilson, P. (1982) *Black Death, White Hands.* Allen and Unwin: Sydney.

3. Corrections in Taiwan (Republic of China)

Lee-Jan Jan
West Georgia College

Abstract: This paper describes the correctional system in Taiwan. It includes the current policy, organizational structure, rehabilitation programs, and up-to-date crime and prison statistics. The focus is to highlight some of the differences between U.S. and Taiwanese correctional systems. For example, the administration of all prisons in Taiwan is under the centralized authority of the Ministry of Justice, prison guards do not carry firearms while on duty, etc.

The data are collected from government and professional publications and observations are made by the author who has visited several different types of prisons in Taiwan.

Corrections in Taiwan, ROC

The organization of the correctional systems in Taiwan is based on the criminal Code article I: "The objectives of imprisonment and detention are to help the convicts to repent, to improve, and to adapt themselves to social life" (Lin, 1984, p. 39). Thus an emphasis on rehabilitation instead of punishment permeates practice.

The prisons are centralized under the supervision of the Department of Prison and Detention Facilities of the Ministry of Justice. There is comprehensive planning for prison construction and modification, personnel recruitment and training, and uniform administration and custodial standards. Therefore, there are few differences in the quality of custodial personnel, rehabilitation programs, and treatment of prisoners among the prisons.

There are 16 adult prisons; the prisons can be classified according to the type of prisoners they house.

1. General Type: These house mainly medium security prisoners, although each may have a maximum security section or an open prison attached to it, such as the Taipei prison.
2. Maximum Security: These house mostly the serious and dangerous offenders, such as the Green Island, Taichung, and Hue Lien Prisons.
3. Prison for the Habitual Offenders: These house prisoners who are convicted within five years after the completion of the sentences for previous crimes (Ministry of Justice, Crime Analysis, 1986), such as the Kao Hsiung Prison.

From Lee-Jan Jan, "Corrections in Taiwan (Republic of China)" in International Journal of Comparative and Applied Criminal Justice (12 (1): 95–100 Spring 1988).

4. Open Prison or Branch Prison Camp: These facilities house the prisoners who present no security problems. The prisoners usually have daytime work and only come back to stay at the prison at night, such as at the Wu Ling Prison.
5. Prisons for Prisoners with Special Illness that Need to be Segregated: Examples include the prison in Hsing Chuang for prisoners with leprosy and the prison in Tao Yuan for inmates with mental illness.

For juvenile offenders, there are three types of facilities.

1. Youth Jail: These house mainly juveniles between 14 and 16 years old, who have committed a crime which carries a minimum prison sentence of five years. There is only one youth jail, located in Hsing Chu.
2. Juvenile Reformatory: These house juveniles who have committed lesser crimes. There are three juvenile reformatories. The one in Chang Hua also accepts female juveniles, while the other two are only for male juveniles.
3. Juvenile Foster Homes: These homes provide a family type environment for children under the age of 12 who have committed a crime (mostly stealing). The children attend public school during the day.

In Taiwan, according to the most current statistics, in 1985 there were 25,499 prisoners confined in 16 facilities. Among them, 1,921 (7.5%) were female prisoners. The educational backgrounds of the prisoners were: illiterate, 3.91%; elementary school, 38.58%; junior high school and its equivalent vocational school, 31.79%; senior high school and its equivalent vocational school, 20.9%; college and up, 4.61%; and literate but no formal schooling, 0.22%. Concerning the age a person is sentenced to prison, the modal category is between age 30 and 40, which consists of 32.41% of the prisoners. The next three high risk categories are 24–30, 24.34%; 18–24, 16.88%; and 40–50, 14.55%. The most frequently committed crimes among males are theft (20.96%), homicide (7.22%), forgery (6.4%), cheating and con game (6.25%), and drug dealing and using (4.02%). Among females the most frequently committed crimes are cheating and con game (14.26%), theft (11.35%), forgery and bad checks (6.4%), vice (5.36%), and drug related offenses (4.17%). Among the male prisoners, 94.65% are first time offenders, and 5.35% are recidivists; 97.3% of the female prisoners are first time offenders and 2.7% are recidivists (Ministry of Justice, Crime Analysis, 1986). The overall rate of prisoner to general population is 130/100,000. The overall rate of prisoner to general population in the U.S. is 201/100,000. This rate is calculated based on the prisoners confined at the end of 1985 in federal and state prisons. When prisoners in county jails are included, this rate should be higher. The percentage of female prisoners in the U.S. is 4.6% (U.S. Department of Justice Bulletin, 1986).

The purpose of imprisonment in Taiwan is rehabilitation. Therefore, after conviction prisoners are assigned to their prisons according to the following considerations; the distance between the prison and the prisoner's home, the crime committed, prior records of offending, and physical and mental conditions. In each prison there is a reception center. After arrival, prisoners are given an orientation to prison regulations, prisoners' obligations and rights, and grievance and parole procedures. Then a series of tests on personality, motor coordination, vocational aptitude, reading and mathematical skills are given to each prisoner. The results of these tests are used as references to plan the most suitable program for the prisoner's rehabilitation.

Prisoners who have the ability and the interest in academic advancement can attend the prison extension school. The school is an integrated part of the prison rehabilitation program, but it is separate and independent from the prison. The school is accredited by the Ministry of Education and can issue either a junior or senior high school diploma to prisoners who have successfully completed the required courses.

For those who are more vocationally inclined, the prison offers its own machine shops for technical training, such as auto mechanics, electrical appliance repairing, type setting, printing, etc. Every six months prisoners can take the examination conducted by the Department of Labor of the Ministry of Interior and can be issued a certificate upon passing the examination.

Moral teaching is an important part of the rehabilitation program that every prisoner is required to attend. It includes:

1. Group lectures on the moral standards of society, law, and relevant civic issues, with renowned social figures often invited as guest speakers;
2. Individual counseling on personal and emotional problems; and
3. Religious programs that each individual can choose to attend. Community religious leaders are invited to give lectures and perform services.

The prisons also run different kinds of joint factories with private business that produce handicraft, clothing, electric devices, etc. Prisoners who participate in this type of work can receive a wage of at least 20% of the free market rate plus bonuses. These factories not only help some of the prisoners financially, but also serve the purpose of indoctrinating a work habit.

For everyday routine, the prison is run like a military camp. All the activities are organized and prisoners move in groups. There is no individual activity.

To achieve the goal of rehabilitation and to motivate the prisoners to behave there is a Progressive Grade System, which divides a prisoner's sentence into four stages. The treatment in early stages is more restricted, while in later stages prisoners enjoy more privileges. For example, the Grade Four prisoners live in a double occupancy cell (currently three prisoners share one of these cells due to overcrowding), keep more personal belongings, and are allowed more visiting time with relatives. Most important, a prisoner in Grade Four, for each month he/she served in the prison, can reduce his/her overall sentence by

16 days. By contrast, Grade One prisoners, for each month they have served, can only reduce their sentences by two days. And only prisoners in Grade Two and above can be considered for parole or transferred to open prisons. Open prisons have more privileges. For instance, the prisoner in an open prison, when meeting the good conduct requirement, can go home for a three-day visit each month, and every month such prisoners can live with their families for seven days in the conjugal dormitories provided by the prison (Wu Ling Prison, 1985). Prisoners of good conduct are also encouraged to govern themselves by a self-discipline program. To organize all aspects of their life, prisoners, under the supervision of correctional officers, elect among themselves factory assistants, supply clerks, factory quality control personnel, cell-block servicemen, work-table captains, and education assistants. Each month they hold an Inmate Daily Life and Work Seminar to discuss problems and make suggestions to improve their life (Taipei Prison, 1984). The prisoner's promotion or demotion to a different grade is dependent on his conduct as judged by the Prison Administration Committee, and with the approval of the Ministry of Justice.

When prisoners violate the regulations, they can be put in solitary confinement, lose visiting privileges, be downgraded, or transferred to another prison. For instance, violators may be transferred to the Green Island prison, which is isolated on a small island and houses the most troublesome prisoners. On the average, the cost to maintain each prisoner is about $150 per month.

The author has visited two adult prisons, one youth jail, one juvenile reformatory, and one juvenile foster home. The overall impressions of these correctional facilities are described below.

1. The physical environment, although compact, is well landscaped, with a lot of plants and shrubbery. The atmosphere is pleasant. When asked whether the many plants obstruct views and create security problems, the answer was that to achieve the goal of rehabilitation the physical plan and appearance of the prison have to be conducive. Thus, the prison should look more like a school campus. There might be some risk, but it is minimized by the regimented military style activities, and the guards always maintain eye contact with the prisoners. Besides, the prisoners are motivated by the Progressive Grade System to conduct themselves well.
2. Inside the prison the guards do not carry firearms; instead they carry whistles and batons. In the machine shops, which have many metal tools, there is usually just one technical instructor and one guard for thirty or more prisoners. When asked about the safety of the instructors and guards, the reply was that the guards are taught to care and show concern for the prisoners. The relationship between guards and prisoners is friendly, and the prisoners hold no grudge against the guards. However, the structure of the building is such that each section or unit of the prison can be shut off immediately from the rest of the prison. Thus, large scale riots are impossible,

and prisoners are well aware that holding their guards hostage can only aggravate their situation.

3. The guards appeared to be enthusiastic and earnest in their work. Their manner was professional and polite. This may be due to their educational background and training. The guards are required to have at least a high school diploma and pass the civil service examination (currently many of them are college graduates). Then they are sent to the Central Police College for six months of special training on the theory and practice of corrections. This training is followed by a two-month internship in a prison before becoming a regular guard. The workload is heavy; on the average the staff/inmate ratio is 1 to 8, and the guard/inmate ratio is 1 to 12. The average salary is equal to about $400 per month, plus housing. Since most prisons are located in densely populated areas, having the guards on the grounds not only keeps them close in the event of need, but the housing serves as a buffer between the prison and the community.
4. In the prison, there is not the usual tension one can sense between the guards and the prisoners; the overall atmosphere is relaxed. The prisoners are well behaved. In the workshops they work diligently and quietly at their jobs. Casual, personal conversations are prohibited; even visitors did not create much distractions to prisoners. When asked about prison disturbances or escapes, the answer was that they had not had any for many years. Several reasons were given. With the physical planning and the surveillance system, any disturbance or escape can be noticed immediately and handled promptly. Further, when a person is convicted and sent to prison, it causes enough embarrassment to him/her. And through the orientation, prisoners are made to understand clearly the consequences of their behavior, so it is to their disadvantage to cause a disturbance. Finally, prisoners are treated fairly. There are appropriate channels to voice discontent. One is the suggestion box. Prisoners can make suggestions or complaints concerning any procedure that affects their lives. They may make complaints about any officers that treat them unfairly. Only the warden and the executive secretary can open these boxes. Prisoners can also make formal petitions to the Prison Administration Committee, or to the inspector from the Ministry of Justice. As a last resort, prisoners or their relatives can send their complaints directly to the Minister of Justice.

In Taiwan the biggest problem the adult prisons are facing is overcrowding. For instance, the Taipei prison, which the author visited, has a capacity for 2,700 prisoners but in recent years it has always held around 5,500 inmates. Even the auditorium is used for sleeping at night. Each prisoner has a sleeping bag, which is packed away during the day. In the shops, the machines or tools that are supposed to be used by one or two prisoners for training now have an additional prisoner standing by, watching and taking turns. To alleviate this problem, there are efforts to construct new prisons and to expand existing ones. In the meantime, the laws regarding bad checks and forgery have also been changed. The violators no longer serve prison terms. Since these violators constitute more than 6.5% of the prisoners, this can be a substantial reduction in prison population.

Another problem is the lack of an independent female prison; female inmates are usually housed in a segregated section of the median security male prisons. The reasons for not building female prisons are cost efficiency, to keep the female prisoners serving time near their home so that they can have closer contact with their families, and the number of female prisoners in each area is too small to warrant a prison of its own. The problem with female inmates not having their own prison is that they do not have access to the better equipped workshops to learn more sophisticated job skills, and their space for activities is also more restricted. Therefore, female prisoners are not receiving treatment equal to that received by the male prisoners.

Compared to the U.S., rehabilitation is still the main purpose of the institutions in Taiwan. And these institutions are very successful at rehabilitation; recidivism is less than 6%. Although the Taiwanese do not call it participatory management, their prisoner self-discipline programs are very similar to participatory management in concept, and these work well. Although Taiwan has a much lower ratio of confined prisoners when compared to the U.S., Taiwan shares the same problem of overcrowding. To solve the overcrowding problem, the main solution is still to build big prisons, not small community correctional facilities; this is apparently based on cost-efficiency. Corrections in Taiwan is considered serious moral work which should not be associated with business and profit making. Thus, privatization of correctional institutions is still inconceivable to the correctional administrations and probably to society in general.

Looking to the future, the Ministry of Justice has just announced that the "six year plan for improvement of correctional facilities" should be completed by the end of 1987; overcrowding and related hardware problems should be alleviated. Then the focus will be on four major conceptual changes: a) In the past, the correctional facilities have been concentrating their efforts on solving problems as they come along. In the future, attention will be directed toward prevention. b) In the past, emphasis was on achieving stability. In the future, emphasis will be on facilitating progress while maintaining stability. c) In the past, solving overcrowding had the highest priority. In the future, improving rehabilitation programs will take the highest priority. d) In the past, increasing personnel was the major effort. In the future, promoting the quality of personnel, such as their training and work ethics, will be the major effort.

Discussion Questions

1. How do the categories of adult and juvenile prisons which exist in Taiwan compare and contrast with the categories that exist in the U.S.? Could the U.S. gain anything by establishing separate institutions for habitual offenders?

2. Compare and contrast the security and programming procedures employed in Taiwanese prisons with those employed in U.S. prisons. What are the advantages and disadvantages of the varying procedures?
3. How does the lot of female prisoners in Taiwan compare with the lot of female inmates in the U.S.?
4. Assuming that the 6 percent recidivism figure given by the author is accurate, why do you think recidivism is so much lower in Taiwan than in the U.S.? On what grounds might the accuracy of this figure be questioned?

References

1986. *Central Daily News,* September 9, Section 8, in Chinese.

Lin, Chi-Tung. 1984. *Penology.* Shan-Ming Book Publishing Company, Taipei, Taiwan: 39, in Chinese.

Ministry of Justice, Crime Study Center. 1986. *Crime Analysis,* June: 263, 384–396, in Chinese.

Taipei Prison. 1984. *A Brief Introduction to Taipei Prison.* Taiwan, in Chinese.

U.S. Department of Justice, Bureau of Justice Statistics Bulletin. 1986. *Prisoners in 1985,* June.

We Ling Open Prison. 1985. *A Brief Introduction to Wu Ling Open Prison.* Taiwan, in Chinese.

4. Cuban Prisons: A Preliminary Report

Institute for Policy Studies*

Introduction

From February 26 to March 5, 1988, board members from the Institute for Policy Studies (IPS) led a delegation to conduct an inquiry into present prison conditions and the treatment of prisoners in Cuba. This investigation was made possible by an agreement signed in February between IPS and the National Union of Cuban Jurists (NUCJ). The agreement called for NUCJ to:

1. Obtain open access to all facilities in six Cuban prisons chosen by the U.S. delegation; and
2. Facilitate confidential interviews with current and released prisoners selected by the delegation.

In exchange, IPS agreed to seek similar access to United States prisons for a Cuban delegation from NUCJ. A condition in the agreement that U.S. visas for the Cubans be obtained prior to the visit to Cuba was waived by NUCJ, which relied upon good faith efforts to accomplish the reciprocity.

Our principal focus was on current conditions. Our interviews with prisoners dealt primarily with present and recent penal conditions, as well as changes in conditions since the beginning of 1987. In interviews conducted with prisoners, we asked them about the crime for which he or she was charged and the length of sentence, though we did not ask them about why and how they were convicted and imprisoned. We discussed that process with official representatives of the criminal justice system. Investigating detention per se was not part of our mandate. Our mandate was limited to the physical conditions and treatment of prisoners within the prisons.

This visiting program is an initial part of an IPS project to explore possibilities for improving and ultimately normalizing relations between Cuba and the United States. The treatment of prisoners and prison conditions, both in the U.S. and Cuba, has been a festering issue between the two governments for years. The proposal for open reciprocal exchange offered some promise to lay to rest an issue which in fact obscures more serious matters which the two countries must address in a process of rapprochement. Indeed, the exchange shows that citizen diplomacy can pave the way for greater communication between governments.

---

*The Institute for Policy Studies, a leading center of progressive research and public education, is located at 1901 Que Street, N.W., Washington, D.C. 20009.

Reprinted from Vol. 15, No. 2 of *Social Justice*, P.O. Box 40601, San Francisco, CA 94140.

The reciprocity feature is essential to the success of the effort. In late April, four high-ranking Cuban penal professionals applied for visas from the State Department to conduct the tour of American prisons. IPS hopes that the United States administration will recognize and support this program, which will help to advance human rights and open doors to future progress.

Members of the IPS Delegation

The delegation from IPS included IPS Vice Chairman, Diana de Vegh, and an IPS trustee, Adrian DeWind; Peter Bell, the president of Edna McConnell Clark Foundation; Dr. Howard Hiatt, M.D., a former Dean of the Harvard University School of Public Health; Aryeh Neier, Vice Chairman, Americas Watch; and Herman Schwartz, Professor of Law, American University. Julia Sweig, staff coordinator of the IPS U.S.-Cuba Dialogue Project, also accompanied the delegation. All our interviews with prisoners were facilitated by Luis Rumbaut, a professional interpreter who accompanied us from the United States.

Tasks of the Delegation

We visited six prisons and one work camp:

- Combinado del Este, a maximum security men's prison, New Dawn Women's Prison, and Van Troi Work Camp in the province of Havana;
- Boniato Prison, a maximum security men's prison in Santiago Province;
- Kilo 7, a maximum security men's prison, and Granja 5 Women's Prison in Camaguey Province; and
- Nieves Morejon, a maximum security men's prison in Sancti Spiritus province.

Prior to our trip, we requested access to all prisons above except to Granja 5 in which we made only a cursory tour.

We conducted confidential interviews with more than 120 prisoners. More than 40 of the interviews were conducted with prisoners we had asked to see in advance; we selected the remainder of the prisoners at random. At least 50 of the interviews took place with prisoners incarcerated for politically motivated offenses, such as illegal exit from the country, burning cane fields, conspiracy to assassinate Cuban leaders, participation in armed rebellion in the Escambray mountains, espionage, possession of counterrevolutionary literature, draft resisting, and desertion. Most of these interviews were with prisoners whom we had selected in advance.

Americas Watch compiled the list of prisoners by consulting with the Catholic Bishops Conference, Cuban-American families, and sources inside Cuba. More than half of our interviews were conducted out-of-doors at places we chose at random. The interviews that took place indoors were also conducted at places we chose at random. At no time were Cuban authorities present during these interviews. This allowed the prisoners to respond to our questions freely. Though a small percentage of the common criminals and political prisoners we interviewed expressed fear of reprisals, we assured them that the content of our interviews would remain confidential and that the likelihood of any reprisals was very small. We asked those prisoners whom other foreign delegations had interviewed whether they had suffered reprisals and all answered in the negative.

The Cubans with whom we were in contact—NUCJ officials, officials of the Ministry of Foreign Relations, and the Ministry of the Interior which operates the prisons—facilitated our visit throughout, providing access, transportation and lodging, including a plane to make possible our visits to prisons in the provinces.

We visited all areas of the prisons that we chose to see, including dormitories, workplaces, areas for conjugal visits, visiting areas, infirmaries, punishment and segregation cells for prisoners designated as dangerous or high-risk inmates, kitchens, laundries, dining areas, classrooms, and libraries. The Cuban authorities gave us access to all areas of each prison that we asked to visit. Of those prisoners we asked to see in advance, we saw all but a handful. Some few, we were told, had already been released. (We will try to verify this.)

In addition to visiting the prisons, we met with Cuban officials nationally and locally in each of the four provinces to discuss the prisons. Some of us also arranged meetings with Ricardo Bofil and Elizardo Sanchez, leaders of two unofficial human rights groups, to obtain through them the testimony of recently released prisoners about prison conditions.

We did not visit pre-trial detention facilities, military prisons, or reform schools. At Nieves Morejon in Sancti Spiritus province, we inspected facilities and interviewed inmates held in two buildings designated for juvenile offenders 16 years and older.

Philosophy of Cuban Penology

Re-education for the purpose of reintegration into civilian life is the central principle of the Cuban penal system. In carrying out re-education, the system relies principally on:

1. Employing as many prisoners as possible in productive, remunerated labor;
2. Providing prisoners with technical skills that will be useful after release from prison;
3. Providing political education; and
4. Instilling discipline, with an emphasis on group responsibility.

We encountered a very strong sense of mission in most of the prison officials we met. They expressed great faith in their system and, though they concede faults in practice, they seem determined to work increasingly on their plan for re-education and for incorporation of the penal population into work and free society. At present, officials say that 85% of the Cuban penal population works. Their goal for 1990 is to provide 95% of the penal population with work. They claim that at present 80% of the penal system's operating costs are covered by production which takes place within the prisons.

Evaluation

The humane and constructive features of the Cuban penal system, particularly the paid work opportunities and the training in basic skills, as well as the harsh and cruel features, appear to us to be directly attributable to the determination to re-educate prisoners.

The humane and constructive aspects of the system are evident in that:

1. The great majority of prisoners work a regular work week at productive jobs under conditions similar to those of workers not serving sentences;
2. Almost all the prisoners who work are paid. The remuneration is the same as for civilians before a 35% discount for cost of living. The amount remaining to them after this discount is sufficient to provide some support for their families or to accumulate substantial savings (in the case of prisoners without family responsibilities) that can aid their re-entry into normal life;
3. The regular prison facilities we saw were all clean and hygienic, and we heard no serious complaints in this regard;
4. We heard no complaints about the use of instruments of torture to inflict pain; neither did we find any policy of extrajudicial executions or disappearances;
5. A system of conjugal visiting is well established at all the prisons we saw. Visits at conjugal areas range from three to eight hours every one to six months, depending upon prisoners' compliance with prison rules;
6. Many prisoners do acquire practical skills during confinement;
7. Prisoners are provided with education to bring them up to the ninth-grade level. A program is underway for prisoners who have completed the ninth grade to secure further education.
8. We heard no complaints that prisoner-against-prisoner violence is commonplace.
9. The outpatient, hospital, physical therapy, laboratory, and pharmacy facilities we saw were modern, hygienic, and well equipped. Doctors and nurses, as well as laboratory and other personnel, were present in sufficient numbers required for the prison population. Prisoners expressed satisfaction with the care available for major medical problems, but we heard some complaints mostly from prisoners held on politically related charges about failure or delays in access to medical care.

The harsh and cruel part of the system is reflected in the fact that:

1. Those who resist re-education or violate prison discipline—including passive violation such as hunger strikes—are confined for extended periods, sometimes in extremely harsh punishment cells—bare, tiny, dark, cold (or hot, depending on the season)—sometimes with insufficient food. We heard of a few cases of prisoners in these cells without clothes and some cases of prisoners dressed in undershorts and shoes. All but one of the prisoners we saw in punishment cells were common criminals, not those confined for politically motivated offenses.

2. Prisoners in protection cells (due to difficulties living in collective cell blocks) who do not work have only slightly better facilities than those in the punishment cells and go outside only once a week for an hour or two. In some prisons they are then placed in large iron cages which are too small to take walks.
3. Visits have been infrequent in the past, though new rules now make them somewhat more frequent. Up to now, many prisoners could only get visits once every six months; the new rules reduce this to once every 60 days. In the best of circumstances, that is, for prisoners considered to be doing best in the prisons and under the recently implemented rules that considerably liberalize visiting, visits may take place only every 21 days (family visits for juveniles are more frequent); incentives (*estimulos*) for good conduct include additional visiting privileges.
4. In general, letters may be sent with almost the same infrequency as visits, though regulations for some prisoners in certain prisons allowed for letters to be sent and received every two weeks—or more often in some cases;
5. In two prisons, Boniato and Combinado del Este, we encountered frequent complaints that prisoners who did not conform to the prison regime had been beaten with rubber hoses (*mangueras*), or with fists or sticks. We heard of one case in which a prisoner was allegedly kicked to death by guards in 1987, but could not verify this. We heard that the two offending guards faced disciplinary procedures but were unable to verify this. We did not hear such complaints of beatings in the other four prisons we visited.

There was one exceptional prison we visited, the Women's Prison of all Western Provinces in Havana province. It is a model prison in terms of all physical facilities. The working conditions, the cells, including punishment cells, and the facilities for activities were very good. Relations between officials and prisoners seemed generally constructive and respectful. The prison reflects the positive influence of a dedicated warden. Although this is a showplace, intended and paraded as such, the fact remains that some 600 women are imprisoned under humane conditions.

As to some other matters, some prisoners told us the food was good and others called it adequate but tasteless. Except for prisoners in some of the punishment cells, no one told us the amount was insufficient. In those punishment cases, prisoners received a small breakfast and larger supper, but no lunch—a very deprived diet.

Except for the punishment cells and harsh protection cells, toilet facilities were minimally adequate. In the punishment cells, toilets are holes in the ground. Most punishment cells in most prisons contained facilities for running cold water. In one building in one prison the facilities were characterized by stench and inadequate water and ventilation.

Bathing facilities in dormitories in all prisons were primitive but adequate relative to the number of prisoners in each detachment.

In the men's prisons, there was little place for prisoners to keep private possessions. In one prison, inmates could only keep their possessions in a numbered bag hung in a room that is normally locked; access over the course of the day is permitted according to a regular schedule. Elsewhere, particularly in the women's prisons, there was adequate space for the storage of private possessions.

For most prisoners, overcrowding is not a problem. Some prisons we saw have empty dormitories. Typical dormitories had double and triple bunks, though we saw only partial evidence of use of the top bunk in the triple-bunk facilities. We calculated an average of about 30 square feet of floor space per prisoner. For those prisoners, the fact that they work elsewhere, study elsewhere, take part in sports elsewhere, and eat elsewhere prevents the lack of space from being particularly oppressive.

On the other hand, we saw extremely crowded conditions in punishment cells. At their worst, we saw a few three-person cells where prisoners were confined 24 hours a day that measured five feet by seven feet, for a total of 35 square feet or 12 square feet per prisoner. Most punishment cells in most prisons we saw contained one or two prisoners. Some punishment cells were slightly larger, measuring 6 feet by 12 feet. In the punishment cells in three of the prisons we saw, prisoners slept on bare cement slabs without bedding. In others, adequate bedding with mattresses is provided. The toilet (a hole in the floor) is in the cell, as is a spigot for water. Light is minimal.

Complaints by prisoners are supposed to be investigated by the office of the Fiscal General, which performs an inspection function—carrying out unannounced on-site visits to prisons to review compliance with requirements for conditions, prisoners' rights, completion of sentence, parole, and release. We obtained evidence that this system works at least some of the time, though how often we could not determine. Some prisoners expressed skepticism about seeking assistance from the Fiscal General and believed their communications would not reach his office. They told us that letters of complaint must be entrusted to their re-educators. Cuban judicial theory does not provide for independent advocates for prisoners. It is not considered an appropriate function for lawyers to represent prisoners in matters dealing with prison conditions. Pastoral visits by clergy are unknown and are apparently prohibited in Cuban prisons.

Two private, unofficial human rights groups have recently begun to operate, with most of their members fresh from prison themselves. The government is hostile to such groups and they have no rights of access to prisoners, though both have sources of information. In recent years, foreign delegations have visited the prisons. The International Committee of the Red Cross (ICRC), however, has not yet been permitted to establish a presence in Cuba, though there have been recent official contacts with the ICRC and indications are that it may gain entry. At present, officials from the prison system itself or from the office of the Fiscal General alone can be counted upon to protect the rights of prisoners.

The Cuban prison system is made very hard by the prolonged prison sentences that have prevailed. Although the officials with whom we spoke are quick to say that Cuba has a low crime rate (no statistics are published), and though this claim seems valid, the number of prisoners is very high. Assuming that the Cuban government's figures are correct, there are 32,000 inmates currently in prisons and detention centers. We received no figures on reform schools or military prisons. Given a nationwide population of about 10 million, the rate of imprisonment is 320 per 100,000.

In the United States, excluding military prisoners and including juvenile prisoners and county jail prisoners, we have approximately 930,000 prisoners in prisons and jails. Given a population of about 240 million, the rate is approximately 380 per 100,000 (statistics from the U.S. Department of Justice as of June 30, 1987). Even if we added prisoners in the military prisons, including draft resisters and draft evaders, the rate in Cuba would still be lower than in the United States. The United States has a very high crime rate and features one of the world's highest rates of imprisonment. In Cuba, with a low crime rate, the rate of imprisonment indicates extraordinarily long sentences. In the case of those prisoners who experience the worst of the Cuban prison system, it can mean several years in cramped, poorly lighted, locked cells with an hour a week in the sun and infrequent visits.

Cuba has recognized that its sentences are greatly prolonged, and some changes are underway. In 1987, 14,000 prisoners were reportedly released on parole. Some crimes have been eliminated in the new penal code effective April 1, 1988; some sentences are being reduced; parole is abbreviating some sentences; the same is the case with reductions of sentences for good behavior.

We applaud the fact that the Cuban government permitted the IPS delegation access to its prisons. Although our visit was constructive, it is only a single visit and we would hope that present discussions with the International Committee of the Red Cross about a permanent presence in Cuba will come to a successful conclusion.

Discussion Questions

1. A number of positive and negative features of imprisonment in Cuba are identified in the article. Are there examples of similar positive and negative features in prisons in the U.S.? If so, what are they and what impact may they have on the prisoners while confined and, eventually, upon the society into which they are likely to be readmitted upon release?
2. The team visiting the Cuban prisons noted that conditions in the Women's Prison of 211 Western Provinces in Havana province was "a model prison" due, primarily, to the "positive influence of a dedicated warden." What are some of the things a warden (superintendent or chief administrator of a prison) in the U.S. can do to improve the conditions of confinement in the prison he or she administers? What things may be beyond a warden's control?

5. Conditions of Confinement Within Security Prisons: Scandinavia and California*

John R. Snortum, Professor of Psychology at Claremont McKenna College
Kåre Bødal, Director of the program of prison research for the Ministry of Justice in Oslo, Norway

Abstract: Within the past three decades, the Scandinavian countries have acquired an international reputation for the development of innovative and humane prisons. Most of the favorable attention from journalists and social scientists has centered upon the so-called "model prisons," which are typically smaller, newer, and "open." However, the majority of Scandinavian prisoners are still incarcerated in the larger, older, locked prisons that are rather traditional in design and function. One might question whether these traditional prisons are, in fact, superior to American state prisons and whether they would meet emerging U.S. standards for conditions of confinement. This investigation surveyed the nature of prison programs, staffing ratios, living conditions, and visiting conditions within 16 "closed" or secure prisons, including 4 each from Norway, Sweden, Finland, and California. On most measures, the conditions of confinement were most severe in California prisons, much less severe in Finnish prisons, and least severe in Norwegian and Swedish prisons.

In 1978, state prisons in the United States were filled to 111% of reported capacity and 30 states were under court orders or consent decrees to improve prison practices and conditions (Mullen and Smith, 1980: Table 2.4). Five years later, state prison capacity had increased 50% but the prisons were still filled to 109% of capacity because of increases in incarceration rates. By the end of 1983, entire prison systems in 7 states had been declared unconstitutional or were operating under court order. Futhermore, one or more prisons in 24 other states and the District of Columbia were subject to court intervention, and litigation was pending in 9 additional states (Bureau of Justice Statistics, 1984).

---

*This research was supported by a grant from the Norwegian Marshall Fund and was written when the second author was a Fulbright-Hays Professor at the Institute for Advanced Study in Social Work, University of Trondheim, Norway. We appreciate the assistance of the following in coordinating the administration of the surveys: Norman Bishop, The National Prison and Probation Administration, Norrköping, Sweden; Miikku Nieminen, Finnish National Prison Administration, Helsinki, Finland; and Robert Dickover, Department of Corrections, Sacramento, California. Special thanks to Jorgen Balder of the Danish National Prison Administration for his cooperation in pretesting an earlier version of our survey within a small sample of Danish prisons.

Scandinavian prisons, on the other hand, have enjoyed generally favorable reviews from journalists (Durham, 1973; Serrill, 1977) and social scientists (Doleschal, 1977; Morris and Hawkins, 1970; Ward, 1972) for their innovative programs and their humane treatment of prisoners. Certain "model prisons" in Sweden have received concentrated international attention: Tillberga, a prison factory; Studiegården, a prison school; and Gävle, a "therapeutic community" (the Reasoner Report, 1974; Snortum, 1976). The contrast with U.S. prisons was dramatized in 1979 when Sweden's Supreme Court refused to extradite a convicted American sex offender because conditions of confinement in U.S. prisons were judged to be inhumane and the 59-year sentence was considered to be excessive (McCarthy, 1979). Despite the diplomatic tensions aroused by this case, American respect for Scandinavian correctional practice was implicitly acknowledged in 1983 when Chief Justice Warren Burger led a group of business, labor, and government leaders on a tour of Sweden's experimental prisons (Raspberry, 1983).

The present investigation surveyed conditions of confinement within 12 secure or "closed" prisons in Scandinavia. Although it was beyond our scope to attempt a comprehensive survey of secure confinement in the United States, we did obtain data from four California prisons in order to provide an American point of reference. In addition, wherever possible, we have drawn upon the massive survey of 559 federal and state prisons that was conducted in 1978 through the National Institute of Justice (Mullen et al., 1980; see also Greenfeld, n.d.).

It must be acknowledged at the outset that there are reasonable grounds for objecting to such a comparison. First, it might be argued that we are belaboring the obvious and pouring salt into a wound that is already painful to state correctional officials. For example, San Quentin's warden, Reginald Pulley, has been outspoken in criticizing his own facility as "a monstrosity" (Associated Press, 1982: 16) and a "time bomb" (Serrill, 1983: 64). Second, it is misleading to compare correctional systems without providing parallel comparisons of the cultural context within which the prisons function. And, third, it is unfair to compare prison systems facing administrative problems that fall on an entirely different scale of magnitude. For example, Scandinavian prison officials do not have to contend with the violence of organized ethnic gangs, nor have they had to accommodate the massive increases in admission rates experienced in the United States. During a four-year period starting December 31, 1979, the increase in the average daily prison population in California was greater than the total daily prison population in 1979 for Norway, Sweden, Denmark, and Finland combined (Flanagan et al., 1982: Table 6.24; Philip, 1983: 42).

Although these objections cannot be countered completely, there are balancing considerations supporting the usefulness of the proposed comparisons. First, it is not a foregone conclusion that the conditions of confinement in Scandinavia are exemplary. While international interest has centered upon a select sampling of smaller, newer, "model prisons," most Scandinavian prisoners continue to be incarcerated in larger, older, more secure prisons. It will be instructive to apply evolving American standards to some of these Scandinavian "fortress prisons."

Second, although the cultural context of Scandinavian and U.S. prisons will not be examined systematically, some of these issues will be raised by our data and still others have been reviewed elsewhere (Snortum, 1976, 1984a, 1984b). Futhermore, although it is customary to refer to the Scandinavian countries as if they represented a common culture, it was anticipated that some of the most interesting comparisons in this research would be among the Scandinavian countries themselves.

Finally, although it must be granted that California and other states face prison problems that differ both qualitatively and quantitatively from those in Scandinavia, not all of these problems are inevitable (e.g., incarceration rates) and none of these problems absolves a society from the moral obligation to provide its prisoners with humane conditions of confinement.

Orientation

Comparative research in criminal justice typically founders on the lack of common denominators in statistical reporting. However, some preliminary steps toward standardization within the Nordic countries have been fostered through the work of the Nordic Council for Criminal Statistics (von Hofer, 1982) and the Scandinavian Research Council for Criminology (Bishop, 1980). Drawing upon Scandinavian statistics compiled by Philip (1983: 42, 45), Table 1 shows that in 1980 Norway registered the lowest imprisonment rate per 100,000, followed closely by Sweden and Denmark, and with Finland showing a rate roughly twice as high as the other three. In trying to understand these national differences, it appears from Table 1 that the low Norwegian imprisonment rate may be a direct reflection of their low crime rates. On the other hand, the relatively high Finnish incarceration rate cannot be explained by the same rationale, for the crime rates in Finland are quite similar to those in Sweden and Denmark. Nevertheless, this gap may be closing, for from 1976 to 1981 the Swedish incarceration rate per 100,000 increased from 49 to 58, the Danish rate increased from 58 to 68, whereas the Finnish rate decreased from 118 to 101.

When comparing Scandinavian and American prisons, it is important to recognize some basic differences in correctional structure and terminology. Most states in the United States maintain a bifurcated correctional system that allocates state prisons for sentences of at least one year and local jails for pretrial detention and for sentences of less than one year. By contrast, each of the Scandinavian countries is organized around an integrated correctional system in which all sentences are said to be served in prisons. Although it is common Scandinavian practice to distinguish national prisons from local prisons for serving longer versus shorter sentences, the parallel with American prisons and jails is not perfect because of the greater degree of flexibility that is possible in an integrated system. For example, Swedish offenders with sentences exceeding one year are sent to national prisons, but they may be allowed to serve their last four months in a local prison. In Sweden and Denmark, pretrial detention is provided in special remand prisons; and in Norway and Finland, pretrial detention is an auxiliary function of regular prisons.

As an additional complication for American comparisons, national and local prisons in Scandinavia can be further differentiated into closed prisons

Table 1 Criminal Justice Statistics for the Scandinavian Countries

	Norway	*Sweden*	*Denmark*	*Finland*
Average daily prison census per 100,000 population (1980)[a]	43	55	63	106
Average daily prison census (1980)	1,751	4,569	3,213	5,089
Number of prisons by type (1981)				
Open prisons or open section	7	43	8	17
Closed prisons	34	39	5	16
Remand prisons[b]	—	23	45	—
Average places per prison (1980)				
Open prisons	55	39	128	72
Closed prisons	53	58	148	207
Percentage of total capacity in open prisons (1981)	17	33	34	27
Reported crime per 100,000 population 15 (14)–67 years				
Murder (1980)[c]	1	7	7	8
Rape (1980)	5	16	12	11
Robbery (1980)	11	61	42	56
Assault (1980)	146	440	140	414
Motor vehicle theft (1979)	404	839	1,024	247
Other theft (1979)	1,014	5,380	5,146	2,763

a Includes persons remanded in custody. All prison data were obtained from Philip (1983).

b Norway and Finland retain remand prisoners in regular, closed prisons.

c All reported crime data were obtained from von Hofer (1982).

(locked institutions) versus open prisons (unlocked prisons with easy community access for work, education, and social services). It is apparent from Table 1 that Scandinavian policymakers have elected to organize their respective prison systems around a large number of small prisons rather than a small number of large prisons. Futhermore, the broad distribution of open prisons throughout Scandinavia indicates a relatively strong commitment to the principle of "least restrictive confinement." Even so, when cell space for pretrial detention is included, Philip's 1981 data showed that more than 65% of the cells in each country were still devoted to closed prisons.

There are obvious difficulties in trying to equate Scandinavian and U.S. criminal justice statistics; however, the true differences are undoubtedly so large that even relatively crude comparisons may suffice. In 1978, when Scandinavian incarceration rates ranged from 43 per 100,000 in Norway to 113 in Finland (Philip, 1983), the estimated U.S. rate was 223 (Flanagan and McLeod, 1983: Tables 6.15, 6.24). Among these 223 hypothetical prisoners, 135 were held in state prisons, 12 were in federal prisons, and 76 were in local jails. Likewise, the U.S. crime rates per 100,000 for 1980 far exceeded those of any Scandinavian country—for example, murder and nonnegligent manslaughter, 10; forcible rape, 36; and robbery, 244 (Flanagan and McLeod, 1983: Table 3.53).

Narrowing the focus to California, as of 1983 the California state prison system was designed to hold 25,703 inmates (Bureau of Justice Statistics, 1984). The largest unit, Soledad, was built to accommodate 2,981 and the smallest, the California Institute for Women, was intended for 930 prisoners. At this writing, the California system includes two maximum security prisons, nine medium security prisons, two minimum-medium prisons, and a complex of minimum security forestry camps that were designed to accommodate 2,096 (Hurst, 1983a). California's incarceration rate per 100,000 at year-end 1978 was well below the U.S. average rate in state prisons (88 versus 123) and it continued to be below the average in 1983 (150 versus 179). However, in absolute terms, these high California rates signify an increased prison census from 21,325 to 39,360, thereby giving California the largest state prison population in the United States (Flanagan et al., 1982: Table 6.24; Bureau of Justice Statistics, 1984). Even after shuttling 1,244 prisoners to local jails, the 1983 prison population in California state prisons reached 148% of design capacity at year-end 1983 (Hurst, 1983a). In an effort to reduce overcrowding, California added a thirteenth prison to its system in 1983, called "Tent City." Tent City is a medium security enclosure of 42–person tents, designed to hold 958 inmates for up to 60 days, while awaiting assignment to other prisons.

Selection and Procedure

A 59–item inventory of prison facilities, populations, staff, and programs was sent to the senior administrator of selected prisons in Scandinavia (in 1982) and California (in 1983). To avoid asking for more administrative time than could be given, the survey instructions allowed respondents to cite statistics that were already available from previous annual reports or to estimate answers within 5% accuracy. Although a variety of types of prisons were surveyed, this report will present only the data obtained from closed prisons, including 4 each from Norway, Sweden, Finland, and California (Table 2). Our selection of closed prisons is biased toward the larger prisons (including the largest in each country) because these prisons also tend to be older and more traditional in design. Finally, it should be noted that, in each of the Scandinavian samples, at least three of the prisons are national prisons and, therefore, confine the most serious offenders for the longer terms. In short, we wished to examine those Scandinavian prisons that would provide the closest equivalent to state prisons in the United States.

The selection of California prisons included the two maximum security prisons, San Quentin and Folsom, and two medium security prisons, California Rehabilitation Center (CRC) and California Institution for Women (CIW). San Quentin and Folsom are notorious and are in no sense representative of the state system as a whole; however, they do provide an insight into the administrative problems in providing maximum security confinement in prisons built more than a century ago. Like San Quentin and Folsom, CRC and CIW are surrounded by high fences and gun towers; however, they occupy more attrac-

Table 2 Sample of Closed Prisons by Type, Capacity, and Composition

Prison	Prison Type	Sex	Capacity (n)	Census/ Capacity (%)	Pretrial (%)	Violent Crimes (%)	Drug Addicts (%)
Norway							
Oslo	Local	M	466	83	30	—[a]	40
Ullersmo	National	M	180	72	0	40	30
Ila	National	M	133	79	0	62	30
Bredtveit	National	F	37	95	29	14	44
Mean			204	83	15	39	36
Sweden							
Kumla	National	M	211	95	0	48	30
Hinseberg[b]	National	F	85	89	0	18	50
Skogome	National	M	75	89	0	47	30
Norrköping	National	M	39	92	0	37	40
Mean			103	91	0	38	38
Finland							
Helsinki	National	M	462	100	2	30	2
Hämeenlinna	National	M/F	321	141	13	15	2
Konnunsuo	National	M	281	110	0	25	0
Mikkeli	Local	M	89	119	46	32	0
Mean			288	118	15	26	1
California							
San Quentin	State	M	2600	131	0	100	40
Folsom	State	M	2058	121	0	90	50
CRC	State	M/F	2100	119	0	40	35
CIW	State	F	930	108	0	40	12
Mean			1922	120	0	68	34

a Missing data.

b Hinseberg also has an open section that accounts for 41% of cell space.

tive grounds and project a much softer architectural image. CIW, the smallest of the state prisons, is modern in design and is organized around relatively small blocks of 60 inmates. CRC was constructed on the grounds of a former health spa. Thus the prison is composed of an incongruous mix of structures, ranging from quite luxurious administrative buildings to rather spartan dormitories where most of the inmates are housed. Although a small number of female prisoners are incarcerated in CRC, the prison cannot properly be considered a coed prison because male and female inmates are isolated in separate compounds.

From the narrow selection of prisons presented in Table 2, it should be apparent that this study is intended to be illustrative rather than comprehensive; therefore, our analysis will be primarily descriptive rather than inferential. For purposes of verbal economy, we shall make occasional references to national means on several of the variables; however, it should be understood that we can make no generalizations about national prison systems as a whole. For this reason, all tables will include data from individual prisons in order to provide the safest guide to interpretation.[1]

Before examining the conditions of confinement within this sampling of closed prisons, we should acknowledge that differences in the proportion of inmates "who were sentenced for violent crimes" or "who are physically addicted to drugs" may drastically affect the security measures that must be imposed. As shown in Table 2, San Quentin and Folsom appear to be serving their specialized role for the detention of violent offenders and security risks (Gettinger, 1982). Although it is unlikely that "violent crimes" and "drug addiction" have precisely the same meanings across prison systems, it appears that the national prisons in Norway and Sweden must contend with significant proportions of each type of offender.

The drug problem was recently identified as "the single biggest difficulty" facing Swedish prison officials at a time when they are attempting to reduce the use of closed, national prisons (Martinsson and Bishop, 1983: 5). Finland seems to be a special case—the problem of hard drug use has not yet reached there. Although there appear to be smaller proportions of violent offenders in Finnish prisons than in Norwegian or Swedish prisons, we would expect this proportion to increase if there are continued policy developments toward more selective incarceration in Finland.

Results and Discussion

Physical conditions of confinement

A reported from the *Los Angeles Times* (1983: 3) offered these impressions of Alpine Block in San Quentin:

> The light is dim gray. The noise is constant, television and radio programs mix with whistles, clangs, music, shouts. The discordant mixture of noise ricochets off the steel and concrete of the cell block. The air is sour, stale, it smells like men crowded together. It smells like disinfectant and cigarettes and sweat and bad plumbing. And it smells somehow like fear.

Whether reported by journalists, by inmate diaries (Wright, 1973), or by systematic surveys of inmates (Mullen and Smith, 1980: Table A-4.26; Farabstein and Wener, 1982), there are certain recurring themes that seem to typify the hardships of American prisons: overcrowding, lack of privacy, noise, lack of basic amenities, and prison violence. Despite the acknowledged aversiveness of constant solitary confinement, prisoners need an occasional escape from staff surveillance and from the "fight-or-flight" vigilance that is generated by interactions with other inmates.

1. The tabled national means represent a simple average across prisons. We decided not to compute averages that were weighted according to the number of inmates per prison because this would mean that the largest prison would overwhelm the influence of the smaller prisons. For example, if weighted means were applied in Norway, the characteristics of Oslo prison would determine 59% of the national mean on the various items.

Rated Capacity

At the time of our survey, the census in the Norwegian and Swedish prisons was generally below their rated capacities, whereas the Finnish and California prisons were filled beyond their rated limits (see Table 2). By way of caution, it should be noted that rated capacity is an elastic concept that may connote very different standards across countries, across architectural periods within a country, and even across different time periods within a particular prison! In their survey of U.S. prison facilities, Mullen and Smith (1980: 8) observed, "With no modification in physical plant, it was not uncommon to see increases in reported capacity that merely corresponded to subsequent increases in the population." When minimum space-per-inmate standards of the American Correctional Association were applied to U.S. prisons, the rated capacities of state prisons were found to have been overstated by 22% and the capacities of local jails were overstated by 55%.

Despite the apparent adequacy of prison space in Norway and Sweden, administrators in both countries believe that they are short of room. Norwegian prison administrators have been able to avoid overtaxing their resources only with the aid of a queuing system that is currently being pressed to the limit. In spring 1984, approximately 5,000 minor offenders were waiting in line to serve short prison terms. The Swedish National Prison Administration recently obtained governmental approval that the functional limit of their system should be placed at 85% of rated capacity (Edholm and Bishop, 1983: 2). Beyond this limit, administrators begin to lose the flexibility to assure that shorter prison terms can be served in the nearest local prison and that drug-free offenders can be housed away from addicted offenders and dealers.

Privacy

Although dormitory quarters were once thought to be more humane because they are less restrictive than individual cells, recent standards advocate single cells because they "provide privacy and enable inmates to personalize space" (Standards from the ACA Commission on Accreditation for Corrections, cited in Mullen and Smith, 1980: Table 3.1). Where dormitory housing cannot be avoided, the standards require at least 60 square feet of space per inmate, prohibit double bunks, and specify a limit of 50 prisoners per living unit. All of the prisons in this survey, except for CRC in California and Mikkeli in Finland, were constructed to house most of their inmates in cells rather than in dormitories. A second facet of privacy is "occupancy," for a prison cell is not private if it is filled beyond capacity by double- or even triple-bunking. It is clear from Table 3 that all inmates in the Norwegian and Swedish prisons were given private cells, whereas many of the Finnish prisoners and most of the California prisoners were either in group quarters or were double-bunked in a single cell. The California figures are consistent with the 1978 survey of state and federal prisons (Greenfeld, n.d.) showing that 55% of U.S. inmates shared prison quarters with at least one other inmate.

Still a third dimension of privacy is structural screening, for there is no real escape from visual surveillance or auditory bombardment if your single cell is enclosed by open bars rather than by a wall and solid door. Of course, if two inmates are confined to a single cell, a solid door may convert to a liability

Table 3 Conditions of Confinement

Prison	*Private Cell (%)*	*Solid Door (%)*	*Cell Time Hrs.*	*Cell Size Sq. Ft.*	*Desk/ Chair (%)*	*Own Key (%)*	*Mess Hall (%)*	*Lockup Rate (%)*
Norway								
Oslo	100	100	18	108	99	37	37	0
Ullersmo	100	100	11	66	100	70	87	7
Ila	100	100	10	65	100	100	85	6
Bredtveit	100	100	11	79	100	30	43	0
Mean	100	100	13	80	100	59	63	3
Sweden								
Kumla	100	100	11	65	100	0	96	3
Hinseberg	100	100	11[a]	65	100	0	100	0
Skogome	100	100	11	65	100	0	100	0
Norrköping	100	100	11	86	100	0	100	0
Mean	100	100	11	70	100	0	99	1
Finland								
Helsinki	95	75	15	94	100	0	30	3
Hämeenlinna	60	100	12	121	100	0	90	0
Konnunsuo	70	100	12	108	100	0	50	0
Mikkeli	3	100	14	79[b]	100	0	0	1
Mean	57	94	13	101	100	0	43	1
California								
San Quentin	50	0	19	38	0	10	40	47
Folsom	40	15	17	45	15	15	65	28
CRC	3	3	12	—[c]	3	3	100	0
CIW	63	100	8	96	100	1	99	5
Mean	39	30	14	60	30	7	76	20

a Confinement in the open section is only 9 hours per day.
b The average dormitory space in Mikkeli is 48 square feet and in CRC is 70 square feet. (However, the latter figure includes group activity areas as well as sleeping areas.)
c Missing data.

because it may serve to screen the sheer terror imposed by the stronger inmate on the weaker. Solid door construction appears to be almost universal in Scandinavian prisons but was available only in the women's prison in the California sample. The problem is particularly acute in a prison like San Quentin where the three largest cell blocks each contain 500 open-bar cells, stacked in tiers of 100 cells per tier (Davidson, 1974).

Cell Time and Cell Space

Court challenges of prison conditions have tended to target three physical aspects of overcrowding: *occupancy,* the number of inmates per confinement unit, as just discussed; *freedom of movement,* the number of hours per day confined to quarters; and *density,* the number of square feet of living space per inmate. The United Nations has set a minimum standard of 65 square feet per inmate;

however, the most frequently cited U.S. standard is 60 square feet (Mullen and Smith, 1980: 19, Table 3.1). If the inmate is confined for more than 10 hours per day, the U.S. minimum standard is raised to 80 square feet per inmate.

Because our survey yields only a measure of the typical conditions of confinement in each prison rather than a cell-by-cell inventory of occupancy by cell size and confinement time, we cannot calculate a precise rate of crowding as did Mullen and Smith (1980). However, applying our general measures individually and in combination, we can gain a rough gauge of the degree of compliance of these Scandinavian prisons with current U.S. standards. *Cell size:* Among the 12 Scandinavian prisons in our sample, all would pass the minimum U.S. standard of 60 square feet as well as the U.N. standard of 65 square feet. *Cell size constrained by cell time:* Only one Scandinavian prison kept inmates confined to quarters for as few as 10 hours per day; however, five additional prisons compensated for longer confinement time by providing at least 80 square feet of living space. *Occupancy:* Among the six prisons that met the cell time and space standards, only three provided private cells and adequate space for all of their inmates (Oslo, Ila, and Norrköping).

If we follow common accreditation practice in recognizing "substantial compliance," we discover several prisons that met two of the criteria while barely missing a third. One prison exceeded the 10-hour confinement limit by 1 hour (Ullersmo) and, adding greater precision than the tabled figures, four missed the mark by only 30 minutes (Bredtveit, Kumla, Hinseberg, and Skogome). One other prison provided private cells for all but 5% of their inmates (Helsinki). Thus we find that 9 out of 12 Scandinavian prisons appear to be in total or substantial compliance with the criteria for private living space (4 Swedish prisons, 4 Norwegian prisons, and 1 Finnish prison).

None of the 4 California prisons met or even approached these same standards.[2] CIW provides relatively spacious cells and imposes shorter hours of confinement than even the Scandinavian prisons. Unfortunately, population pressures required double celling for more than a third of the inmates. At the most negative extreme, San Quentin and Folsom failed all three criteria by wide margins. These maximum security prisons subject their inmates to very small cells for very long hours each day. To make a bad situation worse, half or more of the inmates were forced to share this small cell with another prisoner.

The 1978 survey of U.S. state and federal prisons painted a somewhat brighter picture of confinement hours—an average of 9.65 hours per day. On the other hand, 65% of all inmates were found to have less than 60 square feet of living space (Greenfeld, n.d.). There was little sign of compliance with the 80 square feet standard for prisoners who were confined for more than 10 hours per day: 61% were held in cells smaller than 60 square feet, 33% were in cells

---

2. Apart from the issues of privacy and hours of confinement, it appears that CRC group quarters would meet the dormitory standard of 60 square feet per inmate. However, our data were not sufficiently refined to evaluate a number of criteria related to dormitory occupancy, such as group size, double bunking, ceiling height, and air circulation.

from 60 to 79 square feet, and only 6% were appropriately placed in cells at least 80 square feet in size (Mullen and Smith, 1980: Table 3.10).

Amenities

There seems to be an implicit understanding within these Scandinavian countries that a desk and chair are no less essential to a prison cell than, say, a bed or a door. In our California sample, on the other hand, such cell furnishings were standard only in the women's prison. Part of the problem may be that in older prisons such as San Quentin, with its 4.5 by 8.5 feet cells,[3] there is very little available space after accommodating the usual bed, open toilet stool, and sink. A survey of basic amenities available in U.S. prison cells was conducted in 1978 through site visits to 21 prisons (Mullen and Smith, 1980: Table A-4.1). An examination of 89 representative cell blocks revealed that a chair or stool was generally provided in 67% of the cell blocks and a desk was provided in 54% of the blocks sampled.

All of the Norwegian prisons provided many or most of their inmates with keys to lock their own doors during daytime hours. (Such keys are also commonly available in open prisons in Norway, Sweden, and Denmark.) Although this practice may confirm the suspicion of many correctional conservatives that Scandinavian administrators have "given away the store," the practice is defended on these grounds. First, cell doors are controlled in most prisons by an independent locking system at night. Second, if the prison cell is truly a refuge rather than a punishment chamber, the inmate should have discretionary access to the cell when not engaged in other activities. And, third, if the cell has in fact been "personalized" with personal belongings, it is essential that the inmate should be able to keep these items secure.

Freedom of Movement

The earlier measure on cell time per day provides the most direct expression of this concept. A narrower but, nonetheless, important facet of mobility centers around the feeding of inmates. In the barren world of prisons, mealtime may represent a high point in the day because food takes on increased significance and because the walk to the dining hall provides a break from cell routine. Some prisons simply do not have a dining hall; still others justify feeding some or all prisoners in their cells because they are assumed to pose a security or management problem. Our sample of Swedish prisons provided almost all of their inmates with the opportunity for meals away from their cells, but the rates for California, Norway, and Finland were generally lower, particularly in their largest prisons.

Even though prisons may report that the average prisoner is confined to quarters for only 10 to 12 hours per day, there may still be a significant proportion of prisoners who are subjected to "lockup"—virtually round-the-clock confinement except for showers and brief periods of exercise. Because of the need to isolate these prisoners from the mainline population, this "exercise" typically occurs in a small enclosure and usually takes the form of ritualized

---

3. San Quentin's West block was reported by Murphy (1983) to be slightly larger (44.5 square feet). Likewise, the cells in San Quentin's Alpine block were reported to be 50.6 square feet (*Los Angeles Times*, 1983).

pacing. Lockup may be imposed for disciplinary reasons or may be granted at the inmate's request for protection from rape and other violence. It is apparent from Table 3 that lockup is rarely used or needed in Scandinavian prisons, whereas there is concentrated use of lockup in California's maximum security prisons.

There is still another constraint upon movement within the prison that was not tapped in our survey—"lockdown." Lockdown means that all or most of the prisoners are confined to quarters (except for meals and showers) during extraordinary institutional crises. The extraordinary is becoming ordinary in Folsom and San Quentin. Folsom was reportedly in lockdown for 37 days in 1982 and for 110 days during the first 11 months of 1983 (Associated Press, 1983). More serious conditions were reported for San Quentin in September 1983 (Murphy, 1983: 6): "Most of the 1,024 mainline inmates have been under lockdown since June 1982, when a riot broke out in the exercise yard. . . . More than 2,000 other inmates are always kept in 'lockup' because of behavioral problems and other concerns. . . . 'Eventually we are heading toward 100 percent lockup,' said McCullough [a prison official]."

Staffing and Services

There is general agreement in Scandinavia (Bishop, 1975; Antilla and Törnudd, 1980) and in the United States that the "treatment model" can no longer serve as a judicial rationale for sentencing. Nevertheless, a number of prison programs, which previously may have been required as a condition for release, continue to be offered to prison "consumers" who desire the services; for example, general education, vocational training, religious services, athletics, and personal counseling.

Staffing Patterns

Table 4 presents ratios of the average prison census to the number of staff in three categories: *custody staff* for security and control; *administrative staff* for managerial and clerical duties; and *program staff*, including teachers, medical personnel, social workers, psychologists, chaplains, and others.

Examining the custody staff levels, we see a rough equivalence in the number of prisoners to guards in Sweden, a two-to-one ratio in Norway, a three-to-one ratio in Finland, and a five-to-one ratio in California. The same rank ordering follows for administrative staff and, with one exception, for program staff. Because this rank ordering parallels the ranks for average prison size (Table 2), it is possible that economies of scale can account for some of these national differences.

There are also some important differences in the pattern of resource allocation for staff positions that would be obscured by relying upon the rank orders alone. For example, dividing the mean level of program staffing by the level of custody staffing within each country yields roughly a three-to-one ratio of custody staff over program staff in Norway (4.5/1.8), a five-to-one ratio in Sweden, seven-to-one in Finland, and eight-to-one in California. Although the strong custodial emphasis in California prisons might be explained by the high proportion of violent offenders (Table 2), the same interpretation would not account for the custodial emphasis in Finland.

Table 4 Inmate-Staff Ratios, Program Participation, and Prison Pay

Prison	*Inmate-Custody Ratio*	Inmate-Admin. Ratio	*Inmate-Program Ratio*	Academic Program[a] (%)	Vocational Program (%)	*Hourly Pay[b] ($)*
Norway						
Oslo	2.6	6.4	4.8	18	6	.52
Ullersmo	1.9	8.1	7.6	26	5	.66
Ila	1.5	5.8	2.3	18	6	.91
Bredtveit	1.3	5.0	3.2	60	44	.45
Mean	1.8	6.3	4.5	31	15	.64
Sweden						
Kumla	.9	6.3	3.6	25	0	.69
Hinseberg	1.1	5.1	3.6	49	7	.77
Skogome	1.3	7.4	4.2	2	0	2.66
Norrköping	.5	6.0	7.2	75	0	.77
Mean	1.0	6.2	4.7	38	2	1.22
Finland						
Helsinki	3.3	20.0	6.3	6	0	.24
Hämeenlinna	2.9	11.3	15.1	1	2	—[c]
Konnunsuo	2.8	11.5	38.8	3	4	.24
Mikkeli	2.2	7.1	15.1	5	0	.24
Mean	2.8	12.5	18.8	4	2	.24
California						
San Quentin	4.5	13.6	34.0	27	6	—[c]
Folsom	4.5	12.5	25.0	13	12	.20
CRC	5.9	25.0	13.9	10	12	.18
CIW	4.2	16.4	83.3	15	15	.11
Mean	4.8	16.9	39.1	16	11	.16

a Academic and vocational participation rates were based upon the number of sentenced inmates in each prison.

b The currency rate on March 17, 1982, pegged the U.S. dollar at 6.02 Norwegian Crowns, 5.82 Swedish Crowns, and 4.55 Finnish Marks.

c Missing data.

Although it is commonly assumed that prison security serves staff goals whereas prison programs serve inmate goals, this dichotomy is too facile. In a landmark class action suit against the District of Columbia Department of Corrections, 400 inmates from Lorton Reformatory won an award of $600,000 on the grounds that the prison had not provided enough guards to ensure the inmates' physical safety (Mullen and Smith, 1980: 96). In this regard, our survey of Scandinavian prisons revealed no prison homicides during the previous 2-year period; however, there were 18 inmates killed in the 4 California prisons (10 in San Quentin and 8 in Folsom). It is noteworthy that one inmate was killed in Ila prison shortly after our survey was completed. A review of prison archives disclosed that this was the first murder within Norwegian prison walls since World War II.

Prison Programs

Table 4 also shows the proportion of prison inmates who were participating in academic and vocational programs. It appears that academic instruction was rather broadly available in the Swedish and Norwegian prisons, somewhat less available in California prisons, and seldom available in Finnish prisons. Vocational training slots were available to a small segment of Norwegian and California prisoners but were almost nonexistent within this sample of Swedish and Finnish prisons.

Whereas implementation of educational and vocational programs in Scandinavia is often hampered by the fast turnover of inmates with short sentences, the problem is just the reverse in California's maximum security prisons. There is very little incentive for inmates to undertake a demanding apprenticeship program if their prison sentences extend into the next century. As San Quentin and Folsom have come to serve an increasingly "hard core" population, there has been a decline in the levels of aptitude and motivation for program participation. For example, the printing apprenticeship program in San Quentin is in jeopardy due to a lack of inmates with sufficient math skills to handle the simple calculations that are required in the work. Furthermore, there are not enough teachers to implement an intensive remedial program. The relatively high participation rate in San Quentin's education program may look impressive; however, the limited capacity of the formal academic program would allow only 186 of the 3,400 prisoners to enroll. The 27% figure cited in Table 4 includes inmates participating in a variety of informal, peripheral programs, including cell study.

Finally, Table 4 shows that the average hourly pay for prison jobs was generally higher in Swedish prisons than in Norwegian prisons, and both prison systems awarded much higher pay than was offered in Finnish and California prisons. The extraordinary pay rate at Skogome prison in Sweden stems from an experimental program in "market adjusted wages" for work in prison industries (a laundry and a clothing factory). Inmates are paid in proportion to their productivity based upon work rates of laborers in comparable outside industries, with a further adjustment downward to balance the fact that inmates do not pay income taxes. Because Skogome inmates pay for their own meals, the pay discrepancy with other prisons is less sharp than the figures in Table 4 would indicate.

Prison employment continues to be a sensitive issue in the California prison system. In February 1983, San Quentin inmates staged a brief work strike to protest the introduction of the state's Work Incentive Program, a credit system whereby working inmates could reduce their sentences by up to one-half. Despite the intuitive appeal of the concept, a number of problems were encountered in the initial stages of implementation. Because of the shortage of jobs, many inmates were assigned to "make work" projects such as repeated washing of walls or moving dirt from place to place. Strict adherence to working hours interfered with opportunities for family visits and canteen purchases.

Furthermore, there were no accrued benefits for inmates serving life terms, and there was no opportunity for inmates in protective segregation to participate in the program despite their willingness to work (Bishop, 1983; Mockler, 1983).

Visiting Conditions

Apart from the purely humanitarian concern that prisoners should be able to maintain contact with their loved ones, there is the practical presumption that supportive relationships are a positive force for success following release (Burstein, 1977). The Scandinavian countries, particularly Sweden and Norway, have continued to push for smaller, more widely distributed prisons in an effort to preserve the inmate's links to family and community. Toward this end, all three Scandinavian countries in this survey allow eligible inmates to make home visits prior to release. Based upon estimates provided by administrators, the national means for prisons in this survey (not tabled) revealed the following proportions of inmates making one or more home visits: Norway, 83%; Sweden, 78%; Finland, 56%; California, 2%.

Statistics provided by Bishop (1984) place Swedish home visits in a clearer perspective. Among 13,798 persons sentenced to Swedish prisons in 1982, 7,753 were serving two months or less and, therefore, were ineligible for home visits. The remaining 6,045 inmates were granted almost 42,000 home leaves, or an average of 7 leaves per inmate. One of the incentives for working in Skogome, a "prison factory," is the possibility of receiving home visits as often as every three weeks.

Another means for supporting the inmate's network of social relationships is to provide prison visiting areas that enhance communication and closeness. As shown in Table 5, all of the Swedish prisons and three of the Norwegian prisons provided individual rooms that afford complete privacy for personal intimacy, including sexual relations. Many of these rooms have curtained doors or windows that can be left open for monitoring in those few instances where security or visitor safety might be in question. An administrative comment accompanying the Swedish surveys noted that "culturally speaking, sexual activity is regarded as a private matter for every person, including prisoners. . . . No rules or regulations are specifically directed toward preventing sexual contact. We assume that virtually all prisoners have some opportunity for sexual contact." Likewise, Norwegian prison administrators do not attempt to screen out casual girlfriends or homosexual friends from making unsupervised visits. Finnish prisons, on the other hand, take a more traditional approach to prison visitors. All four Finnish prisons provided a large group room for visiting, and two of these prisons also offered individual visiting rooms (subject to monitoring by the staff).

The coordination of visits in California's huge maximum security prisons presents enormous administrative problems. Prisoners receiving visitors must be located, cleared, and (depending upon security level) escorted to the visiting room. Visitors, likewise, must be cleared and searched for contraband. Following the visit, family members must be detained until the prisoner has been subjected to a search. Due to a shortage of facilities and personnel, on the busiest days there may be families who have driven hundreds of miles who do not get

Table 5 The Nature of Prison Visiting Conditions

Prison	*Screen or Glass Partition*	Large Group Room	Monitored Separate Day Room	Private Separate Day Room	Overnight Quarters
Norway					
Oslo		XXXXX	XXXXX		
Ullersmo			XXXXX	XXXXX	
Ila				XXXXX	
Bredtveit			XXXXX	XXXXX	
Sweden					
Kumla			XXXXX	XXXXX	
Hinseberg				XXXXX	
Skogome				XXXXX	
Norrköping			XXXXX	XXXXX	
Finland					
Helsinki		XXXXX			
Hämeenlinna		XXXXX			
Konnunsuo		XXXXX	XXXXX		
Mikkeli		XXXXX	XXXXX		
California					
San Quentin	XXXXX	XXXXX	XXXXX		XXXXX
Folsom	XXXXX	XXXXX	XXXXX		XXXXX
CRC		XXXXX			XXXXX
CIW	XXXXX	XXXXX			XXXXX

to see the prisoner before turning around again. To avoid this, many visitors sleep in their cars in the prison parking lot on the night before their visit.

The four California prisons showed the greatest diversity of visiting accommodations. Three of the prisons require that suspected narcotics dealers or users be separated from their visitors by a glass partition and converse over the phone. Even though large banks of phones are available in San Quentin and Folsom, the system is often overtaxed and then conversations must be limited to one hour. (Ironically, CRC, the institution that was once devoted exclusively to drug addicts, is not equipped with glass partitions.) The most common setting for visitations in California prisons is the large group room, with spouses, children, and other relatives gathered around crowded tables. Despite close supervision, there are often scenes of sexual fondling and, occasionally, even desperate attempts at intercourse amidst the noise and chaos. In San Quentin, prisoners on death row are escorted through the group room in manacles and then must meet their visitors in tiny bar-enclosed plexiglas boxes, in full view of the crowd.

California prisons, like those in Norway and Sweden, have provisions for conjugal visiting; however, the California Family Visiting Program differs in form and function from the approach in Scandinavia. The furnished living units that are available for one to two days offer a more natural setting for conjugal visits than the formal reception rooms that are allotted for one to two hours in Norwegian and Swedish prisons. However, it is difficult for California prisoners to gain access to the facilities. As Goetting (1982: 56) noted in her review of the seven states that allow conjugal visits, the philosophical emphasis in California is upon "family unity, as opposed to sexual release. Thus, family visits frequently include children, parents, or siblings in addition to or in lieu of the inmate's spouse." Unmarried inmates in California prisons may use the overnight quarters to visit with parents, siblings, or children but not with a paramour or common-law spouse. This restriction was challenged in a case representing an inmate who had lived for seven years with his common-law wife; however, the California State Supreme Court upheld the state's denial of conjugal visits (Hager, 1982).

Goetting (1982) reported a total of 16,716 family visits in California prisons for the year ending March 31, 1980. Given that about half of these visits involved family members other than the prisoner's spouse and given a year-end census of 24,569 inmates in 1980, it is clear that only a small proportion of inmates received even one conjugal visit that year. Nevertheless, it should be remembered that California is one of a very small number of states to offer any form of conjugal visiting. Furthermore, despite the restrictive qualifications and the shortage of facilities, it is clear from interviews with prisoners and their families (Hurst, 1983b) that the family visiting program is highly valued and holds great symbolic importance to the prison population at large.

Overview and Conclusions

We have surveyed some basic conditions of imprisonment in Norway, Sweden, Finland, and California. To provide the fairest comparison to state prisons, we have limited our selection of Scandinavian prisons to closed prisons and have skewed our sample toward the larger prisons. Furthermore, we have included at least three national prisons from each country because they are typically the most secure prisons where the most serious offenders serve the longest terms. Finally, it should be noted that if our sample might be expected to probe the "worst case" conditions in Scandinavia, the same is true in the California state system because we included both of the state's maximum security prisons in our survey. Although it is acknowledged that the California state prisons are at a relative disadvantage to Scandinavian prisons in having to accommodate a higher proportion of violent offenders, there is little doubt that an examination of California's local jails would have revealed that minor offenders face even worse conditions of crowding, visiting, freedom of movement, and program staffing.[4]

Of all the Nordic countries, Sweden has made the most concerted effort to diversify its prison system by deemphasizing the use of large, national prisons in favor of establishing a large number of small, local prisons—many of which are open prisons. For this reason, the present survey of large, closed, national

4. Figures 3.13 and 3.14 in Mullen and Smith (1980) show that less than 10% of California prison inmates were held in "crowded" confinement units in 1978, whereas more than 55% of California prisoners in local correctional facilities were crowded.

prisons would tend to do the greatest injustice to Sweden if our findings should be misconstrued as representing the total Swedish correctional system. Much the same could be said about Finland for, as in Sweden, Finnish open prisons outnumber closed prisons (Philip, 1983). The total capacity (including pretrial detention) devoted to open prisons in 1980 was 33% in Sweden and 27% in Finland, compared to only 17% in Norway. The closest equivalent to open prisons in the United States is the "community-based pre-release facility." In their survey of American prisons, Mullen et al. (1980: 69) noted that such facilities were "barely visible as a component of adult custodial corrections"; and they accounted for only 4% of the state and federal census in 1978.

The conditions of imprisonment were quite similar in our samples of Norwegian and Swedish prisons. Both prison systems have generous provisions for home leaves and both allow easy access to unsupervised privacy with prison visitors. The closed prisons in both countries are relatively small and, at the time of this survey, prison populations were being held within the capacity limits of their facilities. Norwegian and Swedish prisoners were commonly provided with individual cells measuring 65 feet or greater. The cells were equipped with solid doors for privacy and furnished with a desk and chair for convenience. Thus, applying crude measures, it appeared that all four closed prisons in both samples met or approached current U.S. standards for privacy, occupancy, and density.

There were some areas where Swedish prisons showed a slight advantage over Norwegian prisons. They provided somewhat higher levels of staff support, they placed a slightly higher proportion of their inmates in academic programs, they paid slightly higher wages for prison jobs, and they more consistently provided a separate dining area away from the cells. On the other hand, the Norwegian prisons placed a somewhat stronger emphasis than Swedish prisons upon vocational training and they were more likely to provide inmates with keys for locking their own cells. Nevertheless, in the broader context of comparisons with Finland and California, these slight differences fade in importance and the predominant impression is the similarity of Norway and Sweden in providing relatively humane conditions within their closed prisons.

Conditions of confinement in Finland's closed prisons fell between those in California versus Norway and Sweden—though closer to the latter than the former. Finnish prisons are large by Scandinavian standards but, of course, do not approach the size of California's megaprisons. A small proportion of Finnish prisoners were confined in dormitories, though most were housed in cells. Except for serious problems of overcrowding, Finnish cells are among the most spacious in Scandinavia. And, in fact, the cells in Hämeenlinna could accommodate two inmates by the 60 square feet standard if shorter hours of confinement were imposed. Finnish prison cells shared the classical Scandinavian features of solid door construction and were furnished with a desk and chair. In functional terms, Finnish closed prisons appeared to be operating under a "bare bones" allocation of resources: minimal program staffing, little emphasis upon educational and vocational programs, and low pay for prison work. Although Finnish prisoners were allowed home visits prior to release, there were no private accommodations within the prisons for sexual intimacy during visiting hours.

Despite the somewhat austere picture of secure confinement in Finland, we anticipate long-range comparability of Finnish prisons with those in Norway and Sweden based upon two factors: first, Finland already has a record of political risk taking in introducing sentencing reforms (Joutsen, 1983), open prisons, and union scale wages in certain factory prisons;[5] second, there is the facilitative influence of relative comparisons and competition among the Nordic nations themselves.

To no one's surprise, California prisons anchored the negative extreme on most of the international comparisons in the present survey. However, before reviewing these general findings, we should note three relatively bright spots in the California prison system. First, California prisons were similar to Norwegian prisons and superior to Swedish and Finnish prisons in the proportion of inmates receiving vocational training. Second, CIW imposed the shortest hours of daily confinement among all prisons in the comparison; furthermore, if double celling could be avoided, the cells in CIW would be comparable to the best in Scandinavia in terms of privacy, space, and furnishings. Third, California prisons provided overnight quarters for family visiting whereas Scandinavian prisons did not. (Nevertheless, we hasten to add that the Norwegian and Swedish system of home visits combined with brief but frequent conjugal visits during regular visiting hours is functionally superior to the closely rationed California program in meeting the emotional needs of the inmates.)

California's two maximum security prisons projected a particularly oppressive picture of prison life, including overcrowding, lack of privacy, lack of space, lack of cell amenities, lack of safety, long hours of confinement, prison labor at slave wages, sexual deprivation, and visiting conditions that were, for the most part, chaotic and demeaning. What is more surprising is that the two medium security prisons, CRC and CIW, were only marginally better in most respects. Bad as these conditions may be, they are probably not atypical for state prisons in the United States (Mullen and Smith, 1980: Figure 3.13).

If it is not news that such prison conditions exist in California and elsewhere in the United States, is it possible that they are bad by design rather than by default? In 1978, when the U.S. incarceration rate was already among the highest in the world, 85% of Americans believed that the courts "do not deal harshly enough with criminals" (Flanagan and McLeod, 1983: Table 2.40). By contrast, there appears to be a far less punitive attitude in Scandinavia. When respondents in eight countries were asked to recommend appropriate sanctions for seven major crimes, the stiffest penalties were assigned in Kuwait and the United States, whereas the mildest sanctions were proposed in Sweden, Denmark, Finland, and Norway (Scott and Al-Thakeb, 1977). Interestingly, drunk driving is one offense that seems to elicit a reversed pattern of punitiveness in

5. In Köylio, one of the Finnish open prisons that we surveyed, the average hourly pay was $2.93, which is even higher than the rate in Sweden's Skogome prison.

public attitudes and sanctions in Scandinavia and the United States (Snortum, 1984b). Whereas drunk drivers are seldom incarcerated in the United States, these offenders annually constitute more than a quarter of the new admissions to Norwegian and Swedish prisons. It is sometimes suggested, only half in jest, that because drunk drivers tend to come from all segments of society, the threat of imprisonment for this offense serves to give the middle class a stake in maintaining humane prisons.

California is about to begin a billion dollar construction program to alleviate the problem of overcrowding. However, even this huge investment will not solve the problem if recent incarceration trends continue. According to Dennis Dunne (Hurst, 1983a: 1), deputy director for prison planning, after the new construction is completed, "We'll be at 111 percent of design capacity. And then we'll have to build one 500-bed institution every 60 days into infinity . . . and we'll still lose a little ground at that rate." In opposition to this building program, James Austin (Hurst, 1983c: 1) of the National Council on Crime and Delinquency believes that there is a less costly solution: "With a pencil, you could fix the crowding situation in California." Most proposals for sentencing reform typically derive from either of two basic strategies: to reduce the length of sentences for major crimes or to reduce the number of minor crimes that are subject to imprisonment.

Even after pushing sentencing reform to the limits of political acceptability, it is likely that overcrowding will continue to be a problem in the near future. The construction of additional prison space would seem to offer humane relief; however, opponents warn that no matter what rationalization is offered for building new cells, the end result is to increase incarceration rates (Sherman and Hawkins, 1981). The proconstructionists respond, in turn, that rigid opposition to new prisons amounts to "ideological grandstanding" at the expense of inmates who must continue to live under increasingly degrading circumstances. And, ironically, the anticonstructionist position plays into the hands of ultraconservatives who contend that the imprisonment must be unpleasant for purposes of deterrence. There is no easy choice between these two extremes because it appears that undesirable consequences will follow either policy. We can, at least, support a middle course toward prison reconstruction. For those prisons that are "beyond rehabilitation," we endorse a one-for-one replacement of tiny cells in older megaprisons with larger, private cells in smaller, regional prisons.

There may be a tendency for the casual observer to assume that Norway and Sweden were somehow "blessed" with manageable prison systems because they are small, homogeneous countries with low unemployment and low crime rates. Although these are certainly contributing factors, this interpretation overlooks the continuing series of hard political decisions by Norwegian and Swedish legislators over the past century. In Norway, for example, the average daily prison census per 100,000 population increased from 61 in 1814 to 191 in 1843—a figure that is close to the current U.S. rate (Christie, 1975). An official penal commission in 1841 recommended the construction of 7 new prisons to be built on the Philadelphia model (Mathiesen, 1980). Fortunately, only one of these prisons was built because a strong counter-cycle of reduced incarceration soon emerged. This reversal was augmented by a number of policy reforms, including legal authority for dropping of charges, 1887; introduction of conditional sentences, plus general reductions in lengths of sentences, 1894; decriminalization of selected sexual acts, 1927; abolition of work houses for alcoholics, 1970; reduction of petty theft from a felony to a misdemeanor, 1972; and dismantling of the vocational training schools as well as discontinuation of associated indeterminate sentences, 1975 (Bødal, 1976; Røstad, 1978).

Because of higher crime rates in Sweden than in Norway, Swedish legislators have faced an even more difficult challenge in controlling the incarceration rate and in maintaining quality prisons. Whatever may motivate their large investment in small prisons, it is clear that their policies are not based upon expectations of therapeutic gains (the National Prison Administration, 1980). Quite the contrary, they believe that prisons, though unavoidable, are essentially destructive in their effects and, therefore, prison programs can at best aim to serve as a kind of damage control.

Among the newer Swedish programs designed to attenuate the effects of imprisonment are: (1) *prison sojourns,* extended periods of residence away from the prison for participation in more constructive programs such as drug treatment, vocational training, or military service; (2) *work and study release,* for participation in community programs during daytime hours; and (3) *family placement,* to allow drug-addicted inmates to live and work with families in rural areas. What is striking about these programs is the degree of personalization and trust that is implied. Similar observations were offered in an earlier review (Snortum, 1976: 162) of Swedish "model prisons": "My most salient memory of Swedish prisons is their small size. I was impressed to see that prison administrators knew most of the inmates by name." Thus, although we have quantified a number of physical conditions of confinement that are undoubtedly important to the prisoners, we recognize that subtle experiential elements were not adequately captured by our survey. Perhaps this "human dimension" will eventually prove to be the most crucial factor in determining the quality of daily prison life.

Discussion Questions

1. The authors of this article state that "it is misleading to compare correctional systems without providing parallel comparisons of the cultural context within which the prisons function." Why is the cultural context so important? How might the differences in prison conditions uncovered by the authors be explained in terms of differences in cultural contexts?
2. The authors indicate that policymakers in Scandinavia have decided to have many small prisons rather than a few large prisons. What is gained by having small prisons? Is anything lost by having small prisons?
3. Compare and contrast the problems experienced in the Scandinavian prisons with some of the problems found in California prisons and other U.S. prisons. What could the U.S. do to make its prisons more

humane? Are there political barriers that might impede such efforts? If so, what are these barriers, and how might they be overcome?

4. In your opinion, of what importance are differences in inmate-custody and inmate-program ratios between the Scandinavian and California prisons (see Table 4) in terms of the quality of life found in a prison?
5. Assume, for the sake of discussion, that you were sentenced to prison. In which system (Sweden, Norway, Finland, or California) would you choose to do your time and why?

References

Anttila, I. and P. Törmudd 1980 "Reasons for punishment," in N. Bishop (ed.) *Crime and Crime Control in Scandinavia* 1976–80. Norrköping, Sweden: Scandinavian Research Council for Criminology.

Associated Press 1982 "New warden calls San Quentin a 'monstrosity.'" *Progress Bull.* February 10:16.

———. 1983 "Folsom prison crammed with toughest inmates." *Progress Bull.* 24 (November): 42.

Bishop, C. S. 1983 "Judicial update." *California Prisoner* 12, 3: 3.

Bishop, N. 1975 *Beware of Treatment! Some New Develnpments in Criminology and Criminal Policy.* Stockholm, Sweden: Scandinavian Research Council for Criminology.

Bishop, N. (ed.) 1980 *Crime and Crime Control in Scandinavia* 1976–80. Norrköping, Sweden: Scandinavian Research Council for Criminology.

Bishop, N. 1984 Personal communication, August 7.

Bødal, Kåre 1976 "Fengselsvesenet i Norge." *Nordisk Tidsskrift for Kriminalvidenskab 61.*

Bureau of Justice Statistics 1984 *Prisoners in 1983.* Washington, D.C.: U.S. Department of Justice.

Burstein, J. Q. 1977 *Conjugal visits in Prison: Psychological and Social Consequences.* Lexington, MA: D. C. Heath.

Christie, N. 1975 *Hvor Tett et Samfun?* Tabler MM. Oslo, Norway: Universitetsforlaget.

Davidson, R. T. 1974 *Chicano Prisoners: The Key to San Quentin.* New York: Holt, Rinehart & Winston.

Doleschal, E. 1977 "Rate and length of imprisonment: How does the United States compare with the Netherlands, Denmark, and Sweden?" *Crime & Delinquency* 23, 1: 51.

Durham, M. 1973 "For the Swedes a prison sentence can be fun time." *Smithsonian* 4, 6: 46.

Edholm, L. and N. Bishop 1983 *Serious Drug Misusers in the Swedish Prison and Probation System.* Norrköping, Sweden: Swedish National Prison and Probation Administration.

Farbstein, J. and R. E. Wener 1982 "Evaluation of correctional environments." *Environment and Behavior* 14, 6: 671.

Flanagan, T. J. and M. McLeod (eds.) 1983 *Sourcebook of Criminal Justice Statistics*—1982. Washington, D.C.: U.S. Department of Justice.

Flanagan, T. J., D. J. Van Alstyne, and M. Gottfredson (eds.) 1982 *Sourcebook of Criminal Justice Statistics*—1981. Washington, D.C.: U.S. Department of Justice.

Gettinger, S. 1982 " 'Objective' classification: Catalyst for change." *Corrections Magazine* 8, 3: 24.

Goetting, A. 1982 "Conjugal association in prison: Issues and perspectives." *Crime & Delinquency* 28, 2: 52.

Greenfeld, L. A. n.d. *Assessing Prison Environments: A Comparative Approach.* Washington, D.C.: National Institute of Justice. (mimeo)

Hager, P. 1982 "Justices reject conjugal visits for unwed inmates." *Los Angeles Times,* February 19: I, 1.

Hurst, J. 1983a "Prison-building effort futile, critics charge." *Los Angeles Times,* December 26: I, 1.

———. 1983b "Overnight stays allowed: Wives and children also serve time with prisoners." *Los Angeles Times,* April 18: I, 1.

———. 1983c "Change in sentencing laws could ease prison problem." *Los Angeles Times,* December 26: I, 1.

Joutsen, M. 1980 "The indeterminate incarceration of dangerous offenders in Scandinavia," in N. Bishop (ed.) *Crime and Crime Control in Scandinavia,* Norrköping, Sweden: Scandinavian Research Council for Criminology.

Los Angeles Times 1983 "Life among the ruins behind the walls." September 12: I, 3.

Martinsson, B. and N. Bishop 1983 *Current Problems of Prison Administration in Sweden.* Norrköping, Sweden: Swedish National Prison and Probation Administration.

Mathiesen, T. 1980 "The future of control systems—the case of Norway." *Int. J. of the Sociology of Law* 8: 149.

McCarthy, C. 1979 "The world learns America's dirty secret—its prisons." *Los Angeles Times,* March 20: II, 5.

Mockler, R. 1983 "Where are the prisoners' jobs?" *California Prisoner* 12, 3: 2.

Morris, N. and G. Hawkins 1970 *The Honest Politician's Guide to Crime Control.* Chicago: Univ. of Chicago Press.

Mullen, J., K. Carlson, and B. Smith 1980 *American Prisons and Jails Volume I: Summary of Findings and Policy Implications of a National Survey.* Washington, D.C.: National Institute of Justice.

Mullen, J. and B. Smith 1980 *American Prisons and Jails Volume III: Conditions and Costs of Confinement.* Washington, D.C.: National Institute of Justice.

Murphy, T. 1983 "Grim scene in San Quentin cell blocks." *Progress Bull.* September 29: 6.

The National Prison Administration 1980 *Measures of De-institutionalization in Sweden.* Norrköping, Sweden: Information Unit.

Philip, B. 1983 "Nordisk Faengelsstatistik." Nordisk Tiddsskrift for Kriminalvidenskab 31.

Raspberry, W. 1983 "The prisoners work—but do the prisons?" *Washington Post,* August 15: A, 23.

The Reasoner Report 1974 ABC News, February 9. American Broadcasting Company.

Røstad, H. 1978 "Kriminalitet i Norge i 1875 og 1975 Noen Refleksjoner." *Norsk Juridisk Tidsskrift* 2/3: 91.

Scott, J. E. and F. Al-Thakeb 1977 "The public's perception of crime: A comparative analysis of Scandinavia, Western Europe, the Middle East, and the United States," in C. R. Huff (ed.). *Contemporary Corrections: Social Control and Conflict.* Beverly Hills, CA: Sage.

Serrill, M. S. 1977 "Profile/Sweden." *Corrections Magazine* June: 11.

———. 1983 "A growing crisis behind bars." *Time,* December 5: 64.

Sherman, M. and G. Hawkins 1981 *Imprisonment in America: Choosing the Future.* Chicago: Univ. of Chicago Press.

Snortum, J. R. 1976 "Sweden's 'special' prisons: Correctional trends and cultural traditions." *Criminal Justice and Behavior* 3, 2: 151.

———. 1984a "Alcohol-impaired driving in Norway and Sweden: Another look at 'the Scandinavian myth.' " *Law and Policy* 6, 1: 5.

———. 1984b "Controlling the alcohol-impaired driver in Scandinavia and the United States: Simple deterrence and beyond." *Journal of Criminal Justice* 12, 2: 131.

Von Hofer, H. 1982 *Nordisk Kriminalstatisik 1950–1980.* København: Nordisk Statistisk Sekretariat.

Ward, D. A. 1972 "Inmate rights and prison reform in Sweden and Denmark." *Journal of Criminal Law, Criminology and Police Science* 63, 2: 240.

Wright, E. O. 1973 *The Politics of Imprisonment: A Critical Analysis of Prisons in America.* New York: Harper Colophone.

OFFENDER REHABILITATION AND SELECT PRISON PROBLEMS

section II

Introduction

The prison systems of many, though surely not all, countries share a common desire to achieve offender rehabilitation. Yet the very meaning of the term "rehabilitation" is culture specific. Rehabilitation programs are intended to promote normative behaviors, and definitions of such behaviors depend largely on cultural contexts. Moreover, countries vary widely not only in the extent to which they are genuinely committed to rehabilitation, but also in the way they pursue it. These complexities notwithstanding, rehabilitation continues to be a widely sought after goal and an internationally proclaimed justification for incarcerating offenders.

Despite reasonably widespread agreement as to its desirability, rehabilitation has proven hard to attain on the scale most countries would like. Accordingly, it has been difficult to maintain rehabilitation as an ideological justification for incarceration. In the U.S., for instance, rehabilitation has been an explicitly recognized goal (though certainly not the only goal) of imprisonment since the inception of the penitentiary in the late 1700s. Starting around the last third of the twentieth century, however, subsequent to the reign of the rehabilitative ideal during the 1950s, the concept began to see challenges. Research challenging the efficacy of intervention programs began to accumulate, and this research helped spark the view that little, if anything, by way of intervention "works." The discouraging news from research was combined with allegations from the political right that rehabilitation is too soft or lenient and with allegations from the left that rehabilitation is unjust. The idealistic posture of earlier eras gave way to the so-called just desserts model of the 1970s and 1980s. With this shift from utilitarian to retributive thinking has come cynicism regarding the viability of rehabilitation.

Each of the first three selections in this section contributes to the ongoing debate over rehabilitation, but from very different angles. The lead article, "The Affective Responses of Women Prisoners to Two Discrepant Penal Systems," by Francesca Lundström, studies the affective reactions of two samples of inmates to the material and non-material aspects of their confinement. One sample was drawn from a liberal prison system that is oriented toward rehabilitation (Sweden), whereas the other sample came from a punitive system that is centered around retribution (Ireland). After characterizing the two systems,

Lundström employs interview data to study affective reactions. From the article we learn that, while rehabilitative policies may foster affective satisfaction with the daily routine and material features of a life behind bars, these policies do not guarantee positive affective reactions to the non-material aspects of that life, such as interpersonal relationships and emotions. We also learn that, when viewed within the cultural context of Sweden, the emphasis on rehabilitation may generate more anxiety about life after release than the retributive emphasis of Irish penology.

In the second reading, G. Frederick Allen argues that the move of U.S. penal policy away from rehabilitation may be premature, given what U.S. officials can learn from the Chinese experience. Dispelling the myth that China's system is unusually harsh on offenders because of its grounding in Marxist socio-political principles, Allen encourages U.S. officials to consider both the different way rehabilitation is conceptualized by the Chinese and China's more realistic agenda for rehabilitation. Taken in conjunction with the work by Lee-Jan Jan (see Section I, Article 3), Allen's remarks suggest that penologists in the U.S. who are seriously concerned with rehabilitation ought to take a much closer look at China's penal philosophy than has been the case in the past.

The next article by Rudolph Egg discusses a specific treatment modality known as social therapy, which is practiced at a limited number of prison facilities in Germany. These special facilities are for offenders judged by prison authorities to pose a high risk of recidivism, and offenders must volunteer for program entry. The principles and phases of social therapy are described, as are the political problems faced by these facilities. Readers may notice certain points of comparison between German social therapy and what, in the U.S., is referred to as "milieu therapy" or "therapeutic community."

Shifting attention to prison problems, we find some of the most formidable barriers to achieving offender rehabilitation in a prison environment to be those emanating from problems in the way the prison is structured as an organization. Like any bureaucracy, the prison possesses a formal, flow-chart type structure. Within this structure there exists a quite different (more dynamic and sometimes conflicting) structure, one consisting of informal roles, relationships, norms, and goals. It is in the context of the interplay between the formal and informal elements of prison organization that barriers to rehabilitation present themselves. Concerns about organizational problems have led many commentators to take the position that, if rehabilitation is to occur, it is much more likely to transpire in community-based correctional settings than in prison settings. The remaining articles in this section examine various facets of the prison's organization and highlight some of the problems this organization fuels.

The first two of these articles address prison power structures and, in so doing, alert us to the potential for tension between the goals of controlling inmates and maintaining order on the one hand and the desire to change inmate behavior on the other hand. Rasma Karklins demonstrates how power is organized and exercised in Soviet labor camps of the post-Stalin era. Attending to the differences between criminal and political prisoners throughout the article, Karklins discusses the formal and informal structures of labor camps and examines the various mechanisms employed to control inmates. Contrary to images of control achieved through brute physical coercion, the analysis indicates the far greater importance of subtle psychological coercion and, especially, the importance of cooptation of inmates by camp officials. In the next selection, we see that inmate cooptation is not a practice unique to Soviet labor camps. In one of a series of their papers on happenings in the Texas Department of Corrections, James W. Marquart and Ben M. Crouch expose the vital role of cooptation in maintaining social control in U.S. prisons. The rich descriptions offered by Marquart and Crouch are suggestive of the benefits officials gain by enlisting the aid of carefully chosen inmates to exert power over other inmates. The contradiction between rehabilitation and the tradition of accomplishing control by having prisoners rule others through intimidation should be recognized.

Guards (correctional officers) have always occupied a central position in the prison bureaucracy. Guards maintain the most frequent, direct, and intense contact with inmates. Only in the last 15 or so years have guards become the subject of much scholarly attention in the U.S. (By contrast, scholarly interest in prisoners and the inmate society dates at least to the 1940s.) In line with recent U.S. research on correctional officers, Trevor A. Williams' study of Western Australian prison officers tests for links between officers' attitudes and their custodial organizational roles. Williams shows that officers' over-reliance on hierarchical discipline, negative stereotyping of inmates, and antagonisms toward treatment staff are positively related to their commitment to the custodial role. The article illustrates why the organizational role occupied by officers can be counter-rehabilitative.

The final work in this section deals with an unfortunate but integral problem found in many prison organizations, namely violence. In their paper, Frank J. Porporino and his colleagues extend the developing field of victimology to encompass homicide victimization in Canadian prisons. Hypothesizing that serious episodes of prison violence have become increasingly problematic in recent years due to factors such as crowding and the growing involvement of the inmate subculture in drug trade activities, the authors use official data to document a substantial rise in prison homicides between 1967 and 1984. In presenting the characteristics of victims and victimizations, Porporino et al. observe that, across time, more homicides were committed by multiple assailants. This finding is taken as evidence of increased gang activities revolving around drug- and revenge-related motives. In view of the pervasive element of fear for personal safety that life in the more violent prisons is coming to assume, these environments can hardly be expected to produce rehabilitated inmates.

6. The Affective Responses of Women Prisoners to Two Discrepant Penal Systems

Francesca Lundström, University of Illinois at Urbana-Champaign

Abstract: This article contrasts a retributive penal system (Irish) with a rehabilitative system (Swedish) vis-a-vis the affective responses of women prisoners to incarceration. Previous studies typically have focused on narrow aspects of affect (e.g., interpersonal relationships) in prison. In contrast, the present study takes a more comprehensive approach in order to measure and compare affect over various aspects of prison life. In the more material aspects of life in prison, significant differences were found between the affective responses of Swedish and Irish women prisoners. Surprisingly, this difference did not extend to the less material aspects of prison life (e.g., interpersonal relationships and emotions). The most surprising finding was that women from the rehabilitative Swedish system were more fearful of not having a "normal" life after release than those from the retributive Irish system.

Much of the literature on women in prison considers only one or two aspects of life behind the walls and is specific to a particular country; for example, Ward and Kassebaum (1965), Giallombardo (1966), and Heffernan (1972) highlighted the American experience of interpersonal relationships (generally homosexual) in prison; Fox (1982) and Goodstein, MacKenzie, and Shotland (1984) described aspects of women prisoners' emotional responses to prison in the United States; and Adelbert and Currie (1987) studied women prisoners in Canada. Bondeson (1968) attempted to identify criminal socialization of Swedish women prisoners from their use of argot. Koch (1983) reviewed studies on various aspects of women's life in prison from research in Scandinavia but did not attempt cross-cultural comparisons.

The present study compares women prisoners' affective responses to different aspects of prison life, from two different penal systems (Sweden and Ireland), to determine generalizability in the affective responses of women in prison.

Author's Note: The research was funded in part by BRA (The Swedish Crime Prevention Board) and the Swedish Institute. The author gratefully acknowledges the advice and helpful comments from the Editor, *Criminal Justice and Behavior,* and from Merle Levy, Transition Institute at the University of Illinois at Urbana-Champaign. Requests for reprints should be sent to Francesca Lundström, Transition Institute, University of Illinois at Urbana-Champaign, 110 Education Building, 1310 South Sixth Street, Champaign, IL 61820.

Prisons in the Two Countries

The extensive literature documenting the rehabilitative Swedish penal policies (e.g., Anttila, 1971; Swedish System of Sanctions, 1980) and the less extensive literature on the mainly retributive Irish penal policy (e.g., Department of Justice, 1981; McGreil, 1982) would suggest vast differences in prisoners' affective responses to incarceration in the two countries.

Sweden

There are 14 local, open (minimum-security), mixed (accepting men and women) prisons with accommodations for one to seven women. Two national prisons accommodate 7 and 87 women (as of 1982–1983). The larger has open (moderate-security) and closed (high-security) units, which can be either "normal" or drug-free. The smaller prison is mixed high security. A graded system of confinement requires that prisoners be kept in closed units during initial stages of a long sentence. A person in a closed unit is always locked in for the night from around 8:00 until approximately 6:30 the following morning. The bedroom window is barred or alternatively cannot be opened. Privileges (e.g., in choice of work, types of recreation, and granting of furloughs) are limited. During the course of the sentence, the security regulations are gradually reduced by moving prisoners to an open prison or unit and allowing them more privileges. In principle, individuals are sent to an open prison near the end of a long sentence in order to prepare them for release and to promote contact with family, workmates, supervisors, and authorities (Organization of Prison and Probation Services, 1980).

Alternatively, an individual who has been given a sentence of a year or less can be placed in an open institution. Prisoners are placed as close to their home area as possible according to the policy of "The Local Principle." Security measures are not strict in these institutions, cell doors are not locked by the staff at night, there are no bars or other hindrances to prevent opening the bedroom window, and there is seldom a perimeter fence. Prisoners decide for themselves when to go to bed and are permitted to get up during the night to sit in the dayroom, fix a snack, smoke, or talk to each other. In the mixed prisons (an innovation of the 1970s) men and women share common areas (e.g., dayroom, recreation areas) but sleeping accommodations are segregated.

Drug-free units accommodate selected prisoners who have drug-dependency problems (excluding alcohol). Members of the staff choose those prisoners whom they consider likely to benefit from treatment in a drug-free unit. Prisoners sign a binding contract to involve themselves in group therapy and other activities (e.g., gymnastics), are given daily urine tests, and are constantly monitored for drug abuse. These drug-free units can be of a closed or open nature depending on the status of the prisoner. (See Snortum & Bødal, 1985, for descriptions of and comparisons between Scandinavian and California prisons.) Swedish prisons vary in type and design from the old-style Philadelphia type (which have been remodeled) to extremely modern. (For a history of the development of the Swedish prison system, see Nelson, 1972; Sellin, 1947; Weiselgren, 1895.) Many of the prisons are located in the countryside and are not easily accessible, especially by public transport.

The inmates usually live in modern-style bungalows called ''units'' or ''pavilions'' with accommodations for seven to ten people, which give the appearance of a motel or holiday camp. A typical bungalow has an entrance hall with a glass-walled guard room for the staff off to one side. This room is beside the prisoners' dayroom, where the prisoners eat and relax. The dayroom is comfortably furnished with easy chairs, and there is usually a color television in a corner. Off this room is a corridor containing the cells, bathroom, toilet, and a small kitchen where prisoners are allowed to prepare snacks, coffee, and tea. Main meals are delivered from a central kitchen. Cells are single and of a standard size containing a bed, desk, reading lamp, and cupboards. A prisoner who owns a television set or radio is permitted to keep it in her room. The bungalows are surrounded by well-kept gardens (tended by the inmates) with trees, lawns, and flowers.

Ireland

There are two prisons with accommodations for female offenders in Ireland, both high security, with none of the different options for incarceration found in the Swedish system. One of the prisons is mainly for political prisoners and was therefore excluded from the study. The primary prison for female criminal offenders (where this research was conducted) has places for 24 women.

This high-security prison is situated near the center of a medium-sized city and is surrounded by gray and forbidding high stone walls. To gain access to the women's section, one has to pass through no fewer than five locked doors. With the unlocking of the final door one enters a small hall where there are two ''visiting boxes''—small, dingy rooms furnished with rickety tables and chairs. On the walls hang the framed rules for inmates' visitors. Through a barred door is the prison itself. Inside there is ''the class,'' a long corridor that constitutes the main area. It is bleak and cheerless, painted in what one staff member described as ''prison beige.'' This color dominates in the prison. Heavy gray cell doors with peepholes line the corridor. The interiors of the cells have a somewhat more cheery air as the women have hung up posters and postcards. There is also an oratory, the office of the chief officer, the kitchen, and toilets on ''the class.'' The smell of disinfectant is all-pervasive, as the sewage system is old and primitive. A passageway off ''the class'' leads to the reception area, where prisoners are searched and given prison clothes when admitted to prison. The showers, a workroom (sometimes used for sewing), a laundry, and a recreation hall (cavernous and chilly with a television and record player) are in this part of the prison. There is also a small, paved exercise yard surrounded by high stone walls.

The prison philosophy of the state is that there should be a single occupant per cell (Council for Social Welfare, 1983). Severe overcrowding in the prison has resulted in an occupancy of three or four women in some of the cells. A few prisoners do have their own cells, but this situation is uncommon.

Method

Sampling

To minimize bias, the population available for sampling was defined according to the following criteria. The women interviewed were (a) nationals of their respective countries, (b) serving a sentence of more than one month's duration,

(c) not at the beginning or end of their sentences, but acculturated into the life of the institution (a phenomenon, that according to Wheeler, 1961, follows a U-shaped curve).

The data were collected in (a) four Swedish prisons: two local, open, mixed; one national, closed, mixed; and one national single sex with both closed and open units, and (b) one closed prison in Ireland.

Because sampling in prison is fraught with problems (see Lundström, 1987), random sampling was not feasible. In the smaller prisons in Sweden all women who satisfied the criteria listed above were interviewed. In the larger prison, attempts were made to interview all 35 women who satisfied the criteria, but because of illness, furloughs, early release, and refusals (5), only 24 of the eligible women were interviewed during the two weeks in which this researcher was at this particular prison. Staff discounted the possibility that the refusals to be interviewed were for any particular reason or represented a specific group of people. The sampling strategy yielded 32 Swedish women prisoners. In Ireland, 16 women were interviewed who fulfilled the criteria outlined above and were incarcerated there during the two weeks the researcher was at the prison. Thus interviews in Sweden and Ireland yielded a total sample of 48 women prisoners. (Concerning the relatively short periods of time spent in the prisons collecting the data, see Lundström, 1987, on the importance of minimizing "contamination" and "drift" while conducting fieldwork in prisons and similar settings.)

Table 1 gives demographic and criminological information about the women prisoners who were interviewed in the two countries.

Data

The data on the affective responses of the women prisoners were collected using Emic-type interview techniques. In conducting this type of interview the researcher asks the respondent to tell about her particular world—in this instance the initial request was, "Can you tell me about being in prison?" Based on the reply, and using only the words and concepts of the respondent as keywords for further exploration, the researcher continues: "You mentioned [keyword]; can you tell me a little more about that?" The interviewer persists with this technique until all keywords have been investigated. This strategy potentially offers a culturally unbiased worldview of an individual's frame of reference. The interviewer does not impose categories on the situation, but allows the cultural system to generate its own. (For a description of Emic techniques, see Goodenough, 1970; Hoebel & Frost, 1976; Pike, 1967.) This method averts the difficulties posed in the translation of questionnaires or structured interviews into Swedish and English for administration. The method also bypasses the necessity of translation into a common language for analysis.

All interviews were conducted by the researcher, who has two years of training in clinical psychology and previous research experience (interviewing 54 persons who are mentally handicapped; Lundström-Roche, 1982) using the Emic technique. Interviews were tape recorded (with the permission of the respondents) and transcribed verbatim. Initial analysis entailed reading all of the interviews carefully and noting the different topics mentioned by each person.

Table 1 Demographic and Criminological Information on Swedish and Irish Women Prisoners

Women Prisoners' Demographic Information		S	IRL
Age	Median	28	22
	Mean	30	22
	Range	19–55	17–30
Length of Sentence	Median (mths)	22	12
	Mean	21.5	21
	Range	2–72	9–96
Length Served at time of Interview	Median (mths)	5	4
	Mean	5	4.9
	Range	1–14	1–14
No. of Times in Prison	First Timers N	16	7
	Recidivists N	16	9
Marital Status	Married	20	5
	Divorced	3	–
	Separated	0	1
	Widowed	1	1
	Single	8	9
Children	Overall N	18	11
	Mean	2	1
	Mean	1–5	1–4

Types of Crime of Women Prisoners by Country

Sweden Type of Crime	No.	Ireland Type of Crime	No.
Serious Drug Offence	10	Selling Drugs	1
Drug Offence	3	Manslaughter	1
Serious Assault	1	Wounding	1
Threatening and Robbery	2	Arson, Stealing	1
Serious Smuggling	2	Burglary, Larceny	1
Smuggling	2	Larceny	6
Serious Fraud	4	Shoplifting, Stealing	3
Fraud	3	Receiving	1
Serious Stealing	2	Defrauding	1
Stealing	2		
Receiving	1		
Total	32		16

When this work had been completed, the percentage of people mentioning each of these topics was tabulated so that a picture of which topics were important emerged. Because Swedish was not the interviewer's native language, a 25% random sample of all the interviews, both Swedish and Irish, were assessed by a native Swedish speaker (a criminologist with some training in psychology) to check inter-rater agreement on which topics had arisen. We had previously decided that an agreement rate of 80% would be considered satisfactory; empirically, it was greater than 85%.

In most research designs, variables are designated beforehand, but in this instance we wanted variables to be generated by the respondents (see Hoebel & Frost, 1976, p. 381). Overall, 58 variables emerged during the course of the interviews. Some of these were country-specific, some were dichotomous (i.e., could be rated either absent or present), and others could assume values of negative, neutral, positive, or not mentioned. When the variables were rated for each of the 48 individuals, a 25% random sample of all interviews were assessed by another rater (a statistician, who is a native Swedish speaker as well as fluent in English) for a reliability check, which resulted in an agreement rate of more than 80%. We therefore decided to proceed with further data analysis. Because not all of the 58 variables extracted from the Emic-type interviews were included in the six "segments" (described below), the actual variables used are given in Table 2.

Table 2 Segments and Their Cross-Cultural Comparisons

Segment	Variables
Daily Routine	(a) Work (i.e., the kind of work available within the prison) (b) Recreation (i.e., the recreational facilities) (c) School (i.e., the educational facilities)
Relationships	(a) Relationships (with other prisoners) (b) Relationships (with members of staff) (c) Being locked up[a]
Contacts	(a) Letters, (b) Visits, (c) Furloughs
Release	(a) Release in general (b) Possibilities of obtaining a job (c) Possibilities of obtaining accommodation upon release
Emotions	(a) Having a strategy for coping with the "pains of imprisonment" (b) Presence of anger (c) Feelings of "powerlessness" (d) Feelings of depression

a Some prisoners had rather surprising views on being locked up. One prisoner explained thus: "It's rather nice to be locked up, for all day you are together with lots of people you wouldn't have chosen for yourself." We therefore judged that a positive response toward lock-up was an indication (a) that relationships with peers were not as healthy as might have been, and (b) of negative affective response toward relationships in general. The variable was therefore coded using overt negative responses as positive affect and vice versa.

Themes and Segments

To describe systematically the women's affective responses to different aspects of life in prison, the variables were initially categorized (subjectively) by theme. These themes are represented by three overlapping circles: the Inside World, the Self, and the Outside World. Figure 1 displays the concept of the overlapping yet separate nature of the three themes.

Figure 1 Themes and Segments Representing Various Facets of Women Prisoners Affect Toward Prison Life.

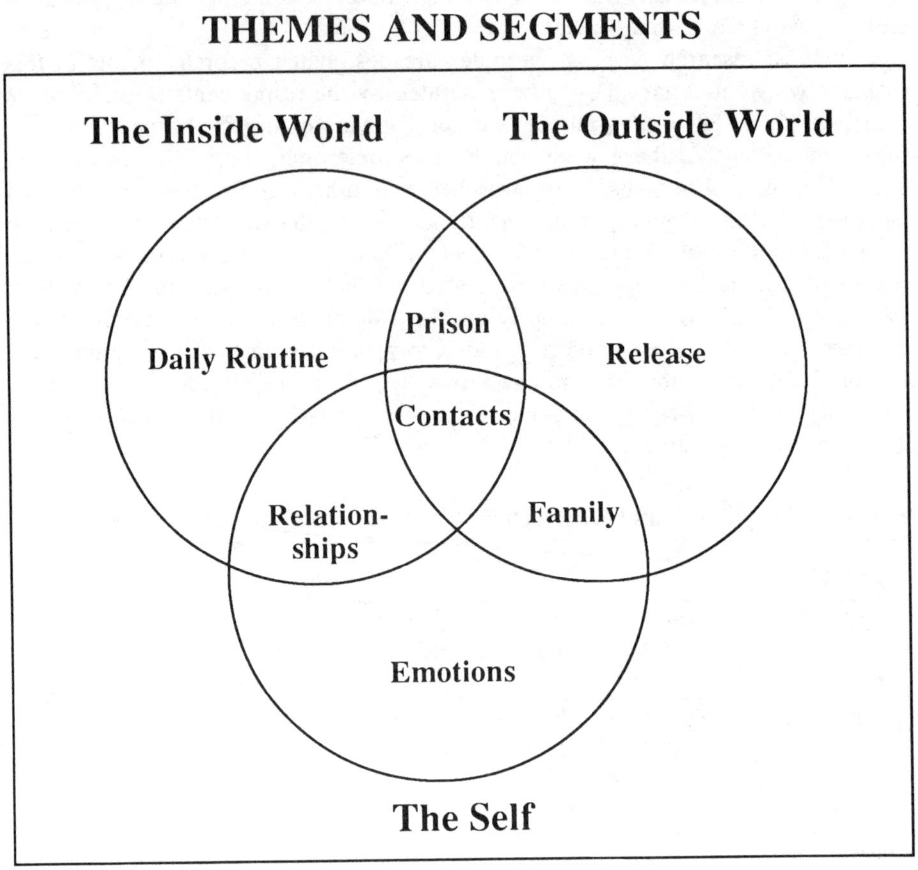

Overlaps of the themes create (eight) segments; three are pairwise overlaps (Prison, Relationships, and Family), and one is the intersection of all three (Contacts). The eighth segment—Wishes—(for improvements in prison life and for themselves in the future) is to be found in the area outside all three circles.

These themes and segments, generated spontaneously by women prisoners in two countries, seem to represent the various facets of their affect toward prison life. It should be noted that the diagram used in Figure 1 and the terms *theme* and *segment* have no empirical basis but are used heuristically for structuring the large amounts of data this type of research design generates.

Because not all of the 58 variables extracted from the Emic-type interviews were included in the segments, decisions were made to eliminate variables that had an overall low rate of response or were country-specific (see Bergman & Magnusson, 1983, on classification and variable choice). When the elimination of the variables had been completed, 23 variables (of the original 58 extracted from the Emic-type interviews) remained for the analysis of the segments. The variables selected for inclusion in each segment will be described below.

We then constructed a rating scale to describe individuals' overall affective responses to each segment. Classification rules were formulated to assign individuals to categories (positive, negative, or neutral affective responses) in the different segments. The following are the general classification rules.

Step 1

Select all individuals with at least one positive rating for the variables constituting the segment. These individuals were classified as the "Positive Affective Response" category for the given segment.

Step 2

Select all individuals with no positive and at least one negative rating for the variables in the segment. These individuals were classified as the "Negative Affective Response" category for the given segment.

Step 3

The residuals (all those with only neutral or not mentioned ratings for the variables in the segment) were classified as the "Neutral Affective Response" category for the given segment. This categorization of the women by affective response yielded contingency tables of Country by Affective Response Classification. Cross-cultural comparisons using chi-square tests of significance for association were made for five of these segments. The segments for which quantitative cross-cultural analysis was not performed contained culture-specific variables, and therefore comparisons were considered meaningless, or the number or type of variables that made up the segments did not lend themselves to analysis. The five segments and the variables that constituted them, which are the basis of the cross-cultural comparisons, are given in Table 2. Because all the variables in the Emotions Segment were dichotomous (i.e., rated present or absent), another method (described below) was devised for classifying the individuals' affective responses in order to make cross-cultural comparisons.

Emotions

The affective responses for Emotions were classified as follows: (a) displaying healthy psychological and emotional survival traits—Positive Affective Response, (b) displaying unhealthy traits—Negative Affective Response, and (c) those falling between these two extremes and therefore considered to be displaying moderately healthy traits—Neutral Affective Response.

The women who described strategies for coping with prison (e.g., "taking it one day at a time") and who mentioned anger and/or powerlessness were classified in the Positive Affective Response category for the segment. We considered a woman's awareness of the effects of these factors on her emotions as indicative of healthy survival traits. (For a discussion of women prisoners' statements about their experiences of powerlessness in the prison setting, see Goodstein et al., 1984, on personal control and Fox, 1982, on infantilization.) The women who did not mention their emotions at all or who only mentioned depression were classified in the Negative Affective Response category. All the other women were categorized as having a Neutral Affective Response because they were considered to have at least a moderate tendency toward psychological survival. The following segments were *not* compared cross-culturally.

Prison

The components of this segment in the two countries were completely dissimilar, and therefore cross-cultural comparisons were considered meaningless. (For example, Swedish prisoners talked about the merits, or lack thereof, of open, closed, mixed, and drug-free units, whereas the Irish prisoners discussed overcrowding in the cells, the failure to segregate remanded from sentenced prisoners, and the lack of any medical facilities.) The purpose of including the Prison segment was to highlight, qualitatively, the extreme material differences between prisons in the two countries. (Facilities in the two countries are described above in ''Prisons in the Two Countries.'')

Family

This segment consisted of only one dichotomous variable: prisoners' sadness concerning their separation from children, spouses, and families. The subject was mentioned by 54% of the women (26/48). Of the 13 Swedish and 9 Irish women who did not mention missing their families, respectively, 8 and 6 of the women had no children. The other 4 Swedish women were recidivists, which suggests that they may have lost contact with their families, an explanation supported by staff members. The 3 remaining Irish women were serving long sentences (24, 36, and 96 months). Anguish at being separated from loved ones has no cultural boundaries: thoughts of home and family were constantly reported by the women, as were worries for the safety, welfare, and well-being of their children (see Fox, 1982).

Wishes

This segment concerned the women's descriptions of what they considered the ''ideal'' way to do time in prison and their hopes for the future. As in the Prison segment, many of the wishes were culture-specific, and therefore cross-cultural comparisons were considered inappropriate.

Results

Chi-square tests of independence were applied to test differences between the Swedish and Irish women prisoners' affective responses in the appropriate segments. The results of this analysis are given in Table 3.

A comparison of the affective responses of Swedish and Irish women toward the Daily Routine shows that the Swedish women tended to have either neutral or positive affective responses, in contrast to the Irish women, who had mainly negative ones. There were significant differences between the national samples, $\chi^2(2, N = 48) = 15.8, p < .001$.

Overall, the tendency is for women prisoners not to have good interpersonal relationships; there are no striking differences between the countries in the distributions. More than 75% of the Swedish women with negative affective responses were over 25 years of age, and all but one of this older group were in closed units. More than 75% of the Swedish women having positive affective responses were in open units. The Swedish women who gave neutral affective responses had a median sentence of 11 months, half that of the other two groups. This finding may indicate that those who have short sentences do not strive to establish relationships in prison. There were no marked tendencies in the Irish prisoners in this segment. A chi-square

Table 3 Affective Responses Toward Prison Among Irish and Swedish Women Prisoners

Segment	Ireland[a]			Sweden[b]		
	Negative	*Neutral*	*Positive*	*Negative*	*Neutral*	*Positive*
Daily Routine	10	1	5	4	14	14
Relationships	7	4	5	15	9	8
Contacts	14	2	0	11	9	12
Release	6	10	0	22	10	0
Emotions	7	5	4	7	13	12

a N = 16.
b N = 32.

test was applied, but no differences were found between Swedish and Irish prisoners, $\chi^2(2, N = 48) = 2.17$, NS.

Overall, Table 3 indicates dissatisfaction with the possibilities for contact. In comparing the two countries, it becomes evident that the dissatisfaction is more prevalent among the Irish women; the Swedish women's affective responses are more evenly distributed. The Irish women's mainly negative affective responses are not surprising given the extreme limitations regarding all forms of contact. A chi-square test yielded significant differences between the two countries, $\chi^2(2, N = 48) = 12.59$, $p < .01$. Table 3 shows that, overall, more than half of the women in prison were afraid of returning to the outside world. Looking at the countries separately suggested that in Sweden the non-recidivists were slightly more hopeful about the future than were the recidivists. Irish women are in general less negative than Swedish women. This attitude could result from the stronger family links found in Ireland.

As there were no women in either country with a positive affective response to this segment, the chi-square table was collapsed into a 2 × 2 format. There were significant differences between the affective responses of the women in the two countries to the Release segment, $\chi^2(1, N = 48) = 4.12$, $p < .05$. It would seem that only one-third (16/48) of the women were displaying healthy psychological and emotional survival traits. We had expected that because more of the Swedish women displayed positive affective responses to the segments dealing with Prison and Daily Routine, their emotional responses would be different from the Irish women's. This expectation is not confirmed. A chi-square test gave no significant differences between the two groups, $\chi^2(2, N = 48) = 3.36$, NS.

Discussion

The Irish penal policy of retribution and containment is reflected in the almost complete lack of work and in the wholly inadequate educational and recreational activities available to the women (see Lundström-Roche, 1985; McGreil,

1982). In contrast, facilities in Swedish prisons have an extremely high material standard and reflect the policy of rehabilitation outlined by Sweden's Kriminalvårdsstyrelsen (National Prison and Probation Administration Board). The daily routines of women prisoners are planned so that the day is ordered and people have work, education, and recreation. This regimen attempts to establish a lifestyle alternative to that of crime, which is often coupled with alcohol and drug abuse (see Lundström-Roche, 1985; Swedish System of Sanctions, 1980). It is not surprising, therefore, that there should be differences in the affective responses of women from the two countries toward their daily routine.

In many studies of women in U.S. prisons (e.g., Giallombardo, 1966; Heffernan, 1972; Ward & Kassebaum, 1965), the interpersonal relationships of women have been ascribed to the forming of homosexual relationships to compensate for the loss of heterosexual ones. In the present study this phenomenon was not encountered in either country. Additional counterevidence comes from Fridlund's (1971) study of women in prison in Sweden. Bondeson (1974) also found that only 2% of her sample admitted to having homosexual relations within a correctional institution. "The dramatic difference between the American and the Swedish prisons is probably real," she states, "the staff in our Swedish institutions have mostly not [even] heard of this phenomenon" (p. 592).

The absence of comments regarding homosexual relationships among the women interviewed in this study has several possible explanations: (a) Getting furloughs fairly regularly in Sweden helps diminish the occurrence of homosexuality (Bondeson, 1974). Nearly all the women had husbands, lovers, or boyfriends on the "outside," and even if their sex lives were not exactly "normal" (Fridlund, 1971), at least there was the possibility of being able to establish and maintain a heterosexual relationship. (b) Homosexuality in Sweden does not seem to be (relatively speaking) as socially accepted as in the United States (Statens Ofentliga Utredningar, 1984). (c) Single-cell occupancy and constant supervision by staff discourage homosexual activity. Sentences tend in general to be shorter in Swedish than in American prisons, which inhibits the formation of homosexual relationships. (d) In Ireland, when two or more women share a cell, a light is kept on all night, and the cell is checked regularly (through a peephole in the door). That women in the materially better milieu of Swedish prisons have similar difficulties in relating to one another is rather startling. This finding suggests that there are universal elements at the nonmaterial level that occur in prison that cannot be alleviated.

Concerning contact with the outside world, Swedish women prisoners have furloughs either once a month or every two months (depending on the type of unit) and are also allowed private visits of two hours' duration once a week, telephone calls, and uncensored letters. On the other hand, Irish women prisoners are allowed to have one supervised visit per week of thirty minutes' duration, to write one and receive unlimited censored letters. There is no access to the telephone, and the possibility of obtaining furloughs is almost nonexistent. The differences between the affective responses of the Irish and Swedish women are therefore not surprising.

The world outside prison is a different place for a Swedish woman who is released compared to an Irish woman prisoner. In Sweden, assistance is available through a network of postrelease agencies geared to help pick up the pieces of a life disrupted by prison and perhaps also by alcohol or drug addiction. In Ireland, little help is available from the state. There are few halfway hostels and almost no help is available for drug problems. But for most Irish women, the family helps as much as it can to rehabilitate, or at least to accept, the prodigal daughter back into the relative safety of the family unit, unlike in Sweden, where family networks appear to be less strong and supportive. That Swedish women were more fearful of release than were their Irish counterparts is a rather surprising finding, given Swedish rehabilitative penal policy.

The Swedish policy implies that the criminal should be reformed in some undefined way and is therefore fit to function as a member of society on release. There should be neither stigma nor shame but a welcoming back of the socially "healed" individual. However, the Swedish women, especially the recidivists, experience the reactions of the ordinary members of society toward them as the opposite of that implied by Swedish penal policy. Their statements of unease at ever being able to live a normal life again and to get a job (especially as a civil servant) or a place to live support this observation, as do their statements about the reactions of employers and acquaintances on learning about past imprisonment. These women claim that they are marked for life, and they are probably correct.

Concerning this aspect of penal policy, Chambliss and Seidman (1982) point out that modifying the codified law does not necessarily enforce automatic changes in the attitudes of citizens. "Even in democracies," those authors claim, "some laws are clearly passed for the specific interest of an individual, others emerge out of lobbying by groups representing substantial portions of the population, yet others, perhaps the majority, are no more than an expression of the views and interests of legislative committees" (p. 139). This last observation may well describe Sweden's penal policy of rehabilitation.

Fox (1982, p. 211) claims that many women in prison are "emotional time bombs, ticking off days and hours of stress, waiting for release." Sykes (1958, p. 64) claims that (male) prisoners somehow must learn psychologically to survive the "pains of imprisonment." He also claims that for the modern prisoner these pains are not rooted in physical brutality, but rather in attacks at the psychological level. Ward and Kassebaum (1965, p. 14) assert that imprisonment is more severe for women than for men because of women's "closer links to the care and upbringing of children." Women, the authors claim, experience anxiety because confinement separates them from their families and renders them unable to fulfill the role of motherhood. This separation anxiety does not arise solely from the physical absence of their children. The continuing care and upbringing of children, those authors argue, is a role intricately interwoven with that of motherhood. That no differences were found between the women for this segment demonstrates the universality of their emotional experiences in prison.

Conclusions

The affective responses of women prisoners to different aspects of prison life were analyzed, and comparisons were made between those of Swedish and Irish inmates. The hypothesis that there would be vast differences between the women prisoners' affective responses to prison life in the two countries was upheld with respect to the more material aspects of prison. Swedish prisons were of a much higher material standard than were Irish prisons; not only the actual buildings but also the facilities for work, recreation, education, and the possibilities for contact outside the prison were all superior in Sweden to those available in Ireland. That these differences did not affect the less material aspects of prison life (e.g., relationships and emotions) is surprising, as is the Swedish women's more negative affective responses toward release. Improving only the material resources of prisons is therefore largely irrelevant to how individuals experience the emotional and related aspects of prison. Further, if a progressive penal policy does not receive general acceptance by the ordinary citizen, then released prisoners will experience stigma and shame, thus neutralizing any rehabilitating effects that serving a prison sentence might have had. Perhaps these observations are of relevance in planning prison reforms.

The crimes for which the women in this study were sent to prison were, in general, petty and even those who were sentenced for drug offenses were mostly women who had sold drugs to finance their own habits. Members of the prison staffs in both countries thought that these women needed another kind of treatment than that afforded by prison. Perhaps it is time to ask ourselves if we really need to incarcerate people who transgress the law but who pose no great threat to society. Whether the penal philosophy is rehabilitative or retributive, it would seem that the damaging effects, psychological and social, both in prison and afterward, are not relevant to general or individual prevention. The concept of prison either as a deterrent or as a rehabilitative agency is patently not working (except to the extent that the prisoner is hindered—not totally prevented—from committing crimes while incarcerated), as indicated by the ever rising crime rates in these two countries and the high incidence of recidivism.

A Swedish staff member (who preferred anonymity) summed up the anachronism of prison with an eloquence born of intimate knowledge of the futility of the system:

> All of them [prisons] should be pulled down with a big tractor, the fence, everything. . . . The system is so outdated, we have been locking up people for several hundred years. Five hundred years ago we couldn't fly to the moon, but we can do that now. Five hundred years ago we locked up people the same way as we do today. It hasn't gone so quickly in this area as it has in all the other areas. But then we haven't invested as much money in this area as we have in the other areas—we haven't done that.

Discussion Questions

1. What can we learn from Irish and Swedish policies to reduce the problems surrounding homosexuality in U.S. female prisons?
2. Why should differences in the material aspects of prison life be unrelated to the way females experience the nonmaterial aspects of prison life?
3. Why do you think a rehabilitative system like Sweden's is associated with more negative affect toward life after release than a retributive system like Ireland's? Will higher levels of negative affect translate into greater recidivism after release? Why or why not?

References

Adelbert, E., & Currie, C. (1987). *Two few to count.* Vancouver: Press Gang.

Anttila, I. (1971). Conservative and radical criminal policy in the Nordic countries. *Scandinavian studies in criminology* (Vol. 3, pp. 9–21). Oslo: Scandinavian Research Council for Criminology, Universitets Förelaget.

Bergman, L. R., & Magnusson, D. (1983). *The development of patterns of maladjustment* (Report from the Project Individual Development and Environment No. 50). Stockholm: University of Stockholm, Department of Psychology.

Bondeson, U. (1968). Argot knowledge as an indicator of criminal socialization: A study of a training school for girls. *Scandinavian studies in criminology* (Vol. 2, pp. 73–107). Oslo: Scandinavian Research Council for Criminology, Universitets Förelaget.

Bondeson, U. (1974). *Fången i fångsamhallet* [Imprisoned in prison society]. Stockholm: Norstedt.

Chambliss, W., & Seidman, R. (1982). *Law, order and power* (2nd ed.). Reading, MA: Addison-Wesley.

Council for Social Welfare. (A Committee of the Catholic Bishops' Conference.) (1983). *The prison system.* Unpublished manuscript. Dublin.

Department of Justice. (1981). *Prisons and places of detention: Survey of objectives.* Unpublished manuscript. Dublin.

Fox, J. G. (1982). Women in prison: A case study in the social reality of stress. In R. Johnson & H. Toch (Eds.), *Pains of imprisonment* (pp. 205–220). Newbury Park, CA: Sage.

Fridlund, G. (1971). *Kvinnor i fänglse* [Women in prison]. Stockholm: Prisma.

Giallombardo, R. (1966). *Society of women: Study of a women's prison.* New York: John Wiley.

Goodenough, W. (1970). *Description and comparison in cultural anthropology.* Chicago: Aldine.

Goodstein, L., MacKenzie, L. L., & Shotland, R. (1984). Personal control and inmate adjustment in prison. *Criminology,* 22, 343–369.

Heffernan, E. (1972). *Making it in prison: The square, the cool and the life.* New York: Wiley-Interscience.

Hoebel, E. A., & Frost, E. L. (1976). *Cultural and social anthropology.* New York: McGraw-Hill.

Koch, I. (1983). *Kvinder i faengsel* [Women in prison]. In C. Hølgård & A. Snare (Eds.), *Kvinners skyld* [Women's guilt] (pp. 44–73). Oslo: Pax.

Lundström, F. (1987). Research design in total institutions: Problems, pitfalls, and possible solutions. *Quality and quantity,* 21, 209–218.

Lundström-Roche, F. (1982). *Our lives: Research to discover the attitudes of mentally handicapped adults to the quality of their lives.* Dublin: International Year of Disabled Persons Committee.

Lundström-Roche, F. (1985). *Women in prison: Ideals and reals.* Stockholm: University of Stockholm, Department of Sociology.

McGréil, M. (1982). The Irish penal system report. In S. McBride (Ed.), *Crime and punishment* (pp. 9–112). Swords, Ireland: Ward River.

National Prison and Probation Administration Information Unit. (1980). *Organization of prison and probation services.* Norrköping, Sweden: Author.

National Prison and Probation Administration Information Unit. (1980). *Swedish system of sanctions.* Norrköping, Sweden: Author.

Nelson, A. (1972). *Crime and responses to crime: An introduction to Swedish criminal law and administration* (J. L. Gets, trans.; Criminal Law Education and Research Monograph Series, Vol. 6). New York: New York University School of Law.

Pike, K. (1967). *Language in relation to a unified theory of the structure of human behavior* (rev. ed.). The Hague: Mouton.

Sellin, T. (1947). *Recent penal legislation in Sweden.* Stockholm: Aktiebolag.

Snortum, J. R., & Bødal, K. (1985). Conditions of confinement within security prisons. *Crime & Delinquency,* 31, 573–600.

Statens Offentliga Utredningar. (1984). *Homosexuella och samhället.* [Homosexuals and society]. Stockholm: Liber.

Sykes, G. (1958). *Society of captives.* Princeton, NJ: Princeton University Press.

Ward, D., & Kassebaum, G. G. (1965). *Women's prison: Sex and social structure.* Chicago: Aldine.

Wheeler, S. (1961). Socialization in correctional communities. *American Sociological Review,* 26, 697–712.

Wieselgren, S. (1895). *Sveriges fångelser och fångvård från äldre tider till våra dagar* [Sweden's prisons and places of detention from ancient to modern times]. Stockholm: Norstedt.

7. Reforming Criminals in China: Implications for Corrections in the West

G. Frederick Allen, Ph.D.
U.S. Probation and Parole Officer,
Northern District of Illinois

Abstract: Visits to three prisons in China revealed that the Chinese penal system, although conceived within a Marxist context, is humanistic, naturalistic, and practical in emphasis. Considering the cultural differences between Orient and Occident, specifically the Chinese respect for power and authority and their belief that the State and its officials serve as guardians of socialist ideology, the author discusses some implications for the West. He concludes that we may have to perceive rehabilitation in more realistic terms. Instead of abandoning rehabilitation, we can learn from the Chinese and translate the concept into providing assistance to offenders that is compatible with the external environment.

Historically, China is prominent among countries that have been unusually harsh towards criminal offenders. In fact, in ancient China the procedure for handling and dealing with prisoners was primarily intended to impress everyone with the majesty of the law and the dreadful consequences of becoming involved with it. The judges, with all the pomp and circumstance of their office and the general procedure of the court, placed all defendants in a subordinate and humiliating position. The defendant had to kneel on the bare floor below the judge and remain in this position throughout the proceedings. Whips were used freely during the interrogation in order to urge the defendant to confess or in response to a statement the defendant might have made that displeased the judge.

The court assumed that every defendant was guilty and it was the burden of the defendants to prove their innocence. In the ancient Chinese view, the defendant was most likely guilty because no law-abiding citizen would ever become involved with the law. Innocent persons falsely accused of a crime were considered guilty since they allowed themselves to become a party to a disturbance in the community. Such disturbances were considered threats to the stability of the community and subject to sanctions. In ancient China, a court appearance was considered a terrible misfortune and an experience to be avoided. As a result of these beliefs, the Chinese learned to settle disputes out of court if at all possible.

Today in China, most of the non-serious crimes are handled through local community control organizations via non-legal mechanisms. These mechanisms

---

From G. Frederick Allen, "Reforming Criminals in China: Implications for Corrections in the West" in *International Journal of Comparative and Applied Criminal Justice* (11(1): 77–86, Spring 1987).

may be compensatory, therapeutic, or conciliatory. Penal sanction arises from serious crimes, is more accusatory in nature, and generally provides for punishment of the offender. By contrast, compensatory, therapeutic, and conciliatory controls are remedial styles and methods of social repair and maintenance.

A recent visit to the People's Republic of China disclosed that the Chinese prison system and the treatment of prisoners have no resemblance to that of ancient China. In fact, it reflects a humane system. The perception of the Chinese system as harsh may stem from the fact that for many years China was closed to the West, and most accounts received were from emigres who were subject to Chinese justice. These individuals were often convicted for political crimes, such as crimes of counter-revolution, corruption, and crimes against the state. Given the Chinese attitude towards such crimes, the punishment could be expected to be harsher than for ordinary offenses.

Much of the author's experience, and this paper which focuses on rehabilitation, is based on the Chinese response to the average domestic crime. It should also be stated that the author's views are based on a western orientation which may influence how the Chinese system is interpreted. Most striking was the impression that the concept of rehabilitation, i.e., the belief that incarceration and other correctional activities can help offenders, is a concept that is embedded deep in the present Chinese penal system. This is especially surprising since in recent years, rehabilitation as a public policy for offenders in the United States has been declining, particularly the concept that prisons can rehabilitate offenders, or that rehabilitation should be a pursued goal of the criminal justice system.

Formal and Informal Processes of Law

The concept of law may be defined as a norm that becomes legal, ". . . if its neglect or infraction is regularly met, in threat or in fact, by the application of physical force by an individual or group possessing the socially recognized privilege of so acting."[1] Using this definition of law, without a designated official or agency who has the authority to enforce rules of conduct, there can be no official violation. In less complex societies with homogeneous groupings, a high degree of face-to-face interaction, and living in a communal style, each individual is subjected to the continuous scrutiny of others. Social control is not delegated to specific individuals or groups, but is shared by all. This collective responsibility system relies on control through ridicule, banishment, or other means which the group may exert on its members. Since 1949, China has developed a new socialist state under the leadership of the Chinese Communist Party. Its model of law is both external and internal. The external law or official model is now a comprehensive code of criminal procedure which became inevitable with modernization and to avoid a re-occurrence of the lawlessness of the Cultural Revolution.[2] The internal model is quite different. Proper modes

1. Hobel, E. 1954. *The Law of Primitive Man: A Study in Comparative Dynamics.* New York: Atheneum.
2. Todd, E. 1984. "The New Code of Criminal Procedure in the People's Republic of China: Protection, Problems, and Predictions." *International Journal of Comparative and Applied Criminal Justice,* 8 (Fall): 43–53.

of conduct are taught not through written laws, but through a lengthy and continuing educational process whereby a person first learns and then internalizes the socially accepted values and norms as a result of external reinforcement. Compliance is obtained not only through fear of governmental punishment, but through a genuine understanding and acceptance of the proper rules of conduct. Where such self-control fails, social scrutiny and social pressure arise spontaneously to correct and to control the deviant.

The Policy of Reforming Criminals

In 1979, the People's Republic of China enacted her first comprehensive code of law. Incorporating the ideas of Marxism-Leninism and Mao Zedong, the new code is formulated in accordance with the policy of combining punishment with leniency. Article 2 states:

> The tasks of the Criminal Law of the People's Republic of China are to use criminal punishments to struggle against all counter-revolutionary and other criminal acts in order to defend the system of the dictatorship of the proletariat, to protect socialist property owned by the whole people and property collectively owned by the laboring masses, to protect citizens' rights of the person, democratic rights and other rights, to maintain social order, order in production, order in work, order in education and scientific research and order in the lives of the masses of the people, and to safeguard the smooth progress of the cause of socialist revolution and socialist construction.

Criminal justice officials indicated they do not simply apply punishment to criminals and make them serve their time. They work to reform offenders mainly through labor and ideological education so they can earn their living through honest labor and become converted to a new life. Deputy Director Jiao Kun of the Beijing Municipal Bureau of Public Security stated the policy succinctly when he said:[3]

> Our principle in handling convicts is punishment and surveillance coupled with ideological remolding, and making them engage in productive labor while giving them ideological education. Maltreatment of prisoners and corporal punishment are strictly prohibited.

The policy of reforming criminals is based on the concepts of education and labor. Entering the prison, offenders are given a month of special prison education. Prison education is designed to help the inmates re-orient themselves ideologically. They are encouraged to "turn over a new leaf," "make a new start towards a better life," "examine and criticize themselves," and "to get to the bottom of why they commit crimes." Assistance from relatives is used to help bring about change in the inmates. Inmates' families are encouraged to visit them, model inmates are used to give talks, and arrangements are made for ex-convicts to return to the institution to share their positive experiences with those in custody.

---

3. Wei Min. 1981. "Reforming Criminals." *Beijing Review,* No. 8, p. 23.

Labor is the second ingredient used in reforming criminals. To insure that inmates learn to support themselves through honest labor, the institution contains industries which provide meaningful work for all inmates.

The First Step

If a preliminary investigation reveals that the nature and circumstances of the crime require official action, the offender is brought before the public security bureau for prosecution. Although the new criminal code provides for defendants to have counsel,[4] it is important to note that a defense counsel in China is not an advocate for the offender as in the West, but an officer of the court in the strictest sense. If in the course of defending the client the counsel discovers the client is guilty, counsel has the legal obligation to come forward and so advise the court. It appears that defendants in China have little to gain by pleading ''not guilty'' if they cannot produce convincing evidence which will support their claim of innocence. They do not enjoy the western luxury of the right to a trial in order for the state to prove their guilt. In China, offenders have much to lose if they insist they are innocent when the evidence indicates otherwise. It is the view in China that the first step towards rehabilitation is a complete confession and admission of guilt.[5]

Rehabilitation Through Labor

For those who have committed serious crimes, especially political and economic offenses, criminal detention and fixed imprisonment terms are ordered by the court. A prison has three functions: a farm, a factory, and a school. The purpose of prison is not only to punish, but to reform and educate the prisoners. Labor is an essential ingredient of the Chinese prison system. Rehabilitation is conceptualized within a Marxist context that explains the causes of deviant behavior in society. Unlike what was prevalent in the U.S. prior to the 1970's when the individual was the central focus, in China little attention is paid to the internal personality dynamics of the offender, but explanations outside the individual, namely the environment, are more closely examined. There are no psychiatrists/psychologists or social service teams available in Chinese prisons. Based on the Marxist ideology of deviance, social service intervention as configured in the West is not a part of a rehabilitation system. Responsibility for deviant behavior is usually attributed to the external environment. In this view, the offender is not looked upon as a deficient person, and certainly not psychopathologically ill, but more than likely as a victim of certain possible negative influences in the environment. These negative influences may not necessarily reflect on the reality of the environment, but on the individual's perception of these realities. Consequently, the entire rehabilitation process is based on the task of re-educating the offender. Re-education involves

4. Article 8, Criminal Procedure Law of China, states that defendants have the right to obtain defense, and the courts have the duty to guarantee that defendants obtain defense.
5. This condition may also exist in the United States, except the order in which it occurs may be different. Yet, although legally, in the West the defendant has the right to a trial, those defendants who plead guilty have traditionally petitioned the court to give them credit for sparing the court a trial.

a process of helping the individual to respond to the environment within a socialist orientation. Essential to this effort is a combination of learning through labor and education. This is based on the assumption that the individual tends to want to receive the benefits from the environment without the consequences. A combination of labor and learning provides the offender with an experience of hard work at manual labor. Again, the assumption is that the offender will see the relationship between hard work and labor as a means to obtain material goods. Prisoners go through a period of work and labor. When the institution and their peers are convinced that they have been rehabilitated, the treatment is over and they return to their communities and jobs.

Inside the Prisons

Three prisons in China were visited: The Tuan Hur Youth Labor Camp in Beijing, the Beijing Municipal Prison, and the Guangzhou Reformatory. Following an inspection tour of the Beijing Municipal Prison, a meeting was held with officials who entertained the following questions:

Question: Could we have some general information about the prison?
Answer: The prison population is 1900 inmates including 130 women. All are sentenced prisoners. Most prisoners were involved in criminal cases and are serving time for such crimes as theft, robbery, rape, embezzlement, and murder.
Question: How many hours do prisoners work in the factories and do they also go to school?
Answer: They work eight hours per day, five-and-a-half days per week, and study two hours a day. They are also allotted one hour for recreation and they sleep eight hours a day.
Question: Do prisoners serve as leaders of other prisoners?
Answer: Both prisoners and staff may serve as leaders of prisoners but generally, cultural courses are taught by prisoners.
Question: What type of basic education is offered to prisoners?
Answer: They have several levels. Some cannot read or write while others are more advanced. So there is the middle school, or self-study with the university.
Question: Can they get diplomas?
Answer: Yes, there are 200 here with middle school diplomas.
Question: How many staff members do you have?
Answer: We have 514 staff members; a little more than 100 are women.
Question: How do you deal with prisoners who misbehave?
Answer: We do have prisoners who come and do not behave well. We try to analyze why they are so and then we try to educate them. Some may feel they have been unjustly punished. We try to help them understand the seriousness of their crime.
Question: What are the ages of prisoners here?
Answer: They are about 30 years old on the average.
Question: What is the average sentence?
Answer: Generally six years.
Question: Do prisoners have difficulty finding work after they serve their sentence?

Answer: Prisoners with a skill have no problem getting work when they go back to society. Sometimes a work group will come to the prison to seek a prisoner who has a special skill.

Question: What percentage of prisoners work in the factories?

Answer: Generally speaking, most prisoners work in the factories but all with working abilities are required to work. It is fundamental to our way that prisoners learn that they must support themselves by work and not just by taking from someone else.

All three institutions visited were clean, with maximum use of the few amenities that were available. The quality of the live-in quarters can only be judged relative to what are average conditions for the Chinese population. Because of the short supply of houses in China, a typical urban residence for a family of four consists of one or two rooms. These institutions were selected for viewing for the Criminal Justice Delegation by the Ministry of Justice. It is not known if they are representative of institutions in China or some of the better institutions. It is reasonable to assume, however, that what we saw were the current facilities serving the detention and correctional needs of the Chinese system.[6] We were free to move about in the institutions, inspect rooms, and talk to prisoners through interpreters. We noted a high degree of discipline. Prisoners were busy doing constructive work and were involved in education. The program provides for manual work on the farm, work in various metal shops, woodwork, craft shops, work in the textile industry making socks and other saleable items, as well as classroom work, dealing with the three R's. Inmates participate in the rehabilitation process, which in some form resembles what, in the West, is considered encounter group sessions. Offenders are put on a stage and criticized by their peers. Those making good progress in the rehabilitation task assume leadership roles in the rehabilitation process. Final evaluation as to the offender's rehabilitation is made jointly with the staff and with the offender's peers. Rehabilitation is considered accomplished when it is collectively decided that offenders have made ideological changes in their perception of themselves in relationship with the larger community and accept the principle of good conduct because to do otherwise constitutes a threat to the community. Thus, Chinese officials are confident that the process of rehabilitation is not generally faked, or the inmates' opportunity to manipulate the staff is significantly reduced since peers with whom they sleep, eat, and work constantly observe them and are involved in the evaluative process. It is, therefore, difficult for an offender to escape the continuous scrutiny and monitoring from either staff or peers.

Inmates are encouraged to learn a marketable skill while in the institution, which will allow them to assume an appropriate role in the world of work after their release. Before the inmate's discharge, an evaluation is made as to what

---

6. What was seen in the institutions visited was consistent with the observations of others on previous visits to China. See Johnson, E. 1984. "Incarceration in the People's Republic of China: Functions and Implication." *International Journal of Comparative and Applied Criminal Justice,* 8 (Winter).

his work assignment should be, an evaluation based on work done in the institution. Once the rehabilitation process is completed, the offender is forgiven and he receives a full pardon. For example, the Chinese stated that should the inmates meet the qualification for working in the institution, and should they decide to do so, as some have, the inmates could assume roles as staff members upon the completion of their sentence. Released prisoners find employment by (1) returning to the work unit where they were employed prior to their imprisonment; (2) returning to the village where they are given jobs by the local neighborhood agency or labor department; and (3) continuing to work in the prison factory or nearby prison community.

There are conflicting reports of how forgiving the Chinese community is towards offenders who have served their time. Traditional Chinese culture reflects that an individual coming in contact with the law constitutes a disgrace on the individual and his family. This view was echoed by many of the Chinese during the tour. According to one report, prisoners returning to their work unit may not be accepted but will experience some rejection.[7] However, the information from prison officials was overwhelmingly positive, indicating that Chinese society does not systematically discriminate against those who have completed their terms; they have paid their debts to society and they may now return to their communities and work units with a fresh opportunity to make a positive adjustment, with all rights and privileges restored and with no official stigma attached to their incarceration, as is common in the West. Recently, procedures have been established by the government to persuade the leadership in work units to accept offenders for employment, as well as to set up quotas in labor recruitment for the offender population.

Can We Learn From the Chinese?

It is the author's conviction that the process of looking at other systems provides us with an opportunity to evaluate and understand our own system. It gives us a perspective that is difficult to gain from within our own system. It was with the view of learning from the Chinese what characteristics of their corrections program would be transferable to the West that the author participated in a criminal justice delegation.

The low crime rate in China has been documented (see Table 1).[8] Explanations provided so far include the handling of much of their deviants in an informal manner, with only the more serious cases being handled by the official courts. The Chinese prefer to emphasize an informal system of justice rather than official enforcement mechanisms. In doing so, much of the deviant behavior is handled locally by family and local community mediation groups.[9] The Chinese concept of rehabilitation is somewhat different from rehabilitation in the West. Although they are committed to the goal of changing the offender, there is an implied tolerance level. This is evident from the recent executions

7. Wei Min. 1981, p. 28.
8. Wei Min. 1981, p. 28.
9. This also affects the recidivism rate, keeping it artificially low, since a large percent of the crimes are handled informally and thus escape official statistics.

Table 1 China's Recidivism Rate

Year	Rate of New Criminal Offenses
1949–66	2–3 percent
1967–76	11 percent
1977–80	3–4 percent

of hundreds of Chinese who were summarily tried for crimes ranging from murders and rape to petty thievery. The Chinese justification for the executions was that those killed were all habitual criminals. So, while in the West, the criminal justice system may lack the rehabilitation initiative, the Chinese initiative will go only so far. If their efforts bear no fruits, they may terminate further efforts. In terms of rehabilitation there are, however, some similarities. Inside the Chinese jails we saw a genuine effort of the staff to help inmates achieve the goal of controlling their behavior and becoming contributing members of society. There was an atmosphere of caring, a genuine commitment to help each inmate, and a direct effort to work with them at a level that is consistent with the inmates' experiences and motivation. The author was impressed with the use of the inmate population in the rehabilitation process. This was reminiscent of the call for using criminals for the rehabilitation of criminals in the West that went unheeded in the 1960's. Cressey's[10] "symbolic interaction" suggested that criminals can be used effectively to introduce guilt and shame into the psychological makeup of other criminals. He states:

> Both sociologists and correctional workers have been grossly negligent, it seems to me, in matters of rehabilitation theory. We have not been able to develop, or publicize an explicit rehabilitation procedure based on solid theory. Further, we have let ourselves fall into a trap inadvertently set by the psychiatrists and social workers, whose psychiatric theory of rehabilitation has been given great publicity and has, accordingly, gained widespread acceptance. So far . . . this kind of theory implies, by and large, that until one has had about ten years of college training he is not qualified to try to rehabilitate a criminal.

Experience gained in the use of indigenous non-professionals, including selected ex-offenders in probation and parole showed that ex-offenders can provide productive and effective service.[11] Work done by Buckley[12] also suggests that there are some offenders whose feelings of resentment preclude their being helped by people they consider "part of the system." We were also impressed with the link between the task/therapy/rehabilitation in the institutions and the role the inmates play after release from these institutions. Unlike what has been reported in some U.S. penitentiaries, where inmates have had to adjust to being

---

10. Cressey, D. 1965. "Theoretical Foundation for Using Criminals in the Rehabilitation of Criminals." *Key Issues*, Vol. 2, 87–101.
11. Beless, W., Plicher, W., and Ryan, E. 1972. "Use of Indigenous Nonprofessionals in Probation and Parole." *Federal Probation*, 36(1), March, 10–15.
12. Buckley, M. 1972. "Enter: The Ex-con." *Federal Probation*, 36(4), December, 24–30.

locked in their cells 23 hours a day,[13] in China, an attempt is made to prepare the inmates for a productive future when released.

The tasks of the Chinese criminal justice systems are to use criminal punishment to defend the values of the community. The official tasks or goals which define the general and publicly acceptable purpose of the Chinese criminal justice system, and the operative goals which define what the system is trying to accomplish, are the same. The inherent ambiguities, inconsistencies, and conflicts that exist in the definition of rehabilitation in the West were not seen in China. While the Chinese emphasize the values of the community at large, in the West we hold the values and rights of the individual as sacred. In weighing the rights of the individual against the interests of the community at large, the controversy persists over how far to extend the rights of the individual and how to apply them in specific cases. The institutions visited seem to share a common goal and their resources and personnel showed evidence of integration and coordination in achieving the goal of rehabilitation. In the West, the criminal justice system faces a turbulent environment in terms of complexity, instability of expectations of various competing interest groups, as well as the unpredictability of resources.

Part of the demise of rehabilitation in the West has been the feeling expressed by many that the concept of rehabilitation has led to differentiation and the impartiality of services by the penal system. Rehabilitation is being abandoned because it is conceptualized by many as being the disease rather than the cure. By focusing on the individual, by relying on the assumption that the cause of deviant behavior is individual deficiency, we have not only ignored the reality of the environment, but we have represented rehabilitation in unrealistic terms. Based on the author's observation of the Chinese system, some implications for the West may be: (1) Instead of abandoning rehabilitation, maybe we can learn from the Chinese and reconceptualize rehabilitation in terms of helping offenders with tangible means and ways that relate to the environment to which they will have to return upon their release. (2) We could eliminate the pursuit of competing theories and consider developing a rehabilitation procedure based on all the useful elements of current theories—rehabilitation, deterrence, punishment, and the justice model. (3) We could expand the use of ex-offenders and non-professionals in correctional programs. And (4) we could try to bring out in the open why our criminals have become criminals.

Discussion Questions

1. How does Allen's description of the Chinese prison system compare and contrast with notions you had about this system before reading the article?
2. Allen discusses labor and ideological education as the principle mechanisms of rehabilitation in Chinese prisons. What possibilities do you see for employing similar strategies in U.S. prisons? What cultural barriers exist?

13. Gonzales, L. 1986. "The New Alcatraz." *Chicago Magazine,* 35(2), February, p. 230.

3. In general, do you agree with Allen's position that Americans can learn something of value about offender reformation from analyzing the Chinese approach? Why or why not?

8. Social Therapy Treatment of Criminal Offenders: A Survey of Pilot Institutions*

Rudolph Egg, Center for Interdisciplinary Research at the University of Bielefeld, Federal Republic of Germany

Abstract: This article reports on the theory and practice of ten social therapy institutions (sozialtherapeutische Anstalten) for offenders with a high risk of recidivism in the Federal Republic of Germany and West Berlin. On the basis of primarily psychotherapeutic concepts, these institutions have developed different approaches to everyday sociotherapy, largely abandoning traditional therapeutic procedures and involving all the staff in the course of treatment. The results achieved by these institutions are encouraging, but the continuity and further development are being jeopardized because of opposition from criminological and political quarters.

1. Introduction

In the German Federal Republic and West Berlin there are at present ten special institutions for the treatment of offenders with a high risk of recidivism. These institutions, officially termed "sozialtherapeutische Anstalten" (SthA), provide about 500 places which represent approximately 1% of all prison places. This article provides information on the foundations, practices, and results of these institutions since the experience gained so far could well assist in solving a question which is being discussed also on an international level, i.e., what method should be employed to bring about a rehabilitation of offenders.

2. Foundations of Social Therapy in the Correctional System

The idea to establish social therapy institutions first arose in connection with a proposal put forward by criminologists in 1966 (Baumann et al. 1966). This proposal envisaged that criminal offenders with more than one conviction for serious offenses who also have a serious personality disorder should, by court order, be sent to such an institution.

2.1 Legal Foundations

In 1969, legislation was introduced which incorporated the main points of the proposal and provided for the establishment of such institutions (Section 65 of the German Penal Code).

In view of numerous difficulties with regard to finance and personnel, the coming into force of the new legislation was twice postponed and has now been scheduled for 1985. There are fears, however, that because of the

*Translated by Adelheid Baker, Center for Interdisciplinary Research at the University of Bielefeld, FRG.

continuing scarcity of public finance, this date may be deferred yet again and the proposed legislation dropped altogether. Even so, this would not mark the end of all social therapy treatment of criminal offenders since, for some years, there have been a number of institutions which originally had been designed to prepare for the implementation of Section 65 mentioned above. However, offenders are not sent to these institutions by a judge, but by the prison authorities after application by the offender if the program of rehabilitation available there promises to be beneficial to the criminal. In this instance, social therapy represents only a special form of correctional treatment, which obviously facilitates administering the treatment, although some of the basic ideas underlying it are changed and, with respect to the future development of SthAs, make a certain stagnation likely.

2.2 Basic Concepts of Content

Institutions in other countries, e.g., the Herstedvester detention institution near Copenhagen (Stürup 1968), the Van der Hoeven Clinic in Utrecht (Roosenburg 1965), and to some extent the Maxwell Jones Clinic in London (Jones 1952, 1962) have served as models for German SthAs; but some small-scale pilot institutions in Germany provided the major impetus in the development of suitable treatment programs.

In the initial phase, the work evolved mainly from certain psychiatric or psychotherapeutic positions which can be characterized summarily as follows (for more details see Bechtel 1971; Engle 1966, 1973; Mauch 1970; Mauch and Mauch 1969, 1971; Rasch 1974, 1977):

a) Psychotherapeutic measures for individuals and/or groups are central elements in the program of treatment. The main aims of the therapy are the treatment and, if possible, elimination of mental disorders which are considered criminogenic as well as the development and fostering of those behavioral traits which are required for living without committing offenses.
b) To ensure the therapeutic orientation of an institution, the administration and other organizational units have to observe the primacy of therapy or therapists. The staff cooperates closely with the specialist team in the tasks of the institution.
c) Therapy in a more narrow sense is accompanied by additional measures with mainly preparatory, supportive, or supplementary functions. In particular, these include education and vocational training, work training, and work therapy, as well as various kinds of social help.
d) Life in an institution is characterized by a liberal correctional setting, e.g., placement in small communal living groups, unlocked cells during daytime, more leisure activities, no internal disciplinary actions or other compulsory measures, no uniforms, light control of mail, telephone calls, visitors, and opportunities for inmates to affect internal matters.
e) In the final phase of treatment, transitional measures, designed to prepare for life "outside," are implemented, e.g., work release

furloughs, parole, and open prisons (reduced external security of the institution).

This concept of social therapy met with opposition, of course. The main points of view can be summarized as follows.

- Instead of institutional measures, there should either be a "treatment in freedom" (Schneider 1978), or such a treatment is rejected on points of social criticism (Heinz and Korn 1973; Hilbers and Lange 1973; Rasch 1977; see also Rasch 1977, pp. 23–30).
- Some proposals are designed to shift the emphasis of the SthAs' work from psychotherapy to other forms of treatment such as social training (Kremer 1977) or to a level of direct conflict-solving (Rehn 1975).

A group of critics must also be mentioned who take a conservative view and regard social therapy as a "socially romantic notion" (Witkowski 1978) and demand a more resolute or rigid enforcement of penal law (see also Fenn and Spiess 1980).

While such conservative attitudes became noticeable through an increase in restrictive regulations and even led to the failure of the initial phase of one model institution (cf. Rasch 1977), the basic therapeutic concept of the institutions was influenced by the following factors.

a) The establishment of large SthAs with highly specialized staff did not materialize because of a variety of financial difficulties. Thus, there was a need during the early stages to look for simpler or other solutions.
b) In concrete terms this meant that few psychotherapists trained in psychoanalysis were employed in the institutions, and therapy was undertaken mainly by psychologists, educators, and social workers who obtained the qualifications mainly through supplementary training courses in one or several therapeutic subjects, especially behavior and client-centered therapy. Different forms of communal living were tested in the residential sections and became integral elements of the program.
c) It was found that forms of therapy developed outside the correctional system could not be transferred automatically to the clientele and situation of SthAs. This applies to both the client-centered group therapy (cf. Leky and Mohr 1977; Lutz 1980) and the therapeutic behavior techniques (Coignerai-Weber 1980; Schmitt 1974). In all cases modifications and mixed forms of "pure" therapies were developed (see also Schmitt 1980, pp. 147–150).
d) At the same time there was a change in attitudes concerning the importance of psychotherapeutic forms of treatment within the overall program. They no longer constituted the essential part of the program; instead, greater priority was given to real-life employment in the small living group, to training programs for learning social

skills and to efforts of integrating the social environment (family, job) of the clients (see also Romkopf 1980a, p. 198).

e) This often led to therapists developing a different view of their role in the institution, i.e., they no longer kept themselves detached from what was happening in the institution, in line with the usually practiced therapeutic abstinence, but started, together with other staff, to participate actively in the everyday activities in the various sections. The work carried out in the small living groups is, therefore, becoming more than a merely preparatory work for the therapy ''proper'' and developing into an independent *sociotherapy*.

The points mentioned show that in various places the attitude toward social therapy is changing, although not all therapists are subscribing to it (e.g., Waxweiler 1980).

3. Practices in German Social Therapy Institutions

There are ten of these institutions in the Federal Republic of Germany and West Berlin and they have a total capacity of 500 places, of which 200 alone are in Tegel, West Berlin. The remainder are spread over relatively small institutions with 30–50 places (see the appended survey).

3.1 General

All institutions are administered by the judicial authorities and usually are headed by a jurist, although therapists, particularly psychologists, also play an important role in decision-making processes. Apart from a small number of psychiatrists or psychotherapists, the majority of individual counselors are psychologists, social workers, and educators. The ratio is one to two counselors per ten inmates. The prison personnel is integrated into the treatment, e.g., by being assigned to individual groups of inmates.

3.2 Inmates

The inmates are admitted to these institutions on a voluntary basis only. Apart from some formal aspects such as age, length of sentence, and type of crime, criteria of admission relate to qualitative aspects which are discussed with the inmate upon admission. It is necessary, for example, that the inmate has a genuine interest in cooperating with the program. Mental and social abnormalities should be significant in character so that special therapeutic measures would be required. Some factors would preclude admission, for instance those relating to security (e.g., high risk of escape) or the possibility that the specific problems of an applicant cannot be treated within the available program. Some of the institutions do not accept drug addicts or offenders convicted of sexual offenses, fraud, or drug offenses. Similar restrictions apply to inmates with disturbances due to mental deficiency.

The majority of inmates are between 25 and 35 years old. They are all male, except in one institution. Nearly all of them previously have spent one or more terms of imprisonment. The sentence length of inmates entering an SthA varies from three to five years. Crimes include offenses against property, especially burglary, as well as crimes of violence (robbery, bodily harm, rape). Inmates convicted of a killing are rare and sex offenders are sometimes not present at all.

Many of the inmates are from broken homes, and many did not finish school and/or have no vocational training. In addition, they are sometimes heavily in debt. Moreover, studies (e.g., Egg 1979; Rasch and Kühl 1977) have revealed a considerable number of psychological problems. To summarize, the inmates in these institutions show levels of psychological and social problems which are above average compared with the general as well as with the prison population.

3.3 Process of Treatment

A stay in a SthA is limited to about 2 years on average and normally consists of three phases:

a) **Initial or trial phase:**
During this phase, the inmate should become familiar with the institution and, with the help of the staff, he should find out which type of assistance offered by the institution would be appropriate and meaningful for him (preparation of a treatment plan). Only after completing this phase is the inmate regarded as a full resident of the institution; but a transfer back to an ordinary prison remains a possibility even after this period.

b) **Main or middle phase:**
During this phase, the actual treatment program is implemented. There are variations among the institutions as to the amount of emphasis given to small living groups, to developing a therapeutic community, to so-called social training (Kremer 1977), to schooling and vocational training, or to individual or group therapy. External measures such as work furloughs, leave, etc., are relatively rare in these institutions, although in one of them (in Hamburg-Bergedorf) working outside the institution with full pay constitutes an essential element of the program. Contacts with friends or relatives are facilitated through liberal visiting regulations (in Hamburg-Bergedorf visitors are allowed into the cells), with very little censorship of mail and telephone calls and the assignment of voluntary helpers from the community.

c) **Final or transitional phase:**
During the final phase, which usually covers the last 6–10 months of the sentence, greater priority is given to the external measures already mentioned. The inmate now has to prepare for his release and his life in a free community. He is granted longer terms of leave, is allowed to visit relatives during parole, and to look for employment. Sometimes he moves from a closed prison to a halfway house.

3.4 Supervision, Further Education, and Concurrent Scientific Evaluation

A thorough team and case-related supervision is practically non-available. On the other hand, there are frequent consultations of team members in conferences, informal discussions, and separate in-service-training periods. An exchange of experience among the various institutions has taken place in a series of supraregional conferences, e.g., at the Center of Interdisciplinary Research (ZiF), University of Bielefeld (Rehn 1976, 1977; Schmitt 1979; Lippenmeier, 1981).

In view of the importance of a concurrent scientific evaluation to ensure the further development of these institutions, there have been repeated demands in this respect (e.g., Kury and Fenn 1977), and it had originally been thought that this would materialize through a proximity to locally situated research institutions. To date, however, there have been hardly any research projects to speak of.

Of the existing publications, those which are oriented toward analyzing processes or sociological and organizational aspects (Driebold 1981; Sagebiel 1979; Schmitt 1980) and especially those which have investigated the success of social therapy in relation to recidivism (Dünkel and Johnson 1980; Johnson and Dünkel 1981; Rohn 1981) or to psychological and social aspects of delinquents (Egg 1979; Waxweiler 1980) are of particular interest in the general discussion of the subject. The findings of these works leave a number of questions unanswered but are on the whole encouraging and should prove helpful in the further development of social therapy programs.

4. Concluding Remarks

In Germany, social therapy institutions have not been able, on account of a multitude of internal and external difficulties, to develop in the way that had been hoped for by prison reformers. The completion or construction of further institutions is slow, and the internal organization is often hampered by a shortage of funds and restrictive regulations so that frequently staff members have to try to manage through savings and alternative solutions. Moreover, in recent years, reformatory endeavors have decreased somewhat. One could even speak of a kind of rollback in penal policies, all of which leaves little hope for the future.

By contrast, the work accomplished so far is encouraging. A number of practical approaches have been developed which seem to be better suited to the needs of those affected and the goals of institutions than some esoteric concepts used in psychotherapy. On the other hand, these new practical developments have caused a certain theoretical deficit which limits the possibilities of teaching and transferring the various pilot programs.

In the autumn of 1980, an interdisciplinary project based on secondary analysis and concerned with developing such an integrative approach was started at the Center for Interdisciplinary Research of the University of Bielefeld (Egg 1981). Preliminary findings will be available in the near future.

The evaluation of SthAs will continue to be of central importance in the research being undertaken in connection with the institutions. The emphasis will not be on supplying evidence in support of the effectiveness of social therapy so as to convince even the most doubtful critics. In fact, this would be impossible since the social therapy approach involves basic principles of ethics and humanity which elude empirical "proof." Even so it seems necessary and useful to weigh the efficiency of the various institutions in relation to one another in order to enable direct assistance with their practical activities.

5. Appendix Survey of Social Therapy Institutions in the Federal Republic of Germany and West Berlin

Location (and Federal State)	Size (no. of places)	Opened in	Bibliographical notes (cf. BUNDESZUSAMMENSCHLUSS 1973, 1977, 1981)
Berlin Tegel (West Berlin)	180 (plus about 50 in work release sections)	1970	COIGNERAI-WEBER 1979 DÜNKEL 1980 DÜNKEL & JOHNSON 1980 JOHNSON & DÜNKEL 1981 KREMER 1977 WAXWEILER 1980
Düren (Nordehein-Westfalen)	32 (plus 28 in the halfway house in Cologne)	1971	BECHTEL 1971 KRETZ 1976, 1977 RASCH 1974, 1977 RASCH & KÜHL 1973, 1978 SAGEBIEL 1973, 1979
Erlangen (Bayern)	40 (6 in the transitional section)	1972	BICKEL 1976, 1977 EGG 1975, 1977, 1979 EGG & SCHUCHT 1978, 1982 SCHLEUSENER 1980
Bad Gandersheim (Niedersachsen)	24	1973	DRIEBOLD 1981 LUTZ 1980
Gelsenkirchen (Nordehein-Westfalen)	54	1974	ROMKOPF 1980 a, b ROTTHAUS 1977, 1981, 1982
Hamburg-Bergedorf (Hamburg)	34	1969	ACKERMANN 1971 HOLZAPFEL 1971, 1972 REHN 1979
Kassel (Hessen)	60	1981	—
Lubeck (Schleswig-Holstein)	17 (women) 42 (men)	1974 1981	BÖHME, BÜHE, SCHUTOW 1978
Ludwigsburg-Bohenasperg (Baden-Württemberg)	59	1969	DOLDE 1982 ENGELL 1972 MAUCH 1964, 1970 MAUCH & MAUCH 1969, 1971
Ludwigshafen (Rheinland-Pfalz)	50	1972	SCHMITT 1974, 1978, 1980

In view of past experience, i.e., a slow rate of progress which has been hampered by many factors, in the future a degree of commitment will be required of scientists and practitioners which extends beyond routine criminological tasks in order that the work begun should not, as a number of previous reformatory projects, be swallowed up in the mainstream of traditional correction.

Discussion Questions

1. Egg discusses a number of problems that have hindered the development of social therapy facilities in Germany. Summarize these problems and explain what might be done to help overcome them.
2. Does the U.S. currently have any kind of penal institution (or modality of treatment) that is similar to what was described by Egg? Explain what is similar and different about U.S. practices.
3. What, if any, promise do social therapy facilities, like those which exist in Germany, have for improving offender rehabilitation efforts in the U.S.?
4. Do you agree with Egg's assertion (made toward the end of his article) that it is not necessary or even possible to supply data regarding the effectiveness of social therapy? Why or why not?

References

Ackerman, E. 1971 Two Years of Experience in the Special Prison in Hamburg-Bergedorf. MschrKrim 54, 367–371.

Baumann, J. et al. (eds.) 1966 Alternative Design for a Penal Code. Tübingen (W. Germ.): Mohr.

Bechtel, J. 1971 The Social Therapy Concept. Pages 43–61 in G. Nass (ed.), Kriminalität vorbeugen und behandeln. Cologne (W. Germ.): Heymanns.

Bickel, A. 1976 The Social Therapy "Treatment" Within and Outside of Prison. Gruppendynamik 5, 338–342.

———. 1977 Intra- and Extramural Social Therapy. Bewährungshilfe 24, 120–128.

Böhme, K., Bühe, H., and Schultow, H. 1978 Social Therapy for Women. Report for the First Project in Lübeck. MschrKrim 61, 180–191.

Bundeszusammenschluss fuer Straffalligenhilfe (eds.) 1973 Social Therapy and the Social Therapy Institution. A Report of the Fachausschuss V. Bonn-Bad Godesberg (W. Germ.): Selbstverlag, Heft 14 der Schriftenreihe.

———. 1977 Social Therapy Institutions. Concepts and Experiences. A Report of the Fachausschuss V. Bonn-Bad Godesberg (W. Germ.): Selbstverlag, Heft 19 der Schriftenreihe.

———. 1981 Social Therapy as a Criminological/Political Task. Recommendations for the Future Legal and Practical Developments of Social Therapy in the Correctional System, made by the Fachausschuss V. Bonn-Bad Godesberg (W. Germ.): Selbstverlag, Heft 26 der Schriftenreihe.

Coignerai-Weber, C. 1979 Ten Years of Social Therapy in Tegel Prison. MschrKrim 62, 338–347.

———. 1980 Therapy of Socially Disintegrated Persons from a Working Class Background. Pages 219–228 in W. Schulz and M. Hautzinger (eds.), Klinische Psychologie und Psychotherapie, Kongressbericht Berlin 1980, Vol. 5, Tübingen and Cologne (W. Germ.): DGVT/GwG.

Dolde, G. 1982 Efficiency Control of Social Therapy Treatment in the Correctional Process. Kriminologische Gegenwartsfragen, Vol. 15, 47–64.

Driebold, R. 1981 Social Therapy in the Correctional System. Possibilities and Obstacles of a Cooperation with Inmates. Weinheim, Basel (W. Germ., Switzerland): Beltz.

Dünkel, F. 1980 Recidivism after Social Therapy Treatment. An Empirical Research on the Criminal Records of 1,503 within 1971–74 Released Prisoners at Berlin-Tegel. Berlin: Duncker and Humblot.

Dünkel, F. and Johnson, E. H. 1980 Introduction of Therapy into Tegel Prison: Evaluation of an Experiment. International Journal of Comparative and Applied Criminal Justice, Vol. 4, No. 2, 233–247.

Egg, R. 1975 Social Therapy in Erlangen. Methods and First Results in a Trial and Test Institution. Bewährungshilfe 22, 87–102.

———. 1979 Social Therapy and Imprisonment. An Empirical Evaluative Research on Social Therapy Measures. Frankfurt (W. Germ.): Haag and Herchen.

———. 1982 Social Therapy Institutions in the Correctional System. MschrKrim 65, 38–41.

Egg, R. and Schucht, H. 1978 Therapy Behind Bars: Into Freedom Step by Step. Psychologie heute 5, No. 2, 39–43.

———. 1982 Psychological Work in Social Therapy Institutions—Tasks and Problems. In F. Lösel (ed.), Kriminalpsychologie, Weinheim, Basel (W. Germ., Switzerland): Beltz.

Engel, S. W. 1966 On the Metamorphosis of the Offender. MschrKrim 49, 151–159.

———. 1973 On the Metamorphosis of the Offender. Foundations of a Treatment Theory. Stuttgart (W. Germ.): Enke.

Engell, R. 1972 Recent Experiences in Social Therapy Work with Delinquents in Baden-Württemberg. Pages 271–284 in H. E. Ehrhardt (ed.), Perspektiven der heutigen Psychiatrie. Frankfurt (W. Germ.): Gerhards.

Engell, R. and Egenhofer, H. 1977 The Social Therapy Institution in Ludwigsburg—Concept and Plan for a Social Therapy Institution. ZstrVollz 26, 164–172.

Fenn, R. and Spiess, G. 1980 Findings of Research into Therapy—Arguments for a Restrictive Imprisonment? Sonderheft der ZStrVollz: Sozialtherapie und Behandlungsforschung 29, 85–89.

Heinz, W. and Korn, S. 1973 Social Therapy as an Alibi? Materials for a Reform of Correctional Treatment. Frankfurt (W. Germ.): Fischer.

Hilbers, M. and Lange, W. 1973 Departure from a Therapy-centered Ideology? Experiences of Modern Forms of Correction in Scandinavia. Kriminologisches Journal 5, 52–59.

Holzapfel, R. 1971 Therapeutic Aspects of Imprisonment. MschrKrim 54, 372–377.

———. 1972 The Special Prison in Hamburg-Bergedorf, Three Years of Practical Experience. Pages 285–291 in H. E. Ehrhardt (ed.), Perspektiven der heutigen Psychiatrie. Frankfurt (W. Germ.): Gerhards.

Johnson, E. and Dünkel, F. 1981 Introducing Therapy into Tegel Prison: Implications from an Evaluation Perspective. International Journal of Comparative and Applied Criminal Justice, Vol. 5, No. 1, 3–10.

Jones, M. 1952 Social Psychiatry. A Study of Therapeutic Community. London: Tavistock.

———. 1961 Social Psychiatry in the Community, in Hospitals, and in Prisons. Springfield, Ill.: Chas. C. Thomas.

Kremer, H. 1977 Action Research "Tegeler Modell"—On the Practice and Strategy of Social Training During Correctional Treatment. Pages 65–82 in W. Hollstein and M. Meinhold (eds.), Sozialpädagogische Modelle. Frankfurt (W. Germ.): Campus.

Kretz, H. 1976 Social Therapy Institution from a Medical Point of View. Pages 77–87 in H. D. Schwind and G. Blau (eds.), Strafvollzug in der Praxis. Berlin, New York: de Gruyter.

———. 1977 Pretensions and Reality of Social Therapy in Germany. Psychiatrische Praxis 4, 135–149.

Kury, H. and Fenn, R. 1977 Social Therapy Treatment and Concurrent Evaluation. Possibilities and Ways of Empirical Research. MschrKrim 60, 227–242.

Leky, L. G. and Mohr, H. 1977 Client-centered Therapy in Groups—Reporting on Experiences. Pages 113–128 in W. Rasch (ed.), Forensische Sozialtherapie. Karlsruhe, Heidelberg (W. Germ.): C. F. Müller.

Lippenmeier, N. 1981 Current Research Problems: Social Therapy on the 5th Meeting of the Workshop on "Social Therapy Institutions in the Correctional System" in Bielefeld. MschrKrim 64, 97–102.

Lutz, H. D. 1980 Group Therapy in a Social Therapy Institution. Pages 229–240 in W. Schulz and M. Hautzinger (eds.), Klinische Psychologie und Psychotherapie. Kongressbericht Berlin 1980, Vol. 5, Tübingen, Cologne (W. Germ.): DGVT/GwG.

Mauch, G. 1970 Social Therapy During Imprisonment. Zeitschrift fur Psychotherapie und medizinische Psychologie 20, 66–75.

Mauch, G. and Mauch, R. 1969 Social Therapy in the Correctional Institution. Possibilities and Limits. Pages 158–176 in W. Bitter (ed.), Verbrechen—Schuld oder Schicksal? Stuttgart (W. Germ.): Klett.

———. 1971 Social Therapy and the Social Therapy Institution. Experiences in Treating Chronic Criminals. Prerequisites, Implementation, and Possibilities. Stuttgart (W. Germ.): Enke.

Rasch, W. 1974 Formal Structure and Basic Organizational Concept of the Pilot Institution in Duren. MschKrim 57, 27–41.

Rasch, W. (ed.) 1977 Forensic Social Therapy. The Experiences of Düren. Karlsruhe, Heidelberg (W. Germ.): C. F. Müller.

Rasch, W. and Kühl, K. P. 1973 Subjective Suffering as a Criterion for a Social Therapy Treatment. (FPI-Test Results with Offenders as Covered by Section 65 of the German Penal Code). MschrKrim 56, 237–245.

———. 1977 Psychological Criteria for Placement in a Social Therapy Institution. Pages 203–259 in W. Rasch (ed.), Forensische Sozialtherapie. Karlsruhe, Heidelberg (W. Germ.): C. F. Müller.

———. 1978 Psychological Findings and Recidivism After Staying at the Social Therapy Institution in Düren. Bewährungshilfe 25, 44–57.

Rehn, G. 1975 Social Therapy and the Social Therapy Institution. Approaches to a Theoretical and Methodological Foundation. MschrKrim 58, 69–82.

———. 1976 Beyond Infancy? Report on the First Meeting of the Workshop on "Social Therapy Institutions in the Correctional System" in Bielefeld. MschrKrim 59, 148–153.

———. 1977 What next? Report on the Second Meeting of the Workshop on "Social Therapy Institutions in the Correctional System" in Bielefeld. Mschrkrim 60, 50–56.

———. 1979 Treatment During Imprisonment. Findings of a Comparative Study into the Role of Recidivism Among Discharged Offenders. Weinheim, Basel (W. Germ., Switzerland): Beltz.

Romkopf, G. 1980a On the Current Treatment Situation of Offenders in the Social Therapy Institution in Gelsenkirchen. Pages 195–203 in W. Schulz and M. Hautzinger (eds.), Klinische Psychologie und Psychotherapie. Kongressbericht Berlin 1980, Vol. 5, Tübingen, Cologne: DGVT, GwG.

———. 1980b The Social Therapy Institution in Gelsenkirchen. Support of the Living Groups by Specialists. Sonderheft der ZStrVollz: Sozialtherapie und Behandlungsforschung 29, 60–66.

Roosenburg, A. M. 1965 Réeducation á la 'van der Hoeven-Klinik.' Schweizerische Zeitschrift fur Strafrecht 18, 391–402.

Rotthaus, K. P. 1977 The Social Therapy Institution from the Jurist's Point of View. Pages 70–77 in H. D. Schwind and G. Blau (eds.), Strafvollzug in der Praxis. Berlin, New York: de Gruyter.

———. 1981 Social Therapy in the Gelsenkirchen Prison. ZStrVollz 30, 323–333.

———. 1982 Experiences in Practical Social Therapy—Comments by a Jurist. Kriminologische Gegenwartsfragen, Vol. 15, 79–99.

Sagebiel, F. 1973 Difficulties in Organizing Social Therapy Structure of Roles and Authority in the Düren Pilot Institution. Kriminologisches Journal 5, 16–30.

———. 1979 On Safeguarding a Therapeutically-oriented Organizational Structure of Social Therapy Institutions. Göttingen (W. Germ.): Schwartz.

Schleusener, J. 1980 Cooperation and Coordination of the Various Vocational Groups in the Social Therapy Institution. Sonderheft der ZStrVollz: Sozialtherapie und Behandlungsforschung 29, 29–32.

Schmitt, G. 1974 Theory and Practice of Social Therapy in Correctional Treatment, with Particular Reference to Behavior Therapy. Pages 1–18 in H. Müller-Dietz (ed.), Kriminaltherapie heute. Berlin, New York: de Gruyter.

———. 1978 The Treatment of Youths and Adults in the Social Therapy Institution. ZStrVollz 27, 146–153.

———. 1979 "What is Possible?" Report on Two Preparatory as well as the Third and Fourth Meetings of the Workshop on 'Social Therapy Institutions in the Correctional System' in Bielefeld. MschrKrim 62, 374–377.

———. 1980 Social Therapy—Brinkmanship in the Correctional System. Concepts and Organizational Structure of a Social Therapy Institution. Frankfurt (W. Germ.): Haag and Herchen.

Schneider, H. J. 1978 Treatment in Freedom. Psychologie heute 5, No. 9, 67–74.

Stürup, G. 1968 Treating the Untreatable: Chronic Criminals at Herstedvester/Denmark. Baltimore: J. Hopkins.

Waxweiler, R. 1980 Psychotherapy During Imprisonment. An Empirical Evaluation of Success Based on a Social Therapy Department of a Prison. Weinheim, Basel (W. Germ., Switzerland): Beltz.

Witkowski, W. 1978 More Severe Punishment and Less Psychology? Or: 'The Absurdity of Punishment.' Kriminalistik 32, 201–205.

Select Problems in the Prison Organization

9. The Organisation of Power in Soviet Labour Camps

Rasma Karklins,* University of Illinois at Chicago

> I am convinced that it is also finally time to speak about what goes on in corrective-labour institutions. . . The rule of openness brooks no exceptions. *Literaturnaya gazeta,* 15 April 1987.

The topic of this paper has been rarely dealt with in recent scholarly work. The contemporary lack of attention to mechanisms of coercion has many reasons, not least of them the difficulty of finding good sources. Yet it is also a question of intellectual fashion. As noted in a comparative analysis of police power in society: "The study of the police as a political institution has fallen unto hard times for a number of reasons and has only recently begun to be resurrected as a worthwhile scholarly topic and a crucial theoretical question in analysing the nature of the state and state rule."[1]

How power is exercised is a core question not only of political science but also of Soviet studies. It is analysed here for a political microcosm, the Soviet labour camp system since Stalin. It lends itself to case study as an underexplored state institution and also because the management of men in prison "presents power relations with naked clarity."[2] Many former camp inmates have even claimed that "nowhere as well as in camp can you penetrate into the very core of a country's—any country's—political system."[3] While this may be an overstatement, I agree with McCleery that "although the prison should

---

*This paper was written under a senior fellowship at the Institute for the Humanities, University of Illinois at Chicago. Data for this study were produced by the Soviet Interview Project. This project was supported by Contract no. 701 from the National Council for Soviet and East European Research to the University of Illinois at Urbana-Champaign, James R. Millar, Principal Investigator. The analysis and interpretations in this study are those of the author, not necessarily of the sponsors. I wish to thank Brian Kemple and Vida Kuprys for their excellent research assistance.

1. Otwin Marenin, "Police Performance and State Rule: Control and Autonomy in the Exercise of Coercion," *Comparative Politics,* XVIII no. 1 (October 1985), p. 102.
2. Rchard H. McCleery, "Policy Changes in Prison Management," in Amitai Etzioni, ed. *Complex Organizations* (New York: Holt, Rinehart and Winston, 1962), p. 377.
3. Eduard Kuznetsov, *Prison Diaries.* Translated by Howard Spier (New York: Stein and Day, 1975), p. 136.

not be taken uncritically as a society in microcosm, the comparative isolation of its social process from the impact of external variables provides a rare opportunity for systemic analysis."[4]

The question is how a small number of men organise to control a much larger number. The typical image of Soviet labour camps is that of a purely repressive institution characterised by the isolation and physical coercion of inmates. But a closer look shows a more sophisticated organisation of power by officials who put a premium on co-opting inmates for self-policing, who manipulate a carefully designed incentive system, and use regimentation and psychological pressure to control and "re-educate" prisoners. Yet the officially intended system of control is weakened in practice by some contradictory goals, faulty execution, and prisoner activity. When they have little choice, guards sometimes compromise with prisoners, and there are elements of inmate power and true self-organisation. As is noted in the highly illuminating comparative literature on prisons, relations between captor and captive are interactive and complex.

Thus I not only analyse how power is exercised but also assess the sources and extent of limitations of control. My approach borrows selectively from several theoretical traditions. The emphasis on organisation means that I use insights of organisational theory as well as Leninist thinking about the power of effective organisation and political propaganda. I also use writings of comparative penologists and the theory about "total institutions" developed by Erving Goffman as a framework of analysis. In this I apply a Weberian approach of exploring the particular features of historical cases with the aid of ideal-type concepts.[5] The conceptual framework of total institutions has proved to be most helpful in making concrete findings meaningful and in reaching for some broader generalisations about the organisation of coercive power.

The primary data sources for this article are the huge store of ***samizdat*** documents, published accounts by ex-prisoners, and 32 in-depth interviews with former camp inmates conducted under the auspices of the Soviet Interview Project (SIP). The sample made accessible by SIP complements dissident sources by consisting mostly of people who were imprisoned on criminal charges and who regard themselves as having been normal Soviet citizens who ended up in camp primarily through bad luck. I also use official Soviet sources on law and penal policy, existing Western scholarly work, and reports by human rights organisations.

The USSR has retained a network of labour camps for the entire period since Stalin's death. Next to regular criminals, these camps hold political and religious prisoners as well as what I call "quasi-criminals," people who in the USSR are considered to be criminals because of economic or other transgres-

4. McCleery, p. 378.
5. Charles Ragin and David Zaret, "Theory and Method in Comparative Research: Two Strategies," *Social Forces,* 61 no. 3 (March 1983), pp. 731–54.

sions that many other polities do not view as crimes.[6] In addition, many have been sentenced under investigative and court procedures that leave much to be desired.[7] The total number of prisoners is uncertain, but most Western sources agree that it is high in comparative perspective and that the inmate population has fluctuated between one and three million during the last 30 years.[8]

The purpose of this analysis is to pinpoint the main political features of the camp system. I look first at the organisational structure of labour camps since Stalin; next I discuss the primary mechanisms of control; and then I examine inmate protests. In these aspects there are some differences by sub-periods, by the type of camp, and by severity of the official camp regime. Some of these differences are pointed out, but elsewhere either a basic pattern holds true or the data are insufficient for more detailed analysis.

Organisational Structure

Soviet law authorises four categories of "corrective labour colonies" (*ispravitel'notrudovye kolonii*). Depending on the severity of their offences and past records, prisoners are sentenced to "ordinary," "intensified," "hard," or "special" regime camps. The more severe the regime, the worse the conditions and the harder the work.[9] Some political and most religious prisoners are imprisoned in regular camps with criminals, but there are also separate political strict regime camps in Mordovia and the Urals.[10]

1. Official Administration

Soviet penal colonies are under the jurisdiction of the Ministry of Internal Affairs (MVD) and are staffed by two types of personnel: specialised civilian employees from among the local population and uniformed custodial officials

6. For details see Louise I. Shelley, "Crimes and Criminals in the USSR," in Michael P. Sacks and Jerry G. Pankhurst, eds. *Understanding Soviet Society* (Boston: Unwin Hyman, 1988), ch. 9.
7. This has been noted in some remarkably candid recent Soviet sources discussing the need for a comprehensive legal reform, such as "Perestroika v. pravovoi sisteme, yuridicheskoi nauke, praktike," *Sovetskoe gosudarstvo i pravo,* 1987 no. 9, pp. 17–43; *see also Moskovskaya pravda,* 17 May 1987, p. 3; *Pravda,* 15 November 1987, p. 3; *Izvestiya,* 23 December 1987, p. 3.
8. The most recent and detailed calculations are by Ger van den Berg, *The Soviet System of Justice: Figures and Policy* (Dordrecht: M. Nijhoff, 1985), chapter VI. See also Peter Juviler, *Revolutionary Law and Order: Politics and Social Change in the USSR* (New York: Free Press, 1976), p. 106; Valery Chalidze, *Criminal Russia: A Study of Crime in the Soviet Union.* Translated from the Russian by P. S. Falla (New York: Random House, 1977), pp. 200–01; Fridrikh Nezansky, "New Information on Soviet Criminal Statistics: An Inside Report." Translated by Peter H. Juviler, *Soviet Union/Union Sovietique,* 6, pt. 2 (1979), pp. 200–11; Peter Reddaway, ed. and trans. *Uncensored Russia: Protest and Dissent in the Soviet Union* (New York: American Heritage Press, 1972), p. 205; Julia Wishnevskaia, "Estimates of the Prison Population of the USSR," *Radio Liberty Research Bulletin,* RL 351/82 (New York: Radio Liberty, 31 August 1982).
9. Juviler, p. 105; see also various official Soviet sources, for example *The Corrective Labour Code of the RSFSR* (1970). Trans. Clayton Yeo, in *The Soviet Codes of Law,* ed. by William B. Simmons, (Alphen den Rijn, The Netherlands: Sijthoff and Noordhoff, 1980), pp. 325–86. It is beyond the scope of this study to comment on other penal institutions such as prisons or special settlement colonies.
10. Some of these camps were closed following the partial prisoner release begun in 1987, but on 12 February 1988 there were still 96 people in Perm Camp VS 389/35. *USSR News Briefs,* 1988, no. 3, p. 4.

organised in a military manner. Among the latter are former army officers and others who have been trained at MVD police schools after attending a general trade school or institute.[11] Many are camp officials only for lack of a better choice and are bitter about the low prestige of their job. Thus a Soviet newspaper mentions a detachment leader who, "like many of his colleagues, when he meets someone for the first time he's in no hurry to tell them that he works in the colony."[12]

Soviet labour camps have a dual identity as both prisons and production units and this is reflected in their organisational make-up. Each camp has a "living zone" and a "production zone"; during most of their waking hours prisoners do hard labour. Since 1957 inmates have lived and worked together in near-permanent detachments (*otryady*), typically consisting of 100 to 130 prisoners (about 50 in stricter camps). Each detachment usually is under an MVD lieutenant or captain euphemistically referred to as "supervisor re-educator." He is responsible for his detachment in all regards: how well the prisoners work, how well they observe the rules and are disciplined, their condition, and their political and re-education work.[13]

The camp director too is responsible both for keeping order and for fulfilling production norms, but many of the other officials are primarily responsible for either order or production. For keeping order each camp director typically has a deputy in charge of "the regime," and another deputy is in charge of political re-education. Then there are a resident KGB operative with his section, a censors' office, and MVD officers in charge of the camp guards. The production personnel are headed by a "director of the ITU enterprise,"[14] civilian work supervisors and engineers. Camps also employ bookkeepers, teachers, medical personnel, and others.

The formal administrative hierarchy is close to the informal one, and even the KGB officers tend to have less power than the camp director.[15] Ex-prisoners refer to him as "the boss" and as having decisive influence over camp life. Nevertheless, there are limits to his power as well. One limit is set by the dual

---

11. Respondents frequently say that officials are uneducated. The only "hard data" I have found are that in 1966, among the *nachal'niki otryadov* in the RSFSR, 11% had higher education and 42% had secondary specialized education, nothing being said about the rest. I. V. Shmarov and F. T. Kuznetsov, *Effektivnost' bratel'nosti ispravitel'no-trudovykh uchrezhdenii* (Moscow: Yuridicheskaya literatura, 1968), p. 169.
12. *Current Digest of the Soviet Press,* XXXV, no. 34, p. 10; also my own interviews.
13. Interview data; see also Shmarov and Kuznetsov, p. 135 and p. 168 and V. P. Shupilov, "Execution of Sentences," in M. Charif Bassiouni and V. M. Savitski, eds. *The Criminal Justice System of the USSR* (Springfield, Ill.: Charles C. Thomas, 1979), p. 212; on the *otryad* system *per se* compare *ibid* pp. 109–10 and F. J. M. Feldbrugge, "Soviet Corrective Labour Law," in *Soviet Law After Stalin,* edited by Donald B. Barry, George Ginsburgs, and Peter B. Maggs, Part I, *The Citizen and the State in Contemporary Soviet Law* (Leyden: A. W. Sijthoff, 1977), p. 36.
14. Shmarov and Kuznetsov, p. 148: "ITU" is the acronym for the Russian "corrective labour colony"; the same source also mentioned that the camp director ranks higher than the enterprise director.
15. The political camps may be an exception. Compare Vladimir Bukovsky, *To Build a Castle—My Life as a Dissenter* (New York: Viking Press, 1979), p. 332.

role of the camps as penal institutions and production units, because achieving the goals of the one frequently conflicts with those of the other. The performance of each camp director is measured both by successful inmate "correction" and by economic productivity, yet organisational imperatives of fulfilling the plan socially may contradict those of fulfilling it economically. To give just one example: for security reasons responsible positions in camp enterprises are supposed to be filled solely by free workers, yet inmates with special skills are sometimes given such work if no one else is available.

Organisational theorists argue that the behaviour of persons occupying organisational roles is principally determined by the requirements of organisational maintenance and enhancement.[16] Applied to camp officials this means that they are eager to have prisoners work well, be disciplined, and avoid unsettling incidents. This need theoretically gives some power to inmates. As argued by Abel, even inmates of concentration camps have leverage over guards because "any ruling personnel is . . . dependent upon its subject population in one way or another and this dependence ensures that control can never be complete."[17] There are other limitations to what is intended to be foolproof organization, for example, limitations set by human nature such as the corruptibility, venality, or humaneness of personnel.

Similar points are made in other writings on prisons. Sykes argues that the power of guards can be undermined not only by prisoner resistance but also by bad implementation:

> Yet the system of power may be defective for reasons other than the fact that those who are ruled do not feel the need to obey the orders and regulations descending on them from above. Systems of power may also fail because those who are supposed to rule are unwilling to do so. The unissued order, the deliberately ignored disobedience, the duty left unperformed—these are cracks in the monolith just as surely as are acts of defiance in the subject population. The "corruptions" of the rulers may be far less dramatic than the insurrection of the ruled, for power unexercised is seldom as visible as power which is challenged, but the system of power still falters.[18]

Looking at organisational power in this perspective we have to ask how diligent, corruptible, or humane are Soviet camp officials? The available data suggest that there is considerable variation in the officials' attitudes. There are only few accounts of humane or friendly treatment, but there are exceptions: guards have been reported to be more humane in reaction to impressive personalities of political prisoners, or when witnessing the suffering of family members, or when they had an ethnic or some other distinctive tie to prisoners. Corruptibility appears to be pervasive, especially in the general camps for criminals, and possibly has increased in the 1970s and 1980s. As for diligence in observing the rules, ex-prisoners emphasise that much depends on the ap-

16. James Q. Wilson, *Political Organisation* (New York: Basic Books, 1973), p. 13.
17. Theodore Abel, "The Sociology of Concentration Camps," *Social Forces*, 30 no. 2 (December 1951), p. 155.
18. Gresham M. Sykes, *The Society of Captives: A Study of a Maximum Security Prison* (Princeton, NJ: Princeton University Press, 1958), p. 53.

proach of the camp "boss." The major differences were summarised by one respondent who had been in three camps: "I had three bosses. One cared only for production and didn't care much what we did after work. He was okay. The other was a former army man. He was only interested in order; he was terrible. We would finish work and had to march in columns all the time. The third was a drunkard and mostly cared about vodka."

If a camp director is of the last type mayhem develops, giving a chance for the more corrupt elements among the guards—and the better organised criminals among the prisoners—to become the unofficial rulers. This situation may be rare, but a few respondents had experienced it. Prisoners seem to prefer the boss who focuses on fulfilling production plans because camp rules are often bent to achieve this. There is great dislike for disciplinarians. One woman who had been in a model criminal camp where the rules were observed to the letter reported that the effect was highly oppressive. In political camps officials tend to observe formal rules more strictly because they are under closer scrutiny. Yet information on protests gets out in part owing to the corruptibility of some guards, and some rules are circumvented in order to avoid more trouble.

Official Soviet sources on job performance of camp officials are very scarce. The "supervision of places of deprivation of liberty" is the charge of a special department of the procuracy, and in a rare article the head of this department for the **RSFSR** wrote in 1975 that his office frequently uncovered illegal activities of penal officials. Examples mentioned include the infringement of prisoners' rights, such as putting them into solitary confinement without due cause, or other camp officials being too soft and giving pay for work not really done.[19] The reason for the latter is not explained, but presumably there was an informal arrangement between guards and inmates to make inmates work at a reasonable rate.

Officials treat collaborative inmates better and also those to whom they feel closer, such as former military officers or party members. The latter are likely to be approached by camp officials who try to co-opt them by playing on "you are one of us" feelings. Personal sympathies or antipathies also play a role as well as whether one has some influential friends or relatives. Generally, however, antagonism between camp officials and inmates appears to be strong. There are also reports of sadism.[20]

Little information is available on the conscript soldiers who guard the camps. They are draftees who—although part of the Soviet Armed Forces—are assigned to the Ministry of Internal Affairs. The letters VV (acronym for "Internal Troops" in Russian) appear on the shoulders of their uniforms. These troops were first formed in

---

19. V. Bolysov, "Ispol'zovat' vse sredstva prokurorskogo nadzora," *Sotsialisticheskaya zakonnost',* 1975 no. 3, pp. 29–31. He also notes that the effectiveness of the supervision by local representatives of the procuracy is low in several regions. Similar problems are referred to in G. I. Brovin and V. T. Mikhailov, *Prokuroskii nadzor za zakonnost'yu ispolneniya prigovorov* (Moscow: Yuridicheskaya literatura, 1977), pp. 38–9.
20. As noted by a respondent, "this type of work brings out the worst in people." From this point on in the text interviews are the source if no other source is cited. On sadist guards see also *Arkhiv Samizdata,* documents 5072, 5322, 5542 (referred to as "AS" from now on).

January 1918 and attached to the Cheka. Their functions—now and then—are to protect internal installations, such as labour camps, and to perform convoy duties.[21] Most former inmates say that they had no contact with the conscripts: "the young men just stand on their watch-towers." Conversations are forbidden and, typically, the only opportunity for them is given when guards escort prisoners outside camp.

One perceptive respondent noted that the isolation of the soldiers from prisoners is strict because they could easily be corrupted owing to their low pay of three rubles a month. He and a few others mentioned that on the occasions when contact was established the soldiers could be bribed to carry letters and bring back money or something else. Next to corruptibility, the effectiveness of the external guards is also limited by the extent to which they ignore their duties or show some human kindness. Information on this is fragmentary. The guards are told that they are dealing with criminals or "enemies of the people," and many apparently take that to be true. Their most important duty is to see that no prisoner escapes, and in this they appear to be quite successful.

Yet for many guards the prison camp experience must be traumatic; this at least is the picture provided in one of the few sources about camp guards, the literary account by Dovlatov who, as a nineteen-year-old draftee, was assigned to be a guard. His book *The Zone* paints a haunting image of the brutalising effect on himself and others serving with him. Dovlatov disagrees with what he sees as a tendency to depict inmates as suffering tragic figures and the guards as monsters, arguing that there is a striking similarity between the camp and the outside.[22]

Prisoners work alongside some free workers, but the official "measures for ensuring isolation of the prisoners" strictly limit interaction.[23] The free workers must pledge that they will limit their contact with prisoners and my interviews suggest that many hardly speak to the ***zeks.*** They also appear to be less corruptible than the underpaid camp guards, though some bring in tea, vodka, letters and other things. Most likely to do so are truck drivers transporting goods in and out of camps.

2. Administration by Co-opted Inmates

Soviet labour camp officials go to great efforts to co-opt prisoners for various positions. Each work brigade is led by an inmate foreman who supervises the work and keeps timesheets. Some brigade leaders are selected because they have superior skills but others get the post for non-economic reasons such as informing. This again illustrates the consequences of the camps' competing goals.

At a higher level there are inmate assistants of detachment leaders who assign work and write reports for the entire detachment. This position gives considerable power over the other inmates and facilitates the officers' task. It is

---

21. Harriet Fast Scott and William F. Scott, *The Armed Forces of the USSR,* 2nd edition (Boulder, Colo.: Westview Press, 1979), p. 222; see also p. 218.
22. Sergei Dovlatov, *The Zone: A Prison Camp Guard's Story.* Trans. Anne Frydman (New York: Alfred A. Knopf, 1985), p. 46.
23. "Rules of Internal Order of Corrective Labour Institutions," trans. Maura L. Lobatto, *Review of Socialist Law,* 12 no. 1 (1986), pp. 29–83, chapt. IX. Henceforth this document will be referred to as "Rules."

characteristic of the organisational approach in Soviet labour camps to co-opt inmates for various purposes. The organisation of work is just one of these purposes and the most straightforward. There is also an intricate system of secret informers as well as formal prisoner "self-administration."

The post-Stalinist camp system differs in several ways from that of the Stalinist era, one of these differences being the emphasis on formal inmate co-optation. A complementary major difference is that in the Stalin period camp authorities more deliberately—but informally—took advantage of the oppressive power of the professional criminals in the camps, who terrorised the politicals.[24] In the contemporary camp system this approach is mostly visible in the use of "pressure cells," discussed below.

Self-administration bodies. The re-educational aspect of camps has been officially emphasised in the post-Stalinist era and this has led to some innovations in camp practice. Among these were "prisoners' councils," a short-lived institution of the early Soviet years revived in 1954 and further reorganised in 1958.[25] According to Article 45 of the Corrective Labour Code of the RSFSR,

> in the aim of developing habits of collectivism in convicted persons serving in places of imprisonment and of encouraging their positive initiative, and also of making use of the influence of the collective for correcting and re-educating convicted persons, voluntary organisations of convicted persons shall be created in corrective labour institutions, working under the leadership of the administration of these institutions.

Official Soviet commentators, as well as my respondents, leave no doubt that it is the purpose of the councils to assist the administration, which has full control over them. To cite the code: "decisions taken by councils of collectives shall be confirmed by the director of the colony or the head of the detachment respectively," and "voluntary organisations shall regularly undertake measures aimed at helping the administration of the corrective labour institutions in their work."[26]

Ex-prisoners use a more direct language: "In the Soviet Union all elected positions are 'elected' by the officials, only collaborators took part." Several respondents said that there had been no elections and rejected the notion of even formal "self-administration." Even they, however, referred to inmate officials as the "helpers" of the guards. One respondent had been the chairman of the *sovet kollektiva kolonii* in his camp. He said that he had not wanted the post, but was forced to take it because he was a former military officer and party member. As the head of all inmates, he commanded them, formed the work brigades, and assisted the camp director in matters involving internal order, culture, and plan fulfillment.

---

24. See, for example, Robert Conquest, *Kolyma: The Arctic Death Camps* (Oxford: Oxford University Press, 1979), pp. 79–80.
25. Paul Barton, "An End to Concentration Camps?" *Problems of Communism*, XI No. 2 (March–April 1962), p. 43.
26. Article 46, p. 345. There is no word about the rights of prisoners. For general comments see L. V. Bagrii-Shakhmatov, ed. *Kommentarii k ispravitel'no-trudovomu kodeksu Belorusskoi SSR* (Minsk Izdatel'stvo BGU im. V. I. Lenina, 1974), pp. 127–32; also Shupilov, pp. 188–9.

Officially the prisoners' council has seven to fifteen members, as well as subsections for a) internal order, b) work and vocational training, c) cultural work, d) general education, e) physical culture, f) sanitation, and g) food and commissary service.[27] Its most visible segment is the camp militia and it is all that many ex-prisoners tend to mention when asked about inmate self-administration. The prefix "self" is understood less to denote individual initiative or autonomy than self-limitation; thus one respondent even used the term "self-guards." Inmates co-opted into the "Internal Order Section" wear red armbands with the letters SVP printed on them. They are a camp militia assisting the administration to impose order; it is connected to the camp KGB section and members report on fellow inmates. Resisting the SVP is punishable in the same way as resisting a warder, yet its members are ostracised and even attacked by other prisoners if opportunities present themselves.

It is difficult to say how many prisoners join the *aktiv*, but one former inmate of a political camp estimated that there were 200 in his camp of 3,000 inmates. Others have indicated that there are more "activists" in criminal camps because politicals refuse to collaborate more often.[28] The council is an effective instrument of the authorities because decisions have the appearance of the will of the prisoners' collective. It facilitates co-opting other inmates and has power over them through means such as participation in parole decisions and the distribution of privileges. The trustees also establish unwritten laws in the camps, such as the practice of giving the inmate mailman who delivers a parcel a share of its contents.

Prisoners allow themselves to be co-opted for various reasons. Cooperation gives some direct benefits such as a man in the health section getting into the bathhouse without queuing. Formal rewards are dispensed by the warders and may entail an additional family visit, a few more rubles for the camp store, or the chance for an early release. If one hopes for a commuted sentence it is crucial to be recognised as being "on the path of correction" and social participation is taken as one indication of this. Situational factors also matter; thus one respondent joined the red armbands for two weeks after he had been in an especially brutal fight with criminals.

The co-optation of some inmates to control the others is typical of total institutions. The co-opted inmate is rewarded both materially and psychologically and is the prototype of the oppressed identifying with the oppressor. Next to the well-known example of the ***kapos*** in Hitler's concentration camps, there are other historical cases such as the black drivers in the American slave community.[29]

Self-policing through informers. One of the more reprehensible duties of the social "activist" is to inform on fellow inmates. But not all prisoner self-policing is overt; there is also a network of secret informers. The informer sys-

27. Bagrii-Shakhmatov, p. 130. According to another Soviet source not all forms of activities are fully implemented in every camp, Shmarov and Kuznetsov, p. 165.
28. Mykhaylo Osadchy, *Cataract* (New York: Harcourt Brace Jovanovich, 1976), p. 123; see also Bukovsky, p. 248.
29. John W. Blassingame, *The Slave Community: Plantation Life in the Antebellum South* (New York: Oxford University Press, 1979), p. 258.

tem is a major element in the system of control within Soviet labour camps. It informs officials about what is going on among the prisoners; it induces compliance and makes prisoners careful in what they say and do; and it increases mistrust among inmates and thus undermines group solidarity and self-organisation. Officials try to co-opt as many informers as possible and they are quite successful in doing so. This work is organised by the KGB section, which receives reports continuously about what inmates are doing or saying. Some informers are blatant and make no secret of their meetings with security officers; others are suspected to be informers because they receive privileges. Estimates are that only about half of the informers are recognised.

If possible, inmates avoid informers. Known informers are sometimes attacked and beaten; killings appear to be relatively rare in the post-Stalin period. The administration transfers informers to protect them and since "professional" informers too tend to move from one camp to another, new transfers are often suspect. Most ex-prisoners argue that the informer system is effective, but more so in camps for criminals than politicals. There are also reported to be fewer or no informers among religious prisoners. Evaluations of the effect of the informer system differ by the pervasiveness of informer presence. The usual estimate is that approximately one-third or one-fourth of the inmates inform on others, but some respondents gave lower estimates and others cited numbers as high as 50% or 70%. In these instances respondents also said that the informer system was totally effective and that inmates had to watch their every word and deed so as not to get into trouble. Informing is negatively correlated with inmate solidarity and autonomous self-organisation. From the point of view of inmates, informing is always viewed as being based on a wish for rewards.[30] Some informers are coerced by the administration, either psychologically or if they are in some trouble, but most indeed do it because it is "easy work" and because they are rewarded by the administration.

Mechanisms of Control

1. Rewards and Punishments

As argued by Erving Goffman, "punishments and privileges are themselves modes of organisation peculiar to total institutions."[31] Post-Stalin Soviet labour camps fit this model in that officials manipulate an intricate incentive structure in a highly calculated manner. It is also characteristic that although physical coercion and other negative incentives continue to be used, the power of positive inducements is emphasised. Similar to the approach used against nonconformists in society at large, punishments are used as a last resort only, presumably because repression can be counterproductive and increase opposition.[32]

Western analysts of the mechanisms of control in modern prisons have noted that prisoners must be led to share in the process of social control

30. Thomas Mathiesen, *The Defences of the Weak: A Sociological Study of a Norwegian Correctional Institution* (London: Tavistock Publ., 1965), p. 51.
31. Erving Goffman, *Asylums: Essays on the Social Situation of Mental Patients and Other Inmates* (New York: Anchor Books, 1961), p. 51.
32. Compare Rasma Karklins, "The Dissent/Coercion Nexus in the USSR," *Studies in Comparative Communism,* XX no. 3/4 (Autumn/Winter 1987), pp. 322–41.

through incentives such as early release and a graduation in custody and privilege that make life within prison walls somewhat more bearable.[33] This approach is carried to an extreme in Soviet labour camps. Prisoners are kept at extremely low levels of physical and emotional sustenance, so that the granting or withholding of even minor privileges has a terrible significance difficult for outsiders to appreciate. Yet one had to read just a few of the desperate *samizdat* appeals by the mothers and wives of prisoners to gain a sense of the great power of this incentive system.

The so-called privileges are simple, even primitive, in nature and go to the core of the prisoner's physical and emotional existence. Prisoners are fed extremely poorly and owing to their perpetual hunger can easily be tempted by the promise of added rations, parcels, or food purchases from the commissary. Similarly, the denial of an expected parcel or food purchase is an effective punishment. But punishment through hunger goes even further in that the minimal daily food rations are cut in half when prisoners are put into punishment cells. The official camp regulations on access to food show it to be the linchpin of a carefully calibrated system of rewards and punishments. Prisoners are acutely sensitive to even minor differentials in their access to nourishment, yet not everyone succumbs to the system's temptations. In fact, the hunger strike is a potent form of protest, maybe precisely because in this instance the prisoners control their intake of food as a means of exercising political power.

The increased or decreased chance of a visit by family members is also a highly sensitive matter, and therefore this "privilege" is widely and effectively manipulated by officials. It is especially effective because the denial of a visit is a psychological trauma for both the prisoner and his family and thus pressures the prisoner in two ways.[34]

There are other effective incentives such as early release, or, on the negative side, the threat of having one's sentence extended.[35] Extension of the term as a punishment has always existed when prisoners committed—or were alleged to have committed—a new crime while in camp, but in 1983 a new article about "malicious disobedience to the requirement of the administration of a corrective labour institution" was added to the criminal code and subsequently used against recalcitrant political prisoners.[36]

---

33. Richard A. Cloward, "Social Control in the Prison," in Richard A. Cloward et al., *Theoretical Studies in Social Organisation of the Prison* (New York: Kraus Reprint Co., 1960), p. 24.
34. Sergei Soldatov, *Zarnitsy vozrozhdeniya (London: Overseas Publications Interchange Ltd., 1984), p. 287.*
35. Shmarov and Kuznetsov, p. 175, call early parole the main stimulus in the resocialisation of prisoners and this is confirmed by the interviews. The hope for early release is a vital part of inmate psychology, although some sentences do not allow the possibility of early release.
36. Julie Wishnevsky, "Resentencing of Political Prisoners in Soviet Camps," *Radio Liberty Research Bulletin,* RL 121/82 (New York: Radio Liberty, 17 March 1983). See also AS 5744. The re-sentencing of prisoners due to be released occurred increasingly frequently in the early 1980s. *See USSR News Briefs: Human Rights,* ed. Cronid Lubarsky, Munich, 1982 no. 23/24; 1984 no. 1/2; 1984 no. 17/18; 1985 no. 15/16; 1985 no. 17; 1987 no. 9.

Significantly, the incentive system has a strong psychological dimension. Officials exert pressure by arguing that a prisoner's own misbehaviour is the source of his suffering. The image the guards project is that of benign paternalism: if the prisoner will be "good," he will be "rewarded." In reality, most rewards are not true rewards but rather food, visits, and similar rights that prisoners are officially entitled to but only receive if they meet three conditions: 1) fulfill work norms, 2) commit no disciplinary infractions and, 3) participate in approved social activity. The officials decide who is a deserving prisoner and who is not, and there is considerable arbitrariness in their assessments.

The basic incentive structure is similar in all camps, although its gradation differs depending on the severity of the camp regime. Visits by relatives, for example, are an inducement everywhere, but fewer visits are allowed in camps with more severe regimes. Incentives are also differently applied according to the officials' assessment of a prisoner. The need for a differentiated and psychologically sophisticated approach to prisoners has been stressed by Soviet prison specialists since the 1960s.[37] An individualised psychological approach is most evident in political camps.

Prisoners are evaluated according to productivity and conduct. Those who cooperate are rewarded; others are penalised. One of the stricter punishments is solitary confinement in a punishment cell where conditions are very harsh; hunger, cold, and sleeplessness are used as means of torture. One could cite many accounts, but one should suffice. A woman respondent who had been imprisoned among criminals and suffered a lot due to her "uncooperativeness" described it this way:

> You are isolated in a concrete cell with no bunk or bedding. The temperature is specially controlled and is below freezing. You start shaking from cold as soon as you get into the cell. You have to sleep on the damp cement, get only water and soup every second day. You come out broken and ill for a very long time.

The severity of treatment in punishment cells has been a prime topic of prisoner appeals and of *samizdat* protests.[38] Some of the conditions these sources have cited—such as the withholding of bedding—are confirmed by the newly available *Rules of Internal Order*. To quote: "Persons confined in punishment cells are not given outer warm clothing. They are not provided with bedding. They are not led out for a walk."[39]

Punishment cells clearly involve intense physical abuse of prisoners, but it is an indirect form of physical coercion. Direct physical coercion through beatings and other violence is relatively rare, especially in the political camps, where it would trigger intense protests. But there are exceptions.[40] One notori-

---

37. Shmarov and Kuznetsov, pp. 7 and 23.
38. See, for example, the 1982 report by the psychiatrist A. Koryagin to the UN Human Rights Commission; AS 4785.
39. *Rules*, Art. 75 p. 65; also AS 2598.
40. *Prisoners of Conscience in the U.S.S.R., Their Treatment and Conditions*, 2nd ed. (London: Amnesty International, 1980). See also AS 4355, AS 5072, AS 5322, AS 5871, AS 5912, interviews and recent Soviet press reports, such as *Ogonek*, 1988 no. 3, mentioning beatings by guards and inmate officials.

ous direct application of physical force is by "pressure cells." In prison slang this refers to being deliberately put into a cell with violent criminals who have been given *carte blanche* for beatings and homosexual rape in order to break the prisoner's resistance to officials.[41]

Although physical coercion is important, the managers of many "total" relationships have recognised its limited effect. This insight existed even among the slavemasters of the American South. The lash was the primary guarantee of slave obedience, yet many of the planters asserted that the frequent punishment of slaves was an indication of bad management. According to one slaveholder, "the best evidence of the good management of slaves is the keeping up of good discipline with little or no punishment."[42] There are several ways of doing so.

2. Regimentation

This is a means of social control emphasised in the comparative prison literature, and it is intensively used in Soviet camps. In the authoritarian prison strict discipline and coercion through force are the main pillars of control. Procedures of regimentation such as frequent head counts and assemblies impose a psychology of domination and place prisoners in a posture of silence, respect and awe. This is also promoted through requirements of saluting and special forms of address in inmate-official contacts.[43] Besides the forced deference pattern in interactions with officials, power is exercised by the lack of personal identity through uniformity of clothing, haircuts, and so forth, and by the loss of privacy. Furthermore,

> in a total institution . . . minute segments of a person's line of activity may be subjected to regulations and judgments by staff; the inmate's life is penetrated by constant sanctioning interaction from above. . . Each specification robs the individual of an opportunity to balance his needs and objectives in a personally efficient way and opens up his line of actions to sanctions. The autonomy of the act itself is violated.[44]

Discipline consists of many petty forms of coercion; their sum and total scale form a sophisticated—and relatively modern—formula for domination.[45]

Strict rules mean that inmates are under constant pressure, but under the guise of order and administrative legality. Extensive regimentation is humiliating and difficult to bear, and assertive prisoners react accordingly. Women political prisoners in Mordovia, for example, staged repeated protests over the obligatory wearing of nametags in 1982. When the prisoner Osipova debated

41. Numerous reports in *samizdat* are summarised in Julia Wishnevsky, "The Use of Torture in Soviet Penal Institutions: The 'Pressure Cell,'" *Radio Liberty Research Bulletin*, RL 39/83 (New York: Radio Liberty, 6 September 1983). See also AS 4937. Of course there are also instances where criminal prisoners on their own beat up other prisoners or steal from them; see AS 3982 and AS 5322.
42. Blasingame, p. 245.
43. McCleery, pp. 382 and 383.
44. Goffman, p. 38.
45. Compare Michel Foucault, *Discipline and Punish: The Birth of the Prison* (New York: Pantheon Books, 1977), especially pp. 137–9.

the issue with the official in charge the latter stated that the purpose of nametags was less to identify prisoners than to punish them and eliminate their arrogance. The official is also reported to have said that in a survey asking "which of the camp regulations are most difficult to bear?", most inmates in criminal camps cited the wearing of nametags.[46]

That Soviet policy makers themselves recognise regimentation as a tool of control is evident from its grading according to the strictness of camps. It is lowest in the "colony-settlements" where prisoners may "move about without having to line up in marching order, do not have to wear distinguishing breast and arm badges, do not have to have their hair closely cropped, or wear special clothing."[47] Specific aspects of discipline, such as drill exercises, are also used as punishment for a transgression.[48]

While rules control every aspect of the highly routinised camp life, prisoners at the same time are uncertain about their details. Most facets of corrective labour institutions are formally regulated by a single, federal instruction—the Rules of Internal Order. This document has never been published in the USSR and for years *samizdat* and Western specialists worked on reconstructing its content; a full official text became available only in 1986.[49] Even though according to Article 23 of the Corrective Labour Code of the RSFSR, "the internal order shall be announced to all convicted persons," most ex-prisoners say that they were only informed of restrictions, their duties, work norms, and the daily regimen.

Access to the official Corrective Labour Code is also limited. The explanation seems to be that the administrators want leeway in applying rules; this became especially important in the early 1970s when they were confronted with the legalistic approach developed by political dissidents. In one instance politicals even used the words of the "moral Code of the Communist" posted on a barracks wall to argue with guards—to the point that they took it down.

This leads to a significant theoretical point: rules are a double-edged sword in that they are supposed to be binding on both officials and inmates. Officials not observing them can get into trouble with their superiors, and yet, from the guards' point of view, bending the rules to the advantage or disadvantage of the prisoners sometimes is the only way they can keep control. I shall return to this point when discussing prisoner protests.

---

46. AS 4967.
47. *Rules,* Art. 18.
48. AS 5322.
49. AS 5828 and *Rules;* see also the introduction to the publication of the latter by F. J. M. Feldbrugge, "The Soviet Penitentiary System and the Rules of Internal Order of Corrective Labour Institutions in Historical Perspective," *Review of Socialist Law,* 12 no. 1 (1986), pp. 5–28.
One set of rules came into effect in 1972 and new ones on 15 March 1978. The latter in most instances were more severe although details remain unclear. See Georgii Davydov, "Changes in Regulations Governing Administration of Labour Camps and Prisons," *Radio Liberty Research Bulletin,* RL 394/86 (New York: Radio Liberty, 22 October 1986), p. 1.

3. Political and Social Re-education of Prisoners

It is typical of total institutions "that a dual language exists, with the disciplinary facts of life given a translated ideal phrasing by the staff that mocks the normal use of language."[50] Again, Soviet labour camps fit the model in the extreme. The formal language used is benign, moralising, and emphasises the "re-education" of convicts. Ex-prisoners make ironic comments about this phraseology and the ubiquitous slogans, yet many are acutely sensitive to the misuse of language and reply aggressively if a term such as "re-education" is used in an interview. This illustrates the psychological pressure exerted by year-long exposure to words that sound well but mask a grim reality. It is an Orwellian world best captured in the work of talented writers such as Dovlatov and Marchenko or the classic work of Franz Kafka, who describes in *The Penal Colony* how a torture mechanism with a needle excruciatingly writes the words "BE JUST" on a prisoner's back.[51]

Soviet officials assert that prisoners are successfully "corrected" only if hard work and discipline are accompanied by re-socialisation.[52] Prisoners are to be changed behaviourally and attitudinally. Behaviourally this means engaging in the forms of approved prisoner activism already described, as well as attending political lectures and participating in other activities, such as the work of the culture section. The duality of language is ever-present, for much is made of all this being self-initiated by the prisoners when in fact it is openly planned and led by camp officials.

Activism is supposed to lead to attitudinal change. Individualism heads the list of attitudes officially designated as anti-social,[53] and it is to be eliminated by group activities. It is hard for prisoners to avoid mobilised participation, especially if they are unwilling to forego the rewards of the system. Prisoners eager not to go against their conscience choose the more innocuous activities such as joining a camp drama circle or choir.

But it is not enough for inmates to go through the motions of communal participation, they are supposed to change attitudinally and the content of activities and slogans is coordinated accordingly. The main themes are repentance and the prisoner's guilt toward the motherland, the beneficial effect of honest hard work, and conscientiously meeting the demands of society. Camp newspapers feature moralising stories about model prisoners who overfulfill the plan, are zealous activists, and are contrite about past misdeeds.[54]

---

50. Goffman, p. 45.
51. Franz Kafka, *The Penal Colony.* Translated by Willa and Edwin Muir (New York: Schocken Books, 1948). See also Anatolii Marchenko, *My Testimony* (New York: Dutton, 1969).
52. A. G. Volchenkov, "Rol' obshchestvennykh organizatsii v vospitanii osuzhdennykh," *Sovetskoe gosdarstvo i pravo,* 1964 no. 1, p. 108. See also A. Kairialis, "Deytel'nost' ispravitel'no-trudovykh uchrezhdenii Litovskoi SSR," *Sotsialisticheskaya zakonnost,* 1967, no. 1, pp. 64–66.
53. Shmarov and Kuznetsov, p. 121.
54. Camp newspapers rarely reach the West, but one issue, *Znamya Truda,* 13 January 1984, is available to the author. On attitudinal correction see also Brovin and Mikhailov, p. 43.

Making prisoners admit their guilt is one focal point of psychological rehabilitation, the other being the voicing of support for the authorities' point of view. This has an especially ominous meaning for people with unorthodox personalities or political and religious convictions, for they are pressured to change their beliefs and to denounce them openly. Some prisoners break down and do so, others just go through the motions, and a third group remains recalcitrant or becomes even more so. The latter pays for it with great hardship.

Political lectures are a large part of resocialisation efforts. Typically, they are held once a week, are obligatory, and absentees are punished. Many religious and political prisoners nevertheless refuse out of principle. The lecture usually consists of the company officer repeating phrases from newspapers. One may debate the effectiveness of this, and many ex-prisoners specifically deny it, but one can also argue that a repetitive ritual leaves an imprint.[55]

Sometimes prisoners get fed up and ask hard questions to embarrass the lecturers. Whoever asks such questions is liable to get punished, but since officials are also embarrassed by such confrontations—especially if the lecturer is from the outside—they sometimes ask "troublemakers" to stay away. This illustrates in a small way the potential of inmate power.

Inmate Protests and Self-organization

Camp officials try to inhibit the self-organisation of prisoners because they see it as a threat to the "healthy" collective,[56] but sub-groups of prisoners nevertheless organise for various purposes, including protest. Resistance to authorities in the prison can be quite passive in the form of avoidance of duties, but here I focus on active resistance in the form of open complaints and protests. Individual complaints and group protests within camps usually deal with questions of food, visits, mail, conditions of work and so forth. While these issues may appear to be of minor importance, they are, as we have seen, significant in the inmates' perspective.

In this instance major differences exist between various types of Soviet camps and over time. Criminal prisoners are much less adept in using complaint writing to their advantage than are political prisoners, and they are also much less likely to try to counterbalance official power by organised protest. If they do protest, it is typically by spontaneous shouting matches, strikes, or riots. As a rule, organised protests occur in camps for political prisoners, and even there their incidence has varied over time.

Complaint-writing. The only legal form of protest is the individual complaint about camp conditions to supervisory organs of the camps. It is notable that the Rules of Internal Order explicitly forbid group complaints.[57] The rationale is presumably a limitation of prisoner solidarity, but it also protects the camp administration from more effective criticism, which could make action by supervisory organs more likely. There is also an implicit denigration of the

55. Andrei Amalrik, *Notes of a Revolutionary.* Trans. by Guy Daniels (New York: A. Knopf, 1982), p. 183.
56. Shupilov, p. 188.
57. *Rules*, Art. 33, p. 46.

merit of complaints since they can be submitted only by individuals, yet individualism is decried as an anti-social attitude.

Criminal and non-criminal prisoners differ significantly in their approach to complaint writing. The criminals usually assume that there is little chance of success, and some do not know how to write or formulate complaints. Others are compliant or intimidated. There are reports that prisoners who wrote too many complaints were punished for uncooperativeness or that letters never got out of camp.[58] At least some criminal prisoners are aware that the politicals are more adept in all this; one former political prisoner reported that criminals would shout encouragements: "continue the fight, write complaints and petitions; they hope that things will get better for them too if we achieve anything."

Political prisoners too have faced obstacles in the transmission of formal complaints, but they have worked relentlessly and resourcefully to make them into effective constraints on the power of camp officials. Like the tactics used by civil rights activists on the outside, political dissidents in the labour camps have taken formally established procedures at face value and demanded that they be observed in the name of legality. This embroils the camp officials in bureaucratic dealings and at the same time boosts prisoner morale.

Many political prisoners have turned effective complaint writing into an art form. One example is that of Andrei Amalrik who, when complaining about the starvation diet in his camp, chose not to appeal to humanitarian sentiments but rather to accuse the kitchen personnel of systematically stealing socialist property. He had a partial success.[59] Denouncing one official to another has been successfully used by others as well. Another tactic is to flood the bureaucracies with short complaints to each of which they have to respond according to established administrative procedures. This has brought the bureaucratic machine to a near standstill and resulted in concessions.[60]

This is not to say that complaints *per se* are very effective. Hundreds of the complaints by prisoners and their relatives reproduced in the *Arkhiv Samizdata* reflect a lack of official responsiveness.[61] Successes occur mostly if the complaint writing is based on a well thought out strategy or is part of a larger protest.

Protest in ordinary camps. When asked about protests, many respondents argued that they were inconceivable or that there were minor incidents only. Awareness that it is forbidden even to write group complaints is widespread. Many inmates of general camps believe that officials are well informed about what goes on among prisoners, and some specifically add that this is why no

58. Interviews. See also *Literaturnaya gazeta,* 15 April 1987, p. 11, and AS 5542; the withholding of paper and pen and confiscation of drafts of complaints is mentioned in AS 5871. In at least one case complaints were even included in a charge against an inmate given an additional sentence while in camp, AS 4937.
59. Amalrik, p. 115.
60. Bukovsky, pp. 33–7 and 256–7. Bukovsky taught inmates of a general camp how to write complaints and engaged them in major successful campaigns.
61. See for example AS 4787; AS 2647; and AS 5912.

organised protests or ''plots'' are feasible. There is a clear negative correlation between the effectiveness of the informer network and protests.

Therefore, if protests occur, they occur as spontaneous strikes and riots.[62] Protests typically are triggered by a change of conditions for the worse or by a blatant abuse of prisoners. Often the result is that both prisoners and officials are punished and transferred—the prisoners because they have misbehaved, and the officials because protests are taken as a sign of their having mishandled things. It seems that for this reason administrators try to avoid protests; one respondent who was close to officials reported that the camp director was always afraid of a ***bunt.***

There are both minor and major protests. Minor incidents include cases where transferred prisoners feel that the conditions in the new camp are too harsh and start to shout or commence a sit-down strike and end up with additional sentences. Prisoners also tend to refuse to work or cooperate when confronted by a new and abhorrent condition. One example from a women's camp was ''when there were worms in the ***kasha.*** You could see the little black heads in your bowl. Everyone sat in the dining room and beat their spoons on the table. No one would eat it or go back to work. They sent the doctor in and she ate a spoonful to show that it was okay, but none of us would eat it. We got no punishment, but we also got no meal.''

One respondent who was in a general hard regime camp reported that strikes occurred, ''usually because the administration had beaten or abused a prisoner. Such strikes simply resulted in the head of the camp being transferred.'' Another ex-prisoner reported a major riot in an ordinary regime camp in Karelia in 1972. The riot was triggered by the accidental killing of a *zek* by a shot from a guard tower. ''Everyone rose up. Everything was burned. The thieves (*blatnye*) were killing the SVP-niks'' (Internal Order Section men).[63] As a result all inmates were given harsher sentences and the camp officials were either dismissed or demoted. This outcome illustrates the counterproductivity of brutality by officials and also the lack of success of inmate protests if it is just an eruption of pent-up frustrations. Results are different in political camps where the approach to protest is different.

62. There are few sources on protest in general camps. Some are reported in U.S. Congress, *Report by the Commission on Security and Cooperation in Europe,* November 1982, p. 148. In a riot in the Pravieniskes camp in Lithuania in 1981, 15 prisoners were killed and about 50 were injured during fighting with special military forces. After the revolt numerous prisoners were transferred to camps in the RSFSR; *USSR News Briefs,* 1982 no. 16, p. 8. On earlier riots see Walter C. Donnor, *Deviance in Soviet Society: Crime, Delinquency, and Alcoholism* (New York: Columbia University Press, 1972), p. 222.

63. Bukovsky, who spent time in a camp for criminals between 1967 and 1970, says that riots were common in the 1960s whenever conditions became unendurable, and that informers and other collaborators were killed; pp. 249, 260. Unbearable camp conditions and the killing of an informer also started the riot in the Pravieniskes camp in 1981. See a report in the Lithuanian *samizdat* journal *Ausra,* September 1981. With *glasnost* camp riots have also been mentioned in the official Soviet press; see for example a report on two riots in a juvenile camp in 1983 and 1986 in *Ogonek,* 1988 no. 3, pp. 19–21 and 26.

Political protest. While protest in general camps typically occurs when something changes for the worse or a flagrant abuse occurs, a much more deliberate struggle for the rights of prisoners characterises political camps. Over time, this struggle has been quite successful and has changed the balance of power. We cannot outline the entire history of political protest within the labour camps, but two examples will indicate the main thrust of change over time. There was an intensification of protest both in frequency and form in the course of the 1970s. One illustration from the political camps for men is that in the late 1960s and early 1970s prisoners circumvented the rule against group complaints by several prisoners filing the same individual complaint, but beginning with the mid-1970s they have just gone ahead and sent group protests.

An even more dramatic change occurred in the political camp for women in Mordovia which had few organised protests in the 1960s, but became more active in the 1970s and emerged as a veritable centre of protest in the 1980s.[64] Starting with the early 1980s the women political prisoners in Mordovia staged repeated protests, engaged in hunger strikes, and wrote numerous complaints, some of which reached the West. Probably because the camp became too much of a political embarrassment it was dissolved in early 1987. What greater success could a prisoner hope for?

How were the protests and successes possible? One principal reason noted by theorists is that under certain conditions the ability to resist power bravely becomes equivalent to ability to manipulate power.[65] This principle has spurred Soviet dissident activities since the late 1960s and has been reflected in their behaviour in the camps. In the words of Bukovsky, "Power is dependent upon public obedience, upon a willingness to submit."[66]

Officially a refusal to work is considered one of the sharpest violations of the regime,[67] yet work refusals have been one of the more frequently and successfully used forms of active protest by political prisoners. Work refusals tend to be effective because they not only disrupt the official "re-education" programme but also undermine the fulfillment of production plans. As noted by respondents, camp officials try to avoid strikes and confrontations involving work as much as possible. This gives some leverage to inmates willing to risk the grim punishments.[68]

Another prevalent form of protest by political prisoners is the hunger strike. There have been many such strikes over the years, for many reasons, and with varied rates of participation. When hunger strikes occur officials typically argue that prisoners are "only hurting themselves," yet they are an im-

---

64. Between autumn 1983 and summer 1984 the women held altogether 193 strikes and 218 hunger strikes, *USSR News Brief,* 1984 no. 16, p. 7. See also AS 4967, and Amnesty International, "USSR: Conditions for Women Prisoners of Conscience in the 'Small Zone' " London, July 1985. Photocopy. On the situation in the early 1960s compare Helena Celmina, *Women in Soviet Prisons* (New York: Paragon, 1986).
65. McCleery, p. 385.
66. Bukovsky, p. 32.
67. Shupilov, p. 209.
68. On work refusals see also *USSR News Brief: Human Rights,* ed. Cronid Lubarsky, 1984 no. 9 (Munich), p. 7.

portant weapon. Inmates have reported that it is only during a hunger strike, or immediately after one, that representatives of higher bodies visit the camp and request an explanation of conditions in the camp; typically some accommodation follows.[69]

The success of these strikes has depended on a number of factors. For one, there is the power of inmate solidarity. Even though officially inmates are prohibited from writing complaints—and of course protesting—for others, it has happened more and more over time. Many protests trigger a chain reaction; that is, somebody protests and is punished for it and other prisoners start protesting in support of their comrade.[70]

Another crucial aspect is solidarity and publicity outside camp. Most protests by political and religious prisoners become known to their supporters in the human rights movement. As a result there have been, since the late 1960s, numerous protests outside camp, such as by the various Helsinki groups in the USSR. And this has usually triggered publicity and concern abroad, embarrassing the USSR internationally.

Once a protest has gained publicity outside camp, official Soviet administrative organs are certain to get involved, if they have not done so before. The official commissions sent in to check things frequently are not only interested in solving the problem at hand but also use the opportunity for bureaucratic infighting and getting rid of rivals. Even if things do not go that far, officials try to avoid protests or keep silent about them because they make them appear ineffective and this hurts their careers. This point has been well-formulated in the theoretical literature: "to a large extent the guard is dependent on inmates for the satisfactory performance of his duties; and like many individuals in positions of power, the guard is evaluated in terms of the conduct of the men he controls."[71]

As a result, officials in political camps have become more circumspect in their behaviour. This success has been achieved at a high cost: hunger strikes are difficult to bear and some protestors have died from cumulative deprivation; other leading activists have paid with strict punishments such as added sentences and strict isolation.

Conclusions

The underlying theoretical perspective of this paper is that even in total institutions such as prisons the intended system of power does not always coincide with the way actual power is exercised. In order to assess how far this thesis holds true I have outlined the main elements in the official organisation of

69. Interview with prisoners from Perm Camp No. 35, *Survey,* 21 no. 4 (Autumn 1975), pp. 210–11. Several demands of political prisoners were met after a hunger strike in February 1969, especially the concession that certain punishments would only be instituted with approval of the Procurator. Reddaway, pp. 206–7. On the success of major protests in a Perm political camp in 1973 over intolerable medical provisions, see Bukovsky, pp. 333–4, who also reports on a month long hunger strike started by forty prisoners and later joined by nearly everyone in camp; Bukovsky, p. 337.
70. For example, AS 2168, AS 2598.
71. Sykes, p. 56; also Blassingame, p. 280.

power in Soviet labour camps and have tried to assess its strengths and weaknesses in practice.

The main strength of the official system is that the direct exercise of power by officials is supplemented by co-opted inmate "self-administration," self-policing, and mobilisation. By these means inmates are divided, made to control each other, and are pressured to change both their behaviour and attitudes. While co-optation exists in prisons the world over, it plays an unusual role in the Soviet labour camps: "self-organised activity" and "self-administration" are magic words in the vocabulary of the officials, yet at the same time true self-organisation by inmates is undermined. The officially instigated "voluntary" activities are a vital power source to camp officialdom and have not been recognised as such in the past. Studies of the Soviet political system have commented upon the role of mobilisation,[72] yet it plays a unique and fascinating role within camps. It represents more than mobilisation *for* the regime; it has a pre-emptive role as well as a strong element of self-policing.

Co-optation not only provides added manpower and control within the camps, it is also a major tool of resocialisation. The most active inmates come to identify with the administration and others are pushed in that direction by more innocuous mobilisation for social and political activities and constant exposure to the message of "re-education." The goal is to modify prisoners' behaviour and attitudes. The way of achieving this is the manipulation of a calculated reward system effective mostly because prisoners are held at such a low level of physical and emotional subsistence that even minor increments are significant incentives. And, if needed, there are also strong negative incentives and punishments.

Discipline and regimentation are other tools of control little recognised in the past. The details of legally established rules are kept from the prisoners and at the same time guards present them as being absurdly strict so that inmates live in fear. There is always a way to punish recalcitrance. Punishment is possible, for example, for a button being unbuttoned, headgear not being removed when meeting an officer, being late for roll-call, and many similar details of daily routine. Since it is impossible to conform in every detail, this mechanism allows for arbitrary pressure on inmates under the guise of order and administrative legality. Regimentation imposes a psychology of domination and can be more effective than physical repression in keeping subjects in line. It is worth pondering the argument of one respondent that the same approach is being used in post-Stalinist society at large.

What then are the weaknesses of this elaborate system? The principal one is that prisoners are not mere puppets but human beings who develop their own outlook and activities. Inmates devise ways to counteract the power of officials. Political prisoners have been most dedicated and successful in this by, for example, limiting the pervasiveness of informers in their midst and by developing

72. For a recent assessment see William Zimmerman, "Mobilised Participation and the Nature of the Soviet Dictatorship," in James R. Millar, *Politics, Work, and Daily Life in the USSR,* (Cambridge: Cambridge University Press, 1987), pp. 332–52.

successful protests. They have learned to generate inmate power by taking advantage of weaknesses in the formal system such as incompetence and in fighting among officials, sensitivity to adverse publicity, and legal provisions prescribing the administrative supervision of camp officials. Formal rules are a double-edged sword that can also be turned against the guards. Some conditions in political camps are better than in general camps owing to the resourceful and assertive activity of inmates based on the belief in the power of each individual to counteract coercion by refusing to submit. Although less purposeful and organised, regular prisoners also undermine the official system by recalcitrance and attempts to corrupt the guards.

It also appears that the camp personnel constitute a weakness in the official organisation of power. Guards tend to be corruptible and many seem to have low morale. Thus, the official intent is frequently circumvented by negligence, too much drink, and other human weaknesses. Guards also tend to make unofficial deals with the prisoners to avoid trouble and to fulfill the formal organisational requirements of the camps to produce order as well as economic goods. Such *de facto* negotiated relationships are necessary in part to reconcile the dualistic goals of the camp system. The camps have both an economic and a socio-political purpose, and this constitutes a structural weakness. Sometimes what advances the one does not advance the other. A total institution has many potent means of controlling its inmates, but if economic productivity is added to its goals, strains on its internal working are increased.

Appendix

Interview sample and methods approach. Soviet publications contain only limited information about the "corrective labour colonies." Given this difficulty, the primary data used here are intensive oral interviews with 32 ex-prisoners who left the Soviet Union between 1978 and 1987. The interviews were based on a structured questionnaire consisting of more than one hundred open-ended questions; average interview length was about four hours. Most respondents were imprisoned in the post-Stalin era, but a few were in camps before Stalin's death, or both before and after. The rationale was to get statements that can be used for comparative purposes.

Problems of selectivity and bias. The general criticisms of emigrant interviewing as a research approach are well known, but in my view, if used carefully, interviews provide important insights not otherwise available. By no means are all emigrants bitter regime enemies. For many, the main reason for emigrating is not one of politics, but rather is linked to economic well-being, ethnic or religious concerns, and family. The statements of respondents are often surprisingly evenhanded and some emigrants are regime supportive, either in full or in part.

The sample is selective in that it does not include hardened criminals, but rather people who ended up in camp for political reasons, circumstance, or minor infringements of the law. There is also a demographic selectivity discussed below. Nevertheless there is no reason to assume that the experiences of the respondents are grossly atypical. The sample is sufficiently diverse to provide a sense of what are general experiences and the analysis is conducted accordingly.

Sample. The camp returnee sample located through the Soviet Interview Project has the advantage of allowing access to a variety of people who regard themselves as having been normal Soviet citizens and who would not have recorded these experiences on their own. This is a significant complement to existing materials on camps largely compiled by dissident ex-prisoners who felt a duty to write about the topic.

The interviews were conducted with the support of the Soviet Interview Project which built a list of emigrants who had come to the USA between 1978 and 1985 with the cooperation of domestic resettlement agencies. For more details, see James R. Millar, "History, Method, and the Problem of Bias," in James R. Millar, ed. *Politics, Work, and Daily Life in the USSR: A Survey of Former Soviet Citizens* (Cambridge University Press, 1987), pp. 3–30. People who indicated that they had been in labour camps constitute the basic sample frame population for this study.

Of a total of 135 identified camp returnees, 56 were of prime interest because they had been prisoners in the late Stalin or post-Stalin period. Interviews were successfully undertaken with 25 of these individuals. The others could not be interviewed owing to difficulties with addresses, time and travel constraints, the ill health or death of the respondent, or refusal to be interviewed. Most of the refusals (9) mentioned fear of the KGB as the primary reason. In these instances our assurances of the strictest confidentiality and of the scholarly nature of the project were to no avail. Participation in the research project was, of course, entirely voluntary. In order to secure more cases a "snowballing" technique was used to reach 7 additional respondents.

Tables 1 and 2 show that the interviewees represent a variegated group. Unavoidably, however, there is a problem of demographic selectivity. Respondents are disproportionately Jewish, from cities, relatively highly educated, and most were in the camps before 1975. There are few female respondents (women make up less than 10% of the camp population).

TABLE 1 Demographic Profile of Respondents

(N = 32)

Gender	Male:	26
	Female:	6
Age when arrested	16 to 25:	10
	26 to 35:	11
	36 to 45:	10
	over 45:	1
Years of education	10 or less:	12
	more than 10:	20
Nationality	Russian:	10
	Jewish:	15
	Other:	15
Region of residence	Moscow/Leningrad:	16
	Other RSFSR:	1
	Other:	15

Table 2 Characteristics of Labour Camps in Which Respondents Had Been

(N = 32)

Type of regime	ordinary:	14
	strict:	7
	hard:	10
	special:	1
Type of camp	primarily for criminals:	24
	primarily for politicals:	8
Region	Moscow/Leningrad:	6
	Other RSFSR:	21
	Other:	5
Period of reference*	before 1953:	8
	1953–64:	15
	1965–75:	18
	after 1975:	8

*If respondent refers to two periods, both are counted

Discussion Questions

1. Do you think the term "rehabilitation" has any applicability within the context of Soviet labor camps? If so, what does the Soviet version of "rehabilitation" mean, and how do system officials go about trying to attain it? Are there organizational factors which undermine efforts at achieving rehabilitation?
2. Karklins describes a number of differences between political camps and criminal camps with regard to inmate activities. Summarize these differences, and state why you believe they exist.
3. What, if anything, do Soviet labor camp employees and U.S. prison guards have in common?
4. Compare and contrast the mechanisms used to induce inmate obedience and conformity in Soviet labor camps with the mechanisms used for this purpose in U.S. prisons. What are some reasons for these points of comparison and contrast?
5. Karklins' article was published in 1989, meaning that at least some of the data upon which the study's conclusions are based may not reflect the political *(glasnot)* and economic *(perestroika)* reforms that were implemented in the Soviet Union during the late 1980s and early 1990s. How might these reforms affect labor camp organization? Will the wider reforms help solve any of the problems mentioned by Karklins? And to the extent that U.S. prisons exhibit similar negative organizational dynamics, would wider political and economic reforms have any positive effect on American prisons?

10. Coopting the Kept: Using Inmates for Social Control in a Southern Prison*

James W. Marquart, Mississippi State University
Ben M. Crouch, Texas A & M University

Abstract: The prevailing imagery in most accounts of prison inmate elites is that they are anti-authority. This study, conducted over an 18-month period in one Texas prison, offers an account of elites who have played a significant formal role in order maintenance. These elites, known as "building tenders," have for many years served as an extension of the relatively small uniformed security form. This analysis examines the formal stratification, selection, and socialization of building tenders as well as their relationships to officials. Finally, projections are made as to order maintenance in the future in light of a federal court order ruling that the building tender system be dismantled.

One of the most striking features of prison social topography is the cadre of dominant inmates, the elites. These prisoners have translated pre-prison reputations, physical prowess, or special skills into the power to influence a wide range of prison outcomes. Their prominence in prison accounts for the extensive literature devoted to descriptions and explanations of elite role behavior (Schrag 1954; Irwin and Cressey 1962; Carroll 1974). Beyond descriptions of the "argot" roles they play and the subcultures they represent (Bowker 1977), a central theme in this literature has been these elites' informal contribution to prison social control. For example, Reimer (1937) states that inmate leaders act as agents of social control by defining proper prison conduct for other inmates. More to the point, Cloward (1960: 48; see also McCleery 1960) concludes that "the inmate elite constitute the single most important source of social control in the prison," achieving the order and stability desired not only by the elites but also by the officials. In recent years several researchers have shown that inmate leaders of cliques or gangs foster prison peace by informally arbitrating among hostile groups (Jacobs 1974; Davidson 1974; Carroll 1974).

In most prison organizations these elites share many of the stability-and-order goals of prison authorities. They are not, of course, motivated by a desire to help the staff *per se;* such an orientation is the province of "rats" and "square Johns." Instead, inmate elites control other prisoners to protect their

*Revision of a paper read at the annual meeting of the American Society of Criminology, Toronto, 1982. The revision benefitted from the comments of anonymous reviewers for *Justice Quarterly.*

James W. Marquart and Ben M. Crouch (1984). "Coopting the Kept: Using Inmates for Social Control in a Southern Prison." *JUSTICE QUARTERLY* 1 (14): 491–509. Reprinted with permission of the Academy of Criminal Justice Sciences.

own statuses, their marketable influence with key prison officials, and their control over the prison economy and rackets. This elite power over the inmate masses is necessarily tentative and informal (Cloward 1960; Sykes 1958). Compliance by the inmates rests largely on the elites' ability to reflect the anti-authority values of the traditional convict code. Even where their actions help maintain peace, elites cannot be overly pro-administration—to do so would undermine their status with the inmate population. Indeed, where collusion between elites and prison authorities does occur in the interests of order maintenance, it tends to be situation-specific or based on particular relationships.

Although most accounts depict prison elites as contributing to prison order in the informal manner described above, there are cases in which prison elites, coopted by prison officials, have maintained more formal control over other prisoners. In such cases, the elites' authority over their fellow prisoners rests not on the defiance of or covert cooperation with officials, but rather on a formal alliance with them. Rarely discussed in the prison literature, this practice is not uncommon. The overt or official use of strong, cooperative inmates has been reported, for example, in the Soviet Union (Solzhenitsyn 1973, 1975), India (Adam n.d.; Bhattacharya 1958), Australia (Shaw 1966), and French Guyana (Charriere 1970). Moreover, several writers have indicated that this form of prisoner control is centuries old (see Shaw 1966; Pendry 1974; Klockars 1974). Extreme examples in this country are found in the recent history of the plantation prisons in Mississippi, Louisiana, and Arkansas (see McWhorter 1981; Mouledous 1962; Murton and Hyams 1969). Although the formal use of elites by prison officials disappeared from these southern prisons a decade ago, the practice continued in some Texas prisons into the 1980s. In this model, the elites' control was sanctioned by the authorities, not by the general population or a convict code.

It is axiomatic that in large maximum security American prisons, some inmates or groups of inmates will dominate others. If that dominance is unquestioned and predictable, then the prison environment can be stable, even safe. Conversely, if one power group falls, then others will move in to fill the vacuum; such power shifts within the informal prisoner world are always disruptive and often dangerous (see Colvin 1982). Where elites have been coopted into serving as formal agents of institutional regulation, officials can both increase daily control within the cellblocks and maximize general stability to ensure that there is never a power vacuum.

This paper presents an account of how such control and stability were achieved through the selection and use of strong elite convicts in one prison. Specifically, we offer an analytic description of a pattern of inmate use within the Texas Department of Corrections (TDC) called the "building tender" (BT) system (see Gettinger and Krajick 1978). We examine the stratification, selection, and socialization of Texas prison building tenders who have been an official element in the TDC prisoner control apparatus for decades. Although the building tender system was abolished in January 1983 by a federal court order, it did represent a unique, contemporary, and longstanding use by prison authorities of a subset of inmates. The account reveals how the control strategies within TDC created and maintained a formal role for elites within the inmate society.

Setting and Method of Study

The data reported here were gathered at the Johnson Unit,[1] a large maximum security institution housing nearly 3,200 inmates (47% Black, 36% White, 17% Hispanic), located on 14,000 acres of farmland. Inmates assigned to this prison were classified by TDC as recidivists over the age of 25, all of whom had been in prison (excluding juvenile institutions) three or more times. Johnson has a reputation for tight disciplinary control, and houses a large number of inmate troublemakers from other TDC prisons. Structurally, the prison has 18 inside cell blocks (or tanks) and 12 dormitories, which branch out from a single central hall—a telephone pole design. The Hall is the main thoroughfare of the prison and is almost one-quarter of a mile long, measuring 16 feet (width) by 12 feet (height).

The data collected for this paper involved the classic participant observation techniques to conduct interviews with officers and inmates. Documents, inmate records, direct observations, and informal conversations were also utilized (cf. Denzin 1970; Lofland 1971; Wax 1971). Most prison participant observation accounts come from ''insiders'' such as prisoners (e.g., Bettelheim 1943; Solzhenitsyn 1973, 1975; Abbott 1981) or by ''outsiders'' such as academics (e.g., Sykes 1958; Carroll 1974; Davidson 1974; Jacobs 1977). However, one of the authors occupied a position between these two roles. That is, he was an ''inside-outsider'' (see Merton 1972) who entered the penitentiary as a guard and collected data on social control and order for 19 months (June 1981 through January 1983). The researcher worked throughout the institution (e.g., cell blocks, shops, dormitories) and observed firsthand how the guards cultivated ''rats,'' meted out official and unofficial punishments (beatings), and used cell and body searches as important means of social control. But this role as a researcher-guard had some limitations. Initially, for example, it was difficult for the researcher to establish rapport with the ordinary inmates because of his uniform and position (see Pearsall 1970; Jacobs 1974B).

Despite these difficulties, the researcher worked ''close'' to the data, which enabled him to understand the structure and operation of the guard and inmate societies. In addition, 20 key informants among the guards (sergeants, lieutenants, captains) and inmate elites were cultivated to assist in analyzing control and order as a daily phenomenon. This ''expert'' knowledge about prison life and prison control were essential to the research (see Marquart 1984). Most importantly, the researcher was able to observe and document the control structure before, during, and, for a short period, after the reform measures were implemented. In effect, the data collection was similar to that in a ''natural'' experiment.

Before turning to our account of the BT system at Johnson, it is necessary to explain why the discussion proceeds in the past tense. The BT system in

1. Johnson is a pseudonym.

Texas is undergoing fundamental transition. In May 1982, TDC signed a consent decree with the Federal Court, Eastern District of Texas, in connection with *Ruiz v. Estelle* (1980), stipulating that TDC would abolish the BT system by January 1, 1982.[2] As of this writing, the BT system has been formally abolished. Most, if not all, BTs have been placed in different, less sensitive jobs (laundry, maintenance, shower) and the term "building tender" has given way to "orderlies" to designate inmates working in the cell blocks. For these reasons, the account below will be in the past tense; technically, BTs no longer exist. But the study is important for at least two reasons: first, change in prison is slow and difficult to achieve by fiat; second, an understanding of the new, emerging order in Texas prisons must be grounded in an understanding of the old order.

The Texas Building Tender System

For decades the Texas Department of Corrections (TDC) used select inmates as extensions of the uniformed custodial force. TDC's use of inmates, however, did not parallel the more familiar practices in Mississippi, Louisiana, and Arkansas. In these states, the staff issued firearms to convict guards who provided the security force in the fields, but these "guards" were housed in separate living areas. The BTs in Texas were never given firearms, although they regularly made and had access to weapons (e.g., clubs, knives, blackjacks). Moreover, BTs lived in the same quarters as their inmate "charges." Finally, while the convict-guard roles in Mississippi, Louisiana, and Arkansas were abolished by 1972, the BT system in Texas flourished until 1982.

It is also noteworthy that BTs were not used uniformly in the TDC units. On some prison farms, such as the one designated for young (17–21 years old) offenders with no prior prison record, inmates employed in the cellblocks ("row tenders") were simply orderlies or porters, making no significant contribution to control. However, the BT system discussed in this paper was restricted to those units housing older, more violent, hardcore, and escape-prone multiple offenders. Thus, the following discussion of the building tender system's structure and operation at Johnson is relevant to less than six of the current 22 units in the TDC.

Stratification

The building tender system at Johnson involved three levels of inmates. At the top of the stratification pyramid were the "head" building tenders. Below them, the rank and file were designated as "building tenders" and the lowest stratum consisted of the "runners," "hitmen," or "strikers." Of course, all these inmates enjoyed a higher status than the other inmates in the population. In 1981, there were 18 head BTs, approximately 150 regular BTs, and well over 200 runners, all of whom were evenly distributed within the prison's liv-

2. *Ruiz v. Estelle* (1980) was a massive class action civil suit brought against the Texas Department of Corrections. The case began in the early 1970s and was finally ruled on in 1980. The court mandated that TDC make changes in health care, fire protection, inmate access to courts, disciplinary procedures, administrative segregation, and the training of new prison officers, all aimed at increasing inmate physical safety and/or civil liberties.

ing areas. Each cellblock or tank housed one head BT, along with three to four BTs subordinate to him. The number of runners in a given cellblock varied from six to 12.

Cell assignments of these elites reflected their special status. Because of Johnson's telephone pole design, cells on the first tier (ground floor) and immediately off the main hall are the most convenient cells; head BTs always occupied these cells. Typically, other BTs occupied the middle and last cells on the first tier (furthest from the main hall) and the first cell on the second tier. BTs were rarely housed on the third tier; these tiers were too far to climb and were the hottest ones during most of the year. Runners, who occupied the lowest and least formalized status level in the system, were distributed in no particular pattern throughout the cellblock.

The daily tasks carried out by BTs and runners were consistent with their ranks. Runners were charged with doing the scut work of the tank, sweeping, cleaning windows, and dispensing supplies to the cells. These tasks were carried out after the work day had ended, since runners held officially assigned prison jobs such as laundry, shower room, and sometimes field worker. Runners also passed along information to BTs and occasionally broke up fights. As a reward for this service, runners enjoyed more mobility than other inmates, but much less, of course, than BTs. Since they were selected wholly by the BTs, it was not uncommon for an uninitiated officer, who asked about a seemingly out-of-place inmate, to be told, "It's alright, boss, he (the runner) works for us." Some of these inmates were BT punks, but others possessed the same personal and pro-authority qualities as the BTs, and many eventually were promoted to BT status.

Since BTs did none of the domestic tasks in the tank, they were free to carry out their major role, that of managing or ruling their tank. BTs defined this area as their community or their turf. Indeed, a head BT's proprietorship of a tank was well-recognized by both inmates and officers, who would refer informally, but meaningfully, to "Jackson's tank," for example. Actual tasks carried out by head BTs and the subordinate BTs were functionally similar, primarily involving order maintenance. Such duties included conducting votes on T.V. preferences in the day room, orienting new inmates into the cellblock routine, and helping officers at count time. More directly aimed at control and order were the admonitions, sometimes aggressive, to other inmates in the cellblock to adhere to prison rules (e.g., "knock off the head running," "turn that radio down," "get your asses off the run," "sit down in the day room"). The orders were not always politely given; in most cases they were intimidating and quite derogatory, as is illustrated in the following example about a noisy day room.

> Keep the fucking noise down you bunch of motherfuckers. If you weren't so fucking loud you might be able to hear me (he had earlier yelled at them to be quiet). If I punched one of you fuckers in the mouth, I bet you'd shut up then.

The blocks were their turf and BTs regularly interceded in conflicts among inmates there. Occasionally the BTs would, under their supervision, allow two quarreling inmates to fight it out and settle their differences in the "manly" way. However, intercession or "straightening out" usually meant an initial warning to an inmate(s) who was causing trouble (e.g., disturbing others, stealing, exploiting). A second reprimand was often followed by some form of physical coercion such as a slap across the face or head, or a kick or two in the buttocks. Those inmates who continued to "misbehave" were beaten and moved to another living area. This process, called "whipping him off the tank," functioned primarily to make examples of those inmates who dared to break or challenge the BTs' system of control and order. Most importantly, the staff tacitly approved and sometimes directed their inmate agents to discipline the other inmates.

The following vignette illustrates not only the proprietary feelings of BTs toward their tanks, but their power in the prison as well. A new officer told a head BT to get his tank cleaned up; the order was loudly repeated. The BT went directly to a lieutenant to report that the officer was "messing with me," whereupon the lieutenant advised the officer of his mistake and to keep out of tank business. This particular officer was never assigned to that tank area again. If an officer frequently gave the BTs a "hard time," that officer was often moved to an outside duty post such as gun towers. In short, the BTs (especially head BTs) ruled "their" tanks according to "their" rules, and even controlled the behavior of the lower-ranking guards.

The above incident also illustrates the BTs' chief power base and mechanism for contributing to prison order: personal ties to upper level security personnel. BTs are institutionalized snitches, expected by the staff to ascertain and reveal information about major rule violations or potential trouble. Although this aspect of the BT's role was widely recognized by both officers and inmates, actual passage of information did not follow the formal lines of an army private reporting to anyone with a captain's rank. Instead, BTs reported information only to those officers (sergeants, lieutenants, captains, majors, wardens) with whom they had developed a personal relationship. Some officers were trusted by few, if any, BTs; others had demonstrated sufficient consistency and common sense in handling sensitive information that the BTs came to trust them over time. Indeed, it was a mark of success for an officer if BTs sought him out and confided in him.

Staff members who had a cadre of BTs "working" for them were in a better position to anticipate and control problems in the prison. Somewhat ironically, then, inmates were in a position to confer status on officers, even to affect indirectly their promotion. Of course, BTs expected and received more than just a sense of a job well done if they proffered information. In return, BTs anticipated future favors such as cell moves when requested, special access to the craft shop, promoting runners to BT positions, or help in obtaining a furlough. But the ties in many of these BT-officer relationships transcended a simple *quid pro quo,* or exchange of favors for instrumental purposes. Whereas Sykes (1958) described these relationships as informal and "corrupting," the guards in this prison consciously shared their power with the BTs. In fact, upper echelon staff members were often observed to give credence to a head BT over a cellblock officer and to call their favorite BTs by their first names.

As one supervisor expressed it, "Look, BTs are going to be here awhile and they get to know the cons better than us. I can't depend on some of these officers. You know how they are, they're late, want extra days off, or just don't show up. Hell, you've got to rely on them [the BTs]." And BTs often identified so closely with a particular officer that they would "take care of his business" without specific expectations of a reward. Some BTs were so loyal to the staff that they said they would kill another inmate if so ordered.

Finally, in addition to status and power, head BTs and regular BTs also enjoyed a number of privileges which flowed from and defined their positions. Some of these privileges were relatively minor, yet highly distinctive in a prison—for example, specially pressed clothes or possession of unique green quilted jackets (while all others wore white cotton coats). Some BTs even had aquariums, while others possessed pets like cats, owls, rabbits, and turtles. A more substantial privilege was mobility. BT cell doors were never closed, permitting them to move freely about the tank and to have "visits" from punks. Head BTs also roamed the halls and spent considerable time in and around the major's office, tagging along with "their" officers, or in the craft shop. They were able to eat whenever they wanted and often ate two or three times in one meal period. Part of this freedom stemmed from the fact that BTs were on call 24 hours a day; it was nonetheless viewed by them and others as a privilege.

Traditionally, BTs were permitted to carry weapons both to control inmates and situations that might require considerable force, and to protect themselves as well as the officers. Clearly, they were not only feared but hated by many other inmates. These weapons, usually kept more or less concealed, included clubs, shanks, pipes, blackjacks, "fist loads," and even a ballpeen hammer. A final privilege, correlated with the carrying of weapons, was relative immunity from discipline. If a fight occurred between a BT and another inmate, the non-BT might receive one night in solitary and 10 days cell restriction; the BT might receive a reprimand or, more likely, no punishment at all. This differential treatment reflected both the tacit understanding that the BT was probably "taking care of business" and the tendency of the staff to accept the self-exonerating explanation given by the BT. The BTs also exercised their power to persuade the staff to go lightly on runners who faced disciplinary cases for "helping the man."

Selection

Since BTs were charged with control responsibilities in a large maximum security prison, the selection of inmates who were physically equal to the task was critical. As one officer put it,

> [S]o you try to pick people that are somewhat capable of taking care of themselves, larger guys, more muscular guys, people that generally know how to handle themselves physically, fighting and that kind of thing.

The ability and willingness to use physical force was usually reflected in the criminal histories of BTs. Of the 18 head BTs at Johnson in 1981, for example, eight were doing time for armed robbery, five for murder (one was a professional enforcer and killer), one for possession of a firearm, and one for rape.

The others were in for burglary or possession of a controlled substance. It was no coincidence that violent criminals were selected for BT jobs. In fact, certain types of criminals were favored over others. The following quote from a ranking officer underscores who was selected:

> I've got a personal bias. I happen to like murderers and armed robbers. They have a great deal of esteem in the inmate social system, so it's not likely that they'll have as much problem as some other inmates because of their esteem, and they tend to be a more aggressive and a more dynamic kind of individual. A lot of inmates steer clear of them and avoid problems just because of the reputation they have and their aggressiveness. They tend to be aggressive, you know, not passive.

As a group, these inmate elites tended to be older than the general population in TDC. The modal age category in TDC in 1981 was 22 to 27 (33%) and 72 percent were under 33 years of age (TDC, 1982). The average age for head BTs at Johnson was 39. All the members of these elites were multiple recidivists and all were doing long sentences, with the average sentence being 32 years (see Schrag 1954). This compared with the TDC population average sentence of about 21 years (TDC, 1982).

The guard staff filled the regular BT positions with an almost equal number of whites and blacks, while only a handful of Hispanic inmates were ever recruited for these positions. The staff mistrusted most Hispanic inmates, perceiving them as dangerous, too clannish, and, above all, "sneaky." Hispanic inmates, primarily for cultural reasons, were tight-lipped and generally avoided any voluntary interaction with the staff or other inmates. They feared being labeled as pro-staff because other Hispanics would commonly take reprisals for snitching—inside as well as outside the prison world. The staff had great difficulties in making inroads into the Hispanic inmate society, so they "hired" mostly blacks and whites. However, power was not equally distributed across inmate groups. The predominantly rural white ranking staff kept the "real" power in the hands of the white head BTs. That is, of the eighteen head BTs, there were fourteen whites, three blacks, and one Hispanic. The ranking staff members were prejudiced and "trusted" the white BTs more than BTs from either minority group. In short, with the help of the staff, a white con power structure, similar to a caste system, dominated the inmate society just as the "old con" power structure ruled Stateville (Joliet, Illinois) from the 1930s through the 1950s (see Jacobs 1977).

Although final selection of BTs and head BTs was done by the staff, BTs already in place played a primary role in the process. Indeed, selections made entirely by the staff were relatively rare. One BT was chosen by staff alone when an assistant warden at Johnson learned that a former BT had arrived at the Diagnostic Unit to begin a new prison term—a life sentence for multiple murder. An officer was dispatched to bring him straight to Johnson and a waiting BT job. Similarly, an inmate who had been a convict guard on the Cummins Farm in Arkansas in the mid 1960s was quickly placed by officials in a BT position when he arrived at Johnson.

Much more typical, however, was recruitment by BTs, especially head BTs. Potential BTs were usually, but not always, identified among the runners or strikers whom the BTs had already informally distinguished from the population in the cellblock. If a runner appeared to have "snap," or good sense, and a willingness to work for "the man," then the head BT would talk to other BTs to gather additional information about the candidate. In many cases, a BT would have known the candidate in the "free world" or perhaps in a juvenile facility. If all feedback from the potential BT was favorable, the head BT would tell a captain, major, or assistant warden that he thought the inmate would "make you a good hand."

Once an inmate was recommended for a BT position, he was interviewed by several ranking security personnel on the unit. The interview was essentially a screening device to determine a candidate's loyalty. The following quote from an officer captures the purpose and meaning of this interview:

> I'll ask him things like why he wants to be a BT. Why do you want to work for me? You know people are not going to like you and what do you expect to get out of the job? These are the kinds of things I'm going to ask: what his motives are, are you going to be loyal to me? What are you going to do if an officer gets attacked? These are the kinds of things I want to know. It's very possible for them to lie, but at least you can find out, do they really want to be a building tender or maybe somebody just threw their name out.

Answers to such questions revealed both attitudes toward staff and possible deportment under stress. Those inmates who were inclined toward violence in every situation were typically rejected by the staff. Thus, instead of violence and extreme authoritarian conduct, the major desirable characteristics appeared to have been common sense, the ability to handle and manage men, as well as the ability to use aggression with some discretion. When officers on the unit decided that a candidate would make a good BT, his name was forwarded to the Classification Division, which in turn reviewed the inmate's records. Unit recommendations did not guarantee a job—the Classification Division approved about half of the unit's selections.

Inmates at Johnson and other TDC units were selected, promoted, and rewarded for pro-authority orientations, which were evidenced when BTs would condemn the competence, intelligence, and morality of other inmates during conversation with officers. Indeed, it was common to hear BTs openly refer to the other inmates as freaks, perverts, "pussies," or derelicts, which aided the BTs in isolating themselves psychologically from the "degenerate masses." But such behavior was more than just verbal, since BTs regularly protected officers. If an inmate struck an officer, doubled up a fist as though he were contemplating such an action, or even cursed at an officer, a BT—or more frequently several—would attack the offender. Perhaps the best example of this allegiance to officials and the solidarity among BTs was their involvement in quelling a riot at Johnson in the fall of 1981. As a response to overcrowding, TDC had installed large tents within the compounds of several units, including Johnson. The riot began when inmates housed in the tents started several fires and broke windows in the nearby gymnasium by throwing rocks and other debris. Within a relatively short period of time, officers and approximately 150 BTs and runners converged in the gymnasium. While the officers were armed with riot batons, the BTs had brought clubs and pipes, and several wielded long wooden toilet brushes. One inmate even passed out blackjacks from a paper sack. When all the "troops" were assembled, the warden addressed the inmates: "Anyone who don't want to kick ass can just go on back to his house (cell)." The inmates cheered in support of the warden's declaration and waved their weapons in the air. The door to the gymnasium was then opened and officers and inmate elites (who identified themselves by wearing red bandanas) attacked the 200 or so rioters in the tent area. Most of the rioting prisoners were injured in some way, many quite seriously.

Socialization

It would appear that little socialization would be required for recruits into the elite core of BTs; only those already capable of imposing their will and prison rules on other inmates were selected in the first place. But socialization did occur, especially anticipatory socialization among runners. Their informal development in the tank was the key to maintaining the BT system.

As in the case of all achieved statuses, prisoners who wanted to join the inmate control system first selected themselves. They were motivated by a desire to be part of an elite, to gain the attendant status and privileges, to be able to beat up others with relative immunity, or some combination of these. The BTs in each living area selected the runners—based primarily on the inmate's willingness to work and inform on the other inmates. There was apparently little, if any, tutoring on how to be a BT. Jerry, a head BT, explains this situation:

> You don't pick these people and tell them now you've got to go in there and tell me what's going on inside the day room [a TV and recreation area in each living area]. By becoming a runner it is expected that you will tell me what's going on, it's an unspoken rule that you will inform on the rest of the people in here. If you hear something you are going to come to me with it.

Instead, neophytes were expected to observe the behavior of their superiors (inmates and officers) and respect status differences. For example, a runner never went to an officer if he had information; instead, he relayed it to a BT, who told the head BT, who in turn informed a captain or major. Inmates who could pick up the approved styles of speaking, acting, and relating to the officers would be regarded as possessing the necessary "snap" to become a BT.

Runners were actually apprentices to the head and other BTs in the tank. As such they sought to emulate BT behavior. For example, just inside each tank's barred door off the main hallway was a wooden bench. BTs spent considerable time on this bench, watching and listening to inmates, regulating movement and noise in the day room or cells, and maintaining the living area count. Runners would also sit on this bench, both watching the deportment of BTs and being identified with them. They also, when possible, followed their "bosses" to and from meals, ran errands for them, and laughed, joked, and roughhoused with them.

From his exposure to BTs on this bench, the runner learned the tasks he would perform should he become a BT. He learned about tank business—the counting process, the routines involving meals, the commissary, medication, and the full range of job schedules. (Some of this information, of course, he would pick up simply by living in the tank.) Second, he came to know the "script" for orienting new inmates in the tank. That is, he noted and developed his own version of: "Mind your own business"; "I'll cut you slack the first time and maybe the second, but if you screw up again, we'll go down to the washroom or my cell and get your heart right." A third and related aspect of the prospective BT's education involved discipline. To maintain order, one had to learn that discretion was necessary, that there were certain conditions under which physical abuse was deemed inappropriate.

Finally, the aspiring BT would gradually come to understand the informal organization connecting BTs in the various cell blocks with elite inmates in powerful positions, such as the bookkeeper in the major's office. The removal of an inmate from one cell to go into another illustrates how this network of powerful convicts operated. Most cell changes were initiated by building tenders rather than staff. For example, the BT would learn of a conflict between two cell mates, tell the bookkeeper, and the troublemaker would find himself in another cell in the tank. Using informal contacts in this way seems appropriate; such cell changes solve problems and are in line with prison policy. But other cell changes, especially changes from one tank to another, may be for personal reasons. In exchange for a bag of coffee, the bookkeeper might move a prisoner against his wishes to the cell of a BT, who would want him for sexual purposes.

In short, the socialization of BTs was a gradual process whereby some inmates learned the specific duties of a member of a powerful tank and prison-wide clique. They did not have to learn the traits which led to their initial recruitment: the willingness and ability to control others.

Three Qualifications

The above account of the BT system at Johnson may lead to at least three false interpretations. The first would be that BTs were firm but fair "right guys" in the service of security. Field observations supported such an interpretation in some cases. Certain BTs at Johnson were in fact personable; and they enjoyed a reputation for even-handedness in dealing with inmates and integrity in working with officials. Other BTs, however, were thugs, men who used their positions to coerce, exploit, and engender fear. Many, probably most, BTs held their jobs because they maintained control over fellow inmates through intimidation. It is precisely for these latter reasons that a federal court ordered TDC to abolish the building tender system.[3]

A second false impression potentially derivative from our account is that prison officers were relatively unimportant in the control process. It should be

3. The Texas news media covered the *Ruiz v. Estelle* hearings and press releases provide grisly examples of BT brutality and perversions (see the numerous *Houston Post* and *Houston Chronicle* articles from February 16, 1983 to July 1, 1983).

stressed therefore that BTs were not solely in charge at Johnson, where reliance on BTs was as great as anywhere else in the Texas prison system. Although, as we have indicated, the tanks did in a sense belong to the clique, their actions were generally known to at least the upper echelons of the security staff. When BTs acted, it was usually either by order of officers or to enforce prison policy. Moreover, officers themselves at times meted out the same type of physical discipline attributed to BTs (see Marquart and Roebuck 1984). Indeed, success in Texas prisons has always required not only information-gathering from BTs and other snitches, but also developing a reputation for personal toughness or *machismo* (see Crouch and Marquart 1980). The point is that officers did not simply prowl the prison operations in whatever fashion they wanted.

The third possible false impression would be that the staff had little, if any, control over the BTs. On the contrary, the staff used two important means to control their "inmate-guards." First, the staff obtained information about BT behavior from other BTs, who all observed and regularly informed on each other as much as they did on the other inmates because of pre-prison and prison conflicts. The BTs essentially policed each other; the staff used this information to control, as well as divide, the BT clique. While united when confronting ordinary inmates, many of these elites engaged in "backstabbing" and lying among themselves for the sake of revenge and helping the "man."

The staff's second source of control was the privilege system. Revocation of privileges for numerous rule violations was a heavy price to pay for a BT. The majority of the BTs followed the rules most of the time and could be considered "model" prisoners. Although these inmates were basically immune from disciplinary reports, excessive infractions (e.g., drug trafficking, excessive force, loansharking, protection rackets) brought "termination." During the research, only one BT lost his job when several BTs in a particular block caught him engaging in a homosexual act. The offender was immediately "fired," moved to another block, and he lost the privileges commensurate with the BT job.

Conclusions

The dissolution of the complex and deeply entrenched BT system at Johnson and other TDC prisons raises a number of questions, including why the system emerged as it did (e.g., no firearms for BTs); whether it was necessary in some objective sense (e.g., officer manpower or funding shortages); whether the effectiveness reflected in TDC's reputation for order and low rates of inmate homicide (see Sylvester, Reed, and Nelson 1977; Krajick 1978) was worth the cost of instilling fear among the other inmates; and what the future holds for TDC as it alters control strategies, at least in recidivist units like Johnson. Most of these questions lie beyond the scope of this paper and we will not deal with them. We will, however, consider the last question concerning the consequences of TDC's rapid move away from using inmates for control purposes, a measure prompted solely by the federal court order in the *Ruiz v. Estelle* (1980) court case.

On the positive side, inmates no longer live with the threat of violence at the hands of guards and their inmate agents. This factor alone has reduced the amount of tension among the inmates. Moreover, the surveillance, harassment, and derogation of the ordinary inmates by the BTs has also ended. The ruling has increased the degree of due process available to inmates accused of violating institutional rules; and it has fostered humane treatment of inmates as well as changing their non-person status to that of a person with civil rights. Most importantly, the ruling has placed all control of inmates in the hands of the staff. The staff can no longer rely on an elite group of inmates to help them run the prison and maintain order.

On the other hand, we expect that this shift in control strategies, certainly in the short run, will result in a relative deterioration of control, increasing inmate-inmate violence and decreasing inmate respect for official authority (see Alpert, Crouch, and Huff 1983). This degeneration, already apparent at Johnson, stems from several interrelated and largely unanticipated consequences of the *Ruiz* ruling that abolished BTs.

First, with the breakup of BT cliques in the tanks, there will be an effort by some inmates to fill the power vacuum (see Hartung and Floch 1956; Colvin 1982). The extensive gang hostility which emerged after the demise of traditional control structures at Stateville (see Jacobs 1977) may not occur in Texas prisons, but cliques will develop to grasp power and provide protection in the absence of the heavy-handed, yet predictable, dominion of the BTs.

Second, control will be diminished as inmates need no longer fear the reprisals and punishments traditionally administered by BTs (and by officers) for inappropriate behavior and attitudes. Since BTs often made working a more attractive choice to inmates than refusing to work, the amount and quality of prison labor is likely to decrease. Such a reduction would be seen by TDC officials as a loss of control, given the emphasis placed on work and the work ethic.

A third consequence is that officials will no longer be able to benefit from extensive information gleaned by BTs and runners about potential trouble in the population. Instead of drawing on a wide network which generally channeled information without fear of reprisals, officers will now have to rely on furtive snitches and their own observations. With no cadre of pro-authority inmates to buffer the caste line between guards and inmates, that boundary may become rigid indeed and, to that extent, it will be more difficult to control the ''lower caste.''

The removal of BTs and the litigation which led to this change are also affecting the security force in ways that will make control less certain. The most obvious is the introduction of a large number of officers to compensate for the loss of BTs in the cell blocks. A joint study by the National Institute of Corrections and TDC concluded that 900 officers must be added to the force as soon as possible. Johnson, for example, received nearly 120 officers within two months to replace the BTs. Such a large influx of inexperienced officers may, in the short run at least, undermine rather than strengthen control. Their classroom instruction will be brief and their on-the-job training will be somewhat hampered by the current uncertainty of more experienced officers, who are concerned about what can be accomplished. Moreover, without BTs to ''run interference'' for the new recruits and carry part of the workload, the new officers' mistakes may be magnified.

A more important, yet less obvious, consequence of *Ruiz* litigation is that the resulting paperwork demands on top unit personnel have caused the center of effective control to move down the security hierarchy. Traditionally, wardens and assistant wardens were directly involved in the prison's daily rounds. But as the *Ruiz* case dragged on, with its attendant writs, interrogatories, discovery, official visits and reports, upper level personnel relinquished control to subordinates. As majors and then captains were required to keep more records and complete more paperwork, effective control moved down toward lieutenants and sergeants. The problem is not that lower ranking officers perform poorly, but rather that those top ranking officers who have had to pull away from daily contact with inmates are generally the very persons who were promoted because of their effectiveness in dealing with inmates—the essence of control. After all, as we have noted, BTs historically brought information to these top level officials. Without them or BTs, order maintenance falls largely to mid-level staff and a host of new officers, while the inmates for whom they have responsibility are not only numerous but, in many cases, are jockeying to carve up the power relinquished by BTs. In the short-term, then, the rise of a new prison order may be painful for all parties.

Discussion Questions

1. How might a system of control and order maintenance such as the BT system impair the prospects of offender rehabilitation? Is there any sense in which such a system could facilitate rehabilitation? If so, how?
2. Overall, would you say the BT system was a good or bad thing? Explain. What alternative(s) could be used to maintain order as effectively?
3. Is inmate cooptation for purposes of order maintenance likely to be a cultural universal in penology? Why or why not?
4. Compare and contrast the nature of inmate cooptation in Soviet labor camps (as discussed in the previous article) with the nature of cooptation in the Texas Department of Corrections.

References

Adam, H. L. (N.D.). *Oriental Crime*. Clifford's Inn, London: T. Werner-Laurie.

Alpert, G., B. Crouch, and R. Huff (1983). "Court Intervention and Prison Reform: The Case of *Ruiz v. Estelle*." Paper presented at the American Society of Criminology annual meetings, Denver.

Berk, B. B. (1966). "Organizational Goals and Inmate Organization." *American Journal of Sociology* 71(5): 522–534.

Bhattacharya, B. K. (1958). *Prisons*. Calcutta, India: Sarkar and Sons, Ltd.

Bowker, L. H. (1977). *Prison Subculture*. Lexington, MA: Lexington Books.

Carroll, L. (1974). *Hacks, Blacks, and Cons: Race Relations in a Maximum Security Prison*. Lexington, MA: Lexington Books.

Charriere, H. (1970). *Papillon*. New York: Pocket Books.

Cloward, R. L. (1960). "Social Control in the Prison." *Theoretical Studies in Social Organization of the Prison*. New York: Social Science Research Council.

Colvin, M. (1982). "The New Mexico Prison Riot." *Social Problems* 29: 449–463.

Crouch, B. M. and J. W. Marquart (1980). "On Becoming a Prison Guard." In B. M. Crouch (Ed.), *The Keepers: Prison Guards and Contemporary Corrections*. Springfield, IL: Charles C. Thomas.

Davidson, R. T. (1974). *Chicano Prisoners: The Key to San Quentin.* New York: Holt, Rinehart and Winston, Inc.
Gettinger, S. and K. Krajick (1978). "Are 'Building Tenders' the Key to Control." *Corrections Magazine* 4, (March): 22–24.
Grusky, O. (1959). "Organizational Goals and Informal Inmate Leaders." *American Journal of Sociology* 65(1): 59–67.
Hartung, F. E. and M. Floch (1956). "A Social Psychological Analysis of Prison Riots: An Hypothesis." *Journal of Criminal Law, Criminology, and Police Science* 47: 51–57.
Irwin, J. and D. Cressey (1964). "Thieves, Convicts and the Inmate Subculture." In H. Becker (Ed.), *The Other Side.* New York: The Free Press.
Jacobs, J. B. (1974). "Street Gangs Behind Bars." *Social Problems* (21) 3: 395–409.
Jacobs, J. B. (1977). *Stateville: The Penitentiary in Mass Society.* Chicago: University of Chicago Press.
Klockars, C. B. (1974). *The Professional Fence.* New York: The Free Press.
Krajick, K. (1978). "They Keep You In, They Keep You Busy, and They Keep You From Getting Killed." *Corrections Magazine,* 1 (March): 4–8 and 10–21.
Marquart, J. W. (1984). "Participant Observation Behind Bars in the Role of a Guard." Paper presented at the Southern Sociological Association annual meetings, Knoxville.
Marquart, J. W. and J. B. Roebuck (1984). "The Use of Physical Force by Prison Guards: Individuals, Situations, and Organizations." Unpublished manuscript.
McCleery, R. (1960). "Communication Patterns as Bases of Systems of Authority and Power." *Theoretical Studies in Social Organization of the Prison.* New York: Social Science Research Council.
Merton, R. K. (1972). "Insiders and Outsiders." *American Journal of Sociology* 78: 9–47.
McWhorter, W. L. (1981). *Inmate Society: Legs, Halfpants and Gunmen: A Study of Inmate Guards.* Saratoga, CA: Century Twenty Publishing.
Mouledous, J. C. (1962). "Sociological Perspectives on a Prison Social System." Unpublished master's thesis, Department of Sociology, Louisiana State University.
Murton, T. and J. Hyams (1969). *Accomplices to the Crime: The Arkansas Prison Scandal.* New York: Grove Press.
Pendry, E. H. (1974). *Elizabethan Prisons and Prison Scenes.* Vol. 1. Salzburg: University of Salzburg.
Reimer, H. (1937). "Socialization in the Prison Community." *Proceedings of the Sixty-Seventh Annual Congress of the American Prison Association:* 151–155.
Schrag, C. (1954). "Leadership Among Prison Inmates." *American Sociological Review* 19: 37–42.
Shaw, A. G. L. (1966). *Convicts and the Colonies.* London: Faber and Faber.
Solzhenitsyn, A. I. (1973). *The Gulag Archipelago.* New York: Harper and Row.
———.(1975). *The Gulag Archipelago II.* New York: Harper and Row.
Sylvester, S., J. Reed, and D. Nelson (1973). *Prison Homicide.* New York: Spectrum Publishing.
Sykes, G. (1958). *The Society of Captives: A Study of a Maximum Security Prison.* Princeton, NJ: Princeton University Press.

11. Custody and Conflict: An Organizational Study of Prison Officers' Roles and Attitudes

Trevor A. Williams, Senior Lecturer, Department of Management, University of Western Australia, Nedlands WA

Abstract: The study reports on survey research into prison officers' attitudes in the Western Australian Department of Corrections. Drawing on research on a variety of organizations, which provides evidence for the prevalence of ''occupational orientations'' or ''task orientations'' among employees, the research tested for significant and systematic relationships between prison officers' attitudes and the characteristics of their organizational roles and role problems. Three commonly observed attitudes of prison officers are their reliance on disciplinary authority, their negative stereotyping of inmates, and their antagonism towards non-custodial staff. The research findings support the hypothesis that such attitudes are directly related to the primary task of prison officers as confining inmates in custody and the conflict with inmates which arises from performing the custodial task. The characteristics and demands of the work itself evidently comprise an important variable in explaining prison officers' attitudes, whereas in most published research on prisons this factor is largely neglected.

Introduction

With few notable exceptions, the organizational roles and role-related attitudes of prison officers have received little direct attention in the published literature about prisons. The two dominant themes of research on prisons have been prisoners and prison reform. When the principal concern of research is prisoners, the officers generally are regarded as elements in the environments of the inmates. When the central issue is prison reform, they are viewed as elements in the prison which could help, but more likely obstruct, reformist aims. Without questioning the importance of these dominant themes, apart from the work of a few sociologists such as Emery (1970) and Thomas (1972), the roles and attitudes of prison officers have been largely neglected as subjects of systematic study in their own right.

In order to understand the work roles and attitudes of prison officers, it is necessary to stand back from the question of what social purposes the prison as an organization ought to serve and consider the purposes that it does serve. Ideas about the prison as an agent of punishment, deterrence and rehabilitation gain and lose currency periodically. The one purpose that the prison has been constantly used for is custody, or segregating prisoners from the rest of society

From Trevor A. Williams, ''Custody and Conflict: An Organizational Study of Prison Officers' Rules and Attitudes'' in *Australian and New Zealand Journal of Criminology* (16(1): 44–55, March 1983).

in varying degrees of confinement. Any serious study of prison officers must take this into account because, whatever other goals a prison might serve, custody appears to be the goal that the prison officer's role is most directly related to (Thomas, 1972).

The direct relationship between custody as *de facto* the primary task of the prison and the role of prison officers in maintaining safe custody has important implications for understanding prison officers' attitudes towards their work, the prison organization, and the roles of others within the prison—inmates, non-custodial staff, and senior administrators. Writers on prisons have often noted (at least in passing) certain attitudes such as denigration of inmates, reliance on hierarchical authority, and opposition to non-custodial staff that are prevalent among prison officers. The tendency is to attribute these attitudes to the "ideology" of prison officers or even to "personality deficiencies" (for example, H. L. Jones, 1965, pp. 108–9). However, such attitudes may also reflect the nature of the work which prison officers perform and the problems of task performance which they encounter. Research on a variety of organizations suggests that shared attitudes tend to develop among people engaged in similar kinds of work. Likewise, even within single organizations, people whose work ostensibly contributes to the achievement of certain common organizational goals tend to develop different orientations and attitudes if they are engaged in different kinds of work (Burns and Stalker, 1961; Harvey, 1967; Lorsch, 1965; Lorsch and Lawrence, 1970; Perrow, 1970; Sayles, 1958; Woodward, 1965). Undoubtedly, the attitudes which individuals hold about their work are, to some extent, personal. Moreover, it has often been noted that the "cultures" of particular occupations and work places are transmitted to new entrants through education and various socialization processes. Nevertheless, orientations and attitudes in work do appear to reflect the characteristics and demands intrinsic to the work itself. They are usually referred to as "occupational orientations" or "task orientations" (Emery and Phillips, 1976; Lorsch, 1965; Lorsch and Lawrence, 1970). In view of this, it may be superficial to dismiss prison officers' attitudes as expressing traditional ideologies, authoritarian personalities, lack of education, and so forth. Social scientific understanding of the prison might be better served by enquiring more directly into the work which prison officers perform and their perceived problems of work performance to establish whether their attitudes are significantly and systematically related to characteristics of their organizational roles.

Prison Officers' Task Orientations: Theoretical Propositions

Prisons, in varying degrees, deprive inmates of their freedom and access to numerous gratifications which are enjoyed by other members of society. Their status within the prison is the lowest. To the extent that prisoners perceive their environment as depriving and threatening, they are likely to seek protection from it. Because, in general, they cannot escape from the prison setting, an "inmate community" tends to develop and to resist and subvert the official order (Clemmer, 1940; Cloward, 1960; Emery, 1970; Sykes, 1958; Thomas, 1972). Hence, a major characteristic of prison life is the more or less persistent conflict of wills over the issue of custody and regimented control of the prisoner's existence. Staff and inmates are not always in a state of open or covert warfare but, under conditions of confinement and relative deprivation, human beings tend to develop social relations as a basis for resisting repressive regimes. The prison is a setting where the staff and inmates are in actual or potential conflict. The problem for prison officers is to maintain control over unwilling prisoners in the face of counter pressures from the inmate community. Published research that does deal directly or indirectly with prison officers suggests that this custodial role and the problems associated with performing it have important consequences for prison officers' attitudes in three main areas: authority, inmates, and non-custodial staff.

The State confers on uniformed staff authority over prisoners, and other measures are taken to protect them from inmate pressure by maintaining social distance between the two groups. The organization structure of the typical prison is para-military, and the significance of this for prison officers is that it supports their attempts to control inmates' behavior. The structure provides the legal authority that is necessary to carry out their duties and defines them as having superior status over the prisoners. However, the authority of uniformed staff is subject to several limitations. While they have legal authority, this is not absolute and its exercise is limited by legal constraints, outside pressures, and the capability of inmates to resist. Moreover, staff lack moral authority over prisoners, since the latter are unlikely to be committed to the organizational task of confining them in custody, and generally staff lack an effective range of rewards with which to influence prisoner conduct (Emery, 1970; McCleery, 1966). Therefore, while the hierarchical organization of the prison provides prison officers with an important means of control over the prisoners, formal authority alone often is not enough. In order to avoid serious friction and disturbance within the prison, uniformed staff also find it necessary to penetrate the inmate community by establishing informal relations with prisoners (Emery, 1970; Thomas, 1972). This creates for them the problem of attempting to maintain control in an unstable situation, and under continuous strains between reliance on legal authority and tendencies towards informal relations with the inmates. Prison officers might look to the official hierarchy for authority, support, and protection in performing their tasks but, to some extent, they must also work independently of that hierarchy.

Because the official organization of the prison is unable to provide uniformed staff with complete protection from the tensions and pressures of the prison setting, they are likely to develop psychological defenses as well. Faced with the task of confining and controlling unwilling inmates, a prevalent reaction appears to be the development of generalized beliefs or stereotypes about prisoners that are unsympathetic, denigrating, and hostile. Such beliefs derive also from attitudes towards crime and offenders which prevail in the wider community, and which prison officers may bring with them into the prison (Turner, 1956). Moreover, they may acquire these beliefs from other staff. New officers, in particular, experience pressure to adopt the definitions of inmates that are used by their longer serving colleagues, and may find it necessary and useful to do so. However, the ways in which uniformed staff define and react to inmates seem to be related directly to pressures arising from the performance of their custodial roles. Especially in prisons where officer-inmate tension is high, negative stereotyping of the prisoners provides the officer with some means of self-justification and of obtaining emotional relief from a conflict situation that is personally stressful (Emery, 1970).

These considerations also suggest further explanations of prison officers' attitudes towards non-custodial staff such as psychiatrists, psychologists, social workers and welfare officers. Apart from religious and welfare activities, the expansion of non-custodial functions within prisons is a relatively recent development, and it is commonly observed that many prison officers regard non-custodial staff, especially those concerned with "treatment," with suspicion and antagonism. Such attitudes are more readily understood when viewed in the context of prison officers' custodial roles, the difficulties they have in performing their roles, and their reactions to the nature of the work. With the entry of non-custodial specialist staff, the dominance of custody as the main purpose of imprisonment was thrown into question. Whereas prison officers, by virtue of their custodial roles, were in relations of actual or potential conflict with prisoners, the work of non-custodial and especially "treatment" staff required co-operative relations with prisoners. While prison officers relied upon their authority over the prisoners and looked to the official hierarchy for support, the para-military organization of the traditional prison inhibited the efforts of non-custodial staff to work with the prisoners. Insofar as prison officers had developed negative stereotypes of prisoners as psychological defenses, the approaches adopted by specialist staff generally expressed more positive and sympathetic beliefs about prisoners, which challenged the officers' defenses. The large and rapid expansion of non-custodial staff in prison systems which occurred during the 1960s and 1970s represented a significant change in prison policy, and one which many prison officers believed was at the expense of reducing their own authority and status, undermining their control over the inmates, and putting concern for prisoners' interests ahead of concern for the officers themselves (Thomas, 1972).

Prison officers' preoccupations with authority and control, their tendency towards negative stereotyping of inmates, and their resentment of non-custodial staff may seem commonplace to anyone familiar with prisons. However, such attitudes have received little systematic empirical study, and the possibility that they are directly related to the task orientations of prison officers attempting to perform their organizational functions to date has been subjected to little, if any, rigorous testing. The research reported and discussed below sought to measure the extent of prison officers' reliance on authority and control, negative stereotyping of inmates, and antagonism towards non-custodial staff. It also tested for the existence and strength of any association between prison officers' attitudes and their perceptions of their own roles and role problems.

The Study

The research was carried out in the Western Australian Department of Corrections (recently re-named the Prisons Department) over a period of four years. During that period, the department employed some 450 persons under the **prison officers' award,** of whom 402 held the several ranks of prison officer or **industrial officer** and whose main responsibilities entailed direct dealings with prisoners. They were employed in the department's 14 institutions which included one maximum security prison, an assessment centre, a treatment institution for inebriates, two medium security institutions, and nine open institutions. The department's daily average inmate population was 1,350. From 1966 (when C. W. Campbell was appointed Director) to 1977, the department's official policies changed significantly from almost exclusive emphasis on custody to encompassing treatment and rehabilitative aims as well. This resulted in a rapid and considerable increase in the number of non-custodial staff employed by the department and the establishment of treatment, educational, and work-release programmes. The department offered an appropriate setting in which to conduct the research for several reasons. First, it was possible to study the entire uniformed staff of the department rather than being restricted to one institution or a very few. Second, by including all of the institutions in the study, comparative research could be carried out. Third, the policy changes towards rehabilitative aims and the establishment of non-custodial staff and programmes enabled the research to focus on all three attitudinal areas discussed above. The research was approved and supported by both the department administration and the prison officers' union.

Data on the attitudes of uniformed staff were gathered in four main stages. Initially it was important to acquire some familiarity with the officers and their work settings to learn something of the shared language they used to describe their work worlds and the meaning and significance they attributed to objects and symbols in those worlds (Berger, 1966; Mathiesen, 1971; Schutz, 1964). The problem was one of getting to know the human subjects of the research by spending time in their work settings. Second, semi-structured interviews of two to three hours were held with 60 officers of all grades randomly selected from five institutions. The institutions included the maximum security prison, the assessment centre, the women's prison, a medium security training and rehabilitation centre for young males, and an open institution. They were judged to represent adequately the variety of institutions operated by the department. The interviews were directed towards respondents' perceptions of their work and their attitudes towards authority, inmates, and non-custodial staff. However, respondents were encouraged to develop discussion in directions that they saw as important and relevant. The main purpose of the interviews was to become familiar with the orientations and terminology of the officers. By contacting a variety of institutions, it was expected that a survey instrument could be developed which was applicable to all institutions. Third, a questionnaire was designed and tested with 43 randomly selected officers from four institutions who completed the questionnaire in small groups with the author present. Finally, a substantially refined questionnaire was developed and distributed to 402 uniformed staff in all institutions. Each copy was accompanied by an envelope addressed to the author, in which the completed questionnaire was to be sealed and returned. Usable questionnaires were received from 184 officers or 70.6% of all possible respondents. Response rates varied between institutions but not sufficiently to introduce serious bias. Similarly, the distribution of respondents between the various officer grades closely matched the distribution of the whole population.

The questionnaire contained 150 items organized into four main sections. The first section sought respondents' definitions of the main purposes of imprisonment, their perceptions of their own roles, and the extent of their reliance on authority and control over inmates. The second section dealt with respondents' attitudes towards and interaction with non-custodial staff. Items in the third section were designed to tap respondents' beliefs about inmates. The fourth section obtained information about respondents' backgrounds, because it has often been suggested or implied that prison officers tend to have certain social backgrounds which largely account for the attitudes they are thought to hold. Responses to the items in the first three sections were arranged on Likert scales, generally using five points. Analysis was carried out in three ways. First, the responses of all respondents were correlated and examined using combined hierarchical linkage and path analysis (McQuitty, 1957, 1960; Hilgendorf, Clark, and Irving, 1967). The central research propositions concerned not only the measurement of particular attitudes but also the relationships between attitudes. This form of analysis was appropriate for obtaining a unique pattern of relationships which minimized research bias in manipulation of the data and which could be verified by independent analysts. Mean scores were also computed for all items. This stage of the analysis provided the essential test of the propositions about work roles and attitudes which were put forward in the previous section. The second stage of the analysis was concerned with whether there were significant differences between the attitudes of prison officers in different institutions. The institutions varied, in particular, according to the degree of custodial confinement and control imposed on prisoners and their variation was likely to affect prison officers' work and attitudes. D^2 analysis was used to measure differences between institutions (Nie, Bent, and Hull, 1970). Third, F tests were applied to establish whether there were significant relationships between attitudes and the social backgrounds of officers. Due to space limitations, only the findings from the first stage of the analysis are reported below. Findings from the comparative analysis and the study of respondents' social backgrounds are reported in forthcoming papers.

Research Findings and Discussion

Hierarchical linkage and path analysis of data for all respondents identified six patterns of correlation among the prison officers' attitudes. Two patterns encompass all of the questionnaire items that are most relevant to the propositions about prison officers' roles or task orientations and their attitudes toward authority, inmates, and non-custodial staff. Correlations and the ordering of correlations between the attitudes that comprise the first pattern are shown in Figure 1.

The strongest correlation is between officers' perceptions of being in conflict with inmates and the general beliefs which they hold about inmates. These perceptions and attitudes are also linked closely with officers' definitions of their own organizational roles and conceptions about the purpose of imprisonment. Thus, the core of this pattern is composed of officers' definitions of their roles, their perceptions of conflict with inmates, and their beliefs about inmates.

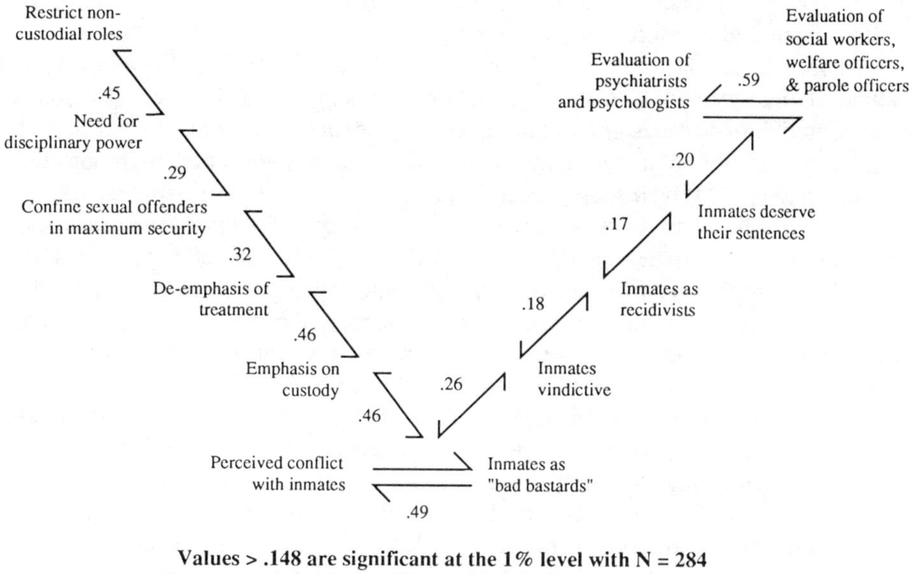

Figure 1

In turn, the extent to which they rely upon disciplinary power over inmates in order to perform their roles enters into the pattern of relationships. Finally, the connections between the central core of attitudes and officers' reactions to non-custodial staff are mediated by reliance on disciplinary power on the one hand and by officers' beliefs about inmates on the other.

The pattern in Figure 1 supports the hypotheses that, the greater the extent to which prison officers see their primary task as maintaining order and security within the prison, (1) the greater will be their reliance on disciplinary authority, (2) the more likely they are to hold negative beliefs about inmates, and (3) the greater will be their antagonism towards non-custodial staff. Also, the pattern suggests that such attitudes are related not only to the custodial role of prison officers but to the problems which arise in performing that role. The more concerned the officer is with custody, the more likely he is to see himself in conflict with the inmates. In order to ensure that the inmates remain in custody, the officer must exercise surveillance and control over most aspects of their daily lives. Not only does the officer stand between the inmates and their freedom to move in the outside community, but he imposes further restrictions on their lives within the prison. The more he tries to reduce the inmates' autonomy, the more resistance he is likely to provoke. Conversely, the more sensitive the officer is to inmate hostility, the more suspicious of them he is likely to be, and the greater may be his willingness to repress them. The central position of the relation between custody and conflict in the configuration of attitudes in Figure 1 suggests that this relation is also central to prison officers' work worlds within the prison. Reliance on disciplinary authority, negative stereotyping of prisoners and antagonism towards non-custodial staff appear to follow from and reinforce this central tension.

The officer who sees himself in the role of confining inmates against their wishes is likely to look to the organization for support in the face of actual or anticipated inmate resistance. Traditionally, the officer's control over inmates has rested on his legal authority to give them instructions and to report them for disobedience. Given that prison imposes deprivations on prisoners, the officer's control has derived largely from his authority to increase or reduce those deprivations. Moreover, the officer's position of formal superiority also serves to maintain social distance between himself and the inmates, thereby helping to protect him from inmate pressures. In consequence, the officer who accepts and acts on a custodial definition of his role can be expected to rely on disciplinary authority as a primary means of managing the inmates.

Figure 1 also supports the proposition that officers' beliefs about inmates are directly related to their roles and role problems. Where an officer perceives his role as confining unwilling prisoners, he is likely to adopt the attitude that he must maintain vigilance against them in order to do his job properly. A custodial definition of the prison officer role leads to a more or less constant interpretation of inmate actions in terms of whether they threaten order and security. Up to this point, the officer is simply regarding the inmates in ways that enable him to perform his custodial role. However, the kinds of beliefs which are linked with officers' perceptions of staff-inmate conflict seem to go beyond mere definitions of inmates as requiring surveillance and control. Figure 1 suggests that officers' attitudes towards prisoners include beliefs that inmates would behave vindictively towards uniformed staff if the opportunity arose, that they are unrepentant and will continue to break the law, and that they are morally inferior to other members of society. In other words, a form of collective hatred may develop between officers and inmates. On the part of the officers, evidently this is expressed in the attitude that inmates are "bad bastards" who should be locked up and punished. Emery (1970) has drawn similar inferences from his study of Bristol Prison, and suggests that:

> The reliance on negative stereotypes serves to keep the officer in the tense prison from personal involvement in the fate of the inmates and hence to avoid the painful and institutionally inefficient responses of sympathy, pity, shame or guilt that would be invoked by his doing or seeing the same things done to ordinary people in his ordinary world. . . . While latent sadistic tendencies would undoubtedly heighten the chances of a particular officer becoming involved (in personal conflict with the inmates) . . . , the same effect can arise from conscientious carrying out of the officer role in a tense prison (pp. 14–5).

Insofar as officers experience tension and conflict in their relations with prisoners, stereotyped beliefs may provide psychological justifications and defenses that are necessary for them to cope with their roles and role pressures.

The rest of the pattern in Figure 1 supports the proposition that officers' attitudes towards non-custodial staff have roots in the officers' occupational or task orientations rather than, or as well as, simply expressing "resistance to change.'' First, such attitudes are influenced by the extent to which uniformed staff rely on disciplinary authority over inmates as means of role performance. The officer who regards disciplinary authority as his primary means of controlling inmates is likely to reject not only alternative ways of performing his own role but also the use of non-authoritarian methods by others. Through their contact with the same inmates, prison officers and non-custodial staff become task interdependent (Thompson, 1967). Hence, they are able to affect each other's roles depending on what they do to or with the inmates. An officer who rejects the use, for example, of treatment-oriented methods for fear of losing control is likely to be suspicious and resentful of staff who do use such methods, especially when they have working contact with inmates for whose conduct he is responsible. Officers' unfamiliarity with the work and methods of non-custodial staff and the often considerable social and educational differences between custodial and non-custodial staff probably increase the strains between them. However, when conflict occurs, it appears to be directly related to the officers' perceptions that non-custodial tasks weaken their control over the prisoners.

Secondly, Figure 1 suggests that the officers' attitudes towards non-custodial staff are bound up with their personal reactions to their roles and role strains as expressed in the negative stereotyping of prisoners. If negative attitudes towards inmates provide means of self-justification and psychological defense, the entry into the prison of staff whose roles are based on positive values and attitudes concerning prisoners challenges the justifications and defenses of the officers. The findings of this research are consistent with Klare's (1960) observation that:

> The very fact of having people in your custody carried the implication that you might be good, otherwise you would not be in charge of them. Prison officers were not sadists, nor were they thoughtless, inhuman or unkind. But having been deprived of a good many satisfactions and of a more positive contentment in their work, at least they needed to feel good by contrast. And every time a progressive governor, or a penal reformer, appeared to take a little badness away from prisoners, it seemed as if a little goodness was being taken away from themselves (pp. 37–8).

Hence, negative stereotyping of the inmates may make it more difficult for officers to accept the roles of non-custodial staff where these appear to emphasize prisoners' potential for learning, change, and development, thereby contradicting the officers' own perspectives on inmates. This second dimension of uniformed staff attitudes toward non-custodial staff points to a complexity in socio-psychological organizations such as prisons.

It seems to be generally true of organizations that differentiation between tasks creates problems of integrating divergent roles and performances into a coherent whole (Lorsch and Lawrence, 1970). To this extent, conflict between prison officers and non-custodial staff may be attributed to the fact that the former are directly concerned with custody whereas the latter are not. However, in the prison, conflict arises also from differences between the values, beliefs, and assumptions of the staff groups. Where staff do not share similar values and beliefs about the inmates, the management and resolution of conflict between them becomes more complex and difficult.

This does not mean that differences between prison officers and non-custodial staff are completely irreconcilable. First, Table 1 indicates that officers distinguish between staff concerned with psycho-therapeutic treatment and staff who provide social work and welfare services to inmates.

Table 1

	Psychiatrists	Psychologists	Social Workers	Welfare Officers	Parole Officers
Effect on inmate rehabilitation	2.96	3.04	3.23	3.70	3.46
Help with inmates' personal problems	1.81	1.99	2.49	3.59	2.69
Effects on prison officers' roles	2.44	2.43	2.98	3.54	2.96

Mean scores of prison officers' attitudes towards non-custodial staff: 1 = very negative, 3 = neutral, 5 = very positive.

Respondents generally perceived psychiatrists and psychologists as having little or no effect on inmate rehabilitation, as providing little help to inmates with personal problems, and as making the work of prison officers somewhat more difficult. On the other hand, social workers, **welfare officers,** and parole officers are rated more favorably in these respects, and welfare officers are consistently regarded favorably. Evidently, non-custodial tasks that entail providing material assistance to inmates and their families and helping to resolve domestic and other personal difficulties are more readily accepted by uniformed staff. These tasks may even be regarded by the prison officers as supporting their own work. Secondly, the correlation pattern in Figure 1 only supports the hypothesis that prison officers' attitudes towards non-custodial staff are related to their own perceived relations with the inmates. An implication is that where officers perceive low tension between themselves and the inmates, they may also hold less negative attitudes towards non-custodial staff. Comparative analysis of uniformed staff attitudes in the 14 institutions studied tends to support this proposition. The comparative research is reported and discussed in a forthcoming paper, but the findings suggest that the interpretation of custodial and non-custodial roles may be more easily achieved in prisons where officer-inmate conflict is persistently low.

Finally, the correlation shown in Figure 2 suggests a further insight into prison officers' attitudes towards discipline and authority.

It indicates that, to some extent, officers who are custody-oriented, and therefore more likely to encounter the staff-inmate conflict discussed above, have another means of dealing with the vulnerability of their roles to pressures within the prison. The official hierarchy of the prison organization maintains the officers' authority and superiority but is unable to do so completely. One way for an officer to increase and maintain the clarity of his role is to adhere

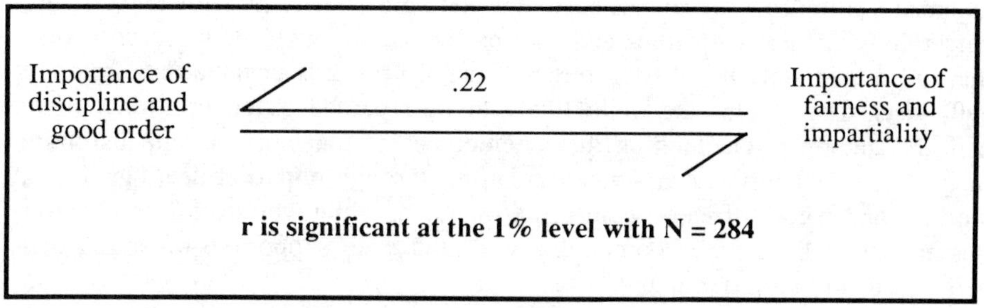

Figure 2

strictly to the rules and treat all inmates alike. Of course, such an orientation may stem from past experience as might be gained, for example, from military service. However, due to the inherently complex and uncertain nature of working with prisoners, the exercise of some degree of personal judgment seems inevitable. This characteristic of the work increases the likelihood of an officer becoming personally involved with the inmates and being exposed to pressures and conflict. Impartiality and fairness in dealing with inmates may help the officer to limit his personal involvement with inmates in ways that reduce tension and conflict. Such an orientation may be contrary to the concern of "treatment" staff with treating inmates in a flexible and individualized manner. On the other hand, it does tend to ensure the basic rights of inmates (Cressey, 1968). Apart from protecting himself, the impartial officer may well contribute to the maintenance of a more stable institutional climate.

Conclusion

The attitudes of prison officers are frequently commented upon in published research on prisons but have seldom received serious examination. The research reported above proceeded from the premise that custodial confinement of prisoners is the primary task of the prison and that custody is the organizational task with which prison officers' work is most concerned. Research on many different kinds of organizations has given rise to the concept of "occupational orientation" or "task orientation" based on evidence that attitudes are significantly and systematically related to the nature of the work which people perform. The findings of this study support the task-orientation hypothesis that the characteristics of organizational roles and problems of role performance significantly affect the attitudes of individuals in those roles. The work of prison officers involves them in confining inmates and exercising control over their lives usually against the wishes of the inmates. In consequence, they encounter resistance and conflict from the inmates, the extent of which appears to depend partly on the amount of custodial control that is imposed. Faced with resistance from inmates, officers' principal organizational means of maintaining control and defending themselves against the pressure of a conflict situation are their legal authority and the support which they receive from the organization. However, they appear to develop individual and collective psychological defenses as well, in the form of negative stereotypes of the prisoners. Suspicious and antagonistic attitudes toward non-custodial staff are consistent with the officers' perceptions of their own roles and role problems, although the research reveals that uniformed staff hostility is directed mainly towards psychiatrists and psychologists. These roles are more likely to be regarded as undermining prison officers' authority, challenging their stereotypes of the inmates, and disrupting their efforts to stabilize staff-inmate relations through impartial dealings. Social workers and parole officers seem to be tolerated, while welfare officers' activities are generally seen as compatible with and even supportive of prison officers' occupational requirements.

All of the above research findings are consistent with the task-orientation hypothesis about the relation between tasks or roles and attitudes within organizations, and suggest that it may be a fruitful way of attempting to understand prison officers' attitudes and behavior. The central relationship between custody and conflict in the prison officers' perceived work worlds also points to an important variable in relations between prison officers, inmates, and non-custodial staff. All prisons are legally responsible for the safe custody of inmates, but the degree of custodial confinement required to meet this responsibility varies considerably. Moreover, safe custody can be achieved by different organizational means and this may affect the level of conflict and the stability of relations within the prison (Emery, Emery, and de Jago, 1973; Thomas and Williams, 1977). Comparative analysis of the research findings for the different institutions involved in the research provides evidence that, the less severe the conditions of custodial confinement, the lower are the levels of officer-inmate conflict and the less hostile prison officers are towards non-custodial staff. The comparative analysis provides further support for the task-orientation view of prison officers' attitudes, since it suggests that they tend to vary with the level of custody and conflict. However, it has been frequently suggested that the social backgrounds of prison officers are also important in explaining their attitudes. More generally, the task-orientation perspective on organizational behavior has been criticized for failing to consider the influence of "prior orientations" which individuals bring to their current occupations (Silverman, 1970). Comparative analysis of the different institutions in the study and examination of the influence of social backgrounds on prison officers' attitudes is reported in forthcoming papers.

Discussion Questions

1. Discuss the implications of Williams' findings and conclusions for offender rehabilitation in Western Australia.
2. Why do you think the officers surveyed by Williams displayed more hostile attitudes toward psychiatrists and psychologists than toward other non-custodial staff? Would you expect this same pattern to be present in U.S. prisons? Why or why not?
3. Is there any relationship between the kinds of officer attitudes studied by Williams and the tendency of officials to co-opt inmates? Explain your answer.

4. What has research on U.S. prison (correctional) officers taught us? How do Williams' findings from the Western Australian sample compare and contrast with what we know from the U.S. research?
5. What are the implications for improving officer attitudes and performance in Western Australia? Do these implications have any relevance for the U.S. prison system? If so, what is the nature of the relevance?

References

Berger, P. L. (1966). *Invitation to Sociology.* Middlesex: Penguin.
Burns, T., and Stalker, G. S. (1961). *Management of Innovation.* London: Tavistock.
Clemmer, D. (1940). *The Prison Community.* Boston: Christopher.
Cloward, R. A. (1960). "Social Control Within the Prison," in Theoretical Studies in Social Organisation of the Prison, Social Science Research Council Pamphlet, No. 15. New York.
Cressey, D. R. (1968). "Achievement of an Unstated Organisational Goal," in *Prison Within Society* (ed. L. Hazelrigg). New York: Anchor.
Emery, F. E. (1970). *Freedom and Justice Within Walls.* London: Tavistock.
Emery, F. E., Emery, M., and de Jago, C. (1973). *Hope Within Walls.* Canberra: Australian National University Centre for Continuing Education.
Emery, F. E., and Phillips, C. (1976). *Living at Work: Australia.* Canberra: Australian Government Printer.
Harvey, E. (1968). "Technology and the Structure of Organisations." *American Sociol. Rev.,* April.
Hilgendorf, L., Clark, A. W., and Irving, B. L. (1967). "The Combined Use of Linkage and Path Analysis in the Development of Causal Models." *Human Relations* 20:4.
Jones, H. L. (1965). *Crime in a Changing Society.* Middlesex: Penguin.
Lorsch, J. W. (1967). *Product Innovation and Organisation.* New York: Columbia University Press.
Lorsch, J. W., and Lawrence, P. R. (1970). *Studies in Organisation Design.* Illinois: Irwin.
McCleery, R. H. (1966). "The Governmental Process and Informal Control," in *The Prison: Studies in Institutional and Organisational Change* (ed. D. R. Cressey). New York: Holt, Rinehart and Winston.
McQuitty, L. L. (1957). "Elementary Linkage Analysis for Isolating Orthogonal and Oblique Types and Typal Relevancies." *Ed. and Psych. Meas.* 17:2.
———. (1964). "Hierarchical Linkage Analysis for the Isolation of Types." *Ed. and Psych. Meas.* 20:1.
Mathiesen, T. (1971). *Across the Boundaries of Organisations.* Berkley: Glendessary.
Nie, N. H., Bent, D. H., and Hull, C. H. (1970). *Statistical Package for the Social Sciences.* New York: McGraw-Hill.
Perrow, C. (1970). *Organizational Analysis.* London: Tavistock.
Sayles, L. (1958). *Behaviour of Industrial Work Groups.* New York: Wiley.
Schutz, A. (1964). *Collected Works.* Leiden: Nijoff.
Silverman, D. (1970). *The Theory of Organizations.* London: Heinemann.
Sykes, G. (1958). *Society of Captives.* Princeton: Princeton University Press.
Thomas, J. E. (1972). *The English Prison Officer Since 1850.* London: Routledge.
Thomas, J. E., and Williams, T. A. (1977). "Change and Conflict in the Evolution of Prison Systems." *Int. J. Crim. and Penol.* 5: November.
Thompson, J. D. (1967). *Organisations in Action.* New York: McGraw-Hill.
Turner, R. H. (1956). "Role-Taking, Role-Standpoint, and Reference Group Behaviour." *Am. J. Sociol.* 61:4.
Woodward, J. (1965). *Industrial Organization.* London: Oxford University Press.

Editorial Note

The forthcoming papers referred to in the text of this article include the following:

Soutar, Geoffrey N. and Williams, Trevor A. (1985). "Prison Officers' Work Attitudes: The Influence of Background and Work Experience." *Australian and New Zealand Journal of Criminology,* March, Vol. 18, No. 1, pp. 17–24.
Williams, Trevor A. and Soutar, Geoffrey N. (1984). "Levels of Custody and Attitude Differences Among Prison Officers: A Comparative Study." *Australian and New Zealand Journal of Criminology,* June, Vol. 17, No. 2, pp. 87–94.

12. Characteristics of Homicide Victims and Victimizations in Prisons: A Canadian Historical Perspective

Frank J. Porporino, Phyllis D. Doherty, and Terrence Sawatsky

Abstract: This article presents an analysis of some of the characteristics of homicide victimizations in Canadian Federal Correctional Institutions. Two historical periods are compared: from 1967 to 1978 and from 1979 to 1984. The findings suggest the incidence of prison homicides has increased over the years, and the character of victims and victimizations has changed. Recent prison homicides were more likely to have been carried out by multiple assailants, were more commonly associated with revenge motives or drug and gambling debts, and involved victims were more likely to have violent backgrounds. The article concludes that a more complete understanding of the causes of prison homicides will require detailed analysis of the process of conflict escalation in these settings.

Introduction

Traditionally, criminal justice systems have dealt almost exclusively with issues relating to the management and treatment of offenders. In recent years, a healthy balancing of this focus has emerged as our justice system has become increasingly responsive to the needs and concerns of victims.

This article integrates the victim and offender perspectives of our justice system in that it concerns itself with offenders who become victims of homicide in prison. Discussions of the nature and extent of victimization in our society generally ignore the fact that many offenders are themselves victimized. In particular, when one examines the pervasive subculture of violence which characterizes many of our correctional institutions, it becomes apparent that many prison inmates are indeed victims—frequently assaulted or killed by fellow inmates.

It is difficult to obtain precise estimates of the extent of victimization within prison environments (Gibbs, 1981). Under-reporting of incidents is the norm since reporting can itself lead to further victimization. In many cases, assailants are neither identified nor charged—and if charged, convictions are rarely obtained since reliable testimony is unavailable.

The problem of effectively deterring violence in prisons has been further compounded in recent years. Overcrowding, a growing concentration of more violent inmates, lengthier sentences, and an increasingly drug-oriented and

---

From Frank J. Porporino, Phyllis D. Doherty, and Terrence Sawatsky, "Characteristics of Homicidal Victims and Victimization in Prisons: A Canadian Historical Perspective" in *International Journal of Offender Therapy and Comparative Criminology* (31(2): 125–136, September 1987).

predatory prison subculture are factors that, in some fashion, seem to be contributing to a definite increase in prison violence (Braswell, Dillingham & Montgomery, 1985; Cohen, Cole & Bailey, 1976; Conrad, 1982; Irwin, 1980; Jacobs, 1977; Scharf, 1983).

Since violence often triggers further violence, the costs of prison violence are not only considerable for the correctional system, but in the long run, for the community. Prisons, in which fear and violence are commonplace, are unlikely to fulfill their social responsibility to change offenders. Aggressive behavior can become a way of life, a means to survive, an attitude and approach to relating with others that is not easily shed when the inmate returns to society.

Increased surveillance and control is one approach to the problem of prison violence, although there is evidence that such generalized "tightening" of security can actually exacerbate the situation (Bidna, 1975). Violence in prisons will continue to the extent that it continues to serve some function for inmates. Understanding the nature of prison violence, and the circumstances under which it occurs, may therefore be the only sensible means of arriving one step closer to effective prevention (Porporino and Marton, 1984).

This article provides an historical description of the backgrounds of victims of prison homicide, and the circumstances surrounding these incidents in Canadian Federal Correctional Institutions from 1967 to 1984. Although prison homicide incidents have been previously examined, analyses typically have not been historical in nature, restricting themselves to examining homicides over only one or two years (Akman, 1967; Sellin, 1967; Sylvester, Reed and Nelson, 1977; Wolfson, 1978). A central aim of the present study was to determine if there has been any change over time in either the characteristics of victims or the circumstances of homicide incidents within the prison environment.

Methodology

The Preventive Security Division of The Correctional Service of Canada provided some basic information on all inmate murders in Canadian Federal penitentiaries from 1982–1984. Data from 1967–1981 were previously obtained by one of the authors (Doherty, 1983) with the permission and assistance of The Correctional Service of Canada (CSC). Every incident of inmate murder in a Canadian Federal penitentiary was included for the years 1967–1984. The data on victims and the information on the circumstances of the incident were gathered from two sources: the inmate institution files and security incident reports maintained at the national headquarters of the CSC.

The definition of inmate murder adopted for this article is: "the killing of a Federal Penitentiary inmate within the penitentiary walls or perimeter of the grounds. The killing may be intentional or accidental, with or without justification." Consequently, this article does not include the murders of inmates on temporary absence passes, or on parole or **mandatory supervision,** or inmates who were the responsibility of the Federal Correctional Service but housed in a Provincial jail.

The data were collected with the aid of schedules prepared to categorize particular kinds of information. The descriptive information on the victims included: age, sex, ethnic origin and languages spoken. The length of the criminal career of the victim was defined as the length of time between first and last adult convictions. Other information on the criminal career included the number of prior convictions and the nature of the current major offence. The length of sentence being served at the time of the murder was noted.

The information on incidents included the number of victims and the year, month, day and hour of the murder. The location of the murder and the type of weapon(s) or other method of murder (i.e., strangulation, beating) were noted. The information included underlying motive, if ascertained; the number of assailants, whether they were charged, sent to trial, and the outcome of the trial. The security classification of the institution where the murders took place was recorded, as was the length of time that the victim had served in the institution just prior to the murder.

The data were analyzed in simple percentage distributions in order to obtain a descriptive profile of incidents and a breakdown of the background of the victims.

Results

As is evident from Figure 1, there has been a noticeable increase in the frequency of prison homicides over the past 18 years within the Canadian Federal Correctional Service. Both the absolute numbers and the rates of homicide per 100,000 inmates have risen significantly.

The number of murders has fluctuated from year to year, ranging between 0 and 12 in any one year. What is striking, however, is that the murder rate increased from 14.14 in 1967 to 118.36 in 1979, beginning a significant trend in prison murders which has lasted in subsequent years. From 1967 to 1978, the murder rate averaged 30.8 per 100,000 inmates. In contrast, since 1979, the rate has averaged 87.3 per 100,000 inmates, an increase of almost three times what it had been in earlier years.

It is also quite apparent that the risk of murder inside a correctional institution is much higher than for males of comparable age in the general population; offenders in Canadian Federal penitentiaries have been on average fourteen times more at risk for homicide than males in the general population (Jayewardene and Doherty, 1985).

A central aim of the present study was to determine whether the nature of victims or victimizations had changed. Over the 18-year period, there were 84 murders which met the criteria for inclusion in the study. Since the data indicated an apparent increase in murders beginning in 1979, it was decided to divide incidents into two historical periods; Group 1 covering the years 1967–1978 and Group 2 covering the years 1979–1984. Group 1 included 32 victims, murdered between January 1, 1967, and December 31, 1978. Group 2 included 52 victims, murdered between January 1, 1979, and December 31, 1984.

Topography of Homicide Incidents

With the sole exception of one incident where two inmates were murdered during a riot, every incident was one with a single victim.

As Table 1 shows, the most likely time for the occurrence of a homicide incident is between 7 p.m. and midnight. The cell is the most likely location. The risk associated with various locations within the prison was fairly similar

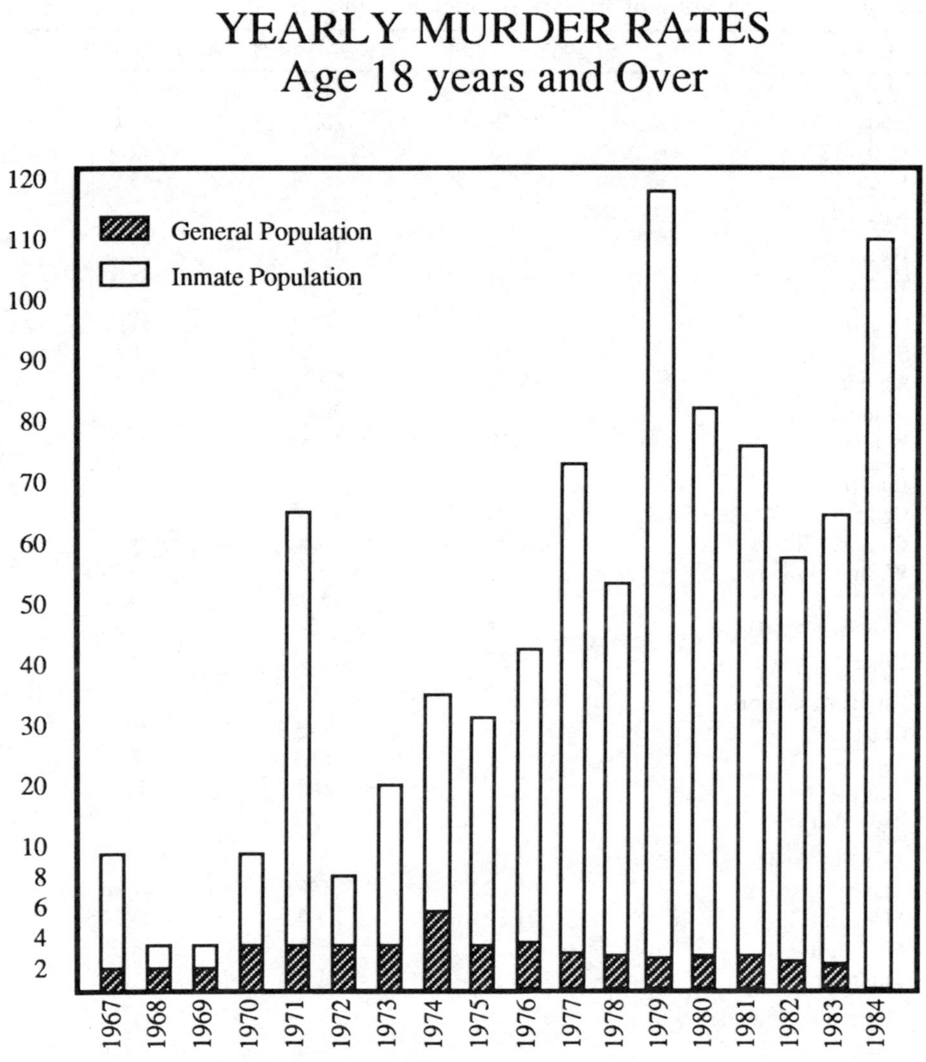

Figure 1

for the two historical periods. Most inmates are killed on a weekend—from Friday to Sunday. A shift seems to be occurring with an increasing proportion of inmates being killed on weekdays in more recent years.

Considering seasonal fluctuations, a curious shift seems to have occurred, with more murders taking place in summer and autumn in recent years.

There was a slight difference during the two historical periods in the number of assailants involved in the murders. In the earlier years, victims were more likely to have been murdered by a single assailant. Three or more assailants have become more common in recent years. The proportion of cases where no assailant is identified has increased slightly from about 16% to 19%.

Table 1 Topography of Inmate Homicide Incidents

Hour	1967–1978 %	1979–1984 %	TOTAL %
Midnight–6:59	6.25	1.92	3.6
7:00–14:59	31.25	26.92	28.6
15:00–18:59	18.75	25.00	22.6
19:00–23:59	43.75	46.15	45.2
Day			
Weekday	28.12	40.38	35.7
Weekend	71.87	59.62	64.3
Season			
Spring	37.50	23.08	28.6
Summer	15.62	30.77	25.0
Autumn	18.75	28.85	25.0
Winter	28.12	17.31	21.4
Location			
Cell	40.62	48.08	45.2
Common Room	12.50	15.38	14.3
Washroom/Shower	6.25	9.62	8.3
Yard/Gym	12.50	15.38	14.3
Corridor	18.75	7.69	11.9
Other	9.37	3.85	5.9
No. of Assailants			
One	46.9	36.5	40.5
Two	18.8	17.3	17.9
Three or more	18.8	26.9	23.8
Unknown	15.6	19.2	17.9
Security Level			
Maximum (6/7)	65.62	59.62	61.90
Medium (5)	21.87	25.00	23.87
Medium (4/3)	12.50	13.46	13.09
Minimum (2)	0	1.92	1.19
Method of Murder			
Knife	68.8	63.5	65.5
Beating	25.00	19.2	21.4
Strangulation	0	7.7	4.8
Multiple	3.1	9.6	7.1
Fire	3.1	0	1.2
Time in Inst. Before Murder			
Up to 6 months	40.6	59.6	52.4
6 months to 2 years	34.4	28.8	30.9
Over 2 years	6.8	11.5	15.5

As would be expected, the largest percentage of murders have occurred in higher security level institutions. During the 18-year period, 85% of the murders occurred in institutions classified as level 5 or higher on a seven-point security scale.

There was little difference in the methods of murder used during the two periods. In recent years, there was more use of strangulation, somewhat less stabbing and beating, and more incidents in which a combination of methods was employed.

The length of time that an inmate was in the institution prior to the murder ranged from one day to 9 years. Overall, over 50% of the victims had served less than six months prior to their murder. The vast majority (83%) had been in the institution for less than two years. Comparing the two historical periods, it is noteworthy that in more recent years a much larger proportion of the victims had been in the institution where they were murdered for less than six months (60% as compared to 41% in earlier years).

Motive

A significant difference was found, from one historical period to the other, in the motive for the murders (see Table 2). In earlier years, inmates were more likely to have been murdered over a sex related matter; more recently inmates have been murdered more often for drug related and revenge motives. Sex related issues may refer to the fact that the victim was a sex offender and was disliked for that reason alone, or had further decreased his status by also being an informer or otherwise alienating other inmates. This was the case with 5 victims in Group 1. Two more victims were not sex offenders, but had become involved in homosexual affairs in the institution and this contributed to their death. One other victim was involved in a homosexual relationship and had gambling problems. It was never definitely ascertained which motive had been the principle cause for his murder.

Revenge or involvement in the prison drug trade was implicated in about 33% of the murders in recent years, but only about 12% of the murders in earlier years. This suggests that a more calculating instrumental form of violence is emerging within the prison setting.

The viciousness of some of the attacks which took place is noteworthy. For example, in one of the incidents the victim received more than 60 stab wounds. In another, the victim was severely beaten, then stabbed repeatedly, and finally doused with a combustible liquid and set on fire in his cell.

Characteristics of Homicide Victims

All of the victims were male. Overall, the victims were on average 30 years of age, and the age group most at risk was between 21 and 25. Close to one-third of the victims (31.3%) fell within this age group during the years 1967–1978; 27% were within this age group from 1979–1984. The median age of victims was slightly higher in more recent years; the median age was 26 during the early historical period, 28 in more recent years.

Over half of the victims were English speaking (55%), 29% were French speaking and 16% spoke both languages. Nearly half of the victims were of French ancestry, the remaining being of other Caucasian origin. Although

Table 2 Motives for Prison Homicide

Motive	1967–1978 %	No.	1979–1984 %	No.
Revenge	3.1	1	15.4	8
Informant	6.3	2	1.9	1
Drugs	9.4	3	17.3	9
Altercation	6.3	2	5.8	3
Sex Offender	15.6	5	1.9	1
Homosexual Affair	9.4	3	0	0
Debts	6.3	2	5.8	3
Other	6.3	2	11.5	6
Unknown	37.5	12	40.4	21

nearly 9% of the penitentiary population are of North American Indian descent, only one Native Indian (1.5%) was a victim of homicide.

There were no significant differences from one historical period to the other on any of the demographic characteristics that were examined.

Criminal Background of the Victims

The victims in both groups were likely to have had convictions as adults, prior to the offence for which they were serving a sentence at the time of the murder. Over 80% of each group had previous convictions (see Table 3).

The majority of Group 1 (58%) were serving their first penitentiary term at the time of their murder; only 48% of Group 2 were serving their first penitentiary sentence. The distribution in the lengths of the criminal careers of the victims during the two periods was very similar. The average number of lifetime convictions was identical.

In more recent years, one quarter of the victims were serving a life sentence, compared to 13% of victims in the earlier years. Victims in recent years were more likely to be serving a sentence of under three years (30.8%) or over 10 years (42%), as compared to the earlier period when inmates in the 4 to 9 year sentence category were at highest risk (47%). The groups were similar in the pattern of violent, property, drug and other offences for which they were serving sentences just prior to their murder. In over 60% of the cases, the victims were serving sentences for a violent offence, another 20% for property offences. A closer examination, however, of the specific offences reveals that a much larger proportion of the victims in more recent years were themselves serving a sentence for first or second degree murder (23% as opposed to 6% in earlier years). In the earlier years, the largest proportion of victims were serving sentences for sex offences (see Table 4).

Table 3 Criminal Careers of Inmate Victims of Homicide

Prior Convictions	1967–1978 %	1979–1984 %
Yes	83.9	81.8
No	16.1	18.2
First Penitentiary Term		
Yes	58.1	47.7
No	41.9	52.3
Length of Criminal Career		
0–3 years	35.5	36.4
4–9 years	32.3	25.0
10 or more	32.2	38.6
Lifetime Convictions		
Range	1–55	1–43
Mean	15	15
Sentence for Present Conviction		
2–3 years	18.8	30.77
4–9 years	47.00	23.08
10 or more	21.9	42.31
Life	12.3	26.92

Criminal Proceedings Against Assailants

Overall, in the 85 cases of homicide that were examined, at least one suspect was identified in about 80% of the cases. There was enough evidence to charge at least one suspect in 53% of the cases. In only 27 cases (32%) was someone sent to trial; moreover, in only 18 cases (21%) was someone actually convicted. Two suspects were found unfit to stand trial.

Conclusion

Data on the incidence of prison murders revealed that inmates incarcerated in Canadian Federal Correctional Institutions are at higher risk of being murdered than other males in free society. Further, this risk seems to have increased over time and is not showing any evidence of diminishing.

Few differences were noted in terms of the topography of homicide incidents over the 18-year period that was examined. The major shifts that seem to be occurring are that in recent years, a large proportion of inmates are being killed on weekdays, earlier on in their institutional stays, and in attacks with multiple assailants.

Meaningful differences for motives underlying the killings were noted, victims in more recent years being killed more often for revenge or because of some involvement in drug trafficking within the institution.

Although there were no significant differences in the age or race of victims from one historical period to the other, it is noteworthy that the greatest proportion of homicide victims were relatively young.

The major background factor which differentiated the victims of former years from those in more recent years was the nature of the offence for which

Table 4 Major Offence of Inmate Homicide Victims

Major Offence	1967–1978 %	No.	1979–1984 %	No.
Violent				
First Degree Murder	3.1	1	5.8	3
Second Degree Murder	3.1	1	17.3	9
Manslaughter	6.3	2	7.7	4
Att. Murder/Accomp.	6.3	2	5.8	3
Robbery	15.6	5	17.3	9
Assault	6.3	2	3.8	2
Forcible Confinement	0	0	3.8	2
Sexual Offences	21.9	7	3.8	2
Sub Total	62.6	20	65.3	34
Property				
Break and Enter	15.6	5	15.4	8
Theft	0	0	7.7	4
Other	3.1	1	0	0
Sub Total	18.7	6	23.1	12
Drugs				
Possession/Traff.	6.3	2	7.7	4
Importing	3.1	1	0	0
Sub Total	9.4	3	7.7	4
Other	6.3	2	3.8	2
Unknown	3.1	1	0	0

the victim was serving a sentence. While murderers make up about 12% of the total penitentiary population, in recent years about 23% of inmate murder victims were themselves serving a sentence for murder. Not only is there an overrepresentation of murderers in the victims category in more recent years, but there is a definite change in the pattern from former years. Then, sexual offenders were at greater risk.

The modal profile for a victim of prison homicide seems to be an individual who is relatively young, with a history of prior convictions and a fairly lengthy criminal career, serving a sentence for a violent offence. This profile suggests that prison homicide victims are not commonly the vulnerable or inexperienced first offenders. Rather, they are individuals steeped in the prison subculture who run afoul of the norms of that subculture. For example, in more recent years a pattern seems to have emerged of more homicides linked to revenge motives or the default of debts from the drug-trafficking in prisons.

A shortcoming of this type of investigation is that it does not provide enough information concerning the kinds of interactions and conflicts that emerge between inmates in prisons. Such level of analysis would seem essential for a more complete understanding of the causes leading to homicide incidents. For instance, through examining motive, it is clear that inmates in recent years are being killed for different reasons. The homicides seem more calculated and focused. There is a suggestion of involvement in the drug trade within an institution—younger inmates may be putting themselves at particular risk for murder. This is compounded by their involvement in gambling or their cooperation with institutional authorities in providing information. There was not enough evidence on the documents which were examined for this study to determine which of the multitude of activities contribute most to the probability of being killed, in what combination or in what sequence.

Future research into the motives underlying inmate murders should include interviews with suspects and other fellow inmates to shed light on the situations which can precipitate and lead up to such brutal deaths (Toch, 1969). Such careful investigation and trend analysis of the process of conflict escalation is essential if we are to further our understanding of the prison situations which contribute to the deaths of inmates.

Discussion Questions

1. Should the characteristics of Canadian prison homicide victims and victimizations be expected to parallel the characteristics of victims and victimization in U.S. prisons? Why or why not?
2. Should the temporal changes uncovered by the authors (and the reasons given for these changes) be anticipated to hold true for the U.S.? Explain.
3. What are the implications of this study's findings for reducing prison homicide in Canada? What strategies and policies are warranted? Might similar strategies and policies assist in reducing homicide in U.S. prisons? Why or why not?
4. How does the ominous threat to personal safety affect life and adjustment behind bars? What do the stress and fear arising from this threat imply for rehabilitation?

References

Akman, D. (1967). Homicides and Assaults in Canadian Penitentiaries. *Harvard Journal of Penology and Crime Prevention,* 12, 102–112.

Bidna, H. (1975). Effects of Increased Security on Prison Violence. *Journal of Criminal Justice,* 3, 33–46.

Braswell, M., Dillingham, S., and Montgomery, R. (Eds.) (1985). *Prison Violence in America.* Cincinnati: Anderson Publishing.

Cohen, A., Cole, G., and Bailey, R. (Eds.) (1976). *Prison Violence.* Lexington: D.C. Heath & Co.

Conrad, J. (1982). What Do the Undeserving Deserve? In R. Johnson and H. Toch (Eds.), *The Pains of Imprisonment.* Beverly Hills: Sage Publications.

Doherty, P. (1983). *Homicides in Canadian Penitentiaries, 1967–1981.* (Ottawa: University of Ottawa, M.A. Thesis.)

Gibbs, J. (1981). Violence in Prisons: Its Extent, Nature and Consequences. In R. Roberg and V. Webb (Eds.), *Critical Issues in Corrections.* New York: West Publishing Co.

Irwin, J. (1980). *Prisons in Turmoil.* Toronto: Little, Brown & Co.

Jacobs, J. (1977). *Stateville: The Penitentiary in Mass Society.* Chicago: University of Chicago Press.

Jayewardene, C., and Doherty, P. (1985). Individual Violence in Canadian Penitentiaries. *Canadian Journal of Criminology,* October, 27(4), 429–439.

Porporino, F., and Marton, J. (1984). *Strategies to Reduce Prison Violence.* Ottawa: Research Division, Ministry of the Solicitor General of Canada.

Scharf, P. (1983). Empty Bars: Violence and the Crisis of Meaning in the Prison. *The Prison Journal,* LXIII, 1, 114–124.

Sellin, T. (1967). Prison Homicides. In T. Sellin (Ed.), *Capital Punishment.* New York: Harper and Row, 154–160.

Sylvester, S., Reed, J., and Nelson, D. (1977). *Prison Homicide.* New York: Spectrum Publications Inc.

Toch, H. (1969). *Violent Men: An Inquiry Into the Psychology of Violence.* Chicago: Aldine.

Wolfson, W. (1978). *The Patterns of Prison Homicide.* Philadelphia: University of Pennsylvania, Ph.D. dissertation.

Author's Note

An earlier version of this paper was presented at the Fifth International symposium on Victimology, Zargreb, Yugoslavia, August, 1985.

Thanks are extended to The Correctional Service of Canada for providing the data.

ISSUES OF POLICY AND MANAGEMENT

section III

Introduction

If imprisonment is to have clearly articulated goals, if those goals are to be realized, and if prisons are to operate humanely, then careful planning of correctional policy and serious attention to management issues are essential. This holds true irrespective of the nation under consideration. The history of penology is replete with policies and management strategies that have been based on political appeal and emotion rather than realistic planning. Furthermore, policies and strategies have typically been reactive instead of proactive, arising as after-the-fact antidotes to problems like crowding and violence that almost certainly could have been diminished in magnitude, or completely avoided, had better foresight been exercised.

Thorough examination of the international literature on prisons indicates that many nations face similar policy and management issues. Paramount among these issues is prison crowding; hence, the first three readings in this section address crowding. In "Prison Overcrowding: Correctional Policies and Political Constraints," Richard Harding operationalizes the term "overcrowding" and employs his definition to identify and forecast the scope of the problem in Australia. Important effects of overcrowding are discussed, including rising costs as well as the reciprocal interplay between official and public reactions to overcrowding. Harding concludes by proposing crowding reduction mechanisms and by examining threats to those mechanisms. This article sensitizes us to the political dimension of the crowding issue.

Two basic ways to reduce crowding of existing facilities are to incarcerate fewer offenders and/or to lessen the length of sentences. In the next article, which especially ought to be read by those who see prison overcrowding as an inevitable product of rising concerns over crime and by those who believe that the only solution is to embark on a massive and costly program of prison construction, H. H. Brydensholt explains how the Danes were able to stabilize and even reduce their prison population in the wake of the escalating crime problem of the 1960s. The Danish response to escalating crime, initiated in 1973, was a rationally planned policy consisting of three elements: (1) the substitution of shorter determinate sentences for longer indeterminate ones, (2) the passage of "depenalization" legislation that reduced the length of prison sentences and rendered fewer offenses imprisonable, and (3) the transfer of resources from institutional to community-based corrections. In the U.S., by contrast, the response to mounting concerns over crime has been one of emotional, retributive outrage—to incarcerate more people for longer periods of time than ever before in the nation's history. It can certainly be argued that the U.S. has a greater problem with crime (particularly violence) than does Denmark. However, this argument is not tantamount to confirming that none of the policies which proved worthwhile for the Danes would be useful in the U.S. In other words, the argument is not a license to conveniently ignore or dismiss potentially viable measures for curbing prison crowding. Parenthetically, the more fundamental questions seem to be *why* the U.S. has such a higher rate of violence than Denmark and what social changes are needed to *prevent* violent crime.

In addition to Denmark, another nation noted for a low rate of imprisonment is The Netherlands. Elmer H. Johnson and Alfred Heijder attribute the low incarceration rate of The Netherlands to the low value accorded imprisonment in that culture and, more specifically, to extensive application of pretrial diversion and the use of short sentences for those who are carefully chosen to be placed in prison. Johnson and Heijder show how penal policy in The Netherlands is grounded in pragmatism instead of pure emotion and moral judgements. Imprisonment, being expensive and of dubious efficacy, is viewed as an unwise business practice to be avoided when possible. Pragmatism is further reflected by the cultural tolerance for differences between people as well as by the willingness to work toward mutual compromise in the event of disagreements. The polity of The Netherlands is structured to balance diverse and conflicting interests; the structure opposes extreme positions of the type that translate into massive prison crowding. As illustrated by the heavy use of diversion, there is an inclination toward less formalized measures of social control.

In the fourth reading in this section, it becomes evident that Japan and the U.S., two of the most economically affluent and technologically developed capitalist nations in the world and with quite divergent cultural traditions, share common problems of prison management. Situating prison management within the framework of broader social change, Elmer H. Johnson and Hisashi Hasegawa identify six pressing issues facing Japanese prison administrators, most of which are only too familiar to prison administrators in the U.S. These are: the need to bring archaic penal laws up to date with modern prison administration; the need to renovate older facilities; problems flowing from a growing divergence between the demographic compositions of the guard force and the inmate population; special concerns surrounding the management of inmates from foreign countries; the impact of greater drug use and drug trade activities on the Japanese correctional system; and difficulties posed by the presence of members of organized gangs among the inmate population. Johnson and Hasegawa also discuss the changing nature of the female prison population in Japan.

As arms of government, prison systems are inherently political. The interaction between politics and prison management is exemplified by James S. E. Opolot in his work "Differing Current Managerial Approaches in the Corrections of Four Selected New States of Africa." Opolot demonstrates that the recent political independence of Botswana, Tanzania, Zambia, and Zimbabwe from British rule has led to a re-examination of colonial administrative practices in each new state. As part of a recurring theme, we see how, at a given period in history, the wider socio-political structure of a nation guides the substance of penal policy and management.

The disruptive behavior of inmates is another basic issue facing correctional administrators in many nations. While disruptive behavior tends to directly vary with crowding levels, the research of W. Davies and P. W. Burgess within the British system indicates that disruptive behavior (or at least the incidence reported by staff) is also a function of institutional management style. The findings suggest that there is an important association between the practices adopted by a prison's top administration and the recorded incidence of disruptive activities among the prisoners. A more fundamental lesson of the article is that the behaviors of inmates and guards alike will inevitably be shaped by the managerial practices to which they are subjected. Managerial practices and the way these are implemented during daily prison operations depend, in turn, on the individual qualities of top administrative personnel and the manner in which such personnel respond to the political environment surrounding their positions.

Measures have been taken in Britain which, among other things, are designed to reduce the pressures that fuel disruptive behavior. For instance, unlike the situation in the U.S., probation officer services are made available prior to, during, and immediately following incarceration. Mike Carlie points out that prison-based probation programs must be carefully designed and backed up by both the institutional administration and the government if they are to successfully assist inmates with their daily lives in prison. Carlie discusses the difficulties confronted by British prison-based probation officers in their attempts to provide helping services during an offender's period of incarceration.

The last reading in this section addresses one of the most perplexing issues confronting prisons today, the management of AIDS. Mark Blumberg begins with a general overview of the disease and then turns his attention to the prison setting. Specifically, he describes how HIV may be transmitted in prison and provides a thorough and balanced analysis of the issues surrounding proposals to manage the problem. These issues include mass screening, segregation, confidentiality, and condom distribution. Blumberg explores the risks of contacting AIDS faced by prison staff and also highlights controversies about the release of HIV infected persons into society. The author helps dismiss some of the myths surrounding the AIDS issue and so corrects much of the misinformation that has guided the formulation of AIDS policy in U.S. prisons.

13. Prison Overcrowding: Correctional Policies and Political Constraints*

Richard Harding**

Introduction

The prison mega-crush has reached Australia; many of our **goals** are bursting at the seams. Most months the problem gets worse. Common sense would suggest that this question of the allocation of scarce resources should be a potent political fact in the development and administration of criminal justice policy. Yet it does not seem to be so. Why is this? Are there, nevertheless, any anomalous, or deviant, cases—jurisdictions where the presumed political constraints seem not to have been quite so stultifying? If so, can we learn anything of general application from such cases? These are the issues I would like to examine in this article.

Overcrowding

There are various measures of prison capacity. I adopt the American terminology, which seems to be the most informative. "Rated capacity" is the number of beds or prisoners *de facto* authorized by correctional administrators to be assigned to a prison; it is an elastic figure, therefore, tending to drift upwards according to exigencies. "Operating capacity" is the number of beds or prisoners which can be accommodated consistent with the maintenance of programmes and services; this too is elastic, though it will only drift upwards as a consequence of the explicit reduction or abandonment of such programmes. "Design capacity" is the number of beds or prisoners originally envisaged by the architects; it is a measure which soon gets left behind in the filing cabinets of penological history—an obsolescent curiosity.

Operating capacity, whilst it is the most difficult to quantify, is, in practical terms, the most significant of these measures. When it is exceeded, one or more of several effects may occur: more lock-up time; diminished access to visiting facilities and interview rooms; diminished access to gymnasia, sports and hobby facilities; lesser availability of work programmes or vocational training; thinner spread of developmental programmes generally; and so on. Also

---

*This article is an amended version of the Third Whatmore Memorial Oration delivered under the sponsorship of VACRO in Melbourne on 7 October 1986.

**Director of the Australian Institute of Criminology. The author wishes to express appreciation for advice and assistance from his colleagues, David Biles, Dennis Challinger, Satyanshu Mukherjee, Anita Scandia and John Walker. Constructive suggestions were also made by Mr. Vernon Dalton, Mr. George Zdenkowski and the Editor of the Journal.

From Richard Harding, "Prison Overcrowding: Correctional Policies and Political Constraints" in *Australian and New Zealand Journal of Criminology* (20(1): 16–32, March 1987).

significant is the intangible but real factor of stress induced when too many people live in too close proximity to each other and must compete for finite space and resources. In combination, such circumstances can, and occasionally do, lead to prison riots.

In June 1986, the Australian Institute of Criminology conducted a survey of the rated capacity and actual occupancy of the total prison system in each jurisdiction. The results, as well as those of a similar 1979 survey, are set out in Table 1.

Table 1 Occupancy Rates of Australian Prison Systems, by State, as against Rated Capacity, 1979, 1986

	Total Rated Capacity		Highest Number of Prisoners		Percentage Occupancy	
	1986	(1979)	1986	(1979)	1986	(1979)
NSW	3,856	(4,097)	3,937	(3,918)	102.1	(95.6)
Victoria	2,030	(1,877)	1,974	(1,590)	97.2	(84.7)
Queensland	1,986	(1,812)	2,230	(1,609)	112.3	(88.8)
Western Australia	1,915	(1,423)	1,741	(1,472)	90.9	(103.4)
South Australia*	779	(1,169)	860	(783)	110.4	(67.0)
Tasmania	477	(449)	360	(293)	64.2	(65.3)
North. Territory**	320	(266)	421	(214)	131.6	(80.5)
ACT	18	(18)	33	(7)	183.3	(38.9)
Australia	11,381	(11,111)	11,502	(9,882)	101.1	(88.9)

*A new remand centre whose design capacity is 168 was opened in Adelaide in September 1986.
**A new prison farm with design capacity for 50 male prisoners was opened near Darwin in August 1986.
Source: Australian Institute of Criminology.

As can be seen, occupancy rates averaged 101.1% of rated capacity, Australia-wide. However, a more telling figure would be occupancy rate as against operating capacity. Roughly speaking, this is 85% of rated capacity. This figure takes account of the fact that both prisons and prisoners have various security classifications, that there are geographical and sexual imperatives in the availability and use of accommodation, and that special programmes such as drug and alcohol rehabilitation are located at particular prisons. On that basis, the Australia-wide occupancy rate was on the order of 118.8%.

Another significant matter which emerges from Table 1 is that pressure on occupancy rates, however they are measured, has increased markedly over the last seven years. In mid 1979, the Australia-wide occupancy rate, as against rated capacity, was 88.9%, that is just in excess of operating capacity. The 1986 rate represents a quantum leap from the point of view of prison management and policy implications.

One point which should be noted in this regard is that those jurisdictions which have done most to expand their capacity—Victoria, Queensland, Western

Australia and the Northern Territory—have not as a consequence made a really significant impact upon their occupancy rates. Quite the contrary: in three of those jurisdictions the position has substantially deteriorated. Faced with a similar observation in the United States, Gottfredson and Taylor (1983:2) commented:

> It is not our intention here to enter the "capacity demand" debate. We merely point out that prison construction has not, to our knowledge, resolved the prison crowding problem in any jurisdiction.

Neither is it my own intention to enter into the capacity/demand debate, which poses many fiendish statistical traps for the unwary (Blumstein, 1983). However, it is a powerful perspective which one should not ignore.

Of course, Australian national imprisonment rates per 100,000 population during the last 40 years (though not necessarily those of some of the constituent jurisdictions) move within ranges which seem congruent with the so-called homeostatic theory of punishment (Blumstein, 1973; 1977). This theory suggests that upper limits are socio-culturally set by prevailing tolerances in the community, and that these tolerances or values do not themselves fluctuate a great deal over time. Thus, the organs of society—police, judges, the media, public opinion, etc.—in some way "sense" the imminent breach of an acceptable rate of imprisonment, and adjust their conduct intuitively, not with deliberate co-ordination, to start bringing the rate down again.

However, it does seem that this theory, to the extent that it still holds good in practice, is really a sub-theme of the capacity debate. This is because, at least in Australia, the highest point in any given cyclical wave seldom exceeds rated capacity, let alone operating capacity, to a gross extent. The limitation in Blumstein's theory is that it was not really tested against current rated capacity but rather assumed that prison accommodation is more or less open-ended. Downward cyclical movements could not really be demonstrated to be purely socio-cultural, therefore, but might have been influenced by the technical questions of capacity. Of course, that is a different proposition from asserting the positive side of the demand/capacity argument—that rated capacity will inevitably be filled up.

Be that as it may, prison construction programmes and commitments in Australia seem to reflect something of each of these perspectives, in that the stated rationale—at least in Western Australia and Victoria—has primarily been that of renewal and replacement of sub-standard plant. Increased capacity has been presented as a minor by-product of this process, rather than an end in itself. Certainly, British experience would suggest that it is playing with fire to reverse the priorities, seeing plant renewal as a by-product of an increase in places. For, hand in hand with explicit commitment to add 13,000 places to capacity over a period of 10 years, there has occurred a drastic increase in the British prison population (Rutherford, 1986; Worrall and Pease, 1986).

The British occupancy rate is in fact currently of the order of 110, against rated capacity, or 130, against operating capacity (Rutherford, 1986). Similarly, the overall United States average rates were approximately 106 or 121 as of 31 December 1985 (*Criminal Justice Newsletter*, 1986a). These average rates concealed wide disparities between jurisdictions (as is also the case in Australia). For example, California was holding 48,000 prisoners in institutions whose total operating capacity was 29,000—an occupancy rate of 165 (*Criminal Justice Newsletter,* 1985). Hawaii's occupancy rate was 180. These figures would seem to suggest that the homeostatic theory, whether it is best regarded as technical or cultural in its mainspring, may be coming to the end of its useful life.

What, then, is the prognosis for Australian prisoner numbers? The total, I would suggest, will continue to increase for several years, with the consequence that prison overcrowding will become more chronic. One should not, of course, be too deterministic about this; concerted policy initiatives are capable of reversing this trend. But in the absence of such initiatives, the drift upwards will continue. This is for a variety of reasons.

First, there are quite strong indicia that penal practices become more severe in times of economic crisis (Young, 1986: 127–9). Whether this effect is directly related to unemployment (Jancovic, 1977; Greenberg, 1977; Yeager, 1979; Wallace, 1981) or mediated by judicial or cultural attitudes (Box and Hale, 1982; Wilkins, 1984) is not entirely clear (Young, 1986: 129). Of course, there are also conflicting indicia, for example, during the post-war reconstruction period in some societies (Young, 1986: 128–9). However, the Australian position over the past four years has been that, as the overall imprisonment rate has risen, so too has the proportion of prisoners who were unemployed at the time of committing the offence (Walker and Biles, 1983–86). Separate figures are not available for received prisoners each year. But it is a fair inference that the evolving pattern of the pool of prisoners reflects also the pattern of receivals. As the likelihood is that unemployment in Australia will increase somewhat over the next two or three years, so too will the underlying upward trend in imprisonment probably be fortified.

In addition, two factors which are already contributing to recent increases in the imprisonment rate have not yet, in my view, made their full impact. These factors are: patterns of female imprisonment and the increase in federal offenders.

With regard to female prisoners, their proportion of the Australian prison population has doubled, from 2.4 to 4.6% in the last 10 years. In actual numbers, we have moved from the low two hundreds to the low five hundreds. This sort of trend is manifesting itself in most developed countries (Mukherjee, 1984; United Nations, 1986: 126–7). In Australia, it is explicable in the following terms: increasing female participation in the commission of drug offences; additional opportunities for women to commit serious property offences; the growth in social security fraud; and, somewhat intangibly, the development of predominantly male judges of decidedly less avuncular attitudes towards female offenders (Fox and Freiberg, 1985: 485–6)—an unanticipated effect, doubtless, of the strong impact of the women's movement during the last decade. It is not fanciful to contemplate that the proportion of female offenders could double yet again over the next decade. If this happens, an additional component of approximately 3.0 per 100,000 would form part of the overall Australian imprisonment rate, which is currently about 70.0. In other words, if the male rate remained unchanged, the overall rate would be of the order of 73.0.

As to federal offenders, it must be said that it is not altogether straightforward to determine exactly who is a federal prisoner. This is principally because some offenders have been sentenced concurrently for both State and federal offences, an eventuality which is made possible by the autochthonous expedient of vesting federal criminal jurisdiction in State courts and by the legal and factual overlap of certain kinds of criminal conduct (Chan, 1986; Kelleher, 1986). However, as at 30 June 1985 as many as 4.3% of all prisoners were in some part federal, of whom 2.5% were federal prisoners only. The advent of a Commonwealth Office of Director of Public Prosecutions in conjunction with increasing use of prosecution powers in matters involving tax evasion, medifraud and social security fraud, along with the imposition of longer sentences in relation to drug importation, seems likely to lead to an increase in this particular component of the prison population. Offsetting this is the fact that, in Victoria, South Australia, Western Australia, the Australian Commonwealth Territory (ACT) and the Northern Territory, the full panoply of State non-custodial sentencing powers is now available in relation to federal offences, by arrangements under s 3B of the Crimes Act of 1914 (Cth). Nevertheless, it could well be that the burgeoning area of federal criminal law could add a component of 1.0 to 2.0 per 100,000 to the overall Australian imprisonment rate over the next 5 to 10 years.

The foregoing factors are not, of course, exhaustive. Some others—such as the spread of genuine efforts to keep fine-defaulters out of prison—should hold back increases. Yet others—such as an increasing punitiveness which is apparently taking root in society (Wilson, forthcoming)—would tend to push imprisonment rates up. All told, the prognosis must be a pessimistic one—that the prison population will continue to increase ahead of general population. On the bright side, this increase is likely to be incremental rather than exponential.

It is important to understand the relationship of these past and likely future trends to serious crime rates. Although I have identified changing crime patterns as having an impact on Australian imprisonment rates at the margins, it should be stressed that at the macro-level greater use of imprisonment is not necessarily driven by, nor will it necessarily drive, serious crime rates. Punishment and crime simply do not conform to identifiable laws of criminological causation.

This point can be demonstrated statistically (Bowker, 1981; Biles, 1982), comparatively (Tulkens, 1979; Downes, 1982) or by analysis of criminal justice systems as a working model (Ashworth, 1986). For every 1,000 index or serious offences committed, no more than one person is sentenced to imprisonment. The reality confronting us is that imprisonment is a minor technique in crime control. That is not to say that, properly honed, it is not an important technique. But if, for example, only 0.9 persons were sentenced to imprisonment per 1,000 index offences committed—that is a reduction of 10% in the number of prison sentences—it could hardly be said that a policy of crime control was being abandoned when, manifestly, this policy draws upon other strategies to such a great extent. The prison overcrowding debate, I suggest, does not really impinge upon the crime control, or law and order, debate.

Practical and Political Effects of Overcrowding

Four main effects can readily be identified. These are: (i) burgeoning costs of the correctional components of criminal justice services; (ii) short-term administrative and political responses made in an effort to alleviate overcrowding; (iii) adverse reactions to these responses by media, public and other arms of the criminal justice system; (iv) further administrative and political responses calculated, if not intended, to exacerbate rather than alleviate the problem whilst also incidentally further increasing costs (Chan and Zdenkowski, 1986: 138). In the course of this spiral, penal policy as a whole becomes distorted, and its position in overall criminal justice policy isolated. As Gottfredson and Taylor (1983: vii) have pointed out:

> Prison crowding is a crisis in the entire criminal justice system, and the active, aggressive and co-ordinated efforts of the entire system are needed for its resolution.

This is certainly true; but it is not to say that some beneficial impact cannot be made by clarifying penal objectives and processes.

(i) Costs

Capital and recurrent expenditures in Australia on corrective services are now of the order of $380 million per annum. In constant dollar terms, real expenditure has increased threefold since 1968. On the recurrent side of the balance sheet, a significant part of this increase is attributable to shift loadings and overtime payments, matters which are themselves associated with the management of overcrowded facilities. The capital component of total expenditure is exactly in line with the overall pattern. Jerome Miller (1986, 231) has recently remarked:

> Having administered three large State correctional bureaucracies, I learned to assess commitment to various stated goals and purposes of a governmental agency by looking at its budget. Where the money goes, the commitment resides.

It is instructive to examine the distribution within Australia of recurrent expenditure between prisons and community corrections: see Table 2.

What stands out is the disparate level of commitment to community corrections programmes by jurisdiction, both in terms of expenditure per offender and of proportion of overall budgetary allocations. Particularly instructive are the cases of Queensland and Western Australia—States whose imprisonment rates have continuously been well in excess of the national average for the last 13 years.

(ii) Primary Administrative and Political Responses

Weatherburn (1986) has traced the efforts made in New South Wales to reduce the prison population. His analysis of median sentence lengths and the distribution of the prison population by time yet to be served leads him to argue cogently that "back-end release" (i.e., release before the expected date of release as computed according to the strict legal entitlements of the prisoner) is potentially the most effective way of reducing the number of prisoners:

Table 2 Expenditure on Prisons and Community Corrections by State, 1984/1985

Jurisdiction (in order of no. of offenders dealt with)	Est.Avg. Cost of Pre-Sentence Report	Avg. Prison Population 1.7.84 30.6.85	Prison Budget $ 1.7.84–30.6.85 (as part of total Corrections budget)	Avg. Annual Cost Per Year of Imprisonment Served $	Avg. Persons under Supervision in Community 1.7.84–30.6.85	Communiy Budget $ 1.7.84–30.6.85 (as % of Corrections Budget)	Avg. Annual Cost per Year of Community Supervision $
New South Wales	$250	3,747	88,379,922 (82.5%)	23,567	13,313	18,693,858 (17.5%)	1,404
Queensland	—	1,940	36,706,112 (91.2%)	18,921	6,879	3,535,685 (8.8%)	514
Victoria	$150	1,878	55,567,000 (84.2%)	29,588	5,502	10,419,000 (15.8%)	2,003
Western Australia	$210	1,481	50,205,000 (94.3%)	33,899	3,115	3,000,000 (5.7%)	908
South Australia	$150	698	27,263,000 (85.9%)	39,059	2,735	4,475,000 (14.1%)	1,028
Tasmania	$320	236	6,318,000 (82.0%)	26,771	1,896	1,444,000 (18.0%)	451
Northern Territory	$200	297	9,701,200 (83.5%)	32,664	477	1,189,800 (16.5%)	2,290
TOTALS	—	10,277	($) 274,140,234 (86.5%)	($) 26,675 (avg.)	33,417	($) 42,755,543 (13.5%)	($) 1,278 (avg.)

The solution to prison overcrowding would seem to depend upon finding a viable mechanism for early release (1986: 134).

Most Australian jurisdictions have, during the last decade, attempted to develop viable back-end release mechanisms. For example, several States legislated for the standard **remission** rate of one-third to apply not just to head sentences but also to minimum or non-parole periods. Others developed work release programmes which, whilst not technically reducing the prison population, in fact alleviated overcrowding inasmuch as work releases could be housed in quite different kinds of accommodation with minimal supervision. Even this, however, was subject to accommodation constraints as well as to the availability of work, so that its efficacy was limited.

More radical mechanisms were explored in New South Wales and Victoria. These were release-on-licence and pre-release.

The New South Wales release-on-licence scheme did not depend on new legislation but rather upon the willingness of the responsible Minister to invoke and utilize an existing statutory mechanism (Weatherburn, 1986: 125). From the start, this approach was controversial, but it was certainly effective. In the course of the 10-month period, March to December 1982, during which it was in full operation, the prison population declined from 3,619 to 3,420. During the 16-month period of the scheme's operation, 1,191 persons were released (of whom only 66 had their licence revoked). Releasees were, by definition, not parolees, that is prisoners who would have left prison at that time anyhow. Although the average outstanding time before "normal" release is not known, it is a fair inference that this programme must have been a major factor in bringing about this decline.

In Victoria, the pre-release scheme was introduced in 1983 by the Community Welfare Services (Pre-Release Programme) Act. The Adult Parole Board was empowered to grant a pre-release to prisoners serving a sentence of 12 months or more, of which no less than three and no more than 12 months remain to be served, provided that the period of pre-release did not exceed one-third of the total sentence. In the first year of the scheme's operation, 1,002 eligible prisoners were considered and 543 applications were granted. Approximately 160 man-years of imprisonment were thereby saved, and the overall impact was to contribute to a reduction of 85 in the prison population over the period of June 1983 to June 1984. One of the significant costs of this achievement was widespread judicial antipathy (Harding, 1984).

Victoria also used other, less conventional methods for coping with overcrowding during the period under review. For example, receival of prisoners might be delayed by leaving them in police lock-ups until space could be found; or, regardless of strict legalities, some might even be put out of the gate to make way for new arrivals. Improvisations such as these are relatively commonplace wherever the problem of overcrowding is acute (De Witt, 1986; *Criminal Justice Newsletter,* 1986b). Australian prison administrators have in fact been compelled to take intolerable legal and political risks to cope with the problems which have been dumped on their doorsteps.

(iii) Adverse Reactions

Inevitably, in these circumstances, something goes wrong—for example, a person about whom it is possible to say that "he really should have been inside at the time" commits a high news value crime, or someone who has committed such a crime is soon released, to a fanfare of publicity. The point is so familiar it barely needs illustrating. Two examples, one from each major jurisdiction, will suffice.

In New South Wales, the February 1986 murder of a nurse, Anity Cobby, was allegedly committed by a group of men who included a prison escapee, Michael Murphy. Murphy had escaped a few months previously from a minimum security institution. Media debate, as public revulsion at the circumstances of the crime grew, revolved around the question of how such a prisoner, serving a long sentence for various offences including crimes of violence, could come to be classified in such a way. The explanation, of course, is the perfectly conventional one that, as prisoners approach the end of their non-parole period minus remission, it is essential to relax somewhat the conditions of detention. But the explanation was far less interesting than the original story. A media furore developed around the escape and the horrendous murder, and everything which might seem to smack of a "soft" correctional regime was drawn into the vortex.

In Victoria, a no less notorious recent case has focused the spotlight upon apparent anomalies in the remission and release systems. The case concerned the manslaughter by neglect of a three and a half year old girl. The parents had treated a minor ailment by putting the child on a water diet for 27 days, at the end of which she died. It was, then, a bad example of a high profile phenomenon, child abuse.

Media attention during the trial was intensive. The father, Marcus Barnes, was convicted. The trial judge sentenced him to 18 months' imprisonment, with a minimum of six months. Yet six weeks and one day after this sentence was imposed and reported, Barnes was released—an event which received as much media attention as the crime and the trial. How had this release come about? The general answer—lawfully and in accordance with conventional practice—was, as with the Michael Murphy case, far less interesting than the original story. For the record, let me explain that Barnes had served one week in custody during the trial and six weeks awaiting sentence, periods which counted towards both sentence and remission. His total time in custody before release had thus been 13 weeks and one day. As for the six-month minimum period, this was subject to one-third remission by order of the Adult Parole Board, bringing the effective sentence down to four months or just over 17 weeks. Where did the additional four weeks go? In further remissions for good behaviour, 21 days by decision of the Director-General of the Office of Corrections and seven days at the discretion of the **Governor** of the prison at which Barnes was being held. Of course, the rationale of these two last-mentioned periods of remission is quite explicitly related to the need to ease overcrowding.

Predictably, police sources jumped on the press bandwagon, The *Barnes* case, it was said, was "a joke" and "a mockery of the judicial system" (*Sydney Morning Herald,* 19 June 1986). Remission was linked to another old chestnut—bail pending trial. Criminals, a police spokesman claimed, "know the system is soft, that there are early release programmes, and that they may get the same sentence for ten robberies as for one or two" (*The Australian,* 5 June 1986). And so on.

Another close-knit occupational group, the judiciary, also reacted publicly. Weatherburn (1986: 125–7) has documented the hostility which the release-on-licence scheme provoked in New South Wales. He has also verified statistically one's distinct impression that superior court judges increased non-parole periods in response to the statutory amendment whereby standard remission rates became applicable to such periods (Weatherburn, 1985). The same process has occurred in South Australia (Dawes and Morgan, 1986) and in the ACT

(Harding, 1984). In such a context, it was not really surprising that the judicial response to the *Barnes* case was a cry of frustration. The Chairman of the Adult Parole Board (a Supreme Court judge) issued a public statement saying that all pre-release powers currently vested in the Office of Corrections should be abolished and that all like powers should be conferred exclusively upon the Board. A primary cause for his concern was that persons released under these provisions were in a penological no-man's land during the pre-release period, inasmuch as parole with its attendant sanctions and controls had not yet commenced in law.

Nevertheless, against all this, the opportunity to make the correctional perspective heard is quite circumscribed. It is too subtle and too beleaguered to be attractive.

(iv) Secondary Administrative and Political Responses

Cases such as those of Michael Murphy and Marcus Barnes, and the debates which they engender, act as a catalyst for changes of direction. Yet the social attitudes and political sensitivities pointing to such changes are pre-existing and deep-seated; there will always be events to set them off.

In New South Wales the Premier, in the wake of political fall-out from allegedly corrupt administration of the release-on-licence scheme, had already rejected a Cabinet submission for new back-end release mechanisms to be set up in relation to the last six months of sentence (*Sun-Herald,* 24 November 1985). This was done on the basis that it would be politically suicidal. In immediate response to the *Cobby* case, a review of the prisoner security classification system was initiated with a view to tightening it up (*Daily Telegraph,* 26 February 1986). This, of course, would put pressure on the capacity of the prison system to cope with its population even without adding a single inmate to the daily roster (Walker and Biles, 1985: Table 18). Finally, legislation was passed to empower sentencing judges to order that normal remissions should not in a particular case be applicable to head and/or minimum sentences: Crimes (Remissions) Amendment Act 1986; Probation and Parole (Remissions) Amendment Act 1986.

In Victoria, the Corrections Bill 1986 will, when it becomes law, cut into pre-release by confining it to sentences of three years or more in relation to which no more than six months remain to be served. This reduction in eligibility will inevitably mean that far fewer man-years will be saved than the number saved under the previous legislation. Moreover, the provision for 21 days leave at the direction of the Director-General is to be reduced to three days, and the seven days Governor's leave is to be abolished altogether. However the Bill is wrapped up, therefore, the reality is that overcrowding has been relegated as a policy consideration to the very bottom of the political totem-pole. In this respect, Victoria matches New South Wales.

Lest it be thought that this is something peculiar to the most populous States, it should be pointed out that comparable moves have been foreshadowed or made in all other States. In South Australia, for example, the Government's 1985 election campaign included an undertaking to give courts wider powers to refuse to set a non-parole period (*Adelaide Advertiser,* 2 December 1985). Legislation along these lines was eventually introduced into Parliament on 28 August 1986. In Western Australia—where the remission rate on non-parole periods is, at three days per month, already the least generous in any jurisdiction—the Attorney-General recently ordered an inquiry into the operation of parole in relation to prisoners serving long sentences for serious crimes (*West Australian,* 4 December 1985). In Queensland, where median sentence lengths for a wide range of offences are the longest in Australia, there has been much talk about increasing sentences. A new form of back-end release now operating in Queensland, home detention (i.e., pre-release under strict surveillance by prison officers), has taken 23 prisoners out of institutions as of 31 July 1986 (*Australian Prison Trends*—No. 122). However, this seems ideologically objectionable in that it takes the prison into the private residence rather than keeping the offender in the community. Finally, the Tasmanian Government at the August 1986 Liberal Party Conference has undertaken to make non-parole periods the toughest in Australia, first by making half of the head sentence the norm and second by empowering judges to provide that there should be no possibility of parole in a particular case.

Amidst all these rumblings, barely a whisper is heard about overcrowding. The fact of the matter is that back-end mechanisms, whilst they may be technically viable, are simply not politically tenable at the present time. If we try to tackle overcrowding predominantly from that end, therefore, no worthwhile progress will be made.

Alternative Approach: Front-end Mechanisms

A primary front-end mechanism (i.e., one emanating from the court itself at the time of sentence), of course, is shorter sentences of imprisonment. No less important, however, is the mechanism I wish to address to this article—community-based correctional dispositions. Weatherburn (1986: 130), after analysing the distribution by sentence length of the New South Wales prison population, has concluded that "front-end solutions directed at sentenced prisoners show little potential for effecting large reductions in the size of the prison population." Chan and Zdenkowski (1986) have reached a comparable conclusion. This view, as I shall try to show, may be unduly pessimistic.

A preliminary point is that receival or admission rates into Australian prisons show striking dissimilarities by jurisdiction. As a matter of common sense, such rates are not totally unrelated to imprisonment rates: see Table 3. The effects of a rigorous campaign about front-end mechanisms conducted in one jurisdiction might spill over into another, particularly as regular meetings of Ministers and administrators responsible for corrections mean that something akin to national correctional perspectives and policies are starting to emerge. This is a factor which a mono-jurisdictional study, such as Weatherburn's, tends to ignore. Moreover, a particular attraction of a front-end strategy is that it would avoid the appearance of subterfuge which, rightly or wrongly, seems to have dogged back-end release mechanisms in recent Australian penological history.

I believe it could be helpful to look at the two mainland States which, in the last decade or so, have traditionally had the lowest imprisonment rate—Victoria and South Australia. One should do so against the following back-

Table 3 Receival and Imprisonment Rates per 100,000 by Jurisdiction, 1985

	Receival Rate	Imprisonment Rate
New South Wales	171.6	75.6
Victoria	111.7	44.8
Queensland	164.2	78.9
Western Australia	273.0	107.0
South Australia	221.8	56.2
Tasmania	156.1	51.5
Northern Territory	955.1	233.6

ground: that, as of 30 June 1986, the South Australian imprisonment rate has increased by 50% from its lowest recent figure of 41.3 (June 1984), whereas the Victorian rate has remained remarkably consistent during the last seven years. (The Victorian rate does not include 17–21 year olds detained in Youth Training Centres. Their inclusion would not, however, erode the force of the points which follow inasmuch as they would add only about 1.0 per 100,000 to the rate of imprisonment.) By contrast, the South Australian community-based corrections rate has remained reasonably steady, whereas that of Victoria, particularly in the last two years, is increasing markedly. These points emerge from Figure 1.

It could, of course, be said that the Victorian total correctional intervention rate amounts to a classic case of net-widening, a proposition which has already been demonstrated in the context of attendance centre orders (Fox and Challinger, 1985). South Australia has apparently been able to avoid this, though only at the cost of embarking on an upward trend in its imprisonment rate.

This observation raises several questions. First, are there areas where the two States differ significantly in their treatment of offenders? If so, is the lesser use of imprisonment in Victoria symptomatic of greater credibility for its community-based corrections programmes?

Necessarily, the answers to such questions are somewhat speculative—judgmental rather than quantitative. This is inevitable, for sentencing and penology are human sciences, not abstract ones. As to the question of differing correctional dispositions, the available data suggest three things. First, Victoria is more likely to sentence sex offenders to community corrections orders of some kind than is South Australia. Second, Victoria is likewise far more likely to sentence burglars to community corrections than is South Australia. Third, the Victoria **remand** in custody rate is significantly lower than that of South Australia. These points all require elaboration.

As to sex offences, the Victorian recorded crime rate is about twice as high as that of South Australia (112:53), and the clear-up rate virtually identical (*Victoria Police Annual Report* 1985; South Australia Office of Crime Statis-

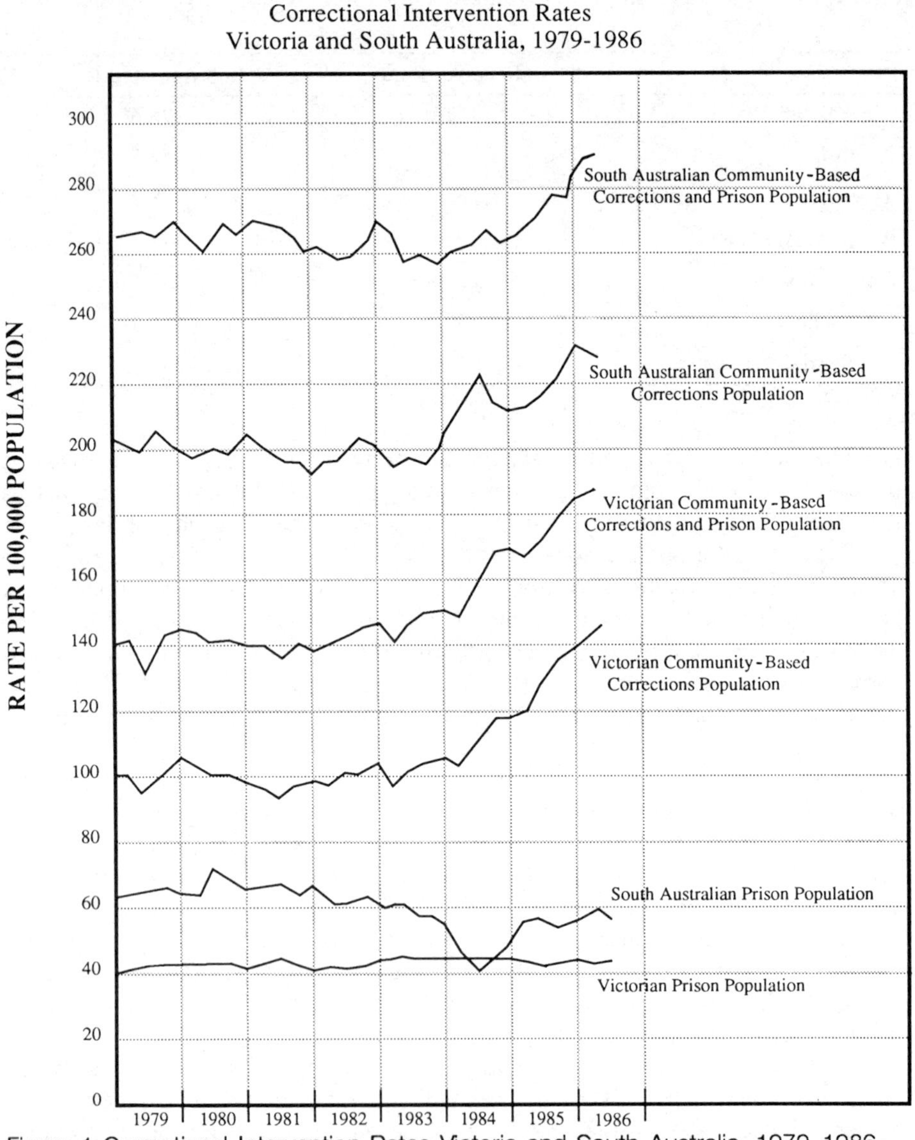

Figure 1 Correctional Intervention Rates Victoria and South Australia, 1979–1986

tics, 1986a. Note, however, that figures to be published by the Police Commissioners' Australian Crime Statistics Sub-Committee will show a slightly higher South Australian rate of sex offences, as against Victoria). Yet current correctional population figures show that in Victoria, 14 convicted sex offenders are serving community corrections sentences for every 10 serving prison sentences, whereas in South Australia the figure is 8 to 10 (Walker and Biles, 1985; Walker and Biles, forthcoming).

With regard to burglary, the sentencing differences are even more striking. Once more the recorded crime rates are comparable (1,890 in Victoria, 1,600 in South Australia) and clear-up rates virtually identical at about 12% (*Victoria Police Annual Report* 1985; South Australia Office of Crime Statistics, 1986). Yet Victoria has 25 burglars serving community corrections sentences for every 10 such offenders in prison, whilst South Australia has only 7 serving such sentences for every 10 in prison (Walker and Biles, 1985; Walker and Biles, forthcoming). Doubtless, several factors have contributed to this disparity. For example, it seems likely (though data are not available to verify this statistically) that the fact that summary jurisdiction in Victoria for property offences extends to situations involving up to $10,000 has tended to reduce sentences of imprisonment, both as to the number imposed and as to their length. Also, it may well be that the property crime/drug dependence link is recognized with some compassion by Victorian sentencers.

Regardless of these possibilities, however, the implications are significant. If Victoria sentenced sex offenders and burglars to imprisonment in the same proportions as South Australia, there would be something of the order of 445 extra prisoners in Victorian prisons. This would increase the current imprisonment rate per 100,000 by some 10.6; it would also mean that the occupancy rate as against rated capacity would be 119 rather than the present 97. Obversely, if South Australia sentenced these two classes of offenders in the same way as does Victoria, its prison population would be reduced by approximately 105—a reduction of 7.6 per 100,000. Consequently, occupancy rate as against rated capacity would have been about 97 rather than the present 110.

Thus, the current imprisonment rate disparities between Victoria and South Australia, and the consequential overcrowding of their prison systems, could be wholly attributed to different sentencing practices in relation to these two categories of convicted offender. Each offence is of a kind which attracts a high median sentence—somewhere in the 2–4 year range for burglary and the 5–9 year range for sex offences. Each, particularly sex offences, is regarded seriously by the community. In that context, it is remarkable that community corrections orders have been used in Victoria in the way that they have.

The other quantitative point that should be made about comparative imprisonment practices of the two States concerns remand in custody. The Victorian rate has in recent years consistently been lower than the South Australian one—something of the order of 5.0 per 100,000 as opposed to 13.0 (*Australian Prison Trends*). Yet in South Australia a far lower percentage (34% as against 55%) of those remanded in custody are subsequently sentenced to imprisonment than in Victoria, and a far higher percentage (24% as opposed to 9%) are sentenced to community corrections orders (Walker, 1985: 18). This would seem to indicate that the philosophy of "a taste of imprisonment" is still alive and well in South Australia (Walker, 1985: 19). One may wonder whether this is not in itself indicative of a lack of credibility in that State for community corrections orders—a supposition which is not necessarily inconsistent with the frequency of their imposition: see Figure 1 on the previous page. In summary, it is likely that the difference in patterns of remand in custody is not merely a technical matter—attributable, for example, to different bail legislation—but is in fact a further manifestation of a lesser commitment to and belief in community corrections as a mode of disposition for hard cases. This may particularly be the case in relation to poor or socially isolated offenders (Office of Crime Statistics (SA), 1986b: 13).

The Victorian Experience

How is it, then, that Victoria seems to have achieved and maintained greater credibility for its community corrections programmes amongst sentencers? To re-state the question in terms used previously, why is Victoria the anomalous or deviant case in terms of successful front-end mechanisms for keeping its imprisonment rate manageable? The answer requires a brief overview of recent correctional history in the State.

During the 1970s, community corrections had fallen into some disrepute, despite the dedication of those in charge. An acute structural defect had inexorably brought about this situation—namely that probation and parole were handled as part of a general social welfare function by the then Social Welfare Department and its successor, the Community Welfare Services Department. Field workers were predominantly trained social workers, lacking a correctional perspective. Apparently, it was not uncommon for a probationer's case never to be formally assigned to a field worker, a hiatus which when it came to judicial attention was the subject of trenchant comments. The classic pre-conditions existed for role confusion, poor performance and low morale (Mawby, 1981; Fielding, 1984; Vanstone and Seymour, 1986).

In 1975, the attendance centre scheme was commenced, followed in 1981 by the community service order scheme. Each had some real success and certainly possessed greater correctional credibility. Attendance centres were run by the same Division of the Department as was responsible for prisons; community service orders benefited from the generally positive image and performance which this new mode of correctional intervention had throughout Australia. However, a basic inequity characterized each of them, that their availability outside the Melborne metropolitan area was severely circumscribed.

Meanwhile, as Victoria entered the 1980s, an air of crisis began to surround the prison system. There were too many escapes, increasing numbers of allegations of misconduct by uniformed staff and, finally, strikes by prison officers. Such events are always symptomatic of low morale and confused objectives.

During 1983 planning was completed to set up a separate Office of Corrections, with comprehensive responsibility for prisons and community corrections (Neilson, 1983). On 1 February 1984, this was done. Commitments were made to construct new prisons, the emphasis being on upgrading or replacing sub-standard plant. The question of officer training was addressed, though conflicting objectives have produced administrative ambiguities which have yet to be resolved. (Harding, 1986).

On the community corrections side, staff were rapidly recruited in large numbers—146 in 1984–85, for example—thus enabling the process to be commenced of making facilities accessible throughout the State. The Office's recruitment policy was deliberately tailored to try to get away from the ''soft'' social welfare/social work perspective which had previously been so marked. Mature persons with a wide range of life experiences were targeted; formal qualifications were discounted somewhat to the point where a minority of new recruits were graduates. The aim has been to emphasize what a *correctional* programme is all about.

In tandem with these administrative changes and political commitments, substantial legislative refurbishing has occurred. The principal move was the passage of the Penalties and Sentences Act 1985. An important aim was to bring within a single Act all general provisions relating to the powers of the courts to impose sentences. No less important and innovative was the objective of bringing all existing community-based modes of disposition—probation, attendance centre orders, community service orders—under the single rubric of a community corrections order. All such orders are to carry core conditions. In addition, the sentencer may choose from amongst a melange of other available conditions, thus indicating the primary nature of the order in pre-1985 terms—for example, as probation or attendance or community service or as a shandy concoction of these possibilities. All such orders will henceforth be administered from a community corrections centre.

A key aspect of the whole scheme is the prompt availability to the sentencing court of advice by community corrections officers. An assessment can normally be made available within an hour or so, particularly in relation to offenders already known to the correctional system. Jerome Miller (1986: 239) has referred to the tyranny of ignorance in the sentencing process, pointing out that, whilst "there may have been a time when the weight of numbers and the lack of appropriate technology dictated that offenders be defined and assigned according to categories fixed in extremes," such a time should now be past. Victoria is attempting to utilize the information available about offenders so that sentencers can in truth individualize sentences on a rational basis. The courts will receive information not only about the suitability and antecedents of each offender but also about the availability of facilities and resources to implement a particular condition of an order. This is immensely important if community corrections are to be fully accepted by the courts.

This part of the Act came into operation on 1 June 1986. Obviously, it is premature to evaluate it. However, the Office of Corrections has initiated from the outset a comprehensive evaluation project, with funds made available by the Criminology Research Council. The main purpose of the evaluation will be to assess exactly what I have been addressing—the efficacy of community corrections as a front-end mechanism to limit prison populations (Henderson, forthcoming). One matter which will also certainly require evaluation is whether the mere fact of providing a greater menu without indicating a "sanction hierarchy" to sentencers is a workable strategy. Fox and Freiberg (1986) fear that "if diversity of choice without guidance is insisted upon, then its price will be disparity" (1986: 234).

Threats to Reform

The judiciary constitute one possible threat; politicians another.

As to the judiciary, their resistance to back-end mechanisms has already been mentioned. Under pressure, legislatures have curtailed the most overt forms of such mechanism. The temptation to increase head sentences and non-parole periods should not correspondingly be curtailed.

However, judicial discretion as to sentence length in any particular case remains wide. Sentencing "law" falls between two stools; it is "legal" enough to raise judicial territorial hackles, but not "legal" enough to be subject to full appellate review according to doctrinal principles. In this respect, the High Court's position has been particularly indefensible (Harding, 1984). The judiciary consequently remains the only public agency which is virtually unaccountable for decisions committing scarce and expensive public resources.

The time is long overdue for the adoption of sentencing guidelines in all Australian States. Principle, equity and rationality in sentencing would thereby be facilitated (Ashworth, 1986; Knapp, 1986). These are in no way irreconcilable with judicial autonomy.

As to politicians, they seem as a breed to find irresistible the temptation to make "law and order" slogans aspects of election campaigns. In this desire, they are richly assisted by the media, particularly in Australia where the quality of reporting about crime and criminal justice policy is generally abysmal, if not positively scurrilous.

In all Australian Parliaments, a mechanism exists—the Standing Parliamentary Committee—to enable complex and sensitive policy matters to be developed on a bi-partisan basis. Members of such Committees can quickly gain sufficient expertise to recognize false diagnoses and quick fixes for what they are. Some continuity can be injected into criminal justice policy development. That is not to say that genuine and profound value differences could, or should, be hidden from sight.

The time has come for a genuine attempt to be made to develop bi-partisan criminal justice policy in Australia. The nature of Australian politics does not make one too sanguine in expressing this hope. But it has happened elsewhere—for example, in the Netherlands—and it could happen here.

Discussion Questions

1. Why is prison crowding a problem in Australia? What points of convergence do you see between the reasons for prison crowding in Australia and the reasons for crowding in U.S. prisons?
2. Why should the economic and political conditions in a society have any bearing on the use of imprisonment and penal practices?
3. Harding outlines four effects of overcrowding in Australia's prisons. Compare and contrast these effects with the effects produced by overcrowding in U.S. prisons.
4. Given Harding's discussion of crowding reduction mechanisms, how do you think Australia should go about reducing the prison overcrowding problem? What should be done to reduce prison crowding in the U.S.?

5. Harding concludes his article by discussing how reforms, designed to relieve crowding, may be threatened. What threats to such reforms do you see in the U.S.?

References

Ashworth, A. (1986) "Criminal Justice, Rights and Sentencing: A Review of Sentencing Policy and Problems," Paper presented at a Conference at the Australian Institute of Criminology, Canberra, March 1986.

Australian Prison Trends, Nos. 1–122, Australian Institute of Criminology, Canberra.

Biles, D. (1982) "Crime and Imprisonment: An Australian Time Series Analysis," *Australian and New Zealand Journal of Criminology,* 15: 133.

Blumstein, A., *et alia* (1973) "A Theory of the Stability of Punishment," *Journal of Criminal Law and Criminology,* 64: 198.

———. (1977) "The Dynamics of a Homeostatic Punishment Process," *Journal of Criminal Law and Criminology,* 67: 317.

———.(1983) "The Influence of Capacity on Prison Population: A Critical Review of Some Recent Evidence," *Crime and Delinquency,* 29: 1.

Bowker, L. H. (1981) "Crime and the Use of Prisons in the United States: A Time Series Analysis," *Crime and Delinquency,* 27: 206.

Box, S. and Hale, C. (1982) "Economic Crisis and the Rising Prisoner Population in England," *Crime and Social Justice,* 17: 20.

Chan, J. (1986) "Federal Offenders: The Search for Statistical Data," ALRO Working Paper, August 1986.

Chan, J. and Zdenkowski, G. (1986) "Just Alternatives: Trends and Issues in the Deinstitutionalization of Punishment," *Australian and New Zealand Journal of Criminology,* 19: 67–90 and 131–54.

Criminal Justice Newsletter (1985) "California Speeds Construction as Prison Crowding Tops 165%," 1 November 1985.

———.(1986a) "Prison Population at All-time High, Passes Half Million Mark," 1 July 1986.

———.(1986b) "Overcrowding Crisis Forcing Extreme Measures in DC," 1 April 1986.

Dawes, J. and Morgan, F. (1986) "Sentencing: Reflections of an Innkeeper," Paper presented at a Conference at the Australian Institute of Criminology, Canberra, March 1986.

DeWitt, C. B. (1986) *New Construction Methods for Correctional Facilities,* National Institute of Justice, Washington, DC.

Downes, D. (1982) "The Origins and Consequences of Dutch Penal Policy since 1945: A Preliminary Analysis," *British Journal of Criminology,* 22: 325.

Fielding, N. (1984) *Probation Practice—Client Support under Social Control,* Florida Parole and Probation Commission, USA.

Fox, R. and Challinger, D. (1985) "Victorian Attendance Centre Orders: An Alternative to Prison?" *Criminal Law Journal,* 9: 3.

Fox, R. and Freiberg, A. (1985) *Sentencing: State and Federal Law in Victoria,* Oxford University Press, Melbourne.

———.(1986) "Sentencing Structures and Sanctioning Hierarchies," *Criminal Law Journal,* 10–216.

Gottfredson, S. D. and Taylor, R. B. (1983) *The Correctional Crisis: Prison Populations and Public Policy,* National Institute of Justice, Washington, DC.

Greenberg, D. F. (1977) "The Dynamics of Oscillatory Punishment Processes," *Journal of Criminal Law and Criminology,* 68: 643.

Harding, R. W. (1984) "Penal Reform," Paper presented to the 6th National Conference of Labor Lawyers.

———.(1986) *Report of the Review of the Objectives and Operational Programs of the Office of Corrections Staff Training College (Victoria),* Office of Corrections, Melbourne.

Henderson, M. (forthcoming) *Evaluating Diversionary Impact of Community-Based Corrections,* Office of Corrections, Melbourne.

Jankovic, I. (1977) "Labour Market and Imprisonment," *Social Justice,* 8: 17.

Knapp, K. (1986) "Discretion in Sentencing," Paper presented at a Conference at the Australian Institute of Criminology, Canberra, March 1986.

Kelleher, M. (1986) "Federal and Australian Capital Territory Offenders: The Future of the Current Laws and Practices," Paper presented at the Australian Institute of Criminology, March 1986.

Mawby, R. I. (1981) *Probation Officers' Views of Probation,* University of Leeds Centre for Social Work, UK.
Miller, J. G. (1986) "Sentencing: What Lies between Sentiment and Ignorance?" *Justice Quarterly,* 3: 231.
Mukherjee, S. K. (1984) "Trends in Women's Imprisonment," in Hatty, S. (ed.), *Women in the Prison System,* Australian Institute of Criminology, Canberra.
Neilson Associates (1983) *Corrections Master Plan, Victoria,* Office of Corrections, Melbourne.
Rutherford, A. (1986) "The Prison System's Expansionist Scenario," *Prison Service Journal,* 4.
South Australia Office of Crime Statistics (1986a) *Crime and Justice in South Australia,* Report No. 14, Department of the Attorney-General, Adelaide.
South Australia Office of Crime Statistics (1986b) *Bail Reform in South Australia,* Department of the Attorney-General, Adelaide.
Tulkens, H. (1979) *Some Developments in Penal Policy and Practice in Holland,* NACRO, London.
United Nations (1986) *Report of the Proceedings of the Seventh United Nations Congress on the Prevention of Crime and the Treatment of Offenders,* New York.
Vanstone, M. and Seymour, B. (1986) "Probation Service Objectives and the Neglected Ingredients," *Probation Journal,* 33: 43.
Walker, J. (1985) *The Outcomes of Remand in Custody Orders,* Australian Institute of Criminology, Canberra.
Walker, J. and Biles, D. (1983a) *Australian Prisoners 1982,* Australian Institute of Criminology, Canberra.
———.(1983b) *Australian Prisoners 1983,* Australian Institute of Criminology, Canberra.
———.(1985) *Australian Prisoners 1984,* Australian Institute of Criminology, Canberra.
———.(1986) *Australian Prisoners 1985,* Australian Institute of Criminology,Canberra.
———.(forthcoming) *Australian Community-Based Corrections 1985,* Australian Institute of Criminology, Canberra.
Wallace, D. (1981) "The Political Economy of Incarceration Trends in late US Capitalism: 1971–77," *The Insurgent Sociologist,* 10: 59.
Weatherburn, D. (1985) "Appellate Review, Judicial Discretion and the Determination of Minimum Periods," *Australian and New Zealand Journal of Criminology,* 18: 272.
———.(1986) "Reducing the NSW Prison Population: Sentencing Reform and Early Release," *Criminal Law Journal,* 10: 119.
Wilkins, L. (1984) *Consumerist Criminology,* Heinemann, London.
Wilson, P. R. (forthcoming) *How the Public Sees Sentencing,* Australian Institute of Criminology, Canberra.
Worrall, A. and Pease, K. (1986) "The Prison Population in 1985," *British Journal of Criminology,* 26: 184.
Yeager, M. J. (1979) "Unemployment and Imprisonment," *Journal of Criminal Law and Criminology,* 70: 586.
Young, W. (1986) "Influence upon the Use of Imprisonment: A Review of the Literature," *Howard Journal,* 25: 125.

14. Crime Policy in Denmark: How We Managed to Reduce the Prison Population

H. H. Brydensholt, General Director, Prison and Probation Administration, Denmark

Abstract: Fluctuations in Denmark's crime rates over the past two decades correspond with major social changes—the rapid spread of industrialization in the late 1950s, the rise in drug use among youths in the 1960s, and the increased unemployment in the 1970s. Despite the rapid increase in criminal activity in the 1960s, the prison population remained stable until early in the present decade. Since 1973, changes in Danish penal laws—the adoption of fixed sentences, the "depenalization" of minor property crimes, as well as the merging of probation and prison administration under a single system—have successfully stemmed the increasing flow of offenders into the prisons. Further efforts at decreasing the number of prison inmates through criminal justice policy change are being considered. However, it is clear that reducing crime itself is an objective that is contingent on more far-reaching social reform.

The Goals of the Criminal Justice System

The Norwegian government's white paper on crime policy, which was published in 1978, stated that the goals of the criminal justice system could be defined as (1) combating crime, while (2) complying with fundamental principles of justice and humanity and (3) maintaining a balance between the cost of criminal justice policy and the benefits to society of that policy.

Although they do not all provide the same definitive statement of their goals, the Scandinavian countries, it is fair to say, do have the same objectives in criminal justice. And, I would guess, these objectives are shared by other countries as well.

With regard to the first goal, we have not been very successful so far. As in other Western industrialized nations, our level of crime has increased. In the last part of this article, I will return to the issue of what should be done about criminality. It is important, however, to stress immediately that while Denmark's depenalization policy, which has been developed over the last decade, has had goals in addition to that of reducing crime, a more lenient crime policy does not necessarily run counter to this fundamental objective. If anything, it seems that a more lenient—and more flexible—penal policy affords more genuine possibilities for avoiding an outbreak of serious crimes than does a stricter system.[1]

---

1. Ulla Bondeson, *Kriminalvård i Frihed* [Criminal Care in Liberty] (Stockholm, Sweden, 1977); Norman Bishop, "Beware of Treatment," in *Some Developments in Nordic Criminal Policy and Criminology,* Scandinavian Research Council on Criminology (Norrköping, Sweden: Kriminålvardsstryrelsen, 1975); and Britta Kyvsgaard, *Straffesystemets Virkning* [The Effect of Punishment], mimeo. (Copenhagen, Denmark, 1978).

Criminality in Denmark

After a peak in criminality during the Second World War, we experienced a relatively stable period in the 1950s. The number of offenses against the penal code reported each year (excluding such minor offenses as traffic violations) was approximately 125,000. However, in the late 1950s and 1960s, Denmark, like other Western nations, saw a tremendous increase in crime rates. This growth in crime was especially rapid during the last part of the 1960s, with the rate of reported crimes rising by 1970 to 300,000. From 1970 to 1974, crime continued to increase, but at a slower rate, reaching 325,000 reported offenses in 1974. During 1975 and 1976 we saw an unexpected but not unwelcome drop in crimes reported per year, to less than 280,000. In 1977 and 1978, crime again increased—to 310,000 reported offenses in 1977 and 340,000 in 1978.

The type of crime accounting for the greatest proportion of these figures is, as in the other Scandinavian countries, offenses against property. Sexual offenses comprise only about one percent of the total number, and violence is a part of less than two percent of the reported crimes. Each year, there occur between 30 and 40 murders among Denmark's over 5 million inhabitants, the majority involving people who know one another. This compares favorably with the number of deaths by traffic accident, which has reached a yearly figure of 800. If the murder rate in the United States were the same as that in Denmark, the number of homicide victims would be about 1,600, instead of 20,000.

What accounts for the changes in criminal activity in Denmark? One thing seems obvious: Crime has something to do with the conditions in which people live. It is impossible to believe that entire generations are biologically different from one another. Rather, the dramatic changes in the level of criminality must be related to citizens' (particularly young males') position in our society. While no one has isolated the causes of the fluctuations in crime levels, and no one believes that simple explanations will cover the entire question, noticeable changes in crime trends can be seen to correspond with major changes in Danish society that occurred around 1958, 1966, 1974, and 1977.

In 1958, with the election of a new government in Denmark, the period of what is called the second industrialization began. During the late 1950s and early 1960s a majority of the farm workers went from the rural areas to the towns, leaving less than 10 percent of the working population occupied in farming. Drug use among youngsters began in Denmark around 1966. The pressing need of drug users for immediate cash could, to some extent, explain the rapid increase in theft and burglaries in the mid-1960s. Moreover, drug use was only one side of the new youth culture, which accepted none of the social norms without question. It is not surprising that respect for other people's property would decrease.

The energy crisis in 1974 meant that for the first time in many years there was a high rate of unemployment, especially among youngsters. One reading the textbooks on crime would expect widespread unemployment to result in an increasing number of criminals. Yet we saw a noticeable fall in criminality. It has been suggested that this decline can be attributed more to a slowdown in crime by recidivists than to a decreased number of new offenders.

Several explanations for this curtailment of crime among ex-offenders have been offered. First, the decrease in crime may be a result of Denmark's policy of providing unemployment insurance. Danish citizens who are forced into unemployment receive about 90 percent of a "normal" income as unemployment compensation. Ex-offenders, who often have difficulty holding jobs, will not be offered jobs for a longer period and thus be able to continue to collect their high unemployment payments. If jobs were available, they would be transferred quickly by the employment authorities to the general social welfare system, where they would receive only about half what is considered a normal wage. According to this explanation, society paid criminals so well that they stopped their criminality. A second explanation attributes the fall in crime to a process of destigmatization. While the person who is out of work in a society with full employment may be severely stigmatized, if many ordinary citizens are forced to be unemployed, the ex-offender's status automatically rises.

But what is the explanation, then, for the upturn in crime two years later? Many youngsters in Denmark remain unemployed, so why has the crime situation changed?

Perhaps this is a result of the large number of youngsters entering into criminality for the first time. It may well be that many youths are bored with forced inactivity and thus are easily attracted to any offer of excitement. If this is true, it indicates a very dangerous situation. There will be no more important crime prevention measure in the next years than to secure work for these youngsters.

The Decrease in the Prison Population

The prison population remained amazingly stable through the 1960s, even while criminality was growing rapidly.[2] Although crime figures more than doubled during the 1960s, the daily prison population remained at about 3,500. However, the early 1970s brought an increasing number of inmates. We were in the situation of either having to secure more prison space or to change our criminal law so that imprisonment was used less frequently.

When the prison population was at about 3,500, this figure could be divided as follows: 800 persons were being held in custody before trial, 500 were serving a short, fixed term of imprisonment (called "*haefte*") often used for minor offenders (especially drunk drivers), 300 were serving indeterminate or "semideterminate" sentences (most of these inmates were youths serving a specific semideterminate sentence called "youth prison," lasting between one and four years), and about 1,900 were serving fixed prison sentences.

About 30,000 people pass through the prison system each year, a large proportion of them being persons held for short periods in the local jails who later receive a sanction which does not involve deprivation of liberty. In addition, there is a high turnover of drunk drivers, who normally receive ten to thirty days of *haefte*.

---

2. Nils Christie, *Hvor Tett et Samfunn?* [How Close a Society?] (Copenhagen, Denmark; Oslo, Norway; 1975).

In 1973, when the prison population was rising, Danish penal law was changed in several fundamental respects. We eliminated the indeterminate and semideterminate sanctions. Today a judgment involving deprivation of freedom is nearly always a fixed sentence. Use of indeterminate sanctions had been shown to result in prolonged periods of incarceration—periods disproportionate to the offense committed. Moreover, neither indeterminate nor semideterminate sanctions resulted in significantly lower rates of recidivism than did fixed periods of incarceration.[3]

This was an important change. But the "depenalization" law passed simultaneously was even more significant. Under this reform, the relatively minor property crimes were handled more leniently. More people were placed on probation. Shorter sentences were given to property offenders: The maximum sentence for first-time property offenders, including burglars, was lowered from two years to one and one-half years, and repeat offenders now face two and one-half instead of three years of incarceration.

Part of this law reform was a major administrative change. Until 1973, the probation administration was a publicly funded, separate organization in the criminal justice system. With fewer people being incarcerated and more placed on probation in the community, it was necessary to transfer some of the resources from the penal institutions to probation. Such a transfer could only be accomplished if the responsibility were placed under the same management as the prison system.

The penal policy in Denmark has been a success in decreasing the prison population. The daily average number of persons incarcerated has dropped from 3,500 to 3,000. We now have 700 persons in custody before trial, 500 serving brief, fixed sentences, and 1,800 serving prison sentences.

Why Do We Wish Fewer People in Prison?

In a report on alternatives to imprisonment which was published in 1977, we find in the introductory remarks a summary of some of the viewpoints which have governed the diminishing role of incarceration in the Danish penal system.[4]

First there are general humanitarian concerns. Incarceration is difficult to tolerate. The harm caused by confinement often extends beyond the deprivation of liberty itself to broken family life, loss of work, and stigmatization. While presumably the deprivation of freedom has always been a harsh punishment, the ill effects of incarceration appear more pronounced today. Perhaps this is because there is a more common understanding of the criminal's situation. In addition, compared with previous conditions, the society from which the inmate is excluded has more to offer—in terms of more spare time, better working conditions, and more material welfare. It can be argued that exclusion from society today is a greater punishment than was true in the past.

3. Karl O. Christiansen et al., *Effektiviteten af Forvaring og Soefoengsel* [The Effectiveness of Indeterminate Compared with Determinate Punishment] (Copenhagen, Denmark, 1972).
4. *Alternativer til Frihedsstraf—et Debatoplaeg* [Alternatives to Deprivation of Liberty—Information for the Debate] (Copenhagen, Denmark, 1977).

Another part of the debate has focused on the effectiveness of incarceration as a penal measure. Deterrence has long been regarded as an important goal of punishment. But opposed to the belief that offenders are deterred from future criminal activity by temporary incapacitation is recent research focusing on inmates' personalities. The findings here do not support deprivation of freedom as a suitable means of resocialization; on the contrary, it seems that deprivation of freedom more often strengthens feelings of insecurity, apathy, and aggressiveness toward the community, damages further the inmate's self-respect, and promotes identification with those who display patterns of criminal behavior.[5] Studies of recidivism also indicate that deprivation of freedom is less effective than other forms of punishment in preventing repeated offending.[6] Even if the methodological problems apparent in the research to date force us to view the results with certain reservations, it is important to note that no research has yet been able to show that deprivation of freedom is more effective in preventing recidivism than are other penal measures.

A third reason for reassessment of the role of incarceration is that offenses against property, which dominate the Danish crime statistics, are looked upon today differently than was the case in the past. The general growth in wealth and the prevalence of theft insurance mean that this offense is not as burdensome for the victim as in previous years. Consequently, offenses against property are seen as not necessarily requiring such serious sanctions. Incarceration can be resorted to less often.

Finally, it has been argued that incarceration is a costly measure. In Denmark, it costs about $90 million per year to run the prisons.

These arguments are not in themselves decisive. Deprivation of freedom normally prevents the offender from committing new offenses during the period of incarceration. This effect should not be ignored. Even if it is difficult to prove that deprivation of liberty does have a general deterrent effect, this severe sanction may be decisive in establishing the authority of the criminal justice system—an important condition for maintaining a general law-abiding attitude among members of society. Incarceration is sometimes a necessary means for society to express its sincere disapproval of a criminal act. This is particularly true in a country that does not have—and does not wish to have—capital punishment.

Thus, Denmark's depenalization policy is not a matter of abolishing the use of incarceration. It is a matter of using incarceration more carefully, for shorter periods. Probably the best argument for our depenalization policy is to envision the situation we would have had if we had not set about reforming the penal system.

In the beginning of the 1970s, the number of prisoners in England and that in Denmark were comparable. England, with its 50 million inhabitants, had about 35,000 persons incarcerated, whereas Denmark, with about 5 million inhabitants, had approximately 3,500 inmates. England did not depenalize; if any-

5. Ulla Bondeson, *Fången i Fangsamhället* [The Prisoner in the Prison Community] (Stockholm, Sweden, 1974).
6. Bishop, "Beware of Treatment."

thing, the sentences became longer. The result is that they now have more than 42,000 prisoners and severe problems in the prison system. The policy in Denmark has made it possible during the same period to regulate the prison population and conditions and to transfer resources from the institutions to the probation service. This has enabled us to intensify our work with offenders at an earlier stage.

The End of the Depenalization Period—and Then What?

Denmark, like the other Scandinavian countries, is still in the process of depenalization. Committees reviewing policies in all these countries recommend further depenalization—a criminal justice system with fewer incarcerated.

In order to comply with these recommendations, sentences could be shortened still more. This could be done either by more lenient judgments by the courts or by earlier release of inmates. In Denmark, we are presently discussing whether inmates might be released after having served one-half of their sentences rather than waiting until they have served two-thirds of their terms, as is now the case. New alternatives to incarceration are also being discussed, such as community service, which is not yet used in any of the Scandinavian countries.

The consequence of the suggestions under debate in Denmark would be a further reduction in the daily prison population, from approximately 3,000 to about 2,500 inmates.

As was mentioned at the beginning of this paper, we have not been successful in achieving the main goal of criminal justice, namely, to reduce crime. One can foresee that a crime policy which is able to meet only part of the goals of criminal justice cannot continue. It may be that we will achieve our goals only by looking outside the criminal justice system for the answers.

The declining birth rate today indicates that the number of youngsters in the most crime-prone years will drop by the 1980s. We may expect that the decreased birth rate will mean more employment opportunities, although this is difficult to predict with certainty. In the meantime, it is crucial that our school systems, our social welfare system, and our communities work to involve youngsters in our society. The criminal justice system must be able to participate in that effort.

In Denmark we created some ten years ago a central crime prevention board, where public officials joined with representatives from the private sector to create crime prevention programs. Initially, this board was most concerned with what is called target hardening, to stem the rising number of property crimes. Now, however, the interest has broadened, and the board is working to stimulate planning in the local communities. The board follows with great interest town planning and its impact on criminal activity. The idea of considering crime prevention when we develop our towns is relatively new.

There is also the recent development of what are called "anti-institutions," a type of living collective housing both staff and their "clients." These seem to be particularly successful with comparatively difficult clients.

Finally, it should be mentioned that we are trying to link the criminal justice system and labor organizations. In some ways this is probably more difficult in a country like Denmark, which depends on a national social welfare system, than it would be in a country like the United States, where private enterprise is still very important in maintaining the standard of living. We believed too long that our criminal justice and other social problems would be solved by hiring expertise. We ought to have learned sooner that it would not be possible to solve those serious problems without involving the public. A country like the United States has an advantage in this respect that we lack—namely, the survival of the citizens' willingness to volunteer. We still have much to learn about that.

Discussion Questions

1. How does the way a country conceptualizes crime theoretically affect the way the country's criminal justice system reacts to offenders? Consider the similarities and differences between the theoretical explanations for fluctuations in Danish crime rates, as advanced by Brydensholt, and explanations that are commonly offered to account for crime in the U.S. Might differences in theoretical conceptualizations of crime lead to differences in penal policies?
2. What aspects of Danish crime policy could be applied to reduce U.S. prison populations (e.g., would you favor shorter fixed sentences; what offenses, if any, would you consider depenalizing; etc.)? Could Denmark gain any benefits by adopting certain aspects of U.S. penal policy? Explain.
3. Is it reasonable to think that the reforms implemented to reduce the Danish prison population could be replicated in the U.S., given the higher rate of crime (particularly violent crime) in the U.S.? Why or why not?
4. Toward the end of his article Brydensholt poses and answers the question of why the Danes wish fewer people in prison. In view of recent U.S. incarceration trends, it is appropriate to ask why U.S. citizens wish more people in prison. How would you answer this?
5. Does (can) a society's prison policy have any noteworthy effect on the society's general level of criminal activity? If so, what kind of prison policy might result in a reduced crime rate? If not, what other social policies would you suggest for reducing crime?

15. The Dutch Deemphasize Imprisonment: Sociocultural and Structural Explanations

Elmer H. Johnson
Southern Illinois University
Alfred Heijder
Procurator-General, Court of Appeal, The Hague

Abstract: The low imprisonment rate of The Netherlands is attributed to a combination of Dutch cultural values and social and political developments since World War II. Police and, especially, prosecutorial discretion are basic to administrative expression of Dutch preference that imprisonment be avoided when possible. However, significant increase in the imprisonment rate has followed a fivefold rise in the crimes known to the police. Future prospects for deemphasized imprisonment are examined.

Advocates of community alternatives to penal confinement have been particularly fascinated by the Dutch reluctance to send convicted criminals to prison. This paper will explore the sociocultural and structural factors that contribute to the reluctance. The Netherlands continues to have the lowest imprisonment rate among urbanized nations, even though the Dutch rate has begun to increase in recent years. Then, a key question is whether the persistent and significant rise of the Dutch crime rate will ultimately persuade the people of The Netherlands that greater reliance must be placed on imprisonment. The paper will conclude with an assessment of this issue.

The fundamental premise here is that the sociocultural system is basic to understanding any society's responses to crime, even when a remarkable increase in the prevalence of criminality is being experienced. The effects of the particular sociocultural system are mirrored by the administrative patterns of criminal justice agencies. The remarkably low imprisonment rate is attributable to three administrative patterns. First, a major portion of arrested persons are diverted prior to trial out of further criminal justice processing. The functions of public prosecutors are crucial in this regard. Second, of those offenders who are tried and convicted, less than two of ten are sent to prison. The majority are given fines. Third, among the relatively few sent to prison, only a very few are given terms of a year or more.

From Elmer H. Johnson and Alfred Heijder, "The Dutch Deemphasize Imprisonment: Sociocultural and Structural Explanations" in *International Journal of Comparative and Applied Criminal Justice.* (7(1): 3–19, Spring 1983).

Table 1 Crude Crime Rates, Percent of Crimes Cleared by Police, and Percent of Crimes Referred to Public Prosecutor for Selected Years: The Netherlands

Year	Crimes Known to Police per 1,000 Population	Percent of Crimes Cleared by Police (A)	Percent of Crimes Referred to Public Prosecutor (B)	Referral Ratio (B Divided by A)
1960	1093.2	57.0	53.4	93.7
1965	1345.6	51.5	45.7	88.8
1970	2023.1	40.7	37.1	91.2
1975	3301.8	32.6	26.7	82.1
1980	4943.6	29.3	25.2	86.0

Responses to Rising Criminality

When measured by crimes known to the police, the incidence of criminality has consistently risen in the last twenty years (see Table 1). The crime rate per 100,000 persons in Holland has increased almost fivefold. Further, gain has been consistent and without fluctuation when each of the years in this period is considered. However, the full impact has not been felt by the public prosecutors because the percentage of crimes cleared by the police has significantly declined. That trend has been quite consistent for the specific years, with only minor breaks in the pattern.

It is to be expected that not all crimes cleared by the police would be turned over to the public prosecutor, but the Dutch data indicate referrals are usual. Of the crimes known to the police, 53 percent were referred to the public prosecutor, compared with 57 percent of those crimes cleared by the police. The referrals also show a decline proportionately with a highly, but not completely, consistent year-by-year trend (Table 1). Are the referrals less likely as the crime rate increases? The referral ratio indicates a rough tendency in that direction, but the referrals continue to compare well with police clearance rates over the decades of the increase in criminality.

The public prosecutor has unlimited power to waive prosecution, either conditionally or unconditionally. If prosecution is undertaken, the prosecutor has the choice of sending the case either to full-chamber district courts (three-judge courts) or to single-judge chambers (police magistrates). The police magistrates, unlike English magistrates or "examining judges," are the same as the judges in the district courts who rotate as police magistrates. The police magistrates are legally competent for all cases, as with district courts, but they can only impose imprisonment of less than six months. Because the Code of Penal Procedure authorizes referral of all cases without complications in presenting evidence, the police magistrates offer a ready means of dealing with the bulk of the courts' work.

The majority of dispositions are either by the police magistrates or by the prosecutor's waiver, ranging from 83 percent in 1960 to 92 percent in 1980

Table 2 Distribution of Dispositions by Type of Court and by Waiver by Public Prosecutor for Selected Years: The Netherlands

Year	Three-Judge Courts	Police Magistrates	Juvenile Judges	Prosecution Waived by Public Prosecutor
1960	10.7	48.1	6.7	34.5
1965	9.9	45.8	7.2	37.1
1970	8.3	42.5	6.6	42.6
1975	6.3	44.4	6.2	43.1

Source: Netherlands Central Bureau of Statistics, *Statistical Yearbook of The Netherlands, 1981*, The Hague, 1982.

(Table 2). The percentage has increased consistently over the decades. More significantly, the waivers of prosecution have represented an increasing share of total dispositions over the decades of rising crime rates. The year-by-year trends have been a general but erratic decline in the share of police magistrate dispositions and a more consistent increase in the share of the prosecutor's waivers. The conclusion is that the increase in the judicial workload, because of more criminal cases referred to the prosecutors, has produced greater reliance on the prosecutor's waivers.

What has been the net effect of those administrative patterns of disposition on the imprisonment rate? The responses to higher criminality have been to increase even more the heavy emphasis on fines and to place decreasing reliance on imprisonment proportionally. The absolute number of prison sentences increased 29 percent from 1965 to 1981, but the characteristic avoidance of incarceration has persisted.

In 1970, only 19 percent of the total sentences involved imprisonment, but by 1981 only 15 percent were unconditional imprisonment (Table 3). In the intervening years, the trend was erratic but generally downward, especially in the years 1971–1980. Meanwhile, fines have followed a converse trend of increasing proportional importance. In 1970, fines held 66 percent of total sentences but 72.2 percent in 1981.

In spite of the persistent avoidance of imprisonment, the growing crime rate has raised the gross imprisonment rate as a consequence of the increased intake at the prosecutor's level (Table 4). The rate was 15.27 in 1965 and 24.54 in 1981. Except for 1978 and 1979 the pattern of growth was consistent.

The policy of imposing short prison sentences helps reduce Holland's imprisonment rate because fewer inmates are present at a given moment to be counted in prisoner sentences. Other nations following a policy of long prison sentences will accumulate a greater number of inmates over a given time, even if the number of prison admissions were the same as The Netherlands.

Table 3 Distribution of Sentences by Type, 1970–1981: The Netherlands

		Percentage Distribution			
Year*	Total Sentences	Unconditional Imprisonment	Partly Conditional	Conditional Sentences	Fines
1970	43,894	19.1	10.4	4.5	66.0
1971	44,832	21.0	10.6	4.6	63.0
1972	45,986	20.9	10.3	4.7	64.1
1973	45,941	19.9	10.1	5.0	65.0
1974	46,345	19.6	9.7	4.5	66.2
1975	51,501	19.2	8.9	4.9	67.0
1977	55,721	17.2	9.2	3.8	69.8
1978	66,897	15.4	7.9	3.6	73.1
1979	67,141	14.3	8.1	3.4	74.2
1980	72,712	13.8	8.6	3.4	74.2
1981	75,209	14.8	9.2	3.8	72.2

*1976 data not available.
Source: *Public Report of the Public Prosecutors for the Year 1981*, The Hague, 1982.

Table 4 Dutch Prison Population and Imprisonment Rates for Selected Years*

December 31 of Given Year	Number of Inmates Present	Gross Imprisonment Rate per 10,000 Population**
1965	1,877	15.27
1970	2,410	18.69
1975	2,645	19.45
1977	2,913	21.11
1978	2,738	19.70
1979	2,891	20.65
1980	3,235	22.92
1981	3,465	24.54

*1976 data not available.
**The term "gross" is used to indicate that the data includes pretrial detention, but criminals in mental hospitals are not included.
Source: Netherlands Central Bureau of Statistics, *Statistical Yearbook of The Netherlands, 1981*, The Hague, 1982.

Table 5 Length of Prison Sentences, 1970–1981: The Netherlands

		Percentage Distribution of Sentences by Length		
Year*	Total Prison Sentences	Less Than Six Months	6 to 12 Months	One Year Or More
1970	8,407	90.0	7.4	2.6
1971	9,409	88.6	8.3	3.0
1972	9,613	89.5	7.4	3.1
1973	9,165	90.2	6.8	3.0
1974	9,097	89.7	6.7	3.7
1975	9,925	88.8	6.9	4.3
1977	9,767	88.3	5.0	6.7
1978	10,306	87.4	5.4	7.1
1979	9,571	86.1	5.3	8.5
1980	10,062	85.6	6.0	8.4
1981	11,142	83.7	6.6	9.7

*1976 data not available.
Source: *Public Report of the Public Prosecutors for the Year 1981*, The Hague, 1982.

The distribution of Dutch prison sentences by length is heavily tilted toward sentences of less than six months (Table 5). In 1970, 90 percent were for less than six months and only 2.6 percent were for a year or more. However, the trend since then has been towards less but still dominant representation of the short sentences and greater representation of sentences of a year or more. That change has been especially marked since 1975. Data not presented here for lack of space indicate that the most noteworthy development in recent years has been a significant increase in the relative importance of sentences of one to five years. For sentences of less than six months, there has been a modest shift toward sentences of one to three months and away from sentences of one month. Holland is losing some of the benefits of the emphasis on short sentences for maintaining a low imprisonment rate.

Parenthetically, The Netherlands imposed a life sentence in 1977 as a noteworthy exception. A Dutch war criminal had been seized in the previous year. After his trial, the need for psychiatric treatment was determined, and he was placed in a state mental hospital. After escaping from the hospital, he threw himself in front of a train and was killed instantly.

Tolerance Grounded in Pragmatism

At first glance, "tolerance" appears to explain the low imprisonment rate, but the word is subject to too many interpretations to be informative. It frequently conveys the notion of "Christian duty," a humanitarian concern for the other fellow in the spirit of "I am my brother's keeper," but this sentiment is found among other peoples and has also stimulated a form of paternalism that has been among the motives for building prisons. Further, generalized tolerance would have to have a long cultural heritage and does not account for the decreased use of imprisonment in The Netherlands after World War II.

The central thesis of this paper is that the decreased use of imprisonment has been the product of a combination of social and political developments that capitalized on pre-existing elements in Dutch culture favorable to the withholding of criminal sanctions. Post-World War II conditions were favorable to the release of the pre-existing cultural elements. The overall outcome was stimulated by basic changes in the Dutch social structure in this century. The effects of these changes on the structure of the criminal justice system are fundamental for explaining the decreased use of imprisonment.

Thus, forbearance is an expression of the general Dutch sociocultural system, rather than an expression of a particular humanitarian concern for lawbreakers. The psychology of Dutch tolerance is pragmatic in its unwillingness to invest financially in the crime control policy, its doubts that imprisonment is cost effective, and that use of alternatives to arrest in management of conflicts is simply "good business." Moral judgments are considered to be of secondary importance in applying criminal sanctions. These attitudes are significant because they are particularly characteristic of contemporary Dutch prosecutors who occupy a strategic position in the structure of legal decision making (Rosett, 1972). A public prosecutor said:

> I am not judging about good or bad. The decisions have nothing to do with moral standards. I just want to stop someone from bothering another person. As prosecutors, we try to make the atmosphere so everyone can live free and walk freely without being bothered by others. We simply are not used to giving a prison term for someone caught for the first time, except for important offenses. Just a theft is not to be punished by an unconditional prison term.

Culturally, the Dutch prefer to see themselves as good people, willing to experiment, experienced in governing themselves since the sixteenth century, committed to softening socioeconomic distinctions adverse to the underprivileged, holding basic trust in one another, and prepared to bargain with one another when there are disagreements. Holland is a small but densely populated country with a history of struggle against the sea, of a combination of individualism and community responsibility, of a long-standing defense of liberties, and of defenses against invasions from Spain, France and Nazi Germany. Yet the Dutch have a religious and political tolerance that has welcomed dissenters and given the Reformed Church and the Roman Catholic Church significant roles in providing social services and political leaders.

The relatively low crime rate and the capacity to withhold criminal sanctions have much to do with the distribution of personal wealth through heavy inheritance taxes, progressive income taxes, and a substantial program to provide resources for meeting personal socioeconomic crises. Conrad (1970: 113) believes that the "careful organization of a welfare culture" has been necessary because of the high population density; social planning and prosperity have achieved "irrefutable success in crime and delinquency."

For these reasons, the citizens are not inclined to see one another as a threat which otherwise would stimulate demands for more severe punishment (d'Anjou et al., 1978). They are likely to seek some compromise when there is a conflict, because the pragmatism they have developed as a trading people favors accommodations. It is "good business" to tolerate differences among people.

Holland is a stable, effective, and legitimate democracy, Lijphart (1975: 124–148) says, in spite of deep religious and class cleavages, because of "a politics of accommodation" that follows several principles. Politics is not regarded as a game of delay and equivocation; rather, the traditions of a merchant nation are that doctrinal disputes should not stand in the way of getting "the job" done. Because, as in politics at the international level, consensus is neither strong nor extensive, ideological differences are accepted as basic realities; but they must not be resolved simply by overriding minority interests. Crucial issues are to be solved at the summit level by the leaders of the political blocs who are shielded from publicity during negotiations with the final stage of the accommodation process worked out publicly. The Dutch tend to accord greater latitude to their leaders under the strong belief that the general interest should have priority over the special interest of one's own bloc. The "government," which refers primarily to the cabinet, must do the job of government, and the parties in parliament should allow them to do so without undue harassment.

Socio-Political Changes and Policy

It was on these sociocultural foundations that the movement towards lower rates of imprisonment began after World War II. For about a year after liberation, conditions were most unusual, but by 1947 Dutch society had returned to what it had been, as though there had not been a war. In the period 1918 to 1966, only World War II had broken a period of stability in which it was exceptional for a person to experience a significant change in social status. Because people felt safe and most of the Dutch press does not sensationalize crimes and criminal proceedings, the Ministry was not unduly pressed to protect citizens from criminals. In fact, the setting of criminal justice policy operates largely detached from public monitoring.

The research of a Dutch sociologist (ter Hoeven, 1976) indicates that a small professional elite, with a fringe of complementary groups, dominates practice in the field of criminal justice. Shared training, positions, norms, and values provide an effective boundary maintaining system that shields the operations of criminal justice from public opinion. The insulation of criminal policy from public controversy, however, may be removed when a particular issue stimulates conflict among power blocs. One occasion was the public uproar that prevented implementation of a proposal to grant amnesty to the last of the Germans convicted of war crimes. Then, we argue, the changes that brought a reduced imprisonment rate should be sought within the structure of criminal justice administration, with the general sociocultural environment permitting these changes.

All the elements mentioned above played a part in the decline in the imprisonment rate after World War II, but Van Weringh would place their conjunction within a context of basic changes in the Dutch social structure that had been operating before the war and that had their effects through issue-oriented bargaining among political parties, none of which held absolute power. The latter effects have been crucial to criminal justice policy, Van Weringh[1] believes, because the long-term rejection of imprisonment by Social Democrats became politically significant in this bargaining among contesting parties. He explains:

> Before 1917 the right to vote was not broadly distributed, but then it became an important part of the Dutch social and political structure. The unions became more and more important in Holland, more and more accepted by the Government and also employers' organizations. Before the war there was a significant Social Democrat party, but it was not represented in government. The first Social Democrat ministers were in the so-called "crisis cabinet" one or two months before the war. Although inclined to pacifism, the Congress of the Social Democrat party in 1938 accepted the need for an army for defense against Germany. In 1939 two Social Democrats were taken into the coalition government of the Christian Democrats and Liberals. The first prime minister after the war was a Social Democrat, and there were Social Democratic prime ministers for many years thereafter. Under these governments, many measures against imprisonment were introduced.

It is important to realize that three political parties hold about the same share of the voting electorate. Because no single party can come to absolute power, there always are coalitions, usually between the Christian Democrats and the Liberals or between the Christian Democrats and the Social Democrats. This political structure opposes extremist positions in Dutch politics. In seeking certain legislation, one of the parties in power sometimes affiliates with the opposition. The Christian Democrats are inclined towards a "law and order" policy in dealing with abortion, homosexuality, pornography, drug abuse, and similar issues because of religious conviction. The Liberals share economic conservatism but do not agree with the Christian Democrats on moral issues. So the Liberals make accommodations with the Social Democrats in support of tolerant policies.

Police Discretion as an Element

All criminal justice systems withhold the full penalties permitted by law for some cases of offenders at particular points in administrative processing. The Netherlands is unique in that all stages of processing, from the police through the prosecutors and judges, are convinced that criminal sanctions should be avoided when possible. The general policy of withholding punishment has the effect that arrested Dutchmen do not fear the courts because of the low level of penalization. Guilty pleas are common; foreigners unsocialized to the Dutch ways are the chief exception. Also the mild penalization helps explain the near absence of violent confrontations between the police and criminals.

1. Interview with Jac Van Weringh, Professor of Criminology, "Bonger" Criminological Institute, University of Amsterdam.

Traditionally, the police have regarded themselves as civilians in uniform and, therefore, are rooted in society. The general expectation is that officers are peacekeepers, preferring to use means other than arrest to mediate problem situations. The older, more experienced officers tend to be more lenient than younger, less experienced colleagues. Versatility rather than force appears to be the superior route to promotions. An Amsterdam officer commented:

> My personal experience is that neighbors accept you as an ordinary person living with your family in the neighborhood. There is no sharp division, but it depends on what district of the city in which you live. I lived where there are many criminals. They would look at me differently. Now I live 20 miles out of Amsterdam. Everyone treats you as normal. First of all you are a civilian, a normal human being.

As evidence of the ''civilians in uniform'' approach, the police and the public tend to share evaluations of the seriousness of offenses whereas prosecutors rank the offenses less harshly. Buikhuisen and Van Dijk (1975) polled a sample of 131 public prosecutors and groups of municipal police, districts of the National Police, and regional National Police.[2] The weights attached to 50 offenses were compared with weights given by another representative sample of the Dutch population. When an offense was judged to be serious, the rating score was greater. Overall, the highest average rating for the 50 offenses was given by the public (6.6). The average scores declined in this fashion: National Police regions (6.0), National Police districts (5.8), municipal police (5.5), and public prosecutors (5.3).

The prosecutors, the three police groups, and the public agreed essentially on the seriousness of manslaughter and instrumental violence. For other offense categories, the police groups were intermediate between the prosecutors and the public. The police groups departed to the greatest degree from public interpretation of ''failure to observe statutory regulations'' and ''intentional injury.'' They approached public attitudes and differed from those of prosecutors to the greatest extent in the evaluation of ''contravening sexual morality.'' In contrast to the homogeneity of attitudes among prosecutors, policemen differed considerably among themselves in attitudes. The older, more experienced, and Amsterdam police were inclined to consider offenses to be less serious than did their counterparts.

The willingness to forego arrests seems to be less a matter of sentimental leniency and more of a desire to avoid unnecessary effort because of policies that drift down from the offices of public prosecutors. The attitudes differ among officers, but, as an example of the effect of previous actions, one officer said: ''When the judge puts them in jail, it is worthwhile to take them off the streets; but, when the judge sends them away as quickly as you can send them, you become tolerant.''

Even in Holland, police discretion is a gray area elusive for reliable measurement, but Schaffmeister[3] believes it is among the distinctions that help ex-

---

2. In The Netherlands the National Police is a unified force, policing rural districts and smaller towns.
3. Interview with Dr. Dieter Schaffmeister, referent for Dutch penal law, the Max Planck Institute for Foreign and International Criminal Law, Freiburg-im-Breisgau, Federal Republic of Germany.

plain the relatively mild reactions to lawbreakers there. He cites official Dutch statistics for 1973 which show that only 114,138 of the 130,731 total accused cases were passed on to the prosecutors. For comparison, Schaffmeister points out that in West Germany, where the law demands more strictly that the police report all cases to the prosecutors, the prosecutors typically drop out about half the cases and 28 percent reach the courts. Because the Dutch police do not pass on all cases, their prosecutors begin with a smaller number of cases. The net effect of both police and prosecutorial discretion in The Netherlands is that only 15 percent of the cases reach the courts, compared with 28 percent in West Germany.

Prosecutors and Principle of Expediency

Prosecutorial discretion is particularly significant. First, this office entails the power to refrain from punitive measures in situations where the accused person is not in a position to bargain for leniency. The psychology of the prosecutors is not necessarily that of wanting to reduce their workload but to find a solution to the difficulties involving the accused without referral for trial. Second, changes in the prosecutor's role norms, rather than changes in laws, have modified the workings of the legal structure since World War II.

Leaving misdemeanors aside, for about half the crimes that the evidence indicates conviction would result, the public prosecutors refrain from bringing the accused persons before the court and substitute other responses. To go to trial, the defendant must be accused of a serious crime or have committed a series of petty offenses. For some first offenders, the experience of being arrested and held two days for police investigation is deemed to be a sufficient deterrent. In other instances, the damage produced by the offense is minor or the evidence is insufficient. Perhaps a warning is sent to the arrested person: "I have received a police report on the crime, but I have decided not to prosecute. But I warn you, that if it happens again, I will be forced to take action." Sometimes, a letter demands that damages must be paid to the victim within a month. If a receipt is sent to the prosecutor's office, the case is dropped. When personal and social problems are indicated in the police report, probation (reclassering) officers are asked to make an investigation which might initiate a helping program without prosecution.

The important functions of the Dutch prosecutor, Schaffmeister explains, are legally contingent on the exclusive monopoly of prosecution and the principle of expediency provided by the Criminal Procedure Code of 1921. The discretionary power is used differentially according to region and offense, but efforts are being made to coordinate nationally the offices of public prosecutors in keeping with principles of consistent administration of discretion. These efforts are promising in The Netherlands because all public prosecutors are under the national Ministry of Justice and because, as discussed below, the prosecutors are developing a sense of occupational identity. Since the 1920s, the Ministers of Justice have been politically astute in framing policies and have leaned increasingly toward reducing the level of penalization.

Earlier the principle of expediency was applied as an exception to the rule of legality—"going by the book," roughly speaking—when obligatory prosecution would conflict with the general interest. But the principle of expediency has come to mean that prosecution can be avoided, even when illegality and guilt are present, when the general interest does not require prosecution. Under the caption "prosecution," the Report of the Public Prosecutors to Parliament for the year 1972 said:

> An important element in our meetings seems to be the fact that the public prosecutor has more and more means available other than prosecution to correct illegal behavior. A corrective talk at his office, a conditional dropping of the case, with or without the imposition of certain conditions, waiving the right of prosecution if the suspect is willing to pay a certain sum in the statutory cases or a discussion with the suspect and the victim can have a better effect than prosecution and disposal of the case in court.

As Schaffmeister puts it, the Dutch prosecutors must give reasons why they take the case to trial and ask for imprisonment, because it is normal *not* to prosecute. The crucial point in Dutch justice, Schaffmeister says, is "to find what is exactly right for *this* man without long discussions about what he did and what the facts are. There is no broad effort to deal with the evidence as the prime consideration." He continues:

> In The Netherlands there is training how to make decisions without emphasizing so strongly that a man has done a crime. As judges they are more likely to understand what people are doing and what criminality is. After their education at the university, the prosecutors in Germany learn their work—what is written in the codes, the sentencing procedures of courts—by training in prosecutors' offices, courts and similar places. Only what is relevant to the judicial education; they do not learn about how to speak with a suspect, how to handle the assessment of the total evidence. The German judges and prosecutors are trained only to follow what "the book" says. They learn to relate this to real human situations only on the job on their own. He learns at home if he is a judge who interprets written codes against human realities, not as part of the official obligatory education.

The role norms of prosecutors have changed in recent decades to make the office, in and of itself, a desirable career for talented graduates of law schools. The office is apolitical and a strong sense of independence is cultivated. Dutch prosecutors seldom are identified by name in newspapers unless there is a most unusual case, such as prosecution of notorious war crimes. Public visibility is of little value and can be damaging because career chances are determined by the legal hierarchy.

The classical prosecutors were individuals, each doing their own job by following their own judgment. More recently, prosecutors have begun to develop a sense of occupational community, in their terms, capable of influencing and coordinating justice policy. They meet to consider issues and reach agreements separate from the judges. Further, the social orientation described above appears to have developed since the early 1960s among a new breed of Dutch prosecutors as a result of changes in law school curricula, of qualities of the new recruits, of weakening of the influence on the senior prosecutors, and, perhaps, of a more general questioning of traditions that arose in the 1960s.

Reclassering: Merits of Volunteer Agencies

"Reclassering" is a term encompassing probation, parole, and other helping services from arrest through prisoner aftercare. The history of Dutch reclassering goes back to 1823, the third oldest in the world,[4] but a coordinated system has emerged only since World War II. Volunteer societies continue to comprise the reclassering organization, giving their programs a linkage with the community and insulating them against the excesses of impersonal bureaucracy, but the financial support now is largely that of government subsidies. An important asset is that there is no special organization of services for the criminal justice system. The chances for reintegration of offenders are promoted by their referral to regular service agencies as ordinary clients. However, the public acceptance of offenders as proper clients for services had to develop, rather than being part of the Dutch culture in the early history of reclassering.

The founders of early volunteer societies were warm-hearted and social-minded businessmen without professional qualifications. In spite of opposition, they eventually were permitted to visit prisoners and to befriend them on discharge. Near the end of the nineteenth century, the fierce public condemnation of this work began to ease, and the government granted in 1905 the first modest subsidy for probation and aftercare to private organizations. This work was carried out by the Salvation Army, the Roman Catholic Rehabilitation Society, the Protestant Rehabilitation Society, a non-denominational society, and many others who were mainly of religious orientation. For example, the Dr. F. S. Meyers Association specialized in the rehabilitation of mentally disturbed prisoners.

The volunteer basis, as explained below, has important advantages, but this nature of reclassering also has serious disadvantages. There has been a history of wasteful, overlapping rivalries among agencies, a tendency to regard humanitarian zeal as a sufficient equivalent of well-directed professional competence, and general weaknesses in providing services appropriate for coordination with the police and courts. Now the agencies employ full-time social workers to lend professional substance and coordination to the efforts of volunteers. As early as 1912, the various small societies tried to integrate themselves. Regulations, dating back as far as 1947, lent some order to the relationships between the societies and the government. Nevertheless, it was necessary after World War II to establish regional reclassering councils in every court district, composed of representatives of the reclassering, a judge, a barrister, the director of the local prison, a forensic psychiatrist and some other experts. Their functions are to coordinate the allocation of subsidies, to assure the government that funds are used effectively, to increase the relevance of presentence reports and other services to the courts, and to expand court use of these services.

The emphasis on volunteers has advantages for developing a network of personalized contacts and for enlisting participation of churches, trade unions, and many other groups in broadening public support for including former offenders among the clients for regular services. The societies endeavor to recruit

4. In the United States the Philadelphia Society for the Alleviation of the Miseries of Public Prisons was founded in 1787 and the British Society for the Diffusion of Knowledge upon Punishment of Death and for Improvement of Prison Discipline in 1808.

volunteers from every walk of life to improve the chances that client and supervisor can be matched. Probably, the primary asset is that volunteer agencies, when compared with government bureaucracies, are in a superior position to represent the interests of their clients, elicit their trust, and, especially, to guarantee the confidentiality of information given by the client when appropriate. Ledeboer[5] explains:

> The attitude about probation officers is different than in the United States. There, the probation officer has the duty to report everything, but not here in Holland. The officer says, ''I have a relationship with my client. He trusts me. I cannot write everything in the presentence report.'' The prosecutor is willing to listen to the social worker because he also does not like jail as a solution. He agrees: ''I do not want such information because I like an alternative that puts a man in the community and helps him to solve his problems.''

The combination of voluntary effort and significant finance from public bodies has produced a remarkable range of services which are made available to clients of justice agencies with development of a special delivery system for them. This development is consistent with an emphasis on reintegrating former offenders into the community as though they are essential ordinary persons requiring services. A particularly relevant development is the emergence in recent years of various agencies for helping in the crisis situations of youth. Advice Centers offer information and referral on a walk-in basis. Judicial Consultation Bureaus specialize in legal counsel for arrested youth. One private organisation specializes in finding housing accommodations for disadvantaged groups because of Amsterdam's serious housing problem. Another provides a short-term hotel. These institutions concentrate on helping in a direct and practical way without offering unsought advice and judgments. They are nonconventional in their skepticism toward the ''establishment,'' yet the authorities extend to them a cautious tolerance that often includes financial support without conditions (Tollemache, 1973: 297–300).

The Regional Reclassering Council in Amsterdam strives to have workers present in the police station as early in the processing cycle as possible. Although representation in all stations has not been accomplished, the premises are that the offense is symptomatic of some fundamental problem and that the time in the station is crucial for the offenders and most likely to lead them to accept a helping relationship. The early contacts are regarded to be more promising than later contacts spread over many years. Further, reclassering is in a position to provide the prosecutor with information vital to intelligent decisions on remand, on referrals for trial, and on the appropriateness of alternative dispositions.

---

5. Interview with Wesselium B. Ledeboer, Secretary of the Regional Reclassering Council, Amsterdam.

Will Penalization Become More Stern?

As indicated above, The Netherlands is experiencing a greater incidence of crime and the imprisonment rate has risen in recent years. It is feared that "heavy" foreign criminals, including armed bank robbers, prefer Holland's relatively mild penalties in calculating risks. Diversion of other kinds of offenders has increased the proportion of recidivists and violent criminals among prison admissions. Amsterdam has suffered an increasingly serious problem of heroin traffic. There have been scandals of policemen accepting bribes from dealers. A portion of the press has been warning of increasing crimes and complaining about what they regard as inappropriately mild penalties for criminals. Some political groups press for more and longer sentences.

Although the Dutch do not have a drug-oriented culture and have one of the lowest rates of alcohol consumption in Europe, there was some abuse of amphetamines, LSD, and opiates in the late 1960s. In 1967–1968 the police responded with arrests of users but soon dropped this policy to concentrate on trafficking. An attitude of watchful and concerned tolerance has been expressed in permitting hashish smoking in certain youth centers (Hardt and Brooks, 1973: 86–87). The Amsterdam police have long permitted opium dens in the Chinese neighborhood under an informal agreement that younger Chinese, non-Chinese, and organized drug operations could not be involved. At least one den still exists, but the agreement has broken down as members of the Turkish ethnic group challenge the Chinese drug ring for control of the heroin traffic.

As in many prosperous European countries, Holland has an appreciable number of foreign workers. Within the Common Market, labor has a new and extensive freedom to cross national boundaries. After becoming familiar with Dutch customs, workers usually have accepted Dutch attitudes toward criminal justice. Another group is made up of black emigrants from Surinam, a former Dutch colony in South America that recently became an independent nation, who migrated to Holland when it was a colony and are, therefore, qualified under the Social Assistance Program. However, they have a serious unemployment problem and, as a largely rural people, are not familiar with urban life. They are a particular example of the growing difficulty of assimilating foreign workers and the second generation of immigrants who are caught between their parents' culture and the culture they have learned at school.

Will the policy of forbearance survive the contemporary impact of a soaring crime rate? The question is especially appropriate because the policy emerged since World War II and then might be only a temporary aberration. The evidence presented above supports the view that the policy and its implementing structure are intact and, in fact, are operating with increased intensity. Otherwise, the recent gain in the imprisonment rate would be even greater. To an increasing extent, the prosecutor's waiver of prosecution and the use of fines instead of imprisonment continue to be dominant strategies in managing convicted offenders. Sentences of a year or more are more frequent, but lesser prison terms continue to be most characteristic. Nevertheless, the trend of one to five year imprisonments has the most potential for producing a further upsurge in the Dutch imprisonment rate.

Future developments will determine whether the current increase in the Dutch imprisonment rate is temporary or whether there will be a return to pre-war level of imprisonment. The homeostatic punishment postulate argues that the imprisonment rate of a given society fluctuates around a level characteristic of that society (Blumstein and Cohen, 1973). When the deviance exceeds the tolerance level, imprisonment rate is likely to increase. When the imprisonment rate has risen greatly, the overcrowding of prisons and the higher costs of administering punishment would tend to bring the imprisonment rate back to the typical level. Which is the typical level for Holland—the pre-war level or the post-war level? Whether or not the ultimate answer will continue to place Holland as the least among nations in the resort to imprisonment, special cultural ambience will not vanish. Even more significantly, public officials are relatively insulated from the public pressures which in other countries would oppose continuance of conditions of a mounting crime rate.

Discussion Questions

1. What are the specific factors that account for the low rate of imprisonment in The Netherlands? What factors do you think account for the comparatively high rate of imprisonment in the U.S.?
2. Early in the article, Johnson and Heijder state "that the sociocultural system is basic to understanding any society's response to crime. . . ." Elaborate on this statement by showing how it applies to The Netherlands and to the U.S.
3. What, if anything, do you think U.S. policymakers can learn from the Dutch as regards the problem of prison crowding? Which Dutch policies could be adopted in the U.S. to address the crowding problem?
4. Do you think that the lack of emphasis placed on imprisonment by the Dutch will be able to withstand the growing concern about crime in The Netherlands? Why or why not?

References

D'Anjou, L. U. M., Cozyn, C., Van Der Toorn, L., and Verkoyen, C. M. R. 1978 Demanding More Severe Punishment. *British Journal of Criminology* 18 (No. 4): 326–347.

Blumstein, A., and Cohen, H. 1973 A Theory of the Stability of Punishment. *Journal of Criminal Law and Criminology* 64 (No. 2): 198–207.

Buikhuisan, W., and Van Dijk, J. J. M. 1975 Official Police Reporting of Criminal Offenses. Research and Documentation Centre Ministry of Justice, The Netherlands (November).

Conrad, J. P. 1970 *Crime and Its Correction: An International Survey of Attitudes and Practices.* Berkeley and Los Angeles: University of California Press.

Downes, David 1982 The Origins and Consequences of Dutch Penal Policy Since 1945. *British Journal of Criminology* 22 (October): 325–362.

Hardt, C. R., and Brooks, R. 1973 Social Policy on Dangerous Drugs: A Study of Changing Attitudes in New York and Overseas. *St. John's Law Review* 48 (October): 48–102.

Heijder, A. 1967 The Recent Trend Towards Reducing the Prison Population in The Netherlands. *International Journal of Offender Therapy and Comparative Criminology* 18 (No. 3): 233–240.

Hoeven, P. J. A. 1976 Politieke Grenzen Van Strafrechtshervorming (Political Boundaries of Penal Reform). *Delikt en Delinkwent* 6 (No. 5): 251–262.

Lijhart, A. 1975 *The Politics of Accommodation: Pluralism and Democracy in The Netherlands,* 2nd edition. Berkeley and Los Angeles: University of California Press.

Rosett, A. 1972 Trial and Discretion in Dutch Criminal Justice. *UCLA Law Review* 19 (No. 1): 353–390.

Tollemache, R. 1973 Crisis Agencies and the Treatment of Offenders in The Netherlands. *Howard Journal of Penology and Crime Prevention* 13 (No. 4): 297–317.

EDITORIAL NOTE

Data obtained by the editors from the Dutch Ministry of Justice while this book was in press, as well as recent correspondence with Dr. Johnson, suggest that the imprisonment rate of the Netherlands is on the rise. According to the Ministry of Justice data, this rise is primarily due to longer sentences being given in response to an increase in the seriousness of crimes committed. These data (see especially Table 11a) can be obtained by contacting the Dutch Ministry of Justice, Research and Documentation Centre (director: dr. J. Junger-Tas), P.O. Box 20301, 2500 EH The Hague and requesting a copy of *Dutch penal law and policy: Notes on criminological research from the Research and Documentation Centre. Key figures on the Dutch criminal justice system.* 02 04 1991, by A. C. Berghuis and P. van Hooff.

16. Prison Administration in Contemporary Japan: Six Issues

Elmer H. Johnson
Center for the Study of Crime, Delinquency, and Corrections Southern Illinois University at Carbondale
Hisashi Hasegawa
Warden, Fuchu Prison, Tokyo, Japan

Abstract: Like all prison systems, the Japanese Corrections Bureau faces problems emanating from the host society and requiring competent managerial responses. This article illustrates that point by presenting six issues stemming from changes, both internal and external to the prison environment, that challenge administrators even in this stable society, which enjoys a relatively low crime rate.

A prison system reflects the society it serves and thereby is a barometer of many of the changes being experienced by the society. The prisons of Japan are well administered and enjoy the advantages of a society that has one of the lowest crime rates in the world. However, even in Japan, prison administrators are being tested by developments that mirror changes stemming from sources both internal and external to the prison environment. Six developments are considered in this article.

First, the Prison Law of 1908 requires basic revision. Second, major reconstruction is necessary to replace obsolete and aging facilities. Third, the increasing discrepancy between the average ages of staff and inmates raises difficulties. Fourth, foreign prisoners raise several issues. Fifth, the greater prevalence of stimulant-drug abuse is associated with the increased presence of professional gangsters in prisons. Sixth, the presence of gangsters and the stronger representation of drug abusers—especially among female inmates—have produced an increase in the number of inmates who typically resist rehabilitation programs, in contrast to the usual attitudes of Japanese prisoners.

Background: The Japanese Prisons

Like all correctional systems, Japanese prisons are fundamentally influenced by the social, cultural, and political patterns of the people they serve. The kinds of persons incarcerated in prisons, their typical behaviors as inmates, the duties of personnel, and the quantity and quality of resources provided—all are shaped by the sociocultural patterns of Japanese society. The strong sense of duty of the Japanese people is reflected in a remarkably low crime rate among highly urbanized and industrialized nations, a long-term decline in the number of prisoners, and the typical diligence of the prisoners. In the postwar year of 1950 there were 85,254 convicted prisoners, compared with 45,304 in 1983, in a nation of about 120,000,000 people.[1] The internal order in the prisons is suggested by these remarkably low statistics for a six-year period: only thirty-five escapes, six assaults upon prison officers, and one murder and thirteen assaults on inmates by inmates.[2]

The history of the Japanese prison system can be traced back to 1872, when the Kangokusaku (Prison Rules) were enacted. Now the Corrections Bureau and the Rehabilitation Bureau, both in the Ministry of Justice, provide the advantages of a unified and coordinated correctional system. The Rehabilitation Bureau administers probation, parole, and after-care services. The Corrections Bureau operates fifty-eight adult prisons, nine juvenile prisons, fifty-nine juvenile training schools, seven detention houses, one hundred and six branch detention houses, nine branch prisons, fifty-one juvenile classification homes, a branch home, and three women's guidance homes. This article is concerned only with the adult prison institutions that manage convicted offenders. Among the fifty-eight adult prisons there are four women's prisons, three medical prisons, two prisons for traffic offenders, and one exclusively for foreign prisoners.[3]

The prisoner classification procedures, substantially changed in 1972, are carried out at classification centers located in a prison within each of the eight correctional regions. There selected new prisoners[4] are oriented to prison life, evaluated by several psychological methods, and differentiated according to allocation categories: W, female; F, foreigners; I, sentenced without forced labor; J, juveniles; L, serving terms of eight years or more; Y, adults over twenty-six years of age. Second, they are differentiated into the categories A, not advanced in criminal inclinations; or B, advanced in criminal inclinations. Third, those prisoners with mental or health abnormalities are identified. Fourth, the new inmates are classified according to specific treatment needs, including eligibility for open institutions or recommendation for assignment to some kind of prison maintenance work.[5]

The foreign visitor is impressed by the diligent labor of inmates and the operation of prison industries offering products for sale on the open market. In June a two-day sale of a wide variety of prisoner-made goods in downtown Tokyo typically draws a great crowd of bargain hunters. Like the Japanese people generally, the prisoners work a five-and-a-half-day week, in furniture manufacture, printing, clothing and shoe making, and a variety of other enterprises. Well over ninety percent of the inmates are so involved.

1. Supporting data for the statistics in this article, unless otherwise indicated, were taken from *Summary of the White Paper on Crime,* 1984.
2. Source: *Correctional Institutions in Japan,* p. 20.
3. *Ibid.,* pp. 1, 4–5; there were three guidance homes at the time of this report, but on March 30, 1985, two were abolished.
4. By "selected," we mean male prisoners, less than twenty-six years of age, with prison sentences of one year or more. The remaining prisoners are classified at the pretrial detention facility.
5. Source: *Correctional Institutions in Japan,* pp. 21–23.

Other programs include vocational training, social and academic education, and correspondence courses.[6]

These programs are predicated on the conviction that the vast majority of the inmates will respond to treatment programs and that their rehabilitation is a viable objective. The beliefs receive some support from recidivism rates that compare well with the experience of penologists in other countries. In 1981, of prisoners who had been released on expiration of sentence, 12.6 percent were returned to prison for new crimes within a year, 38.3 percent within two years, and 51.6 percent within three years. (The percentages are accumulative.) For parolees as of 1981, the equivalent figures were 4.1, 19.3, and 29.7 percent.

Penal Law and Management

Correctional management, of course, must operate within the structure of the penal law. Japanese prisons have been managed under a very old law that was promulgated in 1908. Only slight changes have been made in the ensuing seventy-seven years in spite of attempts to accomplish basic revision several times before and after World War II. There are serious defects in the Prison Law of 1908, but, since it only defines fundamental principles, the management and treatment of prisoners have been improved either by modifying the details of implementation of the old law through its expression in rules and regulations or by new interpretations of the text of the old law.

Nevertheless, the 1908 law has serious defects. The guarantees of prisoners' rights, a quality of modern prison administration, are not specified. For instance, receiving visits is not stipulated as a prisoner's right. Also revision is necessary to permit introduction of such programs as work release and furloughs.

In that context the Corrections Bureau, Ministry of Justice, has been endeavoring diligently in the last several years to obtain necessary revisions of the 1908 law. The efforts have been handicapped by disagreements among political constituencies about the proper balance between the rights of prisoners and the restrictions that should be placed on them.

Reconstruction of Older Facilities

The penal law requires revision because the conditions faced by correctional administrators reflect the rapid social changes to which the society at large has been particularly subject in modern times. Similarly, the facilities are subject to physical aging and functional obsolescence. In Japan, there are over fifty facilities, both large and small, that await reconstruction.

Construction of Fuchu Prison was begun in 1923 and completed in 1935. When construction was begun, the site was largely open with only a few scattered houses in the vicinity. Now it is in the middle of a city of 200,000 inhabitants. Sometimes, political constituencies call for the removal of the prison from the city. Political candidates have promised, if elected, to get the prison out of the city and use the land for a park or other project.

Usually, when prisons are moved, the Corrections Bureau sells the land occupied by the old prison to the local government and uses the money to buy

6. Ibid., pp. 10–12.

cheaper land elsewhere and construct the new prison. However, the high value and the central location of the land occupied by Fuchu Prison make its purchase too expensive for the city government of Fuchu.

To replace Fuchu Prison would cost a million U.S. dollars. There are also five B-type prisons in urgent need of reconstruction, which would cost additional millions. Further, the residents near proposed locations for new prisons raise objections. Third, serious personnel problems would arise because the prison employees have residences in Fuchu and send their children to local schools. If a replacement prison were built in a distant mountain area, the officers would have to give up their Fuchu homes and transfer their children to other schools. Like all Japanese, they are greatly concerned about the quality of their children's education. The schools in rural areas lack the academic quality of Fuchu schools.

Demographic Change: Staff and Inmates

The quality of personnel is crucial to every prison system, and Japan has benefited from effective recruitment and training procedures that are matched by a high staff-inmate ratio.

The Corrections Bureau recruits correctional officers from candidates who have passed a special examination administered by the National Personnel Authority. The recruits take a 220-day primary course at one of the eight regional centers administered by the Training Institute for Correctional Personnel. Training institutes for correctional personnel have existed since 1890, but the present Institute was established in 1969. The Institute also conducts three-month secondary and six-month advanced courses for selected personnel.[7]

In recent years widening discrepancies have been emerging between the average ages of staff and inmates. That demographic trend may be roughly described as a movement toward "grandchildren" supervising their "grandmothers," as an effect of several factors. Staff members retire at age sixty years, and their retention in the service to that point increases the average staff age over time. Many prisons do not receive convicted offenders less than twenty-six years of age; the aging of long-term inmates adds to the average age. A large cadre of prison officers had to be recruited for several years immediately after World War II because that period of socioeconomic chaos produced a great increase in the number of prisoners and because many prison officers were killed in the military struggles. Now members of that cadre are retiring and must be replaced by younger recruits. Table 1 illustrates the effect on the changing age distributions of staff and inmates of Fuchu prison.

A decade or so ago female prisoners generally presented positive attitudes toward prison rules and rehabilitative programs. The administration could expect their dedicated work in prison industries and their positive participation in recreational and other treatment-oriented activities. Further, there was a staff of experienced and talented female prison officers. Half of those at Tochigi Prison, for example, were fifty or more years of age because many had been

---

7. Ibid., pp. 26–36.

Table 1 Age Distribution of Staff and Inmates of Fuchu Prison for Selected Years

Staff or Inmates for Selected Years	Age Distributions in Percentages				
	Under 30	31–40	41–50	50-over	Total
Prison staff					
1971	31.3	13.6	35.4	19.6	99.9
1976	35.8	14.8	27.0	22.3	99.9
1981	47.1	18.1	9.5	25.2	99.9
1985	45.9	23.1	10.8	20.2	100.0
Inmates					
1971	26.5	40.6	22.8	10.1	100.0
1976	15.4	41.5	28.5	14.5	99.9
1981	14.4	41.4	28.5	15.7	100.0
1985	10.2	37.1	32.2	20.5	100.0

recruited from widows of soldiers killed in World War II. They were traditional Japanese women strongly committed to duties, who lived in small cities of 50,000 or fewer inhabitants that lacked the industries providing the employment opportunities they needed as widows. Now they have retired because of their advanced age.

To replace them, the prison service has recruited young women, aged 18 to 29 years, who are eligible for and have passed the national examination for prison officers administered by the National Personnel Board. Actually, the eligible candidates are predominantly younger women, aged 18 to 24 years. About half of them have graduated from two-year or four-year institutions of higher education. The remainder are graduates of senior high schools who have completed twelve years of education.

Wardens of women's prisons frequently face problems because female graduates of the primary training course for prison officers often return from the course and immediately resign to be married. Many of them meet their future husbands as fellow students in the course. Because there are few positions for male officers at women's prisons, the resignation of the female officer is almost inevitable.

This personnel turnover and the relative youth of female prison officers produce a discrepancy between their average age and that of the prisoners. Newly admitted female prisoners in 1965 had a median age of 35.6 years; in 1983 their median age was 38.6 years.[8] The aging of long-term prisoners would further increase the average age of female prisoners present. The young officers do well in maintaining discipline, but the age discrepancy has some influence on their counseling functions because they lack the social experience of older officers.

8. The medians were calculated from statistics of the Corrections Bureau.

Foreigners in Japanese Prisons

With Japan's rising popularity among tourists, larger numbers of foreigners are in the country at least temporarily. Of course, only a small minority engage in crime, but, with the greater number from overseas each year, that minority contributes an increasing absolute number of foreign prisoners. In 1984 there were forty-eight foreign prisoners in Fuchu Prison; in 1985 there were 103, and even more are to be expected in the future.

In Fuchu Prison special provisions are made for foreign inmates. A special cell block provides a bed instead of the floor mat upon which the Japanese customarily sleep. Western-type meals are provided to those who cannot tolerate a Japanese menu. Showers have been installed in a special room as an alternative to the usual large bathing pools.

The term "foreigner" does not refer to nationality only in the prisoner classification system. It identifies those inmates who do not speak Japanese, who do not understand the customs, and who cannot tolerate Japanese food. Otherwise, foreign prisoners are treated with the same concern accorded Japanese prisoners.

Three prisons receive foreigners. Yokosuka Prison confines only those offenders from the American military forces in Japan, according to a treaty between the countries. All female offenders, after sentencing, are sent to Tochigi Prison. Fuchu Prison accommodates all foreign male offenders except those from the American military forces.

The major difficulty is language; the 103 prisoners at Fuchu Prison represent seventeen nationalities. The prison staff includes several who understand English; one person is competent in Chinese, and another in Spanish. No other foreign language is understood by the staff. The Prison Law and Regulations require that all correspondence and reading materials be censored for security and treatment purposes. All visits must be conducted in the presence of an official.

The cost of translation, when necessary, must be borne by the prisoner. Since he or she is unlikely to be able to afford that service, the absence of mail and visitors can be emotionally upsetting. To ease the situation, Fuchu Prison turns for assistance in language translation to the police, the immigration service, embassies, and the United Nations Asia and Far East Institute. Most embassies have been very helpful, but some show no interest in their citizens who have been convicted of crimes in Japan.

The problems associated with foreign prisoners are not limited to Japan. More and more countries are concluding treaties whereby convicted offenders may be transferred to their home countries under certain conditions. In May, 1983 the Council of Europe prepared a Convention for Transfer of Foreign Prisoners. Another possible solution is parole at an early stage of imprisonment. In Japan prisoners are eligible for parole after serving one-third of the sentence or ten years on a life sentence. However, parole of foreign inmates raises at least two problems. Supervision is a key feature of parole. The receiving country may not be in a position to provide supervision. Second, public opinion is likely to oppose early parole of certain kinds of criminals, for example, the foreigners who smuggled large quantities of stimulant drugs.

Impact of Greater Stimulant-Drug Abuse

Since 1945 Japan has experienced three periods of heavy drug abuse.[9] Before World War II drug abuse was limited to a few opium and cocaine addicts. In the social chaos after the war (1946–1956), abuse of stimulant drugs became prevalent throughout Japan. The Stimulants Control Law of 1951, amended in 1954 and 1955, increased penalties, and the Mental Health Law was amended to compel hospitalization. Stimulant abuse declined after 1956 and appeared to have been overcome by 1958.

Narcotic abuse also arose immediately after the war. It reached a level causing serious concern in the period 1957–1963 and was aggravated by the heavy involvement of the Boryokudan in illicit traffic. Government ministries formed the Minister's Council for Narcotics Countermeasures in 1962; the Anti-Narcotic Drug Headquarters was the action arm of the Council. The Narcotics Control Law was amended in 1963 to stiffen penalties, supervise license handlers, and to provide new means of compulsory hospitalization. Coupled with an intensive public information campaign, those actions contributed to a sharp reduction of heroin abuse after 1964.

Stimulant-drug abuse—largely involving methamphetamine that is smuggled from Korea, Taiwan, Hong Kong, and a few countries in Southeast Asia—surfaced as a major problem in 1970 and has continued to the present day. The Stimulants Control Law was amended again in 1973 to raise the penalties to the level of those imposed for heroin offenses. The incidence declined in 1974, but only temporarily. Approximately 18,000 persons were arrested in 1978 under that law, and the number of annual arrests thereafter has tended to increase by twenty to thirty percent. In 1983 the police cleared 23,635 stimulant-drug offenders. However, the number of abusers is estimated to be some ten-fold greater than offenses known to the authorities.

Next to methamphetamine abuse, marihuana use is a problem, primarily among teenagers and adults in their twenties, but the violation rate is considerably lower than in other nations. Narcotic violations, including use of heroin and LSD, are at a very low level.

Official statistics indicate that persistent use of stimulant drugs is becoming more prevalent. In 1979, of 18,297 persons involved in the stimulant-drug cases cleared by the police, 63.0 percent were first offenders. Of 23,301 similar persons in 1983, 54.1 percent were first offenders. Among admitted prisoners convicted of stimulant-drug abuse, a similar pattern was shown. In 1979, 35.9 percent of 5,674 admitted prisoners had served a previous sentence for that offense, but 58.8 percent of 8,007 prisoners admitted in 1983 had served such a previous sentence.

The greater number of stimulant-drug suspects cleared by the police is largely the result of more arrests of drug users. In the years 1977–1983 the absolute number of arrests was relatively constant for persons accused of possession or of deliv-

9. This discussion is based on *A Brief Account of Drug Abuse and Counter-Measures in Japan*, pp. 2–6. For the purposes of this article, "substance abuse" is limited to stimulant drugs in later discussion because the special recent Japanese concern with that particular form of abuse has produced effects on prison management.

ery/receipt. The number of persons accused of illegal import/export or illegal manufacturing declined sharply. Meanwhile, there were 4,085 in 1977 and 11,350 in 1983 accused of illegal use. More intensive police activity is one explanation, but, since many first offense users have been released early in administrative processing, it appears that the official statistics underestimate the extent of stimulant abuse.

Criminal Organization in Japan

Because organized criminals play a major role in the stimulant-drug trade in Japan, their existence and the social psychology of their members constitute one of the six basic prison management problems highlighted in this article.

These gangs, according to DeVos and Mizushima, may be traced back to the Tokugawa period (1603–1868), when unemployment among the feudal samurai became common. During those years, the warrior traditions of the samurai were extended into the marginal activities of private violence. The *tekiya* were related to street venders who were likely to engage in shady business practices and to be vulnerable to extortion. The *bakuto* organized gambling establishments. Both of these groups collectively came to be called the *yakuza,* a term referring to "eight-nine-three" to denote a useless or losing number in gambling. The implication is that those criminals are good for nothing (DeVos and Mizushima, 1967: 293–95). The Japanese police now prefer to identify the contemporary criminal gangs as *boryokudan* (violent gangs) (Rome, 1975:260).

In recent decades, DeVos and Mizushima have reported, the *yakuza* have lost much of their prewar power and are less committed to the earlier gang ethic that prohibited force against ordinary people. The mystique of loyalty and fictive kinship has been replaced by "fairly impersonal relationships" between bosses and underlings. The Japanese gangs have informal relationships, DeVos and Mizushima noted, with professional criminal groups in Hong Kong, the Philippines, Hawaii, and other parts of the United States. Gambling is the most prevalent activity, they have reported, but smuggling of narcotics, guns, and illegal currency is quite common. The relative lack of narcotics activity in Japan, DeVos and Mizushima have speculated, may stem from the reluctance of the Japanese to use narcotics or from the unwillingness of the *yakuza* to push those drugs (DeVos and Mizushima, 1967: 293–95).

The National Police Agency has reported that the *Boryokudan* have been dominant in the importation and domestic distribution of illicit drugs. Of all stimulant drugs seized, 35.5 percent in 1979 were in the possession of the *Boryokudan.* The share has fluctuated over the years, reaching 59.7 percent in 1981. The gangsters have striven to increase the number of users, adding to the use of stimulant drugs among female students, because sale of these drugs is their primary source of income (National Police Agency, 1978: 4–5). Their success is suggested by the 473 percent gain among nongangsters arrested for stimulant-drug abuse between 1974 and 1983. The increase was 186 percent for *Boryokudan* members.

Among the gangs are the Yamaguchi-Gumi,[10] Sumiyoshi Rengo, Dainippon Heiwakai, Inagawakai, and Matsubakai. Members have been arrested for such offenses as homicide, assault, extortion, unlawful assembly with weapons, and involvement in prostitution, gambling, and trade in and use of illicit drugs. The numbers of violent incidents between gangs, the National Police Agency reported, were nineteen in 1979 and thirty-four in 1983, for example. About a thousand weapons are seized from gangsters each year.

The Criminal Department of the National Police Agency has reported that the number of gangster groups has declined slightly from 2,517 in 1979 to 2,330 in 1983 and their membership from 106,754 in 1979 to 98,771 in 1983. The *Boryokudan* are disproportionately represented among prison inmates. On the final day of 1975 there were 37,744 Japanese adult prisoners, of whom 7,932 were gangsters (21 percent); on the final day of 1983 there were 44,869 total prisoners and 12,325 gangsters (27.5 percent). Not only do the *Boryokudan* comprise a significant share of prisoners but that share is increasing.

These prisoners constitute a serious problem for prison security and treatment programs. As dedicated and professional criminals, they are committed to a subculture that resists rehabilitative programs. Criminal behavior and imprisonment do not shame them; conversely, imprisonment raises their prestige among their associates. They bring their underground subculture with them to prison. If prisoner A belonging to X gangster group has a fight with prisoner B belonging to Y gangster group, their fellows rush to help the respective prisoners, regardless of the particular issue.

Boryokudan prisoners try to bribe or intimidate correctional officers to obtain prohibited items (cigarettes, for example, are prohibited in Japanese prisons) or to smuggle out an uncensored letter. Those inmates have a disproportionate share of disciplinary violations. At Fuchu Prison, they were responsible for over ninety percent of the disciplinary punishments in 1983. Most of those violations were for disobedience, violence against inmates, and fighting among themselves.

Their recidivism rate exceeds seventy percent, although a real effort is made to eliminate their criminal tendencies. Perhaps the only hope for their rehabilitation is to persuade them to withdraw from the *Boryokudan*. Prison policy is to attempt such persuasion, but the effort is usually futile. Prospects appear to be better for young gangsters facing a long period of confinement because of anxieties about their future position in the gang after a long absence and because of greater time for exposure to correctional activities.

The difficulties of achieving rehabilitation are suggested by a frequent ritual outside the gate of Fuchu Prison almost every morning. Of the 1,200 *Boryokudan* members in the prison—half of the prison's average population—at least one is likely to be released on a given day. Usually, they are released very early in the morning—for example, at 4:00 or 5:00 a.m. and sometimes even at midnight—to avoid traffic congestion outside the prison gate. Several

10. For a popularized description of the *Yamaguchi-Gumi*, see Rome (1975).

automobiles often bring a score or more—sometimes over 500 when a boss is released—to welcome the released *Boryokudan* prisoner.

Because of their incorrigibility and because their misconduct stands in sharp contrast with the compliance of the typical Japanese inmate, the gangster prisoners are usually classified in B allocation category, which consists of those inmates with advanced criminal tendencies, and are sent to one of the twenty-three prisons that receive B-class inmates. In 1975 there were 6,775 *Boryokudan* prisoners in B category, or 28 percent of all prisoners in that category. In 1983 there were 11,315 *Boryokudan* prisoners in B category, or 39.7 percent of all prisoners in that category. In other words, the gangsters make up a significant and increasing share of all inmates believed to have advanced criminal tendencies. Because they can undermine the internal order of the correctional institution, it would be desirable to keep them in different prisons, separate from one another, but their large numbers make that impossible. Within a given B-type prison, special care is taken in assigning them to workshops and cell blocks.

Stimulant Abuse and Female Prisoners

The increased proportion of women among Japanese prisoners is consistent with trends in many other countries, but in Japan that trend is particularly associated with stimulant-drug abuse and the *Boryokudan*. The female drug-abuse prisoners had to have access to the *Boryokudan* to obtain the drugs and therefore have come under the influence of gangsters. These women are a new type of prisoner in that regard.

Increased convictions for stimulant-related offenses have had remarkable impact on the size of the total prisoner population and on the relative presence of female prisoners. Table 2 shows that the representation of stimulant-related offenders has increased for both sexes from 1979 to 1983 in prison admissions, but the proportionate representation was greater among women. Further, the rate of increase of the proportion was greater for women. The total number of admitted men grew from 28,240 in 1979 to 29,568 in 1983; the rate of increase was 4.7 percent. The number of men admitted for stimulant-drug offenses was 5,318 in 1979 and 7,404 in 1983; the rate of increase was 39.2 percent. For total admissions of women, there were 847 in 1979 and 1,157 in 1983; a rate of increase of 35.4 percent, signalling a trend toward increased convictions of

Table 2 Admitted Prisoners and Those Admitted for Stimulant-Drug Offenses by Year and Sex, 1979–1983

	Total Admitted Prisoners (A)		Stimulant-Related Prisoners (B)		Ratio: B Divided by A	
Year	Male	Female	Male	Female	Male	Female
1979	28,240	847	5,318	356	18.8	42.0
1980	27,531	843	5,864	383	21.3	45.4
1981	29,340	996	6,746	503	23.0	50.5
1982	30,276	1,121	7,475	588	24.7	52.5
1983	29,568	1,157	7,404	603	25.0	52.1

women. But the admission of female stimulant abusers was even more remarkable. In 1979 there were 356 women admitted because of stimulant-related offenses, compared with 603 in 1983, a rate of increase of 69.4 percent.

If the number of admissions for stimulant-drug offenses is removed from the total number of prisoner admissions, the effect on the size of the prison population is shown even more dramatically. The number of men admitted then would have declined from 22,922 in 1979 to 22,164 in 1983. For women, the adjusted number of admissions would be 491 in 1979 and 554 in 1983, or an increase of 12.8 percent compared with the 69.4 percent for women admitted for stimulant-drug offenses alone.

Like the *Boryokudan,* who usually are concurrently dealers in and users of drugs, the women serving sentences for stimulant-drug abuse strongly resist programs intended to change their behavior. These women have no sense of responsibility or guilt. They typically say, "I did nothing wrong to others. I bought the stimulant with my own money. I injected it into my own body. I felt happy. Why should I be imprisoned?"

That attitude opposes the penance that was typical of female prisoners of a decade or so ago. Then, even when the crime was the result of their victimization by another person, women inmates were positive in their participation in correctional activities. Their penance was the beginning point for turning them toward constructive lives.

Conclusion

In conclusion, like all correctional systems, Japanese prisons were fundamentally influenced by the social, cultural, and political patterns of the society. Those patterns help explain the notably low crime rate of Japan among highly industrialized nations. The Japanese also have been willing to make the investment essential to creating Japan's progressive correctional system. Nevertheless, as demonstrated by the six issues considered here, correctional management is always tested by changing circumstances that stem from sources outside and within the prison environment.

Discussion Questions

1. Explain how changes that are internal and external to the prison environment have created challenges for institutional management in Japan. Have internal and external changes created any challenges for institutional management in the U.S.? Explain.
2. Compare and contrast the extent to which each of the six administrative issues discussed by Johnson and Hasegawa are of concern to prison administrators in the U.S. What reasons do you see for these comparisons and contrasts?
3. What do you consider to be the six most pressing prison administration issues in the U.S.?

References

A brief account of drug abuse and counter-measures in Japan. (1979). Tokyo: Ministry of Health and Welfare.

Correctional institutions in Japan. (1982). Tokyo: Corrections Bureau, Ministry of Justice.

DeVos, G., and Mizushima, K. (1967). Organization and social functions of Japanese gangs: Historical development and modern parallels. In *Aspects of social change in modern Japan,* ed. R. P. Dore. Princeton, NJ: Princeton University Press.

The horror of white powder. (1978). Tokyo: National Police Agency.

Rome, F. (1975). *The tattooed men.* New York: Delcorte Press.

Summary of white paper on crime. (1984). Tokyo: Research and Training Institute, Ministry of Justice.

17. Differing Current Managerial Approaches in the Corrections of Four Selected New States of Africa*

James S. E. Opolot, Atlanta University

Abstract: Like the other colonial powers, the British tended to apply the same management model in corrections to virtually all their colonies, protectorates, or possessions in Africa, as elsewhere in their empire. What differences lay between the management of corrections in various colonies, protectorates, or possessions tended to reflect the uniqueness of socio-cultural conditions. However, with the advent of independence there have been some isolated instances of a radical departure from the colonial model. It is this continuity and discontinuity, therefore, that this paper seeks to examine.

Introduction

Most people have a very simplistic view of how African corrections are managed. There is a widespread belief that corrections are simple bureaucracies characterized by neat pyramidal hierarchies with the Commissioner at the top, clear "chains of command," and careful patterns of formal communication. People higher in the systems are assumed to be the bosses of the people under them in the chain of command. People at the top perform long-range planning and budget management, and the people down the line execute those decisions. This view of the African corrections from a management perspective is common, and in some situations it is fairly accurate. However, the current management of the current African corrections is not so neat and simple. What is not realized is the fact that African correctional systems, as organizations, vary in a number of important ways. They have different kinds of clients; they employ workers with varying skills; they work with various types of technologies; they develop divergent styles of structure, coordination, and governance; and they have differing relationships to their external environments. To be sure, there are some common elements in the ways correctional systems operate. No two organizations are really the same, however, and any adequate theory of decision making and governance must take their differences into account. Moreover, significant changes have taken place in recent years, both in the pattern of correctional administration and in the degree of control which is exercised from the

*Paper presented at the Southern Corrections Conference at Tallahassee, Florida, March 25, 1983.

From James S. E. Opolot, "Differing Current Managerial Approaches in the Corrections of Four Selected New States of Africa" in *International Journal of Comparative and Applied Criminal Justice* (7(2): 237–246, Winter 1983).

center. It is with such general changes in the control and direction of corrections, primarily in selected four new states of Africa, that this paper is concerned.

Brief Introduction to the Selected New States of Africa

The new African states selected for analysis in this paper are Botswana, Tanzania, Zambia, and Zimbabwe. They have been selected for a number of reasons. For one thing, they were British possessions until their attainment of independence. For another, each country has been involved in unique political experimentation, thereby making its observers raise questions regarding the extent to which its institutions have changed or not changed relative to those of the others of the same colonial power.

The Socio-Political Context of Each Country

There is some need to briefly describe here the socio-political context of each of these countries since attaining independence. In this way we hope to put into perspective the managerial approach adopted in each country.

1. *Botswana:*

This country (formerly known as Bechuanaland) is located in the heart of Southern Africa. Completely land-locked, rivers that are generally dry form the greater part of Botswana's borders. Surrounded by Namibia (Southwest Africa) to the west and Namibia's Caprivi Strip, Zambia to the north, Zimbabwe to the northeast, and South Africa to the south and southeast, Botswana lies at the center of the Southern African Plateau.

2. *Tanzania:*

Tanzania was established with the union on April 26, 1964, of two formerly independent states—Tanganyika and Zanzibar. The two came under the same constitution until 1979 when a separate constitution was approved for Zanzibar.

The country has come to be known internationally for its experimentation with a one-party system, on the one hand, and African socialism on the other. The former is entrenched in Tanzania's constitution. The set of structures and relationships defined as the single party has been modified many times and continues to be the key political institution in Tanzania.

African socialism is distinguished from capitalism which works to build a happy society on the basis of exploitation of man by man; and it is equally opposed to doctrinaire socialism which seeks to build its happy society on a philosophy of inevitable conflict between man and man. The foundation and objective of African socialism is the extended family. All men are regarded as brethren—as members of an ever-extending family.

3. *Zambia:*

The Republic of Zambia (formerly known as Northern Rhodesia) is a land-locked country in South Central Africa. Tanzania and Zaire border Zambia to the north, Malawi and Mosambique to the South, and Angola to the West.

The Zambian Constitution, which was adopted on August 1973, created a one-party state.

Zambia's United Independent Party vigorously embraces the philosophy of humanism, using it as the foundation of government programs.

It is a humanism based on the biblical text: "Thou shall love the Lord thy God with all thy whole heart and thy neighbor as thyself." As such, it is considered a way of life which attaches great importance to man—his faculties, affairs, and earthly aspiration. It is a humanism which derives from Zambian cultural heritage which asserts the dignity and worth of every individual and his capacity for self-actualization.

This philosophy also believes in egalitarianism and the equal rights of all its citizens. To promote this orientation the government offers free medical services and free education at all levels and has nationalized essential services like public transportation.

4. *Zimbabwe:*

The newest of the four states (formerly called Rhodesia) is the southernmost country of intertropical Africa. It is a relatively small, compact country. Ian Smith, former Prime Minister, brought it to the world map when he broke away from British control of the territory; he ruled it for over a decade. But since April 1980, it has been under the premiership of an avowed Marxist, Robert Mugabe, who intends to make it a one-party state. Thereby Zimbabwe is in a state of transition from established colonial institutions and traditions to those aspired to by its present leader.

The Colonial Correctional Management

Correctional management in these four new states of Africa, as elsewhere on the continent, is a creature of colonial rule. That is, in all these countries the British introduced prisons, probation, aftercare, and juvenile institutions. To this end, William Clifford says about the Zambian penal system: "The treatment of offenders in Zambia has followed a pattern of development similar to that in most of the former British territories of Africa."[1]

Unlike the other colonial powers, the British have been known to rule their territories through established local rulers or chiefs, and in the absence of them, to create their equivalents. The District Commissioner, the lowest ranking central government representative, supervised them. This has been labeled as the policy of Indirect Rule.

The rulers or chiefs maintained law and order in their localities. With this arrangement came the establishment of local prisons, jails, or lock-ups in many locations. The colonial central government maintained central and local prisons, thereby producing a dual approach to penal administration. A classical example was found in Northern Rhodesia (now Zambia) which had twenty-nine local prisons.[2] Of the Nigerian situation Milner writes:

> For well over half a century, Nigeria had a dual prison system, just as its administrative and judicial systems were dual. Government prisons were under the jurisdiction of what ultimately became the Federal Prisons Department; local prisons in the west and north were the primary responsibility of the local authorities.[3]

---

1. W. Clifford, "Zambia," in A. Milner, *African Penal Systems,* p. 241.
2. Ibid., p. 242.
3. A. Milner, *The Nigerian Penal System,* p. 218.

This penal organizational structure apparently was of some concern to the British authorities, at least as evidenced by the proposal for the central government to take over administration of local jails in Uganda. Read puts it this way: "It was the Protectorate Government's long-term aim to take over responsibility for all prisoners sentenced to at least one year's imprisonment but it was never possible to accomplish."[4] The post-Amin Uganda government effected this plan as part of the general national rehabilitation program. Nigeria unified its penal system in April 1968.

Colonial corrections were not planned in that each component evolved over time; "different functions were added at different times regardless of relationships to other functions," as David Duffee and his associate would put it.[5] For example, in Southern Rhodesia the Director of Prisons, the Director of Social Welfare and the Commissioner for Juvenile Welfare are under different jurisdictions, the first under Home Affairs and the other two under Housing.

In Tanganyika, shifting of the approved school was described as follows: ". . . 1960 the responsibility of the approved school was transferred from the Prisons Department first to the Ministry of Education and later to the Probation of Welfare Division of the Ministry of Community Development."[6]

Naturally, under these conditions it was difficult to maintain long-term plans. After all, each department had its own high as well as low priorities.

The management of colonial corrections, especially prisons and jails, was conducted in an authoritarian manner, with the line of authority clearly going down from the position of the head of the prison service, probation and aftercare, or juvenile institutions. The authority of a person came not from himself, as a person, but from his position. The strict chain of command from the Commissioner of Prisons, for example, down to the prisoners was emphasized by the military type of environment of most agencies and institutions (the wearing of uniforms, the salutes, the marching, the use of job titles, the saying of "yes, sir" or "no, sir," etc.).

Under the bureaucratic model the head of the department was seen as the hero who stood at the top of a complex pyramid of power. The hero's job was to assess the problems, consider alternatives, and make rational choices. Much of the organization's power was held by the hero, and great expectations were raised because people trusted him to solve problems and fend off threats from the environment. The imagery of the authoritarian hero was deeply ingrained, especially in the mentality of most colonial Commissioners of Prisons.

Another feature characteristic of the colonial corrections was the position of correctional personnel in relation to those of other government employees. The correctional personnel were civil servants; and they were, therefore, ex-

---

4. J. S. Read, "Kenya, Tanzania, and Uganda," in A. Milner, *African Penal Systems* (New York: Frederick A. Praeger, 1969), p. 131.
5. David Duffee, et al., *Criminal Justice: Organization, Structure, and Analysis* (Englewood Cliffs, N.J.: Prentice-Hall, 1978), p. 400.
6. James S. Read, "Kenya, Tanzania, and Uganda," in A. Milner, *African Penal Systems*, p. 158.

pected to be neutral. As Rawling points out, this principle of public service neutrality implies that:

> He (public servant) is not to indulge in political or party controversy and must, in short, maintain a reserve in all political matters. This civil servant in fact is to dress up as a sort of moral and political eunuch . . . as an idealized entity without passion or parts. . . . Sterilized and immunized he can then be expected to withstand the rude shocks of events which shake ordinary mortals to their foundations. Politically the only personal act which presumably will not conflict with his public duty will be placing a cross on a ballot paper at the very infrequent intervals.[7]

Once the corrections employee-to-be came on board, he placed certain limitations on himself as a participating citizen. Those limitations had to do with his ability to speak and act freely in politics. The basic philosophy underlying such restrictions was that the employee of the government had a direct and personal vested interest in politics which properly should be controlled and restricted. Nor could the employee engage in collective bargaining or union activities to improve his working conditions. Under these circumstances the indigenous prison personnel accepted whatever conditions management deemed appropriate. In other words, benevolent paternalism was the order of the day.

There was strict division between superior officers and the junior ones, especially in prisons service. All the former were expatriates or recruited in England until the eve of independence. The bulk of the latter were indigenous. Under these conditions terms of service for the junior officers were local (contracted for short durations without the benefit of career prospects) and as such left much to be desired, as noted by James S. Read: "The Warder, whose job is not a popular one, had a harder day than his prisoners, and was less well fed; most recruits were illiterate, although Uganda had pioneered the appointment of college-educated personnel."[8] Also, Acting Governor Low of the Gold Coast (now called Ghana) had this to say on visiting Cape Coast: "I found the Gaoler's Quarters as unsanitary as a pig stye; the Gaoler himself half undressed and sitting conversing with the prisoners, his office in disorder and no copy of the rules available . . ."[9]

> In many cases the conditions of life generally are better for the prisoners than for the Escort Warders, and the prisoners themselves in many instances are intelligent and of superior class to the Warders: the consequence is that the prisoners, instead of being controlled by them, bully their warders . . . on occasions the escort Warders themselves work instead of forcing the convicts to do so, so as to avoid being punished for not having made their gangs do the prescribed amount of work . . .[10]

The above stated plight seems not to have been limited to the British possessions in Africa; it was experienced in Asia as well. Datir writes: "The position

7. R. W. Rawling, *The Civil Service and the People* (London: Lawrence and Wishart, 1945), pp. 89–90.
8. Ibid., p. 117.
9. Quoted in Robert B. Seidman, "Ghana Prison System: Historical Perspective," in A. Milner, *African Penal Systems*, p. 440.
10. *The Gold Coast (now called Ghana) Annual Report 1902.*

of prison guards is very much unsatisfactory, right from the evolution of the modern prison system in India."[11]

In the colonial policy of organizational isolation, both the staff and the prisoners, for example, were directed to keep interaction to a minimum. This was done under the guises of familiarity breeds contempt, protection of the warders, and minimizing trafficking.

Argyris[12] and Selznick,[13] among others, have identified three core activities of all organizations. These are: (1) goal-directed or production activity, (2) internal maintenance activity, and (3) adjustment-to-environment activity. Analysis of colonial correctional administration with these concepts in mind reveals that most prison activity, for example, had been determined largely by its internal maintenance and environmental needs. In other words, the prison as a collectivity of people had spent most of its time developing an organizational identity. What attention was paid to the prisoners and staff—the indigenous personnel with the exception of expatriate personnel—was minimal.

It would follow that at the time of independence the colonial management left behind not only bureaucratized corrections, but also some nagging problems. The success of the new leadership has had to depend on how they have gone about restructuring the former and resolving the latter.

We begin by noting that each of the four countries became a new state under different circumstances and has since sought to steer its own unique course. That is, the correctional managerial approach has tended to reflect the realities of the prevailing socio-political context. In seeking to substantiate these points we will focus on (a) Africanization, (b) political participation-realignment of corrections to one-party rule, (c) collective bargaining-unionizations, and (d) two examples of imaginative thinking.

One of the first orders of business for newly independent African states' corrections, as of other government services, has been Africanization. This is a policy which has been aimed at replacing expatriate or colonial employees with Africans whenever the latter became available. During the author's recent (July–August 1979) tour of the four countries all but one had completed the Africanization process. The one exception is Zimbabwe. Here the director of Prisons and most of the senior penal administrators were still white personnel; the Deputy Director is a Zimbabwean.

The slow pace of change in this country may be attributed to the number of whites in Zimbabwe as well as to the manner in which independence was won. Compared to the other countries Zimbabwe had the highest population of settled whites and hence a pool of white public employees; its independence was won through the longest drawn fight.

Contemporary events in certain new states of Africa indicate a departure from the colonial proposition that correctional personnel should not participate in national politics. Both Tanzania and Zambia are newly established one-party

---

11. R. N. Datir, *Prison As A Social System* (Bombay: Popular Prakashan, 1978), p. 138.
12. C. Argyris, *Integrating the Individual and the Organization* (New York: John Wiley, 1964).
13. P. Selznick, *T.V.A. and the Grass Roots* (New York: Harper and Row, 1948).

states each guided by a unique ideology. Zimbabwe is struggling to follow suit. In the former two cases corrections personnel belong to the ruling party. This means that recruitment takes into account party membership. Botswana does not have this requirement; its recruitment and selection are still based in the colonial tradition of civil service.

Of late, there has been a considerable amount of criticism of the restrictions imposed upon criminal justice personnel in general and corrections personnel in particular in terms of their political rights, especially the right to engage in collective bargaining or to form unions. Time and again, arguments and counterarguments have been given for and against the idea of granting greater political freedoms to these public servants.

This matter has not yet been debated at the level that we see in developed countries. What we see in a few new African states are moderate beginnings of unionization not only for correctional personnel, but also for police officers. Fairly well-documented cases of the former are the Botswana Prison Officers' Association and Zambia Police Association.

The establishment of the Botswana Prison Officers' Association is couched in these words:

> 1. These Regulations may be cited as the Prison's (Botswana Prison Officers Association) Regulation, 1980.
> 2. (1) An association, to be called the Botswana Prison Officers Association (and hereinafter referred to as "the Association"), is hereby established.
>   (2) The object of the Association shall be to enable prison officers to meet in order to consider and bring to the notice of the Director matters affecting the welfare and efficiency of the Service.
>   (3) The Association may consider the general principles governing appointments, promotions, transfers, matters of discipline and salaries within the Service with a view to improving conditions within the Service as a whole; but the Association shall not consider individual cases concerning these matters.
>   (4) The Association shall be independent of and not associated with any association or other body outside the Service.
>   (5) No person other than a prison officer shall become a member of the Association in any capacity whether honorary or otherwise.
>   (6) Every prison officer shall be entitled to become a member of the Association and shall not be so entitled unless he is below the rank of Assistant Director of Prisons.
>   (7) A member of the Association who ceases to be a prison officer or is promoted to the rank of Assistant Director of Prisons or above shall thereupon cease to be a member of the Association.

From an organizational perspective it is stated:

3. For the purposes of these Regulations, the following divisions, to be called Prison Division, are hereby established:
   (a) the Northern Division, comprising all that part of Botswana lying north of the Tropic of Capricorn; and
   (b) the Southern Division, comprising all that part of Botswana lying south of the Tropic of Capricorn.
4. (1) A board, to be called the Branch Board, is hereby established for each Prisons Division.
   (2) Each Branch Board shall consist of 9 members of whom—
   (a) 3 shall be senior officers elected from among themselves by junior officers for the time being serving in that Prisons Division; and
   (b) 3 shall be subordinate officers elected from among themselves by subordinate officers for the time being serving in that Prisons Division.

There are two Police Associations under the provisions of the Zambia Police Act, Cap. 133 of the Laws of Zambia. These are: (a) Zambia Police (Superior Police) Officers Association; and (b) Zambia Police (Subordinate Police) Officers Association.

In the latter, there is an Other Ranks Association. The function of these associations is to bring to the notice of the Inspector-General of Police and the Government (Ministry), all matters affecting the welfare and efficiency of the force.

Officials of each of these associations are elected annually from among service members of the Force.

What can we make of these developments in the African countries in question? It is as yet too early to make any meaningful evaluation. For the moment we may have to be guided by what is said in the literature on collective bargaining by prison personnel.

Tannenbaum and others report that workers feel more satisfied when they feel that they can have some influence on management in policy-making.[14] Similarly, prison personnel who feel that they are participating in policy-making roles, and have a say in what goes on in the prison system, may be more satisfied with their work. To the extent that prison personnel feel involved in important professional decisions, they are likely to be more interested and involved in other professionally creative activities. However, as Tannenbaum warns, some individuals will be less satisfied by involvement and participation in the decision-making process.[15] We may expect that the general rule that involvement leads to greater satisfaction will hold in most cases, with the reverse being true for prison personnel with certain personality characteristics and in prison systems with certain senior officials and certain histories.

14. A. Tannenbaum, *Control in Organizations* (New York: McGraw-Hill, 1968).
15 Ibid.

As indicated earlier, Commissioners of Prisons are in prominent positions to exercise authority and expertise in the management and leadership of prisons affairs. The Commissioner's leadership style may help establish a penal climate and conditions that contain high levels of staff trust. Or, the Commissioner may act in ways that generate or escalate staff distrust and disrespect. Either way, the Commissioner's role is potent.

Although they are part of a larger and more complex system, individual Commissioners generally have considerable operational latitude to make decisions and mobilize resources if they are so inclined. The professional status of Commissioners provides them with substantial autonomy and influence. As a result, various scholars stress the crucial role played by Commissioners in most penal systems in determining what organizational variations do exist, and in contributing to differing levels of staff and prison satisfaction. Duffee[16] articulated the same in these words:

> More than any other type in the correctional enterprise, the one role that will be essential to the construction of an adaptable correctional system is the role of correctional management. This role is crucial because of the function it performs in the organization. The manager is the gatekeeper controlling the quantity and quality of interactions between the organization and the environment. Essentially, it is on the ability of correctional management to adapt and improve—that the evolutionary fate of correctional organizations depends.

These criteria are difficult but not impossible to meet. Certainly the Botswana Commissioner of Prisons appears to have emerged as a gradual reformist, thereby meeting some of the criteria stated above.

The Commissioner of Botswana, unlike many of his counterparts elsewhere in independent Africa, has embarked not only upon revising the Prisons Act, the Standing Orders, and the Prisons Rules—the legacies of colonial administration, but also making available supplementary documents. The preparation of the *Prisons Inspections Handbook* is one case in point. This document is written in plain English; it explains very comprehensively the purpose and nature of prison inspection, including its procedures and inherent problems.

In another document this commissioner has outlined the treatment and rehabilitation of prisoners under his charge. He writes: "The prison Administration shall constantly seek to awaken and maintain in the minds both of the personnel and the public the conviction that this work is a social service of great importance, and to this end all appropriate means of informing and educating the public should be used. To understand or indeed to manage a prison it must be thought of in sociological, and/or socio-psychological terms."[18]

The Botswana Commissioner of Prisons, then, has not only formulated a professional point of view and techniques, but also whether or not he is aware of it, he has also developed a social philosophy confused or clearly designed. This social philosophy has been influenced by certain factors, such as the time

16. David Duffee, *Correctional Policy and Prison Organization* (New York: John Wiley, 1975), pp. 42–3.

and place in which they have lived, the current of ideas about them, and the social and economic tensions which have touched their interests and aroused their sympathies or antipathies. These factors, together with his own personal temperament, have not only conditioned his social thinking, but have also provided him with standards of judgement. Consciously or unconsciously he has applied these standards of judgement to far-reaching correctional issues and problems.

Summary and Conclusions

This paper has sought to outline the history of correctional management in the selected new states of Africa, namely Botswana, Tanzania, Zambia, and Zimbabwe, and also has sought to focus on certain recent innovations. In the former case common British colonial correctional management approaches and problems were identified. In the latter case Africanization and experimentation with diffusion of the colonial civil service orientation, unionization on the part of the correctional personnel, and augmentation of existing laws and operational procedures were cited. Here, we sought to demonstrate common denominators among the four countries, on the one hand, and where they differ, on the other. In every country, however, there is need to inquire how far managerial approaches, as at present conceived, are likely to meet the needs of the future.

Discussion Questions

1. Compare and contrast the issues and difficulties facing correctional management in the four African states with those facing correctional management in the U.S.
2. In your view, what should be the nature of the relationship between prison guards and the inmates they manage? Between line staff and their superiors in the prison organization?
3. Opolot discusses the changes in correctional management that were necessary to make the prisons fit the socio-political climate which emerged after independence was achieved in Botswana, Tanzania, Zambia, and Zimbabwe. How do American prisons reflect the socio-political realities of the U.S.?

18. The Effect of Management Regime on Disruptive Behaviour: An Analysis within the British Prison System

W. Davies, Ph.D., St. Andrews Hospital, Northampton NN1 5DG P. W. Burgess, B.A., Medical Research Council Applied Psychology Unit, Cambridge

Abstract: Discipline reports filed in a local prison over a seven-year period were analysed. During this time four different governors were in office, and the numbers of reports filed during each governor's term were compared. There proved to be a significant difference in numbers of reports filed during each governor's term, suggesting that the management regime instituted by the governor of a local prison may have a strong effect upon either the incidence of disruptive behaviour, its recording, or both. One of the governors in this study, under whom discipline reporting frequency was low, had worked at another prison which had been the subject of the Prescott (1976) report. At that time, this governor had been singled out for mention as the governor who had presided over an apparently peaceful prison as measured by discipline reports, supporting the view that a particular governor's management style may be important in influencing levels of disruptive behaviour in the prison situation.

Introduction

A number of studies have documented ways in which, administratively, it is possible to reduce levels of violence in the psychiatric setting (Armond, 1982; Packham, 1978; Brailsford and Stevenson, 1972). However, few, if any, studies attempt to describe the influence key personnel may have on levels of disruptive behaviour generally, and data gathered from a forensic population are even less available.

Gertz (1980) recommends that in order to minimize the risk of violence in the psychiatric setting, administrative staff should keep policies and procedures related to violent behaviour up to date and should participate in training programmes. Scott (1977) emphasizes the maintenance of personal relationships and good communication, and Armond's (1982) study implicates the minimization of administrative changes in the prevention of violent incidents. While the present study takes a broader view, looking at incidence of disruptive incidents generally, rather than specifically violent ones, it is not unreasonable to propose that the measures described above might also be applicable to the prison situation, and would be likely to minimize not only the frequency of violent inci-

From W. Davies and P. W. Burgess, "The Effect of Management Regime on Disruptive Behaviour: An Analysis within the British Prison System" in *Medicine, Science, and the Law* (28(3): 243–247, 1988).

dents but also that of other disruptive behaviours as well. All of the above preventive measures may be influenced by the management regime and, in turn, by the head of that regime—for instance: adequate training of staff in preventive measures and the defusing of potentially dangerous situations, good communication through regular meetings, the fostering of staff morale, emphasis on the importance of personal relationships with inmates, appropriate staff selection, minimization of administrative changes, etc.

It would not be unreasonable to suppose that some prison **governors** might be more successful than others in fostering the environment which is conducive to the psychological well-being of both staff and inmates, therefore minimizing the likelihood of unrest. This study attempts to test this assumption and to demonstrate the importance of the management regime in the reduction of disruptive incidents and the use of disciplinary measures.

Method

Discipline reports documenting disruptive behaviour by inmates in a British local prison were examined. Over a period of seven years the prison was headed by four different governors and a total of 6,838 reports were filed. The number and frequency of reports filed during each of the governor's terms were compared. This required two sets of data. The first was the number of discipline reports filed for each month over the past seven years (the longest available period). The second was the arrival and departure dates of the four governors in post during that time.

The Nature of the Reports

When an inmate offends against any of the prison rules and this comes to the attention of a member of the prison staff, that staff member has the option of "putting him on report." Filing a report detailing the misdemeanour will lead to the accused person appearing before the Governor-in-charge, who will assess the man's innocence or guilt and award a sentence accordingly. In more serious breaches of rules the adjudication will be by the **Board of Visitors,** or the police may be called to investigate. These, however, are relatively rare. For instance, a two-year sample period revealed that only nine percent of reports concerned acts of violence—the majority were minor offences against prison regulations. In the more serious cases, the law runs its course in the same way as if the offence had been committed outside the prison. In practice, the vast majority of discipline reports are filed by members of the uniformed staff or civilian instructors (in the workshops).

Staff members may use their discretion as to whether to file a report on a prisoner, and may choose instead to give an oral warning; an intermediate course of action is for the member of staff to issue a "formal warning," which is recorded as such in the prisoner's record.

The Prison Population

The data were collected from a local prison which was built in 1854, and originally designed to cater for approximately 600 inmates. However, during the period of examination the mean prison population was approximately 1,000, with no increase in cell space and little increase in staff facilities. The emphasis of the prison, as a local facility, is to cater for a wide variety of prisoners, includ-

Table 1 Number of Discipline Reports Filed During Each Governor's Term, with Figures Adjusted for Term Length Differences.

Governor	1	2	3	4
Number of reports filed	356	3064	2720	698
Period in post (months)	5	41	30	8
Expected number of reports (using chi-squared tests)	407	3338	2442	651

ing prisoners on **remand,** young offenders either serving their sentences or waiting to be allocated to a young offenders' unit, adult male convicts with short- or medium-term sentences who may remain in this prison for the duration of that sentence, and those with long-term sentences (over five years) who will spend only the first part of their sentence in the local prison while they are waiting to be transferred to a more appropriate establishment. In addition, there were occasionally a few (never more than ten) female prisoners.

Results

Table 1 shows the number of reports filed during each governor's period in post, together with the total length of each governor's term. Using the chi-squared test, the number of reports that could be expected during each period could be calculated (This information is also presented in Table 1.) The differences between the numbers of discipline reports filed proved significant at the $p > 0.001$ level ($X^2 = 63.92$, df = 3).

A number of variables other than the effect of management regime might account for these observed differences. It is possible that they were caused by changes in staffing levels, changes in numbers of inmates, a population threshold above which a disproportionate amount of incidents were likely to occur, or merely a general trend regardless of management regime. Two of these variables may be immediately accounted for. The "population threshold" theory was previously tested in this prison and with this population, and found not to be a significant variable (Davies, 1983). In addition, staffing levels during the seven years did not change significantly. However, the above analysis does not account for the other two variables: population change and trend in rule-breaking regardless of management regime. The following hypotheses were therefore tested:

1. that the population of the prison varied during the seven years, and that the observed differences in number of discipline reports filed during each governor's term in post reflect these fluctuations in population;
2. that the effect demonstrated in the above statistic is due not to different governors' management styles, but simply to an increasing trend to break prison rules over the seven-year period.

The first hypothesis was tested by pro-rating the "observed" figures from the above chi-squared statistics. This was performed by adjusting the "observed" figures (for each governor's term) according to the percentage above or below the mean population over the full seven-year period. The results are

Table 2 Number of Discipline Reports Filed During Each Governor's Term, with Figures Pro-rated for Changes in Population.

Governor	1	2	3	4
Observed number of discipline reports	356	3064	2720	698
Expected number of discipline reports	374	3286	2493	685

Table 3 Comparison of Numbers of Reports Filed During the First and Second Halves of the Terms in Office of Governors 2 and 3, with Pro-rated Figures to Account for Term Length Differences.

Governor	2		3	
Term of Office	1	2	3	4
Observed number of discipline reports	1519	1545	1343	1377
Expected number of discipline reports	1486	1578	1398	1322

given in Table 2 and do not support the hypothesis. Even after pro-rating to account for population changes, the difference in numbers of discipline reports filed during the term of each governor proved significant at the $p > 0.001$ level ($X^2 = 36.74$, df = 3).

The second hypothesis was tested by comparing data gathered from the terms of office of the two longest-standing governors, numbers 2 and 3 (accounting between them for 84.5 percent of the seven years under study). If there was a trend towards increase regardless of governor, the second half of each governor's administrative term should see more reports filed than the first half. The results are given in Table 3 and do not support the hypothesis. There were no significant differences in numbers of reports filed during the first and second halves of the term in office for either governor 2 ($X^2 = 0.71$, df = 1) or governor 3.

Since neither of these hypotheses was proved, this suggests that the significant differences (in numbers of reports filed during the terms of office of the four governors) observed in the first analysis are valid.

Discussion

The results presented here suggest that the governor of a prison (or the regime he runs) can influence the number of discipline reports that are filed. This study suggests that discipline reports were less likely to be filed during the terms of office of governors 1 and 2 than under either governors 3 or 4. Governor 1 was in office for only a short time, but under governor 2, for whom we have the most data, consistently fewer reports per month were filed than under the other two, and there is a small (but not significant) trend towards fewer reports with time.

This does not necessarily mean that there are fewer breaches of prison rules. It may mean that the staff are less vigilant, or that though vigilant and

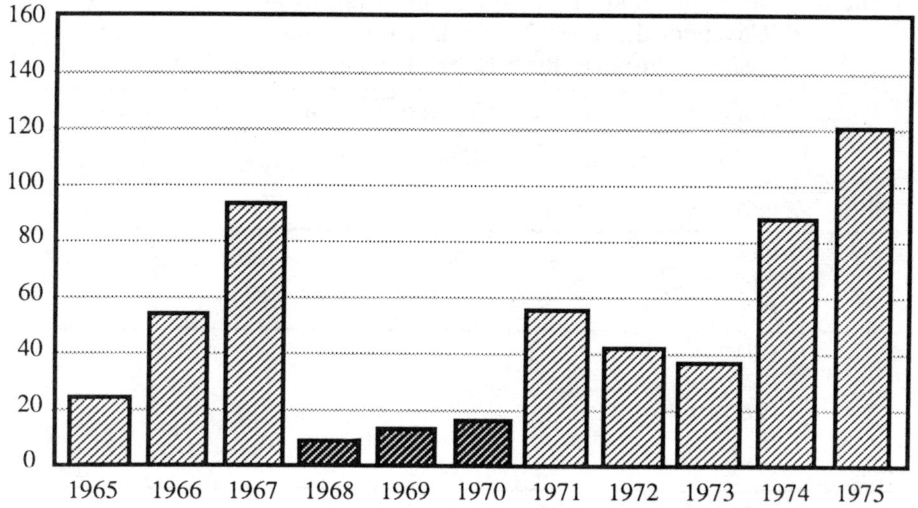

Figure 1 Use of solitary confinement as punishment in Hull Prison 1965–75. Governor's 2nd term of office was from February 1968 to August 1970. Taken from Prescott (1976).

therefore observing breaches of rules, they do not feel so inclined to record the breach formally—and there may be many reasons for this.

Interestingly, before taking up appointment at the local prison described here, governor 2 was in office (in the same capacity) at Hull Prison. Data on the use of solitary confinement as a punishment at this prison are available for the periods during, and surrounding, governor 2's term of office at Hull which was from February 1968 to August 1970 (Prescott, 1976). These data are reproduced in Figure 1. As can be seen, during the period that governor 2 was in office, there were far fewer instances of solitary confinement than there were either before or after; in fact the instances during governor 2's term numbered less than one-third of the total of any other three years during the ten-year period described by Prescott.

In addition, Hull's position in the "league" of offences in **dispersal prisons** appeared to improve markedly during governor 2's term of office (Table 4). Hull was at the bottom ("best-behaved") or in the bottom half of the league from 1968 to 1970 and moved into the top half ("worst-behaved") for four of the five years from 1971 to 1975. Similarly, it was for the most part performing badly in the three years before 1968.

These figures, in themselves, do not conclusively prove anything. However, in conjunction with the findings in this study, they certainly suggest that the management regime instituted by the governor of a prison may have a strong effect upon the reporting and/or use of disciplinary measures for disruptive behaviour. This in turn has many implications for prison crisis management.

Anecdotally, four qualities that staff who had worked with governor 2 consistently highlighted were the following:

Table 4 Hull's Position in "League" of Offences in Dispersal Prisons (Governor 2's Term between Middle Lines). The Higher the Position Number, the "Better-behaved" the Prison.

Year	Number of Dispersal Prisons	League Position
1965	4	1
1966	5	3
1967	6	1
1968	6	5
1969	6	6
1970	6	6
1971	7	3
1972	7	2
1973	7	5
1974	7	2
1975	7	3

a) He was "flexible" and "absorbent" and imparted this to his staff.
b) He established many committees and meetings.
c) He had "charisma."
d) Staff and inmates liked him.

However, the validity of these comments and the mechanics of how a governor and the regime he institutes do in fact influence levels of disruptive behaviour are uncertain, and clarification is left to further study.

Discussion Questions

1. Other than the fact that prison staff may not become aware of certain incidents of inmate disruptive behavior, what else might account for a discrepancy between the number of actual incidents and the number of reported or recorded incidents (i.e., what factors influence staff discretion to report)?
2. Is it reasonable to conclude from this research that differences in management regime *cause* differences in actual and/or reported incidents of disruptive behavior in prison? Why or why not?
3. What variables, other than those examined by the authors, may affect actual and/or reported incidents of disruptive behavior? Explain why each factor you identify is relevant.
4. How might the wider cultural context of a prison influence the level of disruptive behavior displayed by the inmates and the amount of such behavior recorded by the prison staff? That is, what does the study of comparative penology tell us about disruptive behavior?
5. How can the head administrator of a prison minimize disruptive incidents? Take the personal qualities or characteristics of the administrator into account.

References

Armond, A. D. (1982) Violence in the semi-secure ward of a psychiatric hospital. *Med. Sci. Law* 22, 203–9.

Brailsford, D. S. and Stevenson, J. (1973) Factors related to violent and unpredictable behaviour in psychiatric hospitals. *Nursing Times* 18, 9–11.

Davies, W. (1983) An analysis of inmate violence in a local prison. Unpublished Ph.D. thesis. University of Birmingham.

Packham, H. (1978) Violence—managing the violent patient. *Nursing Mirror,* 22 June, 17–19.

Prescott, J. (1976) Report on the Hull Prison riot. In *Report on the Work of the Prison Department*. London, HMSO.

Scott, P. D. (1977) Assessing dangerousness in criminals. *Brit. J. Psychiat.* 131, 127–42.

19. The Role of the British Prison-Based Probation Officer*

Mike Carlie, Director of Criminal Justice Studies
Southwest Missouri State University

Abstract: Unlike probation officers in the United States, British probation officers serve a portion of their time working in a prison providing probation services to prisoners. This policy, referred to as "throughcare," is intended to provide prisoners with probation services prior to, during, and following their incarceration. While the work of community-based probation and parole officers is well documented in the literature of British corrections, the role of the prison-based probation officer is less well researched. This paper reviews the kinds of services provided by prison-based probation officers in England and some of the unique problems they face providing these services in the prison setting.

The author, having spent several months each year over a period of five years (from 1983 to 1987) observing in Her Majesty's prisons, draws upon interview data, official documents, and personal observations to provide the reader with a description and critique of the role of the British prison probation officer. The paper concludes with a review of some of the obstacles prison-based probation officers face in attempting to fulfill their role.

Introduction

Our purpose here is to describe the role of the prison-based probation officer in British prisons and to highlight some of the problems they face in attempting to fulfill that role.

Immediately prior to 1966, when prison probation services were initiated, British prison philosophy was becoming more treatment-than punishment-oriented. One consequence of this shifting philosophy was the creation of the position of Prison Probation Officer which would, ideally, provide inmates with a means of maintaining contact with the outside world, help relieve the stresses and strains of everyday life inside the prison, and, by the prison probation officer's very presence, speak to the then growing concern for treatment and a social work orientation towards offenders.

The prison probation officer's work filled a void in the work of probation officers in the community who, until 1966, dealt only with prisoners prior to and following their incarceration (if paroled). By adding probation services while an offender was in prison, the Probation Service (the national office which administrates all probation officers) created and fulfilled the "through-

*The author thanks Michael Roberts, Senior Probation Officer, Middlesex Area Probation Service, London, England, for his assistance in reviewing and commenting upon this paper during its preparation.

From Mike Carlie "The Role of the British Prison-Based Probation Officer" in *International Journal of Comparative and Applied Criminal Justice* (14(1): 73–81, Spring 1990).

care'' concept. Throughcare requires that the offender be in the care of the Probation Service prior to, during, and after incarceration (during parole or ''aftercare''). Towards this end, the Home Office has stated that ''At the point of sentence, an offender does not cease to be a client of the Probation Service'' (Brown and Whiffen, 1983: 1).

Prison Probation and the Home Office

Among other things, the Home Office is the administrative center for all correctional (and law enforcement) agencies in England. Perhaps the closest analogy to corrections in the United States would be to view England as one state and the Home Office Secretary as the state's Commissioner or Director of the Department of Corrections including prisons, jails, and community-based services such as probation and parole.

Within the Home Office are both the Prison Department (responsible for the day-to-day operation of the prisons) and the Probation Service. The Probation Service is responsible for both community-based and prison-based probation services. While the Prison Department ''. . . holds the responsibility for the care and control of all inmates, the Probation Service contributes to the overall responsibility by making the best use of the particular skills of its staff'' (Sudds, 1987: 1).

Although the Home Office expects prison probation officers to provide a unique service for inmates (a social work orientation rather than a custodial or punitive orientation), in practice it is a different matter. According to the Home Office, ''It is imperative that the Probation Department be seen as an integral part of the overall management of inmate needs whilst in custody and not perceived as an idiosyncratic specialist group'' (Sudds, 1987: 1). As we will see, an administrative philosophy which emphasizes the ''management of inmates'' may not mix well with a social work philosophy.

The Prison-based Probation Officer

Prison probation officers are community- or field-probation officers who live and do their work in the free community and who have been temporarily assigned to duty in one of Her Majesty's Prisons. Their tenure in the institution typically ranges from two to four years and is limited for at least two reasons. First, ''. . . probation officers are supposed to bring into the institution the norms and expectations of the world outside to which the prisoner will return, and for which he must be prepared'' (North, 1986: 4). Keeping the length of service of probation officers short may contribute to this goal.

Secondly, ''. . . the social work needs of prisoners are always in danger of being seen through institutional eyes'' (North, 1986: 4). It is believed that this is most likely to occur when probation officers are asked to serve long terms of duty in the prison. For this reason, the tenure of the prison probation officer is relatively short.

A prison probation officer may have two offices in the prison—one in the administrative area (''outside'') and the second in the inmate living area (''inside''). The outside office is used for everyday desk work, conferencing among staff, and other administrative tasks. The inside office is used for prisoner interviews and help sessions, such as making phone calls, listening to problems, and trying to provide for the social work needs of the inmates (providing counseling, helping prisoners maintain contact with relatives and others in the free community, and being a concerned and interested listener).

The size of a Prison Probation Department depends primarily upon the number of inmates confined in a particular prison. In some prisons, there are only one or two prison probation officers. In the larger prisons, there may be six or more. The structure of the larger prison probation departments includes a Senior Probation Officer with several Probation Officers subservient to that role. There may also be a clerical worker assigned to the probation staff. The position of Chief Probation Officer (similar to the Chief Probation Officer in the United States) remains in the community for purposes of continuity.

Job Description and Job Tasks

In 1967 the Home Office distributed a circular (Home Office, 1967) which outlined and described the role expectations or job tasks for prison probation officers. The list of tasks is lengthy and varies from prison to prison depending upon the age and sex of the inmate/client as well as the nature of the criminal conduct for which the inmate was convicted. Generally speaking, "Probation Officers are in prison principally to bring a social work perspective to the needs of the inmate population and to the care and treatment which they receive" (North, 1986: 6). The impact the prison setting has on the way in which prison probation officers conduct their work is exemplified by Sudds when he states that:

> The nature of the institution and the number of inmates passing through will inevitably dictate much of the work undertaken by probation staff. Experience of others is that much of the work is of a reactive kind but it is however possible to attempt activities in a slightly more pro-active way. (Sudds, 1987: 1)

Representing a link between the institution and the free community, and highlighting the rather complicated role of prison probation officers, Sudds (1987: 2) has stated that prison probation officers:

> will . . . have to make use of not only a detailed knowledge of the Probation Service but also of other community resources. It is a prerequisite of good prison probation work that officers should keep in touch with developments, both in facilities and in practice skills.
>
> Liaison with hostels schemes (i.e., group homes in the community for offenders on probation and/or parole), drug projects, employment schemes (i.e., programs providing job training and placement), local authority housing and social services, ethnic minority advice groups, Department of Health and Social Services, services for women prisoners, etc., all indicate that prison probation work cannot be undertaken effectively without looking outward to the community as well as inward to the prison. [Definitions in parentheses inserted by the author for purposes of clarity.]

North notes that "Turning to consider in more detail the social work methods employed in prisons, many of the . . . practices depend heavily upon shorter term focused work and on crisis intervention techniques" (North, 1986: 2). This is in stark opposition to community-based probation work in which the probation officer has a longer and more definite period of time to establish and implement a treatment plan with a probationer.

While the list of tasks number in the dozens, they may be grouped into a smaller number of categories indicating the kinds of services which, according to the Home Office, should be provided. Included are services for the newly arrived prisoner; meeting the day-to-day needs of prisoners (sometimes referred to as the "welfare role" of prison probation officers); helping inmates who wish to change their behavior; providing training for all prison personnel including prison probation officers and their students; writing reports, reviews, and recommendations; providing throughcare; maintaining contact with prisoners' families; and working cooperatively with other care providers inside and outside the prison.

> A surprising amount of domestic and matrimonial work is also undertaken by Prison Probation staff. In Holoway (a women's prison in London) this frequently centers on the maintenance of ties with separated children. Elsewhere the task is to help men keep their sometimes tenuous links with partners and families. A welfare visit may be used for these and other purposes. Despite its title ("welfare visit") it is in fact a joint interview for inmate and visitor, requiring conciliatory skills not often needed in fieldwork (North, 1986: 3).

North concludes, "From all of this it should be clear that, if there is no standard field Probation Officer's job, still less is there a standard job for Prison Probation Officers. The work varies greatly, both between and within prisons" (North, 1986: 3).

Efforts to establish a welfare-oriented atmosphere in a prison setting are not without problems. It is to this issue that we now turn our attention.

Problems

Three of the most visible problems facing the prison probation officer include those arising from the prison setting itself, the clientele with whom they are expected to work, and the conflicts which arise from sharing responsibility for the inmates' care with prison guards.

> The prison environment inevitably has an impact both on client and worker. The impact of imprisonment on the dignity of individuals—social isolation, powerlessness, dependency, and the breakdown in personal or community relationships—all point to the need for a skilled social work service to be offered to prisoners. (North, 1986: 2)

The prison probation officer attempts to be a buffer between the harsh realities of prison life and the prisoner's need for a modicum of dignity and self-respect. That the prison setting may exacerbate the prisoner's problems makes it "all the more important, and yet all the more difficult, for the traditional value base of the (Probation) Service to be preserved" (North, 1986: 3).

As might be expected, the requirements for "safety, security, and control, and the demands of rehabilitation, training and educational programs" (North, 1986: 4) are at conflict in the prison setting. Essentially, the social work approach (with an emphasis on humanitarian values and a belief in the value of treatment) does not mix well with the oppressive nature of prisons (North, 1986).

Prison overcrowding appears to complicate all of these issues. Overcrowding places excessive demands on educational, vocational, medical, and recreational facilities and staff, and enlarges prison probation officer caseloads. Even procedures within the prison often result in restricting prison probation officers from doing their job as thoroughly as they would prefer. For example, although prison probation officers would like to meet with new prisoners on their first day of confinement,

> The reality is that the variety of statutory activities to be undertaken by the prison within the 24 hours following reception precludes probation officers from having a significantly high profile at this stage and newly received inmates will have a limited capacity to absorb much additional information.
>
> It is nonetheless experienced as a time of some anxiety for these young men who may have unresolved family matters having perhaps not anticipated the remand (being held) in custody that day. It is also thought to be a critical period for those who are potentially suicidal. (Sudds, 1987: 3)

As a result of their training and philosophy, prison officers would prefer to respond to inmate needs with care and patience. In practice, prison overcrowding and staff shortages have necessitated a reactive rather than proactive stance.

Further complicating matters is the fact that, while prison probation officers base their efforts on a social work model and need time to implement their treatment strategy, their clientele are with them for uncertain and often short periods of time. This makes it more difficult to plan a program of assistance for the client/prisoner (Clark, 1985: 2).

Bottomley and Liebling (1987: 10), in an assessment of prison guards and prison probation officers, found that

> According to prison staff, most (prison probation) officer work was dealing with day-to-day problems and consequences of imprisonment; comparatively little involved maintaining family links or tackling underlying problems of criminal behavior—both of which, it was agreed, *should be major aims* of throughcare. (Emphasis is original.)

As clientele, prisoners present a unique set of problems to the prison probation officers. The nature of their needs and the means available for dealing with these needs are different in many respects from the problems probation officers faced while working with probationers in the open community. According to North (1986: 3):

> Some of these prisoners will be emotionally or psychiatrically disturbed. Many will have problems with addiction or with personal relationships or family difficulties. The Prison Probation response can range from long-term counseling to short-term crisis intervention and task-centered work.
>
> Sex offenders, lifers, mothers with babies, deportees, men not yet convicted, men soon to be released, all present their own particular problems and have their own special needs. And above and beyond these come the basic challenges:
>
> A. To deal professionally and sensibly with the stream of demands, anxieties, and enquiries from the inmate population.

B. To deal with offenders, the seriousness of whose offences, or extent of whose past criminal behavior distinguishes them from a conventional field clientele.
C. To find the sense of purpose and commitment to continue with the task of responding positively to the thousands of recidivists and petty, inadequate offenders who choke up our penal institutions, and whom we as a (probation) Service say should not be there.

A criticism often heard among prison caseworkers, social workers, and psychotherapists in the United States is that much, if not most, of their counseling time is spent dealing with matters of immediate concern to their client/inmate. Little time is spent talking about things which occurred prior to the inmate's incarceration, factors which may have contributed to the inmate's criminal behavior in the first place.

As may be imagined, given the conditions under which they must work, prison probation officers appear to be experiencing some difficulties with the role they are supposed to play in the prison setting. Among other things, they are confronted with several structural constraints which make fulfillment of the role difficult. These structural constraints include the fact that the client/prisoner is confined, constantly under supervision, isolated from the community, and otherwise limited in his or her degrees of freedom of choice. Factors such as these may have an adverse impact on the job of the prison probation officer.

Secondly, budgetary constraints within the British government have limited the prison building program, placing even greater pressure on prison administrators and, in turn, their staff. Administrative responses to prison overcrowding sometimes require the use of constraints which may hinder the prison probation officer's efforts. One major aspect appears to be the impact staff shortages and overcrowding have on expectations placed upon prison probation officers and prison guards.

Staff shortages sometimes require that prison probation officers assist custodial staff in the completion of some guard-like duties. According to some prison probation officers, taking a custodial stance towards prisoners compromises and undermines the treatment orientation prison probation officers want to project to their clientele (prisoners). This problem has not gone unnoticed by the Home Office.

> The roles of Prison (guards) and Prison Probation Officers have been under review for some time. In particular, (reports have emphasized) the importance of shared responsibility for prisoner throughcare between the Prison Service and the Probation Service. (These reports) call for setting out of model procedures and guidelines about how Prison (guards), Probation Officers and other specialists can work together. (North, 1986: 10)
>
> The prison guard/prisoner relationship is central to prisoner throughcare. The active involvement of prison (guards) in prisoner throughcare should be considered the norm rather than the exception. Specialist staff, e.g., chaplains, education staff, psychologists and instructors, also have an important contribution to make. (Platt, 1986: 1)

Suggesting that prison probation officers and prison guards "share responsibility for prisoner throughcare" is seen as a threat to the traditional social work orientation of prison probation officers and is a clear example of role duplication. This is what is known as "shared working." Some difficulties have arisen in efforts to clearly delineate what it is prison probation officers are supposed to do. While prison probation officers do not want to act like prison guards, neither do prison guards wish to be solely characterized as the "bad guys," confining their activities to controlling prisoners and being denied opportunities to provide treatment.

Implications of the Findings

While some of the problems identified above carry with them possibilities for resolution, others may not be so easily resolved. The fact that the client is incarcerated, that he/she is a criminal offender, and the consequences this holds for the prison probation officer, may not be changed. However, problems arising from conflicts with administration and guards over the role of the prison probation officer do have some hope of resolution.

To reduce role conflicts, the definition of the roles of prison probation officer and prison guard should be mutually exclusive or sufficiently exclusive so as to appear different to all concerned. This may require the hiring of more prison probation officers (to reduce the effects of overcrowding) so that they are no longer asked to provide custodial services.

Given the degree of role ambiguity and role duplication we have discussed, it may be suggested that there is a need to improve communication between prison probation personnel and other personnel in the prison. "It involves each discipline having a realistic understanding of the other's role, location and availability" (Sudds, 1987: 2).

At one of Her Majesty's prisons (Oxford), probation staff meet in case conference with other prison personnel in order to better coordinate the efforts of the various professionals as concerns each prisoner under discussion (Clark, 1985: 1). It is precisely this and similar kinds of cooperative joint efforts which may help resolve the role complications we have reviewed.

Further research in this area may also reveal the need for administrative clarity as regards expectations placed upon these roles. It has been found that the Governor (warden) of a prison can hinder or enhance the job of the prison probation officer. It was found that the ". . . liaison between the Probation team and all other units within the prison (can be) greatly facilitated by the Governor's decision that within (the) institution there will be no 'no-go' areas as far as the Probation team is concerned" (Clark, 1985: 3).

On the other hand, the Home Office, while encouraging the probation service in its endeavors, has admittedly left the service somewhat shorthanded and without some of the resources needed to conduct their work in the most professional and beneficial manner possible (Platt & Bohan, 1986: 2). England's current financial crisis is having an impact on the field of corrections. The prison building program which is now taking place is straining the correctional budget even further. And the most recent mandates from the Home Office seem to suggest a swing in the pendulum away from treatment (especially throughcare and aftercare) and more towards custody.

In addition to complications arising from the structural constraints and overlapping role expectations, prison probation officers must face both

> . . . outward to the community and inward to the institution; needing to work closely with Probation colleagues from the field and non-Probation colleagues within the prison; and having to exercise skills with no obvious parallel in the wider work of the Service. (North, 1986: 7)

This issue speaks directly to the need for additional training. It has been suggested that an orientation course which would facilitate the role transition from field probation officer to prison probation officer and continual on-the-job training would be most helpful (North, 1986). In the more progressive prison probation departments, training is offered in several different subjects. Some of the programs include 1) training for newly hired prison guards, 2) the training of newly posted prison probation officers as well as their ongoing training, and 3) training of community-based probation officers with whom the prison probation officers regularly work. One of the newest trends is the placement of trainee prison governors (superintendents) with community probation teams.

According to both field probation officers and prison probation officers, although the kinds of training mentioned above might help alleviate some of the problems we have described, there appears to be a consensus that training is not occurring with the frequency, breadth, or regularity needed.

The British have little more than anecdotal evidence that prison probation officers actually make a difference in adult facilities—in recidivism rates, in impacting levels of institutional violence, in increasing prisoners' feelings of satisfaction or self-worth, or apparently in any other way. Data such as these may be found as pertains to the use of probation officers in institutions for juvenile offenders (Bottomley and Liebling, 1987). Similar data on adult prisoners would be helpful for comparative research, as well as for the evaluation and enhancement of existing prison probation services.

There is a need for such research in the future if the British program of prison probation is to continue and become a model for other nations. While a number of difficulties currently surround the provision of probation services in Her Majesty's Prisons, the presence of the social work orientation may positively impact the quality of life in the prisons for the keepers and kept alike. As regards prison probation officers:

> Prison Governors welcome (their) independence, and recognize the professional advantages which this brings for the inmate population. (North, 1986: 6)

Conclusions

The tasks relegated to the role of prison-based probation officer appear, at least in principle, to be potentially meaningful in terms of creating a more humane environment within the prison setting. Future research on this subject should focus on determining to what extent the goals of the prison probation service are being met. Barriers to reaching these goals should be clearly identified and addressed in such a manner as to clarify the role of the prison probation officer as distinguished from prison guards.

Not all contacts between prison guards and prison probation officers result in problems. On the contrary, Bottomley and Liebling (1987: 11) found that:

> There was little significant contact between most prison staff and (prison) probation officers, according to staff from both services whom we interviewed; however, when contact did occur it was seen as valuable on both sides.

The sharing of information about prisoners' day-to-day activities and concerns and the effort to create and maintain a productive working environment (between guards and probation officers) were among the two most visible consequences of prison guard-prison probation officer contact observed by the author.

Discussion Questions

1. Do you think that the concept of throughcare and the use of prison-based probation officers are valuable ideas? Why or why not? How might the use of probation officers in U.S. prisons be advantageous or disadvantageous to institutional management?
2. Do you agree or disagree with the author's assessment of how the British should go about resolving the problems pertaining to the role of the prison probation officer? Explain. Which of the problems do you believe will be the most difficult to resolve and why?

Bibliography

Bottomley, A. Keith, and Alison Liebling, "Young Offender Throughcare: A Study of the Implementation of the Revised Procedures for Young Offenders in Custody. Summary of Final Report to the Home Office," Center for Criminology and Criminal Justice, University of Hull, Hull (England) October, 1987.

Brown, Chris, and Alan Whiffin, *Oxford Prison Team: Policy and Practice,* policy statement, 1983.

Clark, John (Senior Probation Officer), *Probation Team in Oxford Prison—Response to Local Statement of Values, Purpose, Priorities and Practice,* policy statement, August 8, 1985.

Home Office, H M Prison Long Lartin, memo, September 15, 1987.

North, John, et al. (Acting Chief Probation Officer), *The Professional Task of the Prison Probation Officer,* policy statement, February, 1986.

Platt, T. C. (Prison Department), and W. J. Bohan (Criminal Department), *Circular Instruction No. 25/1986, Home Office Circular No. 64/1986, Prisoner Throughcare-Shared Working,* policy statement, August 28, 1986.

Sudds, Alan (Senior Liaison Probation Officer), *Feltham Remand Centre Probation Department,* policy statement, April 3, 1987.

20. Issues and Controversies with Respect to the Management of AIDS in Corrections

Mark Blumberg*

Introduction

Acquired immunodeficiency syndrome (AIDS) is a disease that destroys the body's immune system. Those afflicted with this condition are rendered defenseless against a wide variety of infectious ailments that are not usually harmful to people who possess a properly functioning immune system. AIDS was first diagnosed in the United States in June 1981 (Morgan and Curran, 1986: 459). Yet, during the next seven years, more than 84,000 additional cases were reported to the U.S. Public Health Service (Centers for Disease Control, 1/23/89), and between 1 and 1.5 million Americans became infected with the Human Immunodeficiency Virus (Centers for Disease Control, 12/18/87). It is projected that by the year 1991, approximately 270,000 Americans will develop "full-blown" AIDS and that 179,000 people will have died from this disease (Morgan and Curran, 1986: 461).

In the United States, AIDS first appeared among gay males. Shortly thereafter, cases were reported among intravenous (IV) drug users. Because correctional institutions contain a large number of inmates who have a history of IV drug use and because homosexual behavior is a reality in jails and prisons, it has been feared that these facilities would become breeding grounds for this disease. To assess the actual spread of the virus, in each of the last three years, the National Institute of Justice (NIJ) in conjunction with the American Correctional Association (ACA) has surveyed all 50 state prison systems, the Federal Bureau of Prisons (FBOP), and over 30 large county/city jail systems to determine the number of inmates who have been diagnosed with "full-blown" AIDS (Hammett, 1986; 1987; and 1988). The findings from these annual surveys indicate that the number of AIDS cases is increasing in the nation's correctional facilities, but at a slower pace than in the general population. As of October 1, 1987, a cumulative total of 1,964 confirmed cases had been reported. This represents an increase of 59 percent over the previous year's cumulative total of 1,232 inmates diagnosed with "full-blown" AIDS and compares with a rate of increase of 61 percent for the population as a whole (Hammett, 1988: 23).

---

*Mark Blumberg is associate professor of criminal justice administration at Central Missouri State University, Warrensburg, Missouri. The author would like to express his gratitude to Kenneth Hass, Allen Sapp, and Scott Christianson for providing helpful comments and ideas.

Even though the number of persons with AIDS in prisons and jails has not reached the levels initially feared, the long incubation period associated with this disease has created apprehension that the worst is yet to come. As a consequence, correctional administrators have been forced to confront a variety of new and complex issues as they struggle to develop policies that hopefully will prevent transmission of this ailment within the institutional setting. Many of these are issues that the outside society has already faced: mandatory testing, the question of whether to segregate infected inmates, who should have access to the results of positive HIV tests, the appropriate content of educational programs designed to slow the spread of AIDS (i.e., whether to teach abstinence or "safer sex"), and the question of condom distribution. At the heart of the debate is the following question: Should prisons and jails adhere to the practices of the larger society or is the institutional environment sufficiently unique that deviations from these policies are acceptable?

This article examines some of the key issues that AIDS poses for policy-makers and administrators in the field of corrections. After a brief discussion of the relevant medical and social aspects of the HIV epidemic, the scope of the problem in correctional facilities is explored. The relationship between AIDS in prison and jails and IV drug use is examined. In addition, various studies that have attempted to determine whether the virus is being transmitted within the institution are highlighted. This is followed by an examination of the pros and cons with respect to various policy options that are designed to prevent the transmission of this disease within the correctional system. The controversies that have been raging in the field of corrections over such practices as mass screening, the segregation of infected inmates, confidentiality requirements, condom distribution, and the release of prisoners with AIDS are reviewed.[1]

The Nature of the HIV Epidemic

Scope

Previously, it was noted that between 1 and 1.5 million Americans have become infected with HIV, the viral agent that causes AIDS (CDC, 12/18/87: 804). The great majority of these seropositives[2] appear healthy, but they are able to infect others. Because the incubation period is so lengthy (mean = seven years), it is not known what proportion of seropositive persons will eventually develop "full-blown" AIDS. A recent study suggests the percentage may be as high as 99 percent (Lui, Darrow, and Rutherford, 1988: 1334). At this point in time, the available data indicate that 20 to 30 percent will progress to this stage within five years (Koop, 1986: 12).

Mode of Transmission

HIV is transmitted only through sexual contact, through contact with infected blood, or from an infected mother to a newborn infant (Friedland and Klein, 1987). There is overwhelming evidence that casual contact with infected per-

1. Readers who are interested in learning what practices are actually being followed by most correctional facilities with respect to HIV testing, segregation, and confidentiality requirements are advised to consult Hammett (1988).
2. The term "seropositive" refers to individuals whose blood test indicates that they have been exposed to the Human Immune Deficiency Virus (HIV), regardless of whether or not they manifest symptoms of illness.

sons does not transmit AIDS. Studies of individuals who resided in the same household as AIDS patients and who shared plates, cooking utensils, toilets, and other objects with these infected persons over an extended period of time have concluded that not a single individual has become infected except through sexual contact or by sharing needles (Friedland et al., 1986).

In the United States, approximately 90 percent of AIDS cases have been reported among two risk groups: homosexual/bisexual males and IV drug users (Centers for Disease Control, 1/23/89: 1). Despite exaggerated claims to the contrary (Masters, Johnson, and Kolodny, 1988), there is little evidence to suggest that the disease is ''breaking-out'' of the ''high-risk'' groups into the general population. Only 4 percent of the cases have been linked to heterosexual transmission (Centers for Disease Control, 1/23/89: 1), and the great majority of these have occurred among the female sex partners of IV users (Friedland and Klein, 1987: 1129).

Treatment

At present, there is no cure for AIDS and no vaccine to protect against the virus. In fact, most public health experts do not believe that a general vaccine to prevent AIDS will be available until the mid-1990's, at the earliest (Weisburd, 1987: 329). Physicians are able to treat some of the opportunistic infections that plague AIDS patients. However, the only drug approved to treat AIDS itself is azidothymidine (AZT). Both AZT and the cost of medical treatment for AIDS patients are very high. A recent study estimated that the lifetime medical costs (including AZT) for each person with AIDS will rise to approximately $61,800 by 1991 (Hellinger, 1988: 309).

Social Stigma

Because AIDS is a recent phenomenon evoking fears of the unknown, because it is associated in the public mind with practices that are viewed as immoral by many people (i.e., homosexuality and drug addiction), and because it is a horrible disease, a great social stigma has attached to this ailment. Infected persons have often been treated as outcasts and subjected to various forms of discrimination. Many cases have been reported in which persons with AIDS or individuals merely carrying HIV have been unable to buy insurance, denied housing, terminated from employment, forced to leave school, or subjected to other forms of harassment. In Arcadia, Florida, the home of three infected hemophiliac brothers, who had attempted to enroll in public school, was set on fire (Rosellini and Goode, 1987).

The Relationship Between AIDS in Corrections and IV Drug Use

Outside the institution, male homosexual behavior is the most common risk factor associated with AIDS. Approximately 70 percent of all reported cases have occurred among members of this ''risk group'' (Centers for Disease Control, 1/23/89: 1). Among inmates, however, IV drug use is the key risk factor for developing AIDS. Almost all cases have occurred in prisoners with a history of IV drug use. With the exception of California, IV drug users constitute the majority of inmates with AIDS in all states (Greenspan, 1988: 7). In addition, the largest concentration of confirmed cases has been reported in those states (i.e., New York and New Jersey) where the rate of seroprevalence[3] among addicts tends to be quite high. Epidemiological data indicate that between 50 and 60 percent of IV drug users in New York City and northern New Jersey are seropositive as compared with a rate of less than 5 percent in most other sections of the nation away from the East Coast (CDC, 12/18/87: 2). Because "shooting galleries"[4] are typically found in the northeast, a substantial proportion of addicts in this region have become infected with HIV.

IV drug use also explains the disproportionate number of minority persons who have been victimized by this disease. The National Institute on Drug Abuse (NIDA) estimates that 70 percent of the nation's 1.28 million IV drug addicts are black or Hispanic (Stengel, 8/17/87: 13). For this reason, HIV infection is much more common in poor inner-city neighborhoods. Forty-two percent of AIDS patients are members of these racial ethnic groups (CDC, 3/89: 11). This proportion is approximately double their representation in the general population. One-third of the AIDS cases among minorities are attributed to IV drug use as compared with just 5 percent among whites (Stengel, 8/17/87: 13). Excluding homosexual and bisexual men with AIDS, the ratio of persons with AIDS is 12.0 to 1 for blacks and 9.3 to 1 for Hispanics as compared with whites (CDC, 12/18/87: 10).

Minorities constitute an even greater proportion of those diagnosed with AIDS in the correctional setting. One reason is the greater prevalence of IV drug use in poor, disadvantaged neighborhoods. Another is that prison and jail populations contain both a disproportionate number of minorities as well as IV drug users. Whatever the reasons, the fact remains that this epidemic has placed a tragic burden on some of the most powerless individuals in our society.

Transmission of HIV Within Institutions

Most epidemiological studies have concluded that the rate of seroprevalence within the general inmate population is quite low (less than 3 percent—Hammett, 1988: 29).[5] Nonetheless, many correctional administrators remain concerned that seropositive inmates will transmit HIV to others within the institution through either homosexual activity or by sharing contaminated needles or tattoo equipment. Although no cases have been documented in which an inmate seroconverted[6] during incarceration, "logic and common sense both suggest that even in the best managed correctional institutions, there may be at least some transmission of the AIDS virus occurring among inmates" (Hammett, 1987: 15). On the other hand, there is little doubt that incarcerated IV drug users face far less risk of becoming infected with HIV than do those for addicts who remain on the street.

---

3. The term "seroprevalence" refers to the proportion of individuals in a specific group who are seropositive.
4. "Shooting galleries" are locations where drug users gather to "rent" needles and syringes. It is not uncommon for the same equipment to be shared by numerous addicts in a short period of time.
5. The rate of seroprevalence is somewhat higher in those jurisdictions (e.g., New York) that have a substantial number of intravenous drug users within their correctional population (Criminal Justice Newsletter, 4/15/88).
6. The term "seroconvert" refers to a positive HIV blood status by an individual who formerly was not infected.

Several states have attempted to determine through HIV testing whether the virus is being transmitted within the institution. These studies indicate that very few prisoners who have been continuously incarcerated since the beginning of the epidemic are infected. Maryland authorities observed that only two of 137 such inmates were seropositive (Vaid, 1987: 238). Similar findings have been reported in New York and Florida (Hammett, 1988: 31). However, because the upper limit of the incubation period for AIDS has not been established, it is uncertain whether these inmates actually seroconverted during incarceration.

Mass HIV screening of all inmates *both* upon entry and at release has been instituted in four states (Alabama, Idaho, New Hampshire, and West Virginia [Greenspan, 1988: 6]). These data should eventually provide some indication of how frequently the AIDS virus is being transmitted within the prison. However, because Alabama is the only state among these systems with a substantial number of AIDS cases, it is questionable whether these findings will be generalizable to those systems that contain the largest number of inmates with AIDS (i.e., New York, New Jersey, and Florida).

Mass Screening

In the United States, public health authorities have attempted to control the spread of HIV through education, voluntary testing, and by counseling persons at "high-risk." With the exception of immigrants and military personnel, most testing has been conducted on a voluntary basis. From the beginning of the epidemic, correctional administrators have debated whether this approach is appropriate in prisons and jails. Before discussing the controversy regarding mandatory testing, it is necessary to touch upon the available medical technology for diagnosing HIV.

The current blood test is not able to predict which seropositive individuals are likely to develop "full-blown" AIDS nor at what point symptoms may appear. The test cannot detect the AIDS virus, merely the presence of antibodies to HIV. Because the human immune system will generally not develop antibodies until six to twelve weeks[7] after exposure (Petricciani and Epstein, 1988: 236), persons tested during this period will be seronegative[8] despite the fact that they are able to infect others. These results are commonly referred to as "false-negatives." They pose a real concern for any program of mass screening.

Mandatory mass screening involves testing all inmates or all incoming inmates for HIV infection. A more limited version involves testing only members of "high-risk" groups (i.e., homosexuals, IV drug users, or prostitutes). Proponents argue that mass screening is the best way to identify seropositive inmates. Such a policy provides correctional administrators with an opportunity to target education and prevention programs. In addition, infected individuals can be placed under special supervision to insure that they do not transmit the virus to others. Supporters of this policy argue that institutions must take action to iden-

7. Some persons do not develop antibodies until several months after exposure to the virus.
8. The term "seronegative" refers to those individuals whose HIV blood test indicates that they have NOT been exposed to the virus.

tify infected inmates and to prevent the spread of this virus or they will be held civilly liable. Finally, it is suggested that mass screening could provide a more accurate projection of how many cases of "full-blown" AIDS will eventually develop. This will enable correctional officials to plan more effectively and to seek an appropriate level of funding to meet future needs.

Critics of mass screening do not accept these rationale. They respond to the claim that education and prevention efforts be targeted by asserting that these programs must be directed toward all inmates. It is argued that all prisoners should be encouraged to refrain from "high-risk" behavior, not just those identified as seropositive. Furthermore, opponents of mass screening are opposed to the practice of segregating infected individuals from the inmate population. Because any system of mass screening would produce some "false negatives," it is not possible to even identify all infectious inmates. The problems that this raises with respect to any segregation policy are discussed in the next section.

Opponents of mass screening are also skeptical about the civil liability concern. They note that institutions already have rules that prohibit those types of conduct which can transmit HIV (i.e., sexual contact and IV drug use). As a consequence, inmates who engage in these practices do so at their own risk. Most correctional lawyers argue that the institution would not be held liable unless an inmate became infected through a sexual assault (Hammett, 1987: 35).

The claim that correctional institutions must be able to accurately project the number of future AIDS cases is not disputed. However, critics of mass screening note that anonymous testing procedures can satisfactorily achieve this goal. In fact, the Centers for Disease Control (CDC) are now utilizing this procedure to determine the prevalence of HIV in ten geographically diverse institutions across the nation (Corrections Digest, 6/1/88: 1). Blood samples will be coded in such a manner as to insure that prison officials do not learn the names of infected inmates.

Opponents of mass screening also argue that such a policy is not a wise expenditure of resources and that it will create a class of outcasts within the institution. Fear is expressed that not only will seropositive inmates be subjected to harassment, discrimination, and perhaps even violence within the prison, but that they will also encounter difficulties in obtaining employment and housing upon release.

There is also the question of how prisoners will respond to the knowledge that they are seropositive. Because institutions contain a substantial number of individuals with sociopathic personalities, it can be argued that inmates who learn they are carrying a deadly virus will be more likely, not less, to engage in predatory behavior.

Finally, it is noted that the pressure to conduct widespread testing of inmates has come from politicians, not state correctional officials (Greenspan, 1988: 8). Both the National Association of State Corrections Administrators (Vaid, 1986: 3) and the National Commission on Correctional Health Care (Criminal Justice Newsletter, 5/2/88: 3) are opposed to this policy. In many cases state legislators have proposed statutes that require mandatory testing over the objections of correctional and public health officials.

Segregation

In addition to the controversy with respect to testing, correctional administrators must also decide whether to separate infected prisoners from the inmate population. Segregation can be undertaken for medical reasons,[9] to protect an infected individual from violence, or as a general policy to prevent the transmission of HIV within the institution. It is the latter rationale which raises a great deal of controversy and is thus the focus of our attention.

Proponents of segregation assert that this is necessary to prevent the transmission of HIV within the institution. In making the case for this policy, advocates make the following arguments: (1) previous research indicates that homosexual activity is a fact of life in prison. Nacci and Kane (1983: 35) report that 30 percent of male inmates have had a homosexual experience as an adult in prison. However, data from another institution (Wooden and Parker, 1982: 50–51) noted that 65 percent of the male prisoners have had sex with another male during their current period of incarceration;[10] (2) other sexually transmitted diseases (e.g., rectal gonorrhea) are sometimes transmitted in the correctional setting; (3) tattooing (although prohibited in most institutions) is a very common practice[11] and illicit drug use probably takes place as well to some extent; and (4) studies conducted within various institutions conclude that a small proportion of inmates are sexually assaulted during incarceration (see Bowker, 1980: 2–3).

Civil libertarians are opposed to the practice of segregation except for valid medical reasons or in cases involving protective custody. They argue that because HIV is NOT spread through casual contact, separate facilities are not necessary. In fact, the CDC opposes special housing for AIDS patients except when medically necessary. Critics contend that institutional segregation undermines the basic public health message that AIDS is not transmitted except through intimate contact.

Opponents of this practice also express concern because infected inmates are often placed in substandard living quarters and denied an opportunity to participate in certain work assignments, rehabilitation, and recreation programs or to be eligible for work release. Furthermore, because these prisoners are excluded from many institutional programs, they frequently also lose the opportunity to earn ''good time'' credit toward eventual release.

---

9. Because AIDS patients have an impaired immune system, they sometimes must be isolated to protect them from catching infectious conditions that do not threaten healthy persons.
10. These statistics may overstate the risk of HIV transmission within prisons and jails. Wooden and Parker (1982: 54) note that the overwhelming majority of inmates in their sample (80 percent) report not having been the passive partner in anal sex. Studies that have examined the sexual practices of gay men observe that this type of behavior poses the greatest risk of viral transmission (Winkelstein et al., 1987).
11. Although there are no documented cases of HIV transmission as a result of sharing tattoo needles (Vaid, 1987: 230), there is concern that this common practice among inmates may be quite risky.

The problem of "false negative" HIV test results has already been noted. Vaid (1987) has suggested that a policy of mandatory testing and segregation could actually be counterproductive for this reason. Because individuals who remained in the general prison population would be perceived as HIV-free, inmates might be encouraged to continue engaging in high-risk behavior due to the mistaken notion that all infectious persons had been placed in isolation. Furthermore, such a policy could conceivably place seropositive inmates in greater jeopardy as well. Believing that they have little to lose, these individuals might continue to engage in risky activities. However, it is possible that repeated exposure to the virus may increase the likelihood that a seropositive individual will eventually develop "full-blown" AIDS (Gostin, 1986: 11).

Segregation raises other problems as well. Critics note that it can become very expensive. In those jurisdictions that have a large number of infected inmates, this policy may require the development of what is in fact a second corrections system. Officials may be required to duplicate many existing institutional programs. As the number of cases continues to grow over the next few years, this could become an administrative nightmare.

Clearly, correctional administrators have a legal as well as an ethical responsibility to pursue policies that minimize the transmission of HIV within the institution. However, it is questionable whether a blanket policy of segregation is the best way to accomplish this objective. As an alternative, prison and jail administrators could reduce the incidence of "high-risk" behavior through such steps as increased supervision, hiring more correctional officers, intensive educational programs, and harsh penalties for sexual assault (Vaid, 1987: 238). In addition, the classification process can be used to identify both inmates who are likely to engage in predatory behavior as well as those who are likely to be victimized. Bowker (1980: 11) notes that the latter are "more likely to be middle class, young, inexperienced, convicted of minor property offenses, and slight of build." This is an important piece of information for correctional officials who wish to place potentially vulnerable prisoners under special supervision.

Confidentiality

Another issue that must be confronted by policymakers is the question of who should have access to information with regard to HIV antibody status. Clearly, the attending physician must have these results if the inmate is to be provided with proper medical attention. The case for disclosure to other personnel within the institution is far less compelling. Although correctional officers have sometimes asserted that they have a right to know who is seropositive, relatively few systems routinely disclose this fact to line officers (Hammett, 1988: 97). In fact, state law in some jurisdictions prohibits the disclosure of HIV test results without the written authorization of the infected party.

Correctional officers base their case for disclosure on the rationale that this knowledge is necessary if they are to be able to take appropriate precautionary measures when interacting with seropositive inmates. The latter, on the other hand, are genuinely concerned that they will be subjected to threats, ridicule, or even attack, if their condition becomes known. Policymakers are thus confronted with the task of balancing these competing concerns. In those jurisdictions that do not prohibit disclosure, does the officer's right to know outweigh the inmate's right to privacy? Are line officers put at increased risk when they are forced to operate without this medical information?

Examination of the circumstances under which HIV is and is not transmitted suggests that the inmate's right to privacy should take precedence over the employee's right to know. For one thing, this virus is not transmitted through casual contact. The basic modes of transmission are now clearly understood. If correctional officers become infected as a result of their employment, it is quite probable that they have engaged in activities with inmates that would be cause for dismissal even if AIDS was not a concern. Second, educational programs are designed to teach staff that it is advisable to take proper infection control measures (e.g., wearing latex gloves when contact with blood or other body fluids is anticipated) with all inmates. By providing institutional personnel with a "master-list" of seropositive prisoners, a false sense of security could be created for persons working in the facility. This may lead to a situation in which correctional officers fail to take adequate precautions when dealing with other inmates. Because the available technology for detecting HIV antibodies in newly infected persons is unreliable, this would not be a wise course of action.

Whatever policy is followed with respect to notification of line officers, institutions must insure that the antibody status of infected inmates does not become known within the general prison population. Administrators should develop clearly enunciated policies that prohibit medical personnel and others from making any disclosures to unauthorized individuals. Care must also be exercised in the handling of "master-lists" that contain the names of seropositive inmates. These should be stored in locations that are not accessible to inmates. However, despite the best efforts of correctional administrators, the identity of some infected individuals is still likely to become known. On occasion, inmates will disclose their HIV status to others. In other instances, the fact that an inmate has been denied the opportunity to participate in a particular activity or release program will serve as a "tip-off" for the institution's "rum or-mill." Finally, in cases where the individual has progressed to ARC (AIDS-related complex) or "full-blown" AIDS, the physical manifestations of the disease may become obvious to other inmates. Therefore, educational programs, as part of their mission, must articulate the message that infected prisoners pose no danger to others within the facility (as long as "high-risk" behaviors are avoided).

Distribution of Condoms

Another important decision that correctional administrators must confront is the issue of condom distribution.[12] Because condoms can reduce the risk of HIV infection, many educational campaigns outside the prison have emphasized the use of condoms as a means of avoiding exposure to the virus. Such campaigns have often been controversial with critics, charging that they encourage people

12. A policy that would generate far more controversy is the distribution of clean needles to inmates. Not only would this create a security problem, it would be a tacit admission that authorities are unable to stop the smuggling of illicit drugs into the institution. Not surprisingly, this step has not been considered by any correctional facility.

to engage in casual sexual activity. The debate over "safer sex" vs. abstinence is even more intense in the area of corrections. Although most correctional systems allow inmates to be provided with "safer sex" information (generally through outside speakers), only New York City, Mississippi, and Vermont actually make condoms available for use by inmates within the institution[13] (Hammett, 1988: 92).*

Advocates of condom distribution assert that homosexual behavior is a fact of life in many institutions and that officials should give inmates access to these devices as a means of protecting them from disease. It is asserted that such conduct will occur despite the best efforts of policymakers and administrators to eliminate sexual activity within the institution. Furthermore, they point to desperate attempts by inmates who "are fashioning makeshift condoms out of trash can liners, bread wrappers and other plastic bags" in an attempt to protect their health (Criminal Justice Newsletter, 7/1/88: 5).

Critics of condom distribution note that sexual activity is prohibited within institutions and that many states have statutes that criminalize homosexual behavior. They argue that this step would imply tacit approval of such conduct by correctional administrators. There is also concern about how the public might react and fear that inmates might use condoms to make weapons or hide contraband (Hammett, 1988: 92). Finally, there is the question of whether condoms actually offer significant protection against HIV infection during anal intercourse (CDC, 3/11/88: 136).

Those jurisdictions that have chosen to distribute condoms report few problems. New York City has not experienced any cases in which inmates used condoms to make weapons or conceal contraband (Hammett, 1988: 92). Inmates receive condoms from medical personnel who must dispense AIDS information and counseling with regard to "safer sex" along with these prophylactic devices (Criminal Justice Newsletter, 7/1/88: 6). The same policy is followed by Vermont officials.

Release of Persons with AIDS

Denial of Parole

How should persons with AIDS be treated with respect to parole? Sometimes, correctional officials hear arguments that infected inmates should be denied release on parole (Vaid, 1987: 250). It is asserted that such persons present a serious danger to the health of others and that the state has an obligation to protect its citizens from infection. However, others assert that to deny parole solely on medical grounds would constitute punishment based on illness and therefore violate the constitution (*Robinson v. California*, 1962).[14] Because HIV is not transmitted through casual contact, persons in the community could protect themselves by not engaging in the types of "high-risk" behavior that spread

---

**Prison Journal* Editor's Note: In August 1988, the Philadelphia prisons adopted a policy of making condoms available to inmates.

13. The state of Washington dispenses condoms, but only for conjugal visits. In addition, some jurisdictions provide inmates with condoms upon release (Hammett, 1988: 22).
14. The U.S. Supreme Court noted that even one day in jail for the "crime" of having a common cold would constitute cruel and unusual punishment (*Robinson v. California,* 370 U.S. 660).

this disease. Following this line of reasoning, it would only be appropriate to deny release to a convicted sex offender who was infected with the virus. Other parolees would pose no greater risk to the public than the one million other seropositives already in the population.

Early Release

Others have made the opposite claim, that inmates with AIDS who present no danger to the community should be eligible for early release from prison. Recently, the New York State Division of Parole announced that 50 prisoners who were seriously ill with this disease had been released as soon as they became eligible for parole (Sullivan, 3/7/87: 1). Under this policy, release is not automatic; inmates must demonstrate evidence of good conduct and not present a danger to the community. The state argues that this policy demonstrates compassion toward those who are terminally ill.

Although most jurisdictions with a large number of institutional AIDS cases have not followed the lead of New York, there are several reasons why correctional administrators may wish to consider this approach. One reason is that the cost of treatment for prisoners with AIDS is quite high, and inmates are not eligible for medicaid reimbursement or social security disability. As a consequence, correctional systems that must care for many individuals with AIDS will face enormous budgetary pressures. Second, there is the issue of whether prisons and jails can provide satisfactory medical care. Gido and Gaunay (1987: 28) have concluded that inmates with AIDS in New York survive, on the average, less than half as long as such patients on the outside. This raises the question of whether institutions are able to provide the kinds of treatment that these patients require. Third, there is also a humanitarian consideration. Should gravely ill individuals who pose no risk to the community be forced to spend their final days in prison, isolated from family and friends?

Claims of humanitarian treatment may cut both ways, however. Most inmates suffering from AIDS are not only quite ill, they are also from the most disadvantaged segment of our society. Few of these individuals come from families that have much in the way of economic resources. Because of their physical condition, they are unable to obtain employment or qualify for health insurance. Some are likely to have trouble finding suitable housing if released and may end up on the street. Under these circumstances, there is reason to believe that early release is not always in the best interests of inmates suffering from "full-blown" AIDS. Although some correctional systems may be tempted to release these individuals en masse in order to be relieved of the substantial medical expense that treatment for AIDS entails, this temptation should be resisted. Such a policy would be quite shortsighted. In addition to the hardships that some of these inmates would be forced to endure, the actual savings would be minimal. For the most part, releasees will still be treated at state expense, whether through Medicaid or in public hospitals. Any policy of early release that is truly based on humanitarian concerns must take into consideration the individual circumstances of each particular case.

Conditions of Parole

The HIV epidemic poses other parole related issues as well. Specifically, may a parolee who continues to engage in "high-risk" behavior be subject to revocation for this reason? On the one hand, it can be asserted that the purpose of parole is to prevent the commission of additional crimes and that revocation under these circumstances is therefore inappropriate. However, others argue that the purpose of parole is to protect the community, regardless of the nature of the threat. This debate is complicated by the fact that twelve states have enacted statutes that make it a crime to expose another to HIV (Weisenhaus, 8/1/88: 1). Is it therefore appropriate to revoke parole for this behavior only in those jurisdictions?

Disclosure

Finally, there is the question of disclosure. What obligation does a parole officer have to notify a spouse or sex partner that a releasee is infected with HIV? This is similar to the dilemma that currently confronts physicians. Does the well-being of others outweigh the need to protect patient confidentiality? Clearly, there is no simple answer. In some states, there are statutes that prevent disclosure of HIV test results to third parties without consent. Parole officials in these jurisdictions can protect the health of persons who may be at risk by counseling inmates that they have an ethical obligation to notify all potential sex or needle partners of their HIV status.

Conclusion

It is apparent that the AIDS epidemic has generated a great deal of discussion and controversy regarding the proper management of this disease within the nation's prisons and jails. Policymakers have been forced to wrestle with many of the same issues that have confronted the larger society. Some correctional systems have responded to this challenge by instituting mass screening for HIV and segregating inmates infected with the virus. Although these are measures that are viewed as inappropriate by most public health officials for dealing with AIDS, it is argued by others that the unique circumstances of the institution justify this response. On the other hand, we are now one decade into the AIDS epidemic, and three consecutive surveys of correctional institutions by the National Institute of Justice (NIJ) indicate not a single case of occupational transmission in the United States (Hammett, 1988: 15). With thousands of seropositive inmates in correctional facilities, a rather compelling case can be made that if occupational transmission was a serious concern in prisons and jails, it would have manifested itself by now.

Correctional officers have sometimes expressed concern that they will become infected with HIV as a result of various risks that they face on the job. It has been suggested that staff could become infected as a result of bites, by being spat upon, by having bags of feces thrown at them by inmates, or in the course of breaking up fights between prisoners. However, an examination of the dynamics under which HIV is and is not transmitted indicates that all these modes of suggested transmission are highly unlikely.

HIV is a very difficult virus to transmit. Studies of hospital workers who accidentally prick themselves with HIV infected needles indicate that less than

1 percent of these individuals actually seroconvert (Friedland and Klein, 1987: 1127). To date, there has not been a single case of HIV infection reported that resulted from either a bite[15] or a spitting incident (Hammett, 1988: 2). Not only have laboratory tests revealed that HIV is present in the saliva of very few infected persons (Ho et al., 1985), it is found in such minute quantities as to make transmission under these circumstances extremely improbable. In addition, the virus lacks the ability to pass through intact skin. For these reasons, seroconversion is not likely to occur under either of these circumstances. Assaults against staff that involve the throwing of bodily waste pose even less danger because HIV is not present in the feces of infected persons (Hammett, 1988: 15). Although it is theoretically possible for a corrections officer to become infected as a result of a cut received in the course of terminating a fight (if one of the participants is seropositive), the fact that this has not ever occurred suggests that the threat is more theoretical than real. In fact, staff members who consistently follow prescribed CDC (11/15/85) infection control procedures (i.e., insuring that open wounds are bandaged, wearing gloves when contact with blood or other body fluids is anticipated, etc.) face far less risk from AIDS than from stab wounds or other traditional risks associated with their job.

Not only is the fear of occupational transmission unwarranted, there is also little evidence to suggest that this virus is being sexually transmitted between inmates within the institution. Almost all prisoners diagnosed with AIDS have a history of intravenous drug use prior to entering the institution. In addition, seroprevalence studies indicate that few, if any, inmates who have been continuously confined since the beginning of the AIDS epidemic are infected. As previously noted, the rate of AIDS cases is rising at a slightly lower rate in prisons and jails than in the general population. Taken together, this evidence suggests rather strongly that our correctional institutions have not become breeding grounds for this disease as was initially feared. In fact, for those inmates who have a history of intravenous drug use, the institution probably provides a more secure environment than they would encounter on the street where needle sharing among addicts is far more likely to occur.

Discussion Questions

1. Are you surprised to learn that, while the number of AIDS cases is increasing in U.S. prisons, the number of prison cases is rising at a slower pace than in the general population? Why or why not? How can this finding be explained?
2. In view of Blumberg's discussion, explain your opinion on each of the following issues concerning the management of AIDS cases in prison: (a) mass screening, (b) segregation, (c) confidentiality, (d) condom distribution, and (e) release of inmates with AIDS.

15. In a biting incident, there is contact with blood. However, it is the assailant who comes in contact with the blood of the victim. Unless the former was bleeding from the mouth, it is highly unlikely that the latter would become infected with HIV.

3. Do you agree that the risk of occupational transmission is as low as the author suggests? Explain your position.
4. If you were administering a prison, how would you manage the AIDS problem? What policies would you implement?

References

Bowker, Lee H. (1980) *Prison Victimization.* New York: Elsevier.

Centers for Disease Control (CDC) (1989) *HIV/AIDS Surveillance.* Atlanta: U.S. Public Health Service (March).

Centers for Disease Control (CDC) (1989) *AIDS Weekly Surveillance Report.* Atlanta: U.S. Public Health Service (Jan. 23).

Centers for Disease Control (CDC) (1988) "Condoms for Prevention of Sexually Transmitted Disease." *Morbidity and Mortality Weekly Report* 37 (March 11).

Centers for Disease Control (CDC) (1987) "Human Immunodeficiency Virus Infection in the United States." *Morbidity and Mortality Weekly Report* 36 (December 18).

Centers for Disease Control (CDC) (1985) "Recommendations for Preventing Transmission of Infection with Human T-Lymphotropic Virus Type III/Lymphadenopathy—Associated Virus in the Workplace." *Morbidity and Mortality Weekly Report* 34 (November 15): 681–860.

Corrections Digest (1988) "CDC Funding Study to Measure the Spread of AIDS in U.S. Prison Population." (June 1).

Criminal Justice Newsletter (1988) "Of Inmates from New York City, 15% Show Exposure to AIDS Virus." (April 15).

Criminal Justice Newsletter (1988) "Correctional Health Group Urges No Mass Screening for AIDS." (May 2).

Criminal Justice Newsletter (1988) "Condoms for Inmates at Issue in Philadelphia, San Francisco." (July 1).

Friedland, Gerald H. and Robert S. Klein (1987) "Transmission of the Human Immunodeficiency Virus." *The New England Journal of Medicine* 317 (October 29).

Friedland, Gerald H., et al. (1986) "Lack of Transmission of HTLV-III/LAV Infection to Household Contacts of Patients with AIDS or AIDS-Related Complex with Oral Candidiasis." *The New England Journal of Medicine* 34 (February 6).

Gido, Rosemary and William Gaunay (1987) *Acquired Immune Deficiency Syndrome: A Demographic Profile of New York State Inmate Mortalities,* 1981–1986. New York: NY State Commission of Correction (September).

Gostin, Larry (1986) "AIDS Policies Raise Civil Liberties Concern." *National Prison Journal* (Winter): 10–11.

Greenspan, Judy (1988) "NPP Gathers Statistics on AIDS in Prison." *National Prison Project Journal* (Summer): 5–8.

Hammett, Theodore M. (1988) *AIDS in Correctional Facilities: Issues and Options.* Third edition. Washington, D.C.: National Institute of Justice (April).

———. (1988b) *Precautionary Measures and Protective Equipment: Developing a Reasonable Response.* Washington, D.C.: National Institute of Justice (January).

———. (1987) *AIDS in Correctional Facilities: Issues and Options.* Second edition. Washington, D.C.: National Institute of Justice (May).

———. (1986) *AIDS in Correctional Facilities: Issues and Options.* Second edition. Washington, D.C.: National Institute of Justice (May).

Hellinger, Fred J. (1988) "Forecasting the Personal Medical Care Cost of AIDS from 1988 through 1991." *Public Health Reports* 103 (May–June): 3.

Ho, David D., et al. (1985) "Infrequency of Isolation of HTLV-III Virus from Saliva in AIDS." *The New England Journal of Medicine* 313(25): 1606.

Koop, Everett C. (1986) *Surgeon General's Report on Acquired Immune Deficiency Syndrome.* Washington, D.C.: U.S. Public Health Service.

Lui, Kung-Jong, William W. Darrow, and George W. Rutherford, III (1988) "A Model-Based Estimate of the Mean Incubation Period for AIDS in Homosexual Men." *Science* 24 (June 3).

Masters, William, Virginia Johnson, and Robert Koldny (1988) *Crisis: Hetero-Sexual Behavior in the Age of AIDS.* New York: Grove Press.

Morgan, W. Meade and James W. Curran (1986) "Acquired Immunodeficiency Syndrome: Current and Future Trends." *Public Health Reports* 101 (September–October).

Nacci, Peter L. and Thomas R. Kane (1983) "The Incidence of Sex and Sexual Aggression in Federal Prisons." *Federal Probation* 47 (December): 31–36.

Petricciani, John C. and Jay S. Epstein (1988) ''The Effects of the AIDS Epidemic on the Safety of the Nation's Blood Supply.'' *Public Health Reports* 103 (May–June).

Rosellini, Lynn and Erica E. Goode (1987) ''AIDS: When Fear Takes Charge.'' *U.S. News and World Report* (October 12): 62–70.

Stengel, Richard (1987) ''The Changing Face of AIDS: More and More Victims are Black or Hispanic.'' *Time* (August 17): 12–14.

Sullivan, Ronald (1987) ''New York State Paroles 50 Men Sick with AIDS.'' *New York Times,* 7 March, section I, p. 1.

Viad, Urvashi (1987) ''Prisons.'' In Burris Dalton and the Yale AIDS Law Project (eds.), *AIDS and the Law: A Guide for the Public.* New Haven: Yale University Press, pp. 235–50.

———. (1986) ''Balance Response Needed to AIDS in Prison.'' *Nation Prison Project Journal* 7 (Spring): 1–50.

Weisburd, Stefi (1987) ''AIDS Vaccine: The Problems of Human Testing.'' *Science News* 131 (May 23).

Weisenhaus, Doreen (1988) ''The Shaping of AIDS Law.'' *The National Law Journal* 47 (August 1).

Winkelstein, Warren Jr., et al. (1987) ''Sexual Practices and Risk of Infection by the Human Immunodeficiency Virus: The San Francisco Men's Health Study.'' *Journal of the American Medical Association* 257 (January 16).

Wooden, Wayne S. and Jay Parker (1982) *Men Behind Bars: Sexual Exploitation in Prison.* New York: Plenum Press.

PRISONERS' RIGHTS AND PROTESTS

section IV

Introduction

There is a rather well known principle in penology which states that the humanity of a society can be gauged by the basic rights and living conditions the society accords its prisoners. The notion is that since many people consider prison inmates to be the least deserving class of the citizenry, the treatment of prisoners represents a barometer of social justice. This principle implies that an ethically progressive society will treat its prisoners in a benevolent fashion. There is another penological principle termed "less eligibility," which states that inmates should be granted no services, benefits, or living conditions which are superior to those granted the most disadvantaged class of free citizens. The principle of less eligibility implies that prisoners ought to be treated no better than members of the most disadvantaged class in a stratified society.

As the readings in this section suggest, there is a fundamental tension between the two principles just described which makes the comparative study of prisoners' rights and protests intriguing. The tension is perhaps most evident in Kevin N. Wright and David L. Cingranelli's article entitled "Inhumane, Cruel, and Degrading Treatment of Criminal Prisoners Throughout the World." Employing data compiled by the U.S. Department of State, the authors scrutinize 155 nations for prison practices that violate basic human rights, as defined by the United Nations. In all likelihood, many of the nations surveyed consider themselves to be humane and wish to be seen as such by other nations. Yet violations are discovered in nearly 60 percent of the nations, and Wright and Cingranelli report an inverse association between the likelihood of violations and the degree of economic development. Violations are also linked to religious structure and possibly to political structure. The reading concludes with a discussion of implications for international efforts to better control the abuse of prisoners' rights.

Before prison injustices can be controlled, they must be visible. Injustices become visible primarily through inmates' grievances and protests, the subject of the next two selections. Gillian Douglas compares the grievance procedures available to prisoners in England, Sweden, and Denmark. Issues examined include the access of inmates to information, prison censorship, the bureaucratic hierarchy of appeals, legal aid, inmate councils, prison boards, court appeals, and ombudsmen services. Douglas finds grievance mechanisms in all three nations to be unsatisfactory. Mechanisms internal to the prison are typically not independent enough of the prison administration to be fair, and external mechanisms are often both inaccessible and reluctant to grant redress. We are left with the uncomfortable conclusion that, even in nations like Sweden and Denmark, which possess internationally renowned reputations for progressive penology, much prison injustice may remain concealed and unabated due to the inadequacy of protest machinery.

In a brief and earlier formulation of their larger work entitled *Prisons Under Protest* (Open University Press, 1991), Phil Scraton, Joe Sim, and Paula Skidmore examine prison conditions in Scotland, with emphasis on uncovering the reasons for protests and disturbances by inmates at Peterhead prison. The state's explanation, centered on the pathological characteristics of select individual prisoners, is critically analyzed vis-a'-vis the findings of the independent inquiry conducted by the Gateway Exchange organization. Scraton and associates offer quantitative and qualitative data to challenge the reductionistic official account of the reasons for disturbances. In revealing the material conditions underlying the disturbances, the authors not only make us aware of the potentially volatile consequences of failing to provide legitimate avenues of protest, but also alert us to the manner in which the ideology generated by the state in response to protest can reproduce and indeed exacerbate prison injustice.

Among the most noteworthy developments in U.S. penology over the last three decades have been the inmates' rights movement and, more recently, the privatization movement. Before the 1960s, the courts in the U.S. followed a ''hands off'' policy in regard to prisoners' rights, maintaining that inmates' complaints were the proper domain of correctional administrators in the executive branch of government rather than the domain of the judicial branch. Then, concomitantly with other social movements in the 1960s, the courts slowly began to intervene; the result was a series of landmark appellate rulings meant to remedy some of the more flagrant abuses of executive branch discretion. While it is clear that the judiciary steered a more conservative direction during the latter 1970s and 1980s, certain advances were made in the struggle to bring the treatment of prisoners up to Constitutional standards. For its part, the privatization movement can basically be seen as a response of the state to the need to construct more prison space, coupled with the state's inability to finance such construction. While private industry has long had ties with prison labor and private organizations have traditionally provided the state with various prison support services, the idea of government contracting with the private sector, both to finance the construction of adult prisons and to actually operate these institutions, gained momentum during the 1970s and 1980s. In addressing one of the most salient of the numerous controversial issues surrounding expanded privatization, Harold J. Sullivan explores the ramifications of the privatization movement for the limited gains ensuing from the prisoners' rights movement. Sullivan makes a persuasive case that, in view of legal precedent, there is little to keep governments from circumventing their Constitutional responsibilities to prisoners through privatization. Sullivan's points should be carefully considered by anyone who is seriously concerned with preserving the rights that inmates have attained as well as by nations that are thinking of expanding private influence in their prison systems.

21. Inhumane, Cruel, and Degrading Treatment of Criminal Prisoners Throughout the World*

Kevin N. Wright**
David L. Cingranelli**

Abstract: Recent international policy has focused on assuring the human rights of criminal prisoners. Because of the difficulty and cost of comparative research, little is known about the success of these efforts. In this study, by utilizing a secondary data source, we are able to examine various indicators of inhumane and cruel practices in 155 nations. Substandard conditions and violations of basic human rights are found in over one-half of the nations. The levels of economic development, religion, and political structure are found to be related to a nation's prison practices.

The imposition of punishment is necessary to prevent criminal behavior, to protect citizens, and ultimately to preserve the social order. The most prevalent form of severe punishment throughout the world is incarceration. Governments deny freedom to criminals by detaining them in special facilities in order to make the outcome of their misbehavior painful and to preclude further offenses. But in their zeal to prevent crime and to pursue vengeance, some nations overstep the boundaries of human decency and treat prisoners in cruel and inhumane ways. They deny men and women any shred of human dignity, forcing them to live in extreme squalor with insufficient provisions for survival and health.

Only recently has the world community, through actions of the United Nations, begun to recognize basic human rights and moral obligations owed by governments to all citizens, even convicted criminals and political prisoners. Members of the United Nations have agreed that regardless of how vile and vicious the crime, the incarcerated retain some undeniable human rights. These include the right to a nutritionally adequate diet, the right to housing that is protected from the elements and is not overcrowded, sanitary living conditions, and the right to visitation. Member nations have agreed that prisoners should not be physically mistreated, denied adequate medical care, or forced to work inordinately long hours. Absent these conditions, incarceration reduces prisoners to a sub-human existence, which violates an individual's integrity and makes government as inhumane as the worst criminal.

---

*An earlier version of this paper was presented at the annual meeting of the American Society of Criminology, Denver, Colorado, November 1983.
**Center for Social Analysis, State University of New York at Binghamton.

Kevin Wright and David Cingranelli (1985). "Inhumane, Cruel, and Degrading Treatment of Criminal Prisoners Throughout the World." JUSTICE QUARTERLY 2(3): 345–362. Reprinted with permission of the Academy of Criminal Justice Sciences.

Rights of Prisoners in the United States

The United States tacitly recognized these tenets in framing the Constitution, yet formal guarantees were not established until recently. The Eighth Amendment to the Constitution states that punishments should not be cruel and unusual, but interpretations of which practices and conditions violated this provision were left to prison officials. No governmental agency served as a watchdog of inhumane treatment. Neither the legislature nor professional organizations established any standards for incarceration. Courts refused to review prisoners' allegations of cruel and unusual practices, claiming that they had no right to interfere because such matters were the prerogative of the executive branch of government. One judicial decision went so far as to suggest that prison officials were free to do as they pleased since the convicted felon, "as a consequence of his crime, not only forfeited his liberty, but all his personal rights except those which the law in its humanity accords to him. He is for the time being the slave of the state" (*Ruffin v. Commonwealth,* 62 Va. [21 Gratt.] 790, 794–796 [1871]).

Not until the mid-1940s did the courts begin to reverse their position. In a landmark case, *Coffin v. Reichard* (143 F.2d 443, 445 [6th Cir. 1944], cert. denied, 325 U.S. 887 [1945]), the U.S. Supreme Court stated that a prisoner retains all the rights of an ordinary citizen other than those expressly taken away by law. Extensive protection of prisoners' right to decent treatment did not follow until a series of cases were heard in federal courts during the 1960s and 1970s. Even then, intolerable conditions prevailed in some locations. In a study of United States prison conditions, Goldfarb and Singer (1973: 371) concluded that, "For far too many prisoners, the right to minimum standards of decent food, clothing, shelter, and medical care, the right to be protected from physical assault while incarcerated and the right not to be disciplined by torture exist only in theory and rarely can be enforced."

Coincidental to the Coffin case in the 1940s, the American Prison Association issued its first manual of standards for correctional practices. It published subsequent revisions during the next two decades, but the standards were always offered as suggestions for self-evaluation and contained no enforcement provisions. It was only in 1973, when the National Advisory Commission on Criminal Justice Standards and Goals issued its set of prison standards, that human rights of prisoners were stressed. According to Lee Bowker (1982: 291), when the American Correctional Association was confronted with a set of national standards that could be used by federal agencies to demand compliance as a condition for federal funding, it sought to strengthen its position by forming the Commission on Accreditation for Corrections, a body charged with reviewing the conditions and practices of prisons according to professionally determined standards. The effectiveness of the Commission remains to be determined since participation is voluntary and to date relatively few institutions have accepted the invitation to be reviewed.

International Standards

Action on the international level to assure humane treatment of prisoners has lagged behind American efforts. One reason for this is the lack of a powerful tribunal with the power to force member nations to comply with international standards.

In 1957, the U.N. Economic and Social Council issued its Standard Minimum Rules for the Treatment of Prisoners. This document contains 55 general rules about the treatment of prisoners and 39 additional and specific rules applying to special types of prisoners (i.e., the insane and mentally abnormal, those awaiting trial, and civil prisoners).[1] The general rules define minimal standards for the provision of basic human rights to prisoners—for example, that every prisoner should have a nutritionally adequate diet to assure health and strength. There is a provision that no prisoner should be allowed to discipline another prisoner. The document specifically prohibits corporal punishment, placing prisoners in dark cells, and all cruel, inhumane and degrading punishments as methods of disciplining prisoners.

The United Nations more indirectly endorsed these standards by including a reference to them in the International Covenant on Civil and Political Rights of December 16, 1966. This general human rights agreement states that "no one shall be subject to torture or to cruel, inhumane or degrading treatment or punishments." Unlike the Standard Minimum Rules, the Covenant is an international agreement, requiring formal declarations of endorsement from all participating U.N. nations. Even though it lacks the specificity of the early document, the Covenant could legitimize international standards for imprisonment, but declarations of endorsement are voluntary and have been slow in coming. The U.N. General Assembly reaffirmed the agreement by resolution in 1975, and the Covenant entered into force on March 19, 1976. As late as July 1982, only 70 nations had submitted their written endorsements of the Covenant (United Nations 1982b). The effect of the Standard Minimum Rules and the Covenant on prison conditions and practices remains to be determined.

There are many reasons why one might expect a gap between ratification of formal U.N. agreements and actual national practices. Some governments such as El Salvador, the Philippines, Poland, and Kampuches—well known for their alleged violations of human rights—have formally endorsed the International Covenant on Civil and Political Rights. Many nations that signed the agreement also submitted declarations and reservations along with their endorsements. Australia accepted the general principles of the agreement, for example; but with regard to Article 10 on the rights of prisoners, that country expressed the reservation "that these and other provisions of the Covenant are without prejudice to laws and lawful arrangements, of the type now in force in Australia, for the preservation of custodial discipline in penal establishments" (U.S. House Committee on Foreign Relations 1983: 650).

1. The United Nations Standard Minimum Rules, which were approved by simple resolution in 1957, have been published in Alper and Boren (1972). Copies of international treaties which contain provisions pertaining to the rights of prisoners are included in a recent publication by the U.S. government (U.S. House of Representatives, 1983).

Many essays have been written to express unofficial cultural and regional interpretations of the Covenant and other human rights agreements.[2] Tabandeh (1966), expressing an unofficial Muslim commentary on the Universal Declaration of Human Rights, wrote:

> Some may object that certain provisions (in Muslim law) imposing fines and penalties make differences between people. Thus, if an incontinent Muslim commits adultery, his punishment is 100 lashes, the shaving of his head and one year of banishment. But if the man is not a Muslim and commits adultery with a Muslim woman, his penalty is execution. And if the adulterer and adulteress are both slaves, each of them must be punished with 50 strokes. Similarly, if a Muslim deliberately murders another Muslim he falls under the law of retaliation and must by law himself be put to death by the next of kin. But if a non-Muslim who dies at the hand of a Muslim has by life-long habit been a non-Muslim, the penalty of death is not valid. Instead the Muslim murderer must pay a fine and be punished with a lash (p. 17, parentheses added).

The extent to which cruel and inhuman treatments are practiced throughout the world is the topic of concern in our research. How many nations fail to meet minimum standards of human decency in imprisoning criminal offenders? How far have international documents been effective in promoting humane prison practices? These are questions that, from a humanitarian concern, cry for answers but to date have been difficult to address.

Past Research

Two attempts have been made to evaluate the effects of U.N. activity to regulate prison practices about the world. Daniel Skolar (1975) conducted a series of surveys for the U.N. between 1967 and 1974. In 1974, 58 nations responded to a questionnaire in which they were asked whether they had implemented the Standard Minimum Rules. Fifty percent of the nations reported that they complied with the rules on accommodations and living conditions; 62 percent reported that they segregated different categories of offenders. Standards for medical practices were reportedly met by 65 percent of the sample. Sixty-five percent also indicated that they implemented the rules on discipline and punishment. Sixty-nine percent complied with treatment standards. Classification and individualization were reported by 59 percent, and 52 percent claimed that work standards had been met. Most of the respondent countries indicated that prison law and administrative practices had been influenced by the Standard Minimum Rules.

These surveys entail several problems. They rely upon self-reporting, and nations may distort the portrayal of their prison practices and conditions to cast them in a more favorable light. They may also interpret and implement the standards in a way that is consistent with their culture but fail to establish the desired minimal standards. For instance, what is considered to be an adequate diet will be judged by the nation's own nutritional standards rather than by an international norm. Furthermore, the sample of 58 nations is small compared to the more than 150 nations existing in the world today. Since these nations

2. For a collection of such essays, see Pollis and Schwab (1979).

agreed to participate in the survey, their patterns of compliance may not represent the more general practices found throughout the world.

In an earlier study, Bad-El-Din Ali (1969) conducted a more thorough analysis of the implementation of the Standard Minimum Rules in nine nations. Relying upon expert investigations rather than survey results, Ali determined that subscription to the standards had increased between 1955 and 1969 in all nine nations that he studied. Nations tended to implement the general rules more fully than the specific rules. Israel achieved the highest percentage of rule implementation, meeting 90 percent of the standards; Costa Rica achieved the lowest, with 34 percent. The remaining seven nations—including Hungary, Italy, Australia, and the United States—fell somewhere between these two nations. Third World nations showed greater levels of improvement during the period of study but still tended to have worse prison conditions than did more industrialized nations.

Bad-El-Din Ali's study supports the claim that U.N. standards produce improvements in international prison conditions, yet it too suffers from methodological limitations. The sample is extremely small, making it not only difficult to reach any conclusions about conditions throughout the world but also precluding further analysis of factors that might be related to prison practices.

Evaluating Prison Practices

In this work we compare international variations in the treatment of criminal offenders. Unlike other comparative research that evaluates positive or successful aspects of prison policy, we focus upon those that are negative by identifying nations engaged in cruel, inhumane, and degrading activities. Though disagreements remain, several types of treatment appear to be generally recognized by international tribunals as failing to meet minimal standards and are considered to violate prisoners' human rights. These include harsh and primitive conditions, overcrowded living situations, inadequate sanitary conditions, inadequate nutrition, failure to allow visitation, physical mistreatment of prisoners, substandard medical care, and forced labor for long hours.

Information about the prison practices of countries was gathered through a content analysis of the 1981 volume of the Department of State's report on human rights practices (referred to below as the *Country Reports*). The State Department collects information about the human rights practices of other nations through an annual questionnaire sent to U.S. Ambassadors, reviews of reports issued by American intelligence agencies, and reviews of newspapers and reports issued by other human rights organizations, including Amnesty International. Initial drafts of each country's human rights report are prepared by American embassies. The reports are edited by appropriate area and country experts within the State Department, in consultation with the embassy and the Bureau of Human Rights. One section of the report on each country deals with cruel, inhumane, or degrading treatment or punishment of prisoners. The prison practices described for each country later in this report reflect official U.S. State Department perceptions of practices.

Our purpose was to describe variations in the treatment of prisoners among nations, to identify country characteristics that appear to be related to the violation of prisoner rights, and to draw a conclusion about the success of international efforts to control inhumane practices. Information regarding prison practices and conditions in different nations was gathered through a content analysis of the 1981 report by the United States Department of State on human rights practices during calendar year 1980. Content analysis is defined by Ole Holsti (1968: 601) as "any technique for making inferences by systematically and objectively identifying specified characteristics of messages." It has been used most often to determine authorship of anonymous documents (see Mosteller and Wallace 1964), to make inferences about the motives of communicators (see Litt 1963), and to provide clues to attitudes and behavior not easily studied through other, more obtrusive methods (see Smith 1972). In the present study, content analysis is used to quantify the substantive messages within the human rights report relevant to the prison practices of countries.

In conducting this type of research, we faced several difficult definitional issues arising from the cultural and developmental differences in the world. The most significant problem was to determine the benchmark by which to evaluate conditions. Should we use a universal standard or a sliding scale, which would account for different perceptions of quality of life found throughout the world? In the least economically developed nations, most citizens live in primitive conditions that are not sanitary and subsist on diets that are not nutritionally adequate. If prison conditions greatly surpassed the standard of life for free people, criminal sanctions would lose their deterrent effect and incarceration might appear to be desirable to many citizens. Therefore, we only classified a nation's prison conditions as harsh if they were considerably worse than those available to the average citizen of that nation.

By reviewing the *Country Reports'* descriptions of conditions in two underdeveloped nations, Nepal and Guinea, we can show how these distinctions were made. Nepal prisons were described as reflecting "the general standard of living in one of the poorest developing nations. Jail conditions vary according to the crime committed and the person's status, but all prisoners have access to medical attention and to the traditional Nepalese diet as well as being permitted visitors and goods from the outside" (p. 1059). We classified Nepal's prison system as one that was not harsh or abusive. The *Country Reports* describe conditions in Guinea prisons as "generally very poor. Ill treatment and poor conditions in Guinea prisons are recognized features of the prison system. The Amnesty International Report 1980 expresses fear that many prisoners have been killed in prison or died as a direct result of ill-treatment and poor conditions" (p. 110). We classified Guinea prisons as cruel and inhumane.

Objective measures of human rights practices would be difficult to construct, because there is some disagreement over which rights are fundamental and widespread disagreement over what constitutes the denial of a fundamental human right (Donnelly 1982a; Thompson 1978; Van Dyke 1973). While the State Department reports are obviously not an ideal source of information about human rights practices abroad or even about American government perceptions of those practices, they are comprehensive both in the number of countries reported upon and in the variety of human rights practices described (Heginbotham and Bite 1978). They are consistent in format and are widely respected.

Nevertheless, the reports are the subject of some controversy, and there are those who claim that they are fabricated to support Administration positions. There are a number of reasons to discount this allegation. First, the reports often contain harsh criticisms of the human right practices of nations which have traditionally been friendly to the U.S. and others which have been singled out by particular administrations to receive U.S. aid. The Philippines, South Korea, and China are all examples of nations in the former category; El Salvador is an example of one which falls into the latter category. The State Department report issued in February of 1981, for example, castigated extremist behavior on both sides of the ideological spectrum in its assessment of human rights practices in El Salvador during 1980. These abysmal practices of the El Salvador government are reflected in the study's account of penal practices in that nation. The most recent report of El Salvador's human rights practices has not been content analyzed, but it does not markedly differ from reports that have been issued in recent years. Although El Salvador is a primary recipient of U.S. foreign aid, there is no evidence that reports on its human rights practices have been toned down to render that aid less controversial.

Second, if the reports were obviously biased, they would be roundly criticized by members of Congress (especially those of the party in opposition to the President). In the Fall and Winter of 1982, the authors interviewed State Department officials responsible for producing the annual *Country Reports,* members of foreign affairs committees in Congress, and committee staff members. During our interviews, we encountered very little criticism of the reports. Members of Congress used additional sources of information about human rights practices when making their decisions, but most spoke highly of the integrity of the State Department effort.

Third, there is a close correspondence between the human rights reports issued by the State Department and those issued by other human rights organizations. No report on human rights practices is accepted as "objective," but the annual Amnesty International (1981) and Freedom House (1981) reports represent the two best known alternative sources of information about human rights practices in other nations. Although the emphases of these two reports are different, each contains information which can be compared with the State Department Report. The level of agreement on comparable items is remarkably high.[3]

---

3. It is difficult to make precise comparisons of the human rights reports produced by different organizations because of differing formats, definitions employed, and periods of time reported. However, 100 countries were randomly selected and an independent coder was employed to compare the Amnesty International and State Department reports for calendar year 1980. The coder was instructed to focus upon two items of information which were consistently mentioned in the *Country Reports* and which were usually mentioned by Amnesty International—whether the government practiced torture and whether the government arbitrarily arrested and imprisoned its citizens. The levels of agreement between the two reports in these two categories were 81 percent and 77 percent respectively.

Finally, content analysis of the *Country Reports* as a method for measuring U.S. State Department perceptions of human rights practices in other nations has several advantages over methods employed in previous studies. Most works have not attempted to rank or otherwise quantify human rights practices. Some rough quantification is necessary, though, in order to compare and evaluate the practices of nations. Certain scholars have simply located one, two, or a few nations on a prisoner treatment continuum on the basis of their own expertise (Ali 1969), or have relied on self-reporting (Skoler 1975). The results are often interesting, even compelling, but rarely replicable or generalizable. To our knowledge, the *Country Reports* are the only centralized source of information about human rights practices which address prison conditions and practices throughout the world. The findings reported here in effect summarize the results of the State Department study of those conditions in 1980 and should be interpreted accordingly.

The reliability of measurement is a matter of concern for all quantitative analyses. The problem is especially serious for content analysis, since it is difficult to avoid biases on the part of those attempting to quantify communication content. In order to avoid bias in the coding of information, the investigators did not participate in the actual coding process except for the preparation of the measuring instrument and the written instructions to the coders. Each country's description of prison practices was coded by three individuals, who worked independently and were paid for their research assistance. For the data used in this study, all three coders agreed on 71.5 percent of the items coded. Two coders out of three agreed 28.5 percent of the time.

Findings

Table 1 presents findings regarding violations of the eight conditions of humane prisoner treatment plus a summary assessment of governmental respect for prisoners' rights among the 155 nations. The eight variables were moderately to highly correlated and appeared to form a cohesive cluster indicating one attribute.

Thus, we felt justified in creating a summary variable indicating overall attention to prisoner rights. A nation was categorized as violating those rights if any of the eight inhumane situations listed in Table 1 were classified as present in that country. We see the extensiveness of inhumane practices at the bottom of Table 1: 90 nations (almost 60 percent of the sample) violate prisoners' rights in some cruel, degrading, or inhumane way. In some cases, (Ireland and the United Arab Emirates, for example) the only violation was that of overcrowding. But in Guinea, as indicated above, the treatment is so harsh and inadequate that prisoners die as a direct result of incarceration. The description given of prisons in Brazil is more typical of nations where prison conditions are substandard:

> Detention facilities are overcrowded, and the level of prison health care, diet, and sanitation is low. Officials point out that, as with other social services, the country lacks resources to upgrade detention facilities. There are no legal distinctions in treatment of prisoners based on type of offense, class, or sex. (U.S. Dept. of State 1981: 358–359)

Table 1 Variation Among 155 Nations in Violations of Standards of Humane Prisoner Treatment (N = 165)

Violations	Number of Nations	Percentage of Nations
Prison Conditions Harsh and Primitive	57	36.8%
Prisons Overcrowded	49	31.6%
Sanitary Conditions Inadequate	24	15.5%
Nutrition Inadequate	34	21.9%
Visitation Not Allowed or Seldom Allowed	10	6.5%
Prisoners Physically Mistreated	23	14.8%
Medical Care Substandard	25	16.1%
Prisoners Forced to Work Long Hours	7	4.5%
SUMMARY: Prisoners' Rights Violated	90	58.1%

Table 2 The Relationship Between Respect for Prisoners' Rights and National Ratification of the International Covenant on Civil and Political Rights (N = 165)

		International Covenant	
		Ratified	Not Ratified
Violation of Prisoners' Rights	None	49% (29)	33% (35)
	Some	51% (30)	67% (71)

Cruel, inhumane, and degrading conditions still remain common throughout the world. In over one-third of the nations, they are reported to be harsh and punitive. Nutrition is inadequate for maintaining the health and strength of prisoners in every fifth nation. Sanitary conditions fail to meet minimal standards of decency, prisoners are physically mistreated, and medical care is substandard in every seventh nation.

While U.N. activity to assure minimal standards may have improved conditions throughout the world, these findings lead us to conclude that they have not accomplished all that they were intended to do. Information in Table 2 further supports this conclusion. The International Covenant on Civil and Political Rights prohibited cruel, inhumane, and degrading treatment or punishment and called for ratification by member nations of the U.S. General Assembly. In 1980, 59 of the 155 nations in our sample had so acted; yet 51 percent of those same nations still engage in the mistreatment of prisoners. Of the nations that have not ratified the Covenant, 67 percent engage in harsh and cruel practices.

Since we do not know whether nations more likely to meet minimum standards were also more likely to sign the Covenant, we cannot conclude that the Covenant caused a change in national prison practices.

Guided by indications in these data—as suggested by the Brazilian situation—as well as by previous studies, we next sought to determine the relation between the level of economic development and the treatment of prisoners. We expected the least developed nations to incur practical and financial difficulties in complying with minimal treatment rules. The World Bank's categorization of nations into six levels of development was used in the assessment. This scheme, based upon gross national product (GNP) alone, classifies nations as low-income, lower middle-income, upper middle-income, and industrial market economies. A separate category of high-income oil exporters is created because of their unique and highly skewed distribution of wealth. A sixth category consists of the East European non-market economies. In all, the World Bank classifies 125 nations, deleting countries whose economies play an insignificant role in the world market.

Table 3 shows a very strong relationship between level of economic development and the failure to meet minimum rules of prisoner treatment. Almost all—85 percent—of the poorest countries have prisons where conditions and practices are cruel, inhumane, and degrading. For nations in the second category, that percentage drops to 71.8. For upper middle-income nations it drops even further to 57.9 percent. Less than six percent of the industrial market economies are reported to incarcerate citizens in substandard facilities. The lack of financial resources in poor countries is probably the reason for this pattern of violation. Faced with other weighty economic and social problems, governments in poorer countries cannot afford to upgrade prison facilities.

Table 3 demonstrates that the two special categories—high income oil exporters and East European non-market economies—also appear to exhibit high levels of noncompliance with minimal standards. In the case of the high income oil exporters, this may suggest that they regard prisoners' rights much like poorer Third World nations do, and they are unwilling to expend government resources to upgrade facilities. Since many citizens in these nations remain very poor, leaders may feel incarceration would be too attractive if conditions were improved. An alternative and more plausible interpretation is that a third variable—religion—determines their prison practices. Each of the oil rich nations practices some form of Islam. Islamic principles endorse strong punitive responses to criminal behavior; in some cases, corporal punishments are condoned. Very harsh and substandard conditions would, therefore, be expected. In evaluating this hypothesis, we found that 14 of the 20 Islamic nations of the world (70 percent) fail to meet minimal standards. This percentage is higher than the 58 percent of all nations that fail to meet those standards, thus supporting our hypothesis.

We found that of all the categories, the percentage of nations failing to meet international standards of prisoner treatment was highest for East European non-market economies. Seven out of eight nations, or 87.5 percent, incarcerated prisoners in substandard facilities. Furthermore, when we included all

Table 3 Nations That Violate Prisoners' Rights Categorized by Level of Development

Level of Development	Number of Nations	Percentage Violating Prisoners' Rights
A. Lower Income Economies (n=34)	29	85.3%
Afghanistan Bangladesh [b,d,g] Benin [a] Bhutan Burma [a,b,d,g,h] Burundi [b,c] Central African Republic [a] Chad [a] China [e,f] Ethiopia [a,b,c]	Ghana [a,b] Guinea [a,d,f] Haiti [a,b,c,d,f,g] India [b] Kampuchea [a,c,d,f,g] Laos [a,g] Madagascar [a,b] Malawi Mali [a,f,g] Mozambique [a,d,g]	Nepal Niger [a,b] Pakistan [b] Rwanda [a,b,c,d,g] Sierra Leone Somali Republic [a,d,e,g] Sri Lanka [a,b,c,g] Sudan [a] Tanzania [b,d,g] Toga Uganda [a,d] Upper Volta [a,d] Vietnam [a,d,g] Zaire [a,b,c,d]
B. Lower Middle-Income Economies (n=39)	28	71.8%
Angola [b,c,d,e] Bolivia [a,b] Cameroon [b,d,g] Colombia [b] Congo Republic [d,g] Costa Rica Cuba Dominican Republic [a,b,c,e,f] Ecuador [a] Egypt El Salvador [a,b] Guatemala Honduras [a]	Indonesia [a,b,d,f] Ivory Coast [a,d] Jamaica [a] Jordan [b] Kenya [a] Korean Peoples Rep. [d,e,f,h] Lesotho Liberia [a,b,c,e] Mauritius Mongolia Morocco [a,b,c] Nicaragua [a,b,f] Nigeria [b,f]	Papua New Guinea Paraguay Peru [a,b,c] Philippines [a] Senegal Syria Thailand [a] Tunisia [a] Turkey [b] Yemen-Arab Rep. [a,d,g] Yemen-Peoples Democratic Rep. [a,c,d,f,g] Zambia [b,c] Zimbabwe Rhodesia [b]
C. Upper Middle-Income Economies (n=19)	11	57.9%
Algeria [a,b,c,d] Argentina [e,f,g] Brazil [b,c,d,g] Chile Greece Iraq [b,c] Israel [b]	Korean Republic [a] Lebanon [b,d] Malaysia Mexico [a,b,c,d,f] Panama [a,b] Portugal	Singapore South Africa Trinidad [a] Uruguay Venezuela Yugoslavia [a]

Table 3 Continued

Level of Development	Number of Nations	Percentage Violating Prisoners' Rights
D. High Income Oil Exporters (n=4)	3	75.0%
Kuwait [d,f]	Saudi Arabia	United Arab Emirates [b]
Libya [f]		
E. Industrial Market Economies (n=18)	1	5.6%
Australia	France	New Zealand
Austria	German Fed. Republic	Norway
Belgium	Ireland [b]	Spain
Canada	Italy	Sweden
Denmark	Japan	Switzerland
Finland	Netherlands	United Kingdom
F. East European Non-Market Economies (n=8)	7	87.5%
Albania	German Democratic Republic [a,b,c,d,e,f,g]	Rumania [a,b,c,d,e,f,g,h]
Bulgaria [a,b,f,g,h]	Hungary	USSR [d,g,h]
Czechoslovakia [a,d]	Poland [b,h]	
G. Nations not classified by World Bank (n=29)	8	29.7%
Bahamas [a,b,c]	Gabon a,b	Qatar
Bahrain [e,f]	Gambia	St. Lucia
Barbados	Grenada	Sierra Leone
Botswana [f]	Guinea-Bissau [a,b,c,d]	Seychelles
Cape Verde Is.	Guyana [a,b,f,g]	Solomon Is.
Cyprus	Iceland	Suriname
Djibouti	Luxembourg	Swaziland
Dominica	Mula Is.	Taiwan [g]
Equatorial Guinea	Malta	Western Samoa
Fiji [b]	Mauritania	

a = prison conditions, harsh and punitive
b = prisons overcrowded
c = sanitary conditions inadequate
d = nutrition inadequate
e = visitation seldom or not allowed
f = prisoners are physically mistreated
g = medical care substandard
h = prisoners work long hours

communist nations in our analysis, thirteen of the sixteen, or 81.3 percent, reportedly mistreat prisoners. These are exceedingly high percentages. They may suggest that political structure is even more important than economic development in determining whether prisoners will be mistreated. However, the statistics for these nations, more than the others, are of the most questionable validity. Communist nations represent the United States government's most obvious and threatening enemies. If the *Country Reports* misrepresent or overstate the harshness of prison conditions, it would probably be for these nations. Until we can substantiate this level of inhumane practices through other sources, we should probably not conclude that there is a strong association between government type and prison practices.

Conclusions

Our analysis of the respect shown by governments for the integrity of the person as it relates to criminal prisoners showed that inhumane, cruel, and degrading practices remain common throughout the world. Almost 60 percent of our sample failed to meet at least one international standard of minimal treatment. This finding leads us to conclude that the fight for the human rights of incarcerated men and women is far from over. Our analysis of variables associated with inhumane treatment persuades us that a nation's prison practices and conditions are tied to several very strong determining factors: level of economic development, religion, and possibly political structure. This suggests that the fight to change international conditions will be a difficult pursuit and may require the encouragement and economic support of international organizations and more developed nations. The United Nations, through a number of its organs including the Human Rights Committee and the Committee of Crime Prevention and Control of the Economic and Social Council, attempts to encourage compliance with the Standard Minimum Rules, primarily through the manipulation of symbols. Member nations are requested to submit information about the treatment of prisoners, and, from time to time, this information is published along with statements of concern. For example, a recent report of the Human Rights Committee (1982b) raised concerns about the treatment of prisoners in eight countries—Japan, The Netherlands, Morocco, Jordan, Rwanda, Guyana, Uruguay, and Iran (though it is not clear how these eight were selected).

According to the report, the nation of Morocco was asked to provide the Committee with further information, including:

> what the rules were concerning solitary confinement, for how long a person could be subjected to it, . . . how did the supervisory committees established to monitor conditions in prisons and detention centers operate, how often did they visit each prison, whether prisoners and detainees were able to contact members of supervisory committees and whether the Government considered the possibility of instituting a system of completely independent prison visitors. (p. 32)

The most recent *Yearbook on Human Rights* issued by the United Nations contains an assurance from the United States that the

> Department of Justice, under its authority to file suit against state prisons and jail systems that reflect unconstitutional treatment of inmates, has been very successful

> in its litigative efforts. Favorable rulings have set out timetables that include [prison] population reduction and improvement of facilities. In addition many of the [court] orders have also provided for monitors to be appointed to assure adherence. Thus, prisoners' rights to be free from cruel and unusual punishment are being furthered. (1982a: 106)

But the United Nations has few tangible rewards or sanctions at its disposal to ensure compliance. Developed nations, on the other hand, can attach strings to the financial assistance which they provide to less developed nations, similar to the way in which the U.S. federal government provides federal aid to state and local governments.

The United States already has enacted several public laws which make foreign assistance contingent upon evidence of good or at least improving human rights practices. The most common language used by U.S. policymakers to describe phenomena that should trigger actions in defense of human rights abroad is "a consistent pattern of gross violations of internationally recognized human rights." This language implies that human rights can be measured, at least at the ordinal level, so that the human rights practices of other nations can be ranked from best to worst. It also implies a threshold for the tolerance of human rights violations. When the severity of human rights violations by other nations crosses the implied threshold, the statutes require that the U.S. government cut off military and economic assistance and vote against loans from multilateral lending agencies (Rubin and Newberg 1980; Lillich 1979).

Only human need has been recognized by U.S. policymakers as a more important factor than human rights in the decision to provide foreign economic assistance to repressive governments if the President determines that the aid will directly benefit needy people and reports to Congress how it will do so. Although the analysis is not presented here, our data indicate that nations which violate the rights of prisoners also tend to violate other human rights. Thus, even though the emphasis of U.S. policy is not on prisoners' rights, an indirect effect of that policy is likely to be an improvement in protections against the violation of those rights.

While there is some evidence suggesting that the U.S. policy on human rights has been implemented (Cingranelli and Pasquarello 1985), there is no indication that the policy has caused changes in the human rights practices of other nations. Evidence of this type would presumably strengthen the resolve of U.S. policymakers to continue the policy despite occasional strong criticism from certain government leaders, the press, and the general public. It might also encourage other developed nations to adopt similar policies.

Discussion Questions:

1. Would you agree or disagree that all nations should be obligated to observe certain basic human rights in the operation of their prisons? Why or why not?
2. Why, and in what way, may definitions of basic human rights vary across nations? Is it reasonable to think that a minimal standard can be established and applied across diverse nations?

3. What do you see as the strengths and weaknesses of the research method used by Wright and Cingranelli? How could future research improve on the weaknesses?
4. Wright and Cingranelli report a strong inverse association between economic development and rights violations. Is the fact that a country lacks the requisite economic resources (or the fact that a large class of the country's citizenry lives in degrading and inhumane conditions) a legitimate or illegitimate reason for violating the basic rights of prisoners? Should more economically developed nations be held to higher standards of accountability? Explain.
5. Does the fact that a nation's dominant religious belief system expresses an extraordinarily punitive image of criminals in any way excuse the poor quality of treatment received by prisoners in that nation? Explain.
6. Because of the nature of their data source, Wright and Cingranelli are reluctant to conclude that a nation's political structure strongly affects its adherence to prisoners' rights. Were an improved data source available, do you think it would indicate such a relationship? Why or why not?
7. What are the implications of this research for efforts to curb violations of prisoners' rights? What, if any, role should the U.S. play in these efforts?

References

Ali, B. (1969) "Treatment of Prisoners in Nine Nations: A Pilot Study on Standard Minimum Rules." *Criminologica* 7: 2–18.

Alper, B. S., ed. (1972) *Crime: International Agenda*. Lexington: Lexington Books.

Bowker, L. H. (1982) *Corrections*. New York: Macmillan Publishing Co.

Cingranelli, D. L. and T. E. Pasquarello (1985) "Human Rights Practices and the Distribution of American Foreign Aid." *American Journal of Political Science* (Forthcoming).

Donnelly, J. (1982) "Human Rights and Human Dignity: An Analytic Critique of Non-Western Conceptions of Human Rights." *American Political Science Review* 76 (June): 303–316.

Goldfarb, R. L. and L. R. Singer (1973) *After Conviction*. New York: Simon and Schuster.

Heginbotham, S. J. and V. Bite (1978) "Issues in Interpretation and Evaluation of Country Studies." In U.S. Congressional Research Service, *Human Rights in Selected Countries and the U.S. Response,* prepared for use by the House Committee on International Relations, pp. 341–372.

Holsti, O. R. (1968) "Content Analysis." In Gardner Lindzey and Elliott Aronson (eds.) *The Handbook of Social Psychology*. Reading, Mass.: Addison-Wesley.

Lillich, R. (1979) "U.S. Legislation Relating Human Rights to U.S. Foreign Policy." Paper prepared for the International Human Rights Law Group.

Litt, E. (1963) "Civil Education, Community Norms, and Political Indoctrination." *American Sociological Review* 28: 69–75.

Mosteller and Wallace (1964) *Inference and Disputed Authorship: The Federalist*. Reading, Mass.: Addison-Wesley.

Pollis, A. and P. Scwab (1979) *Human Rights: Cultural and Ideological Perspectives*. New York: Praeger.

Rubin, B. and P. Newburg (1980) "Statistical Analysis for Implementing Human Rights Policy." In P. R. Newburg (ed.) *The Politics of Human Rights*. New York: New York University Press, pp. 268–284.

Skoler, D. L. (1975) "World Implementation of the United Nations Standard Minimum Rules for Treatment of Prisoners." Washington, D.C.: American Bar Association, Commission on Correctional Facilities and Services.

Smith, J. K. (1973) *Political Values in Africa: A Comparative Analysis of Newspaper Editorials in Five African States, 1961–1970*. Ph.D. dissertation, Boston University.

Tabandeh, S. (1966) *A Muslim Commentary on the Universal Declaration of Human Rights*. London: F. T. Goulding & Company.

Thompson, K. (1978) "New Reflections on Ethics and Foreign Policy: The Problem of Human Rights." *Journal of Politics* 40 (November): 984–1010.

United Nations (1982a) *Yearbook on Human Rights for 1977–1978*. New York: United Nations.

———. (1982b) *Report of the Human Rights Committee*. New York: United Nations.

United States Department of State (1981) *Country Reports on Human Rights Practices*. Washington, D.C.: U.S. Government Printing Office.

United States House of Representatives (1983) *Human Rights Documents*. A committee print of the Committee on Foreign Affairs.

Van Dyke, V. (1973) "Human Rights Without Discrimination." *American Political Science Review* 67 (December): 1267–1290.

22. Dealing With Prisoners' Grievances

Gillian Douglas (Bristol)*

This article will examine what methods are provided by the authorities for prisoners to complain against decisions taken by the prison administration in England and Wales,[1] Sweden and Denmark. The two Scandinavian countries have been chosen as a comparison to England because they are regarded as having progressive penal policies, and also because they make considerable use of their ''ombudsmen'' in dealing with complaints against the administration. A comparative study of this type can shed light on universal features of a particular topic and can suggest new perspectives on it. However, it must be borne in mind that procedures in different countries have developed to fit the particular circumstances there pertaining, including their economic situations and their official perceptions of crime and punishment.

Mechanisms for challenging prison authorities' decisions may be divided into two categories: mechanisms within the framework of prison administration, and mechanisms external to the prison administration. It will be seen that both categories are employed by the three countries, but their availability and effectiveness vary.

It is necessary first to examine how far the three systems facilitate challenges, by enabling prisoners to have information and reasons concerning the decisions they wish to complain about, and by enabling them to correspond with persons or bodies outside the prison to obtain advice or assistance.

Facilitating Challenges

In England, a prisoner has no right of access to his file to see if a decision has been based on correct information. The bulk of the detailed regulations which affect him are secret, and he will very often not be given a reason for a deci-

---

*LL.B., LL.M. Lecturer-in-Law, University of Bristol; currently Visiting Fellow, Faculty of Law, National University of Singapore. This article was written following a study-visit to Sweden and Denmark in 1982, made possible by a Council of Europe Fellowship for Individual Criminological Research. I am grateful to all those who made my visit so interesting and enlightening. I am also grateful to my colleagues, Dr. J. J. Fawcett, Mr. S. P. Jones and Dr. H. F. Rawlings who read earlier drafts of this article and made many helpful comments.

Article by Gillian Douglas from the *British Journal of Criminology*. Vol. 24, No. 2 (1984) pp. 150–167. Reprinted by Permission of Oxford University Press.

1. England and Wales are one jurisdiction sharing the same legal and administrative structure; only England will be referred to hereafter. The position in Scotland and Northern Ireland is broadly the same, though governed by separate legislation and administration, and mechanisms for dealing with prisoners' grievances are effectively the same as in England and Wales. For details, see the May Committee Report (1979). Article by Gillian Douglas from the *British Journal of Criminology* Vol. 24, No. 2 (1984) pp. 150–167. Reprinted by permission of Oxford University Press.

(a) Giving Information to the Prisoner

sion. Even where secrecy is not an issue, reasons tend to be cursory and uninformative (Cohen and Taylor, 1979).

The position is very different in Sweden, where the Freedom of the Press Act 1949 Ch. 2 provides that "official" documents are open to public scrutiny. They are defined as documents kept, received, prepared or drawn up by a State or municipal authority. "A consequence . . . is that any party concerned in a case or other matter may study the written material which constitutes the basis for the considerations of the authority" (Holmberg and Stjernquist, 1981). A prisoner may therefore inspect his file to see if the information in it is correct. The prison administration (Kriminalvardsstyrelsen, hereafter KVS) also has the practice of giving reasons for decisions.

The Danish Information Act 1970 is not as wide-ranging as the Swedish legislation (Holm, 1975). An individual may see the documents relating to his own case, but not if they are "internal working documents" which include evaluations and recommendations. However, the presumption of access is at least established. Denmark's Administrative Procedure Act 1964 also requires that parties to an administrative proceeding be given an opportunity to comment orally or in writing before the decision is made, after being fully informed of the facts. Rule 28(1) of the Order on Custodial Treatment accordingly provides for prisoners to be "informed of decisions made in respect of their position and on request they shall be informed of the reasons for the decision" and they must be given an opportunity to present their own views.

From an administrative point of view, the more a prisoner is kept informed and consulted about a decision, the more he may wish to challenge it (Parole Board, 1979). On the other hand, to give reasons and an opportunity to air his views may enable the prisoner to accept a decision more easily. It may also be beneficial from a reformative point of view, in giving him some say and influence on what happens to him in prison.

(b) Allowing Correspondence

A prisoner who is dissatisfied about the conditions in which he is required to serve his sentence, or who believes that an unfair or unreasonable decision has been taken which affects those conditions, may wish to communicate his views to the outside world for a number of reasons. He may wish to seek advice on possible remedies; he may wish to initiate a complaint with an outside body such as a court; he may wish to let off steam; he may wish to publicise an abuse. The rules operating to control communication with the outside world are crucial in respect of all these.

The draconian English rules on censorship, apparently designed to prevent any complaint about the prison from being aired outside, have been heavily criticised by the European Commission of Human Rights in the *Silver* case (5947/72 (1981) 3 E.H.R.R. 475). The Commission, whose Report was substantially adopted by the European Court of Human Rights (2/1981/41/60–66, March 25, 1983), found that three aspects of censorship in particular infringed Article 8 of the European Convention on Human Rights. First, the prisoner had to pursue internal complaints procedures before he could complain to a Member of Parliament, the Parliamentary Commissioner for Administration (the ombudsman) or a lawyer. This was known as the "prior ventilation rule," and since internal procedures can be extremely slow, it had the effect of delaying considerably the external airing of grievances. Secondly, complaints to other persons (apart from the European Commission of Human Rights) could simply not be sent. Thirdly, under r.34(8) Prison Rules, prisoners may only correspond with relatives or friends, unless the Secretary of State allows otherwise.

In the light of the Commission's view that these restrictions were in breach of the Convention, the standing orders governing correspondence were amended, and prisoners may now complain outside provided that they ventilate complaints internally *at the same time*. They may write—and complain—to any person or organisation unless the correspondent is regarded by the authorities as presenting a genuine and serious threat to security or good order in the prison. While representing a considerable improvement over the previous situation, these changes can still be criticised on three counts (although the Court declined to rule on their compatibility with the Convention).

First, only standing orders have been changed. The Prison Rules remain the same. Standing orders are of uncertain legal status and a failure to abide by them may be legally unchallengeable (the point will be further discussed later in this article). Secondly, r.47(12) Prison Rules makes it an offence against discipline to make a false and malicious allegation against an officer, punishable by loss of remission. A prisoner may be reluctant to use the internal complaints procedures for fear of facing disciplinary proceedings (Zellick, 1982a). Finally, the Prison Department retains considerable discretion to decide that some person or organisation represents a threat to security or good order, and so may not be corresponded with.

A very clear difference emerges when one examines the position in Sweden and Denmark. Their liberal prison regimes have been accompanied by liberal rules on censorship. (For Sweden, see the Act on Correctional Treatment in Institutions 1974, ss.25–31. For Denmark, see Circulars B-16, C-2, 4, 7, 8.) Such restrictions as there are exist to detect escape plans or criminal activity inside or outside the institution, in particular, whether drugs are being smuggled in. No attempt is made to prevent complaints being aired outside. Indeed, it is expected that prisoners will complain about their conditions. They may write any number of letters they like and can also communicate by telephone. There is accordingly no difficulty in making their views known outside and in seeking help in pursuing their grievances.

Mechanisms Within the Framework of Prison Administration

(a) Taking a Grievance to a Higher Official

All three systems allow a prisoner to make a complaint to a higher official in the administration.

In England, a prisoner can apply to see the governor of the prison to seek a request or make a complaint. He may also ask to see a visiting officer of the Secretary of State (r.8(1) Prison Rules) by which is meant in practice the Regional Director or his deputy who periodically visit the prisons in the region, the medical officer or the chaplain. Additionally, a prisoner may petition the Secretary of State.

Little is known[2] about the operation of these mechanisms, perhaps because of the secrecy surrounding the administration of the prisons. It appears from cases brought under the European Convention on Human Rights (for example *Silver, Reed* 7630/76 D R 19 p. 113), and from the work of Cohen and Taylor (1979) that the handling of petitions tends to be slow and, since **governors** may be reluctant to break new ground, prisoners must resort to the Home Office for any novel or unusual request. It seems that about one-third of petitions concern disciplinary awards, the Home Secretary acting as an appeal body from the governor or board of visitors who adjudicate on discipline (May Committee, 1979). A prisoner is not entitled to legal representation in any internal adjudication, such as discipline or parole (*Fraser v. Mudge* [1975] 3 All E.R. 78), and this absence of legal scrutiny may not be conducive to encouraging careful documentation and observance of set procedures. Recently, increasing conflict between the uniformed and managerial grades (Zellick, 1982b) may have the effect of constraining a governor into deciding an issue in such a way as to avoid provoking the displeasure of the staff for fear of industrial action, rather than on its merits.

In Sweden, it is a general feature of administrative law and practice that a person may appeal against a decision to a higher tier in the bureaucracy. Most decisions concerning prisoners are taken either by the prison governor or by the regional director, or are made or ratified by the KVS itself. Prisons are divided into local prisons, grouped into 13 regions headed by a regional director, and national prisons, generally for prisoners serving over one year, whose governors are of equivalent ranking to the regional directors. Discipline is decided by the governor, but if he awards the punishment of adding on extra days to the sentence to be served (the equivalent of loss of remission in England) this must be confirmed by the KVS. Governors also decide on granting leaves of absence from the prison, whether for visits, work or study. If leave is abused, the time spent away from the prison can be deducted from that counted as having been served, but only the KVS can make such deductions. Transfer to another prison is decided at a regional level for the local prisons, and by the KVS for the national prisons.

While the KVS *is* prepared to reduce or quash disciplinary awards so as to achieve some general uniformity across the prisons, it will rarely uphold a complaint concerning transfer from an open to a closed prison. This is an extremely common informal penalty; for example, in a 1977 sample, 37 percent of inmates who were moved from open national prisons and 47 percent who were moved from open local prisons were transferred because of misbehaviour (Kühlhorn, 1981). The KVS seems mainly concerned to check that governors are not acting outside their powers, rather than to control too closely how they choose to run their prisons.

If the prisoner is not satisfied with the determination by the KVS, either in its "original" or "appellate" jurisdiction, he may appeal to the administrative

---

2. Research is currently being undertaken by the Home Office Research and Planning Unit, following recommendation by the House of Commons Expenditure Committee in 1978 (H.C. 662–1). Results are not yet available.

court of appeal, the Kammarrätten (KR). This will be discussed below, but should be regarded structurally as an extension of the appeals apparatus which exists in Swedish administration (Holmgren, 1974).

In Sweden (but not, of course, in England) a prisoner is theoretically free to seek legal advice and to ask his lawyer to represent him in any matter, but this rarely happens in practice. The main reason for this is the problem of cost, since legal aid is not available for internal appeals (though it may be granted for appeals to the KR). Also, lawyers are inexperienced in this area, and therefore may be of limited utility.

In Denmark, there is no regional tier in the prison administration. Governors of prisons are of very high standing, ranking as equivalent to judges, district prosecutors and police chiefs. The Prison Department takes important decisions concerning inmates serving over five years, such as parole, transfer to an open prison or leave; otherwise the governor decides. Prisoners must complain to a governor before going on to the Prison Department (Circular C-4). This is equivalent to the English requirement that petitions will be scrutinised by the governor to see if he can provide a remedy without recourse being necessary to the Home Office. Denmark, like England, does have a disciplinary offence of making a false and malicious allegation, though apparently it is rarely used.[3] It may, of course, still have a deterrent effect. The Prison Department will rarely alter a decision taken by a governor. This may be due to the fact that governors will have worked at the Department before being appointed to their posts in the prisons, and so are regarded as familiar colleagues. As in Sweden, legal representation is possible in theory only.

The Court in *Silver* (para. 116) distinguished between complaints to a higher official (there, the Secretary of State) as to the validity of a directive, and those alleging misapplication of such a directive by another official. The Court was satisfied that the latter could be adequately dealt with, so as to provide the prisoner with an "effective remedy" for a breach of the European Convention on Human Rights, as required under Article 13; whereas the former would place the Secretary of State in the position of being judge in his own cause. Such a distinction seems unreal in practice. Rather the main drawback of the internal machinery in all three countries seems to be the reluctance of a higher official to reach a different decision from that of his colleague, unless the latter has clearly gone beyond his legal powers. Such reluctance may be due to various pressures operating on the higher official. He is likely to identify with the staff rather than the prisoners. He may want to avoid undermining the authority of a uniformed officer over the prisoners on his wing. He may feel he must back up an officer in conflict with more junior grades. Such pressures make it difficult for an official to substitute his own opinion on the merits of a decision, most particularly if it means having to choose between the staff and an individual inmate. The latter is hardly likely to have confidence in the grievance procedure in these circumstances.

3. Personal communication from officials at the Prison Department.

(b) Inmate Councils

A more satisfactory means of providing redress may be seen in the setting up of "inmate councils." While the central aim of these is to provide more democratic involvement in decision-making, this can have the effect of providing a mechanism for dealing with complaints in two ways. First, the prisoner representatives on the council may take up a grievance collectively and seek to negotiate a change in practice. Secondly, the representative may act as a go-between for a prisoner in making a personal request or complaint. Forming such a body, and providing for such functions to be performed, brings prisoners somewhat closer to the position of employees who elect union shop stewards to represent them in discussions with management. The device may therefore have the effect of emphasising the conflict between staff and inmates, and perhaps lead to "industrial action" such as refusal to work. It is possible because of fear of such consequences that the English prisons have not set up inmate councils.

In Sweden, however, after the substantial unrest in the prisons during the late 1960s and early 1970s, and the rise of the prison reform organisation, KRUM (Mathiesen, 1974), the re-organising legislation did provide for collective action on the part of prisoners. The Act on Correctional Treatment in Institutions 1974, s.36 provides that "Within the limits set by rules and agreements concerning the operation of the correctional system, inmates shall be entitled to have consultations under some suitable form with the management of an institution concerning matters of common concern to the inmate. They shall also be entitled to hold meetings with each other in some suitable way to discuss such matters. . . ." However, this provision is regarded as having limited utility (Ward, 1979). First, it allows for consultations but not negotiations. Secondly, the entitlement depends on the limits set by rules and agreements. The forum for consultations was expected to be an inmate council, consisting of representatives of the prisoners meeting with the governor and staff. Such councils are largely moribund in Sweden today.

The picture is slightly different in Denmark, where r.18 of the Order on Custodial Treatment provides that prisoners "shall have the opportunity to discuss and influence general matters in relation to their life in the institution either through elected representatives or otherwise." Circular B-12 excludes from discussion "questions concerning individual inmates or individual members of staff." This would seem to prohibit prisoner representatives from pursuing complaints on behalf of individual inmates, but it appears that a governor who is amenable will permit the representatives to fulfill this role. One may conclude from the Swedish and Danish experience that the success and effectiveness of inmate councils depend on the enthusiasm of the governor and staff to permit them to function, and also on the willingness of the inmates to put in the effort needed without taking advantage of the special position they acquire for their own ends. If all this can be achieved, it does seem that inmate spokesmen can help to provide a useful channel of communication between staff and prisoners. Prisoners may have more faith in their own representatives than in a prison official, and the governor can obtain an important insight into the views and concerns of the prisoners. This might compensate for the possible increase in control problems arising from giving inmates more freedom to organise against and to challenge the system.

(c) Prison Boards

The English system has set up bodies which are supposed to be regarded as an independent check and reviewing agency of the prison authorities' decisions. Every prison has its "board of visitors"[4] (Jellicoe, 1975) made up of representatives of the local community, including at least two "lay magistrates" (that is, justices of the peace who seldom have training in law). Their duties are to "satisfy themselves as to the state of the prison premises, the administration of the prison and the treatment of the prisoners" (r.94 Prison Rules). They must inquire into and report upon any matter into which the Secretary of State asks them to inquire; they must direct the governor's attention to any matter which calls for it; report to the Secretary of State any matter which they consider it expedient to report; inform him immediately of any abuse which comes to their knowledge; and report to him annually. They may be seen as inspectors of the prison, as "well informed and acute but friendly watchdogs of the public interest" (May Committee, 1979). However, they have two other duties. First, they hear the most serious disciplinary charges against prisoners, and secondly they "shall hear any complaint or request which a prisoner wishes to make to them" (r.95(1) Prison Rules). Members of the board must visit the prison frequently and a prisoner may always speak to them when they visit. They have the right of access to every part of the prison, and no records may be withheld from them.

Yet the boards do not seem to deal very effectively with complaints.[5] Often, this function is carried out by one or two members, accompanied by an officer, touring the prison and stopping to exchange a few words with any inmate wishing to talk to them. Alternatively, the prisoner can appear before a full board of up to twenty people, with the governor present, which is likely to inhibit him from speaking out freely. Some boards may run a "clinic" system, whereby a fixed time is set each week for private consultations; this method was approved by the Jellicoe Committee but is not required by the legislation. Prisoners are therefore dependent on the approach of the particular board at their prison for whether their complaints are handled in this more sympathetic way.

Jellicoe found that prisoners expected little success from complaining to board members, since they assumed that the boards "side" with the authorities. This seems due to the function of the board in hearing serious disciplinary charges, which undermines their supposedly neutral position. Indeed, the very exercise by the boards of this function itself gives rise to prisoners' complaints, as shown by the number of petitions made to the Secretary of State concerning awards, and by the increasing number of court cases arising out of the conduct

4. In Scotland these are called Visiting Committees. In Northern Ireland, both Boards of Visitors and Visiting Committees exist. Their functions are the same as in England.
5. Research is currently being undertaken by the Centre for Criminological Research, University of Oxford.

of adjudicatory proceedings (this issue is dealt with later in this article). In any case, as the European Court recognised in *Silver* (para. 115), boards have limited powers to deal with complaints, being able only to make reports or recommendations to the governor or Home Secretary and lacking any power to issue binding instructions to prison staff.

Recently, proposals have been made in Sweden to set up boards along similar lines to the English boards of visitors. These would replace the "supervision boards" which currently decide on parole and extended leave of absence for prisoners serving sentences of less than one year. These boards, made up of local experts such as doctors, employment officers and judges, would take on the role of lay representative committees who act as local inspectors of the institution. Such committees already oversee the Swedish police districts. However, the proposals have not been enthusiastically received, and it is suggested that efforts could be more usefully directed towards reviving inmate participation in the running of the prisons.

External Complaints Mechanisms

We have seen that internal mechanisms for complaint may be unsatisfactory in that they may be slow, they may leave a prisoner open to disciplinary sanctions, and they enable the authorities to be judges in their own cause. Prisoners will accordingly very often wish to complain to somebody outside the prison sphere.

(a) Courts

The prime legal external mechanism for challenging discretion is a court action, but courts in the three countries have been reluctant in the past to undertake the task when a prisoner has asked them. This is perhaps partly due to the uncertain legal status of the rules affecting prisoners.

In England, these are contained in the Prison Act of 1952[6]; the Prison Rules 1964 (as amended), which are statutory instruments made by virtue of authority delegated by Parliament to the Secretary of State under s.47 of the Prison Act; and standing orders and circular instructions issued by the Prison Department. It is unclear whether a prisoner may sue for damages in tort for breach of statutory duty; while the early case of *Arbon v. Anderson* [1943] K.B. 252 held in the negative, the Court of Appeal in *Williams v. Home Office (No. 2)* [1982] 2 All E.R. 564 accepted that it was an arguable point (see Zellick, 1982c). However, the courts are prepared, in actions for judicial review, to rule on the meaning and extent of the Prison Rules, in order to declare that the prison authorities have exceeded their statutory authority, and to quash any decision made beyond such authority. They also seem prepared to consider whether the Rules themselves go beyond the authority vested by s.47 (*Raymond v. Honey* [1982] 1 All E.R. 756; Zellick, 1982c; Halsbury, 1982, para. 1139). If it is uncertain what remedies a prisoner has in respect of a breach of the Prison

6. In Scotland, the Prisons (Scotland) Act 1952 and the Prison (Scotland) Rules 1952 as amended. In Northern Ireland, the Prison Act (Northern Ireland) 1953 and the Prison Rules (Northern Ireland) 1954 as amended.

Rules, it is doubtful if breach of the standing orders would be actionable either in tort or by way of judicial review (Halsbury, 1982, para. 1103).

The same confused position exists in both Sweden and Denmark. In the former, the Act on Correctional Treatment in Institutions is filled in by Regulations, drafted by the Ministry of Justice, and rules made by the KVS. In Denmark, the Criminal Code, passed by Parliament, authorises the Minister of Justice to make the Order on Custodial Treatment, and the Prison Department within the Ministry issues the circulars laying down detailed rules and regulations. In both countries the legal effect of these rules and regulations is uncertain.

It is yet to be established in any of the three countries that *rules* made by the authorities are outside their legitimate powers and therefore void. Hence, there may be no effective remedy for a breach of the European Convention as required under Article 13 (see the European Court's judgment in *Silver,* para. 118). The courts have, however, begun to scrutinise *decisions* taken by the authorities, and to rule on their legality. In England, in *R. v. Hull Prison Board of Visitors, ex p. St. Germain* [1979] 1 All E.R. 701, the Court of Appeal held that *certiorari* is available to quash disciplinary decisions of boards of visitors taken contrary to the rules of natural justice. Two of the three judges did not regard adjudications by governors, who, of course, deal with the great majority of prison offences and breaches of prison discipline, as being similarly reviewable, but more recently at first instance in *R. v. Board of Visitors of Dartmoor Prison, ex p. Seray-Wurie* (*The Times,* February 5, 1982), this does seem to have been accepted, and logically there seems to be no distinction between the two. Following the *Hull* case, other prisoners have attempted to use the courts to quash other types of decision, but the courts have kept largely to the area of disciplinary procedure. It is true that censorship of correspondence was condemned in *Raymond v. Honey,* but the case was unusual since the action brought was for contempt of court, in which one may expect the courts to take a concern. In perhaps the most important case so far, dealing with the legality of the "control units" which were set up to impose extremely rigorous regimes on severely disruptive prisoners, the court baulked at facing directly the question of prison policy raised by the issue (*Williams v. Home Office (No. 2)* [1981] 1 All E.R. 1211).

Even if the courts will provide redress, this will be of little use if the prisoner is unable to initiate his action in them. In England, apart from actions for contempt, a prisoner must be represented by a solicitor to start proceedings. Unless he is wealthy, he will require legal aid. The attitude of the local Legal Aid Committee, which grants legal aid, will be of crucial importance, since if it views the proposed action as frivolous or vexatious, it will refuse the application.

In Sweden, as has been pointed out, there is a system of administrative courts of appeal (KR). There are four such courts, hearing altogether about 30,000 cases each year. Appeals from the KVS are assigned to one of these courts, and of its caseload of about 5,700 cases per annum, 600 are appeals from prisoners. Three judges sit to determine a case, and arguments are written rather than oral. Prisoners, unlike other appellants, do not have the *right* to an oral hearing, but must seek the leave of the KR, which is rarely granted. Only

1–2 percent of appeals from prisoners are successful. Yet the subject-matter of these appeals, mainly concerning disciplinary punishments or the denial of leave, is by no means unimportant. Research concerning leave, for example, has shown that the rate of granting leave varies considerably between open and closed, local and national prisons, and is not particularly related to the level of abuse of leave (Kühlhorn, 1981). The variations may therefore appear highly unfair to the aggrieved prisoner, yet the KVS and the KR seem unconcerned to achieve greater uniformity. The actual conditions concerning eligibility for leave are not defined in the legislation but have been evolved by the KVS (KVS, 1980). It is open to the KR to rule on the validity of these conditions, but so far it has not called them into question.

The extremely low rate of success of prisoners in the KR suggests either that prison administration functions particularly smoothly in Sweden or, perhaps more likely, that the KR feels that it is not its role to interfere with discretion so long as it is legally exercised. This does not seem to deter prisoners from appealing, however, and from their point of view they have nothing to lose. Legal aid *can* be obtained for the services of a lawyer, but if not, since the case is decided on documents, a lawyer's skills of advocacy are less necessary anyway, and the prisoners will not suffer unduly by being unrepresented. Also, since the KR can review the merits of a decision, technical points concerning jurisdiction, calling for legal expertise, are not in issue. It quite often happens that the KVS changes its mind while an appeal is pending, and so the prisoner succeeds in his objective. In any event, independent scrutiny of its decisions may encourage higher standards and greater flexibility on the part of the KVS.

The KR can confirm, alter or quash a decision, but it cannot award damages, and so a prisoner would have to use the civil courts for this remedy. In practice this is almost unheard of. Appeals against decisions of the KR may be made to the Supreme Administrative Court, but this only considers cases raising questions of general public importance and hears very few concerning prisoners.

Denmark, like England, has no separate system of administrative courts. The ordinary courts have been even more cautious than their English counterparts in hearing cases from prisoners, but there are signs that their attitude too might be changing. The Supreme Court has heard two prisoner cases recently, and in the second of these it did accept that it had jurisdiction to review the conduct of a prison governor who transferred a prisoner to Herstedvester (which is basically a psychiatric prison), just before he stood for re-election as a prisoner representative. He had apparently been a very active spokesman who had kept the staff very busy dealing with his demands. The Court found nothing wrong with the governor's conduct, but has at least accepted that it *may* control discretion in the prisons (Vestergaard, 1982).

Courts in all three countries may have been reluctant in the past to hear prisoners' cases, for fear of "opening the floodgates" to hundreds of disgruntled prisoners who have nothing better to do than to make things difficult for the prison staff (for example, see Lord Denning in *Becker v. Home Office*

[1972] 2 All E.R. 676, 682h). This view seems to be diminishing as courts realise that they have a duty to safeguard the rights of all citizens, both outside and inside prison. Besides, the limitation of cost and the need for legal aid serve effectively to prevent most "vexatious" actions from reaching the courts (except in Sweden where they can be a problem for the KR). Those cases which do reach a hearing seem generally to raise important questions concerning the administration of the prisons, which it is right for the courts to consider. Growing recourse to the courts, particularly in England, suggests that prisoners certainly feel the need for this channel of complaint.

(b) Ombudsmen

All three countries have "ombudsmen" who investigate complaints concerning the administration, the fame of the Scandinavian ombudsmen leading directly to the setting up of the institution in the United Kingdom. However, the function of these ombudsmen is to scrutinise the workings of the administration rather than to procure redress for the aggrieved individual.

The office of British Parliamentary Commissioner for Administration (PCA)[7] was set up in 1967. Under the Parliamentary Commissioner Act, his task is to investigate complaints from persons who allege that they have suffered injustice as a result of "maladministration." This concept is not defined in the Act, and Commissioners have had recourse to the Parliamentary debates for enlightenment as to its meaning. There, Richard Crossman suggested that it would include, *inter alia,* "bias, neglect, inattention, delay, incompetence, perversity, turpitude, arbitrariness" (October 18, 1966. Hansard, Col. 51). It is clear that the PCA is to be concerned with the manner in which a decision is reached, and not with its merits, and this must weaken his value for an individual complainant who may be aggrieved by the decision itself, and not by its procedure. The institution of PCA has been criticised because complaints must be made to an M.P. first, who then forwards them to the Commissioner. This "filter" has been felt to lessen unduly the number of complaints reaching the PCA. However, it appears that prisoners may write directly to the PCA so long as an M.P. also refers the complaint (PCA, 1981). Also, the change in prison practice from requiring "prior ventilation" of complaints to "simultaneous ventilation" should mean that prisoners are able to complain to the PCA without delay.

Gwyn (1982) has suggested that the small number of complaints dealt with by the PCA (917 received, 228 completed in 1981) is due to the extreme thoroughness with which they are investigated. In addition to scrutiny of the documents involved, complainants and staff may be interviewed at length and full explanations for decisions reached are sent to all complainants. But this cannot account for the small number of cases *received* by the PCA. This seems more likely to be due to the relative lack of public awareness of his office, certainly as compared to that of the Scandinavian ombudsmen. Also, if the PCA does find maladministration, all he can do is to criticise the department or officials

7. The PCA has jurisdiction over prisons in both England and Scotland. Northern Ireland has its own Parliamentary Commissioner, set up by the Parliamentary Commissioner Act (Northern Ireland) 1969 (see Wade, 1982, pp. 92–93).

responsible, and to recommend changes in practice. He cannot bring a court action against those culpable, or order them to pay compensation, though he may suggest that they do so, and so even a successful complainant may be dissatisfied with the outcome of the inquiry, though it has been suggested that to have a complaint investigated "is likely to be a source of prestige, while actually to receive an apology from Prison Department must surely be gratifying to any inmate" (Martin, 1980). It is not, however, an "effective remedy" under Article 13 of the European Convention (see *Silver,* para. 115).

Whatever the reasons for the lack of popularity of the PCA, the fact remains that in 1981 only 39 complaints were received by him concerning the Home Office, including the Prison Department, and he accepted 12 complaints from prisoners for investigation. Yet the average prison population in 1981 was 43,300 (Prison Department, 1981). The "extreme thoroughness" of his investigations may be shown by the fact that he only completed six prisoner cases, in none of which did he find maladministration. (One may compare these figures, for interest, with the overall totals of 24 percent of cases accepted for investigation, 228 completed of which 42.5 percent were found to be justified.) The PCA does not publish reports on all the complaints he investigates, so it is not possible to know the subject of the complaints from all the prisoners. However, Martin (1980), in a survey of twenty cases reported by the PCA from August 1976 to July 1979, found that complainants tended to raise a number of issues at the same time. The most common complaints related to access to, or the quality of, medical or dental treatment, followed by the handling of petitions, particularly the delays involved, and gaining access to a solicitor. Most of the complaints were not upheld, but Martin concluded that the PCA "has real achievements to his credit where the problems were of administrative correctness. Details like the calculation of the date of eligibility for parole, detecting inefficiency in handling petitions, are effectively examined in ways which no other body could do equally well." Martin thought that the very rarity of prison cases investigated by the PCA "has value in that the Commissioner's comments are considered at a very high level in the Department, with the permanent Under-Secretary of State being personally involved."

Yet although the PCA asserts that departments are ready to accede to his recommendations, these are by no means always effective to produce change. For example, in the *Knechtl* case, the prisoner wished to consult a solicitor with a view to suing the Prison Department for negligence in respect of medical treatment. The Prison Department refused to let him do so. He complained to the PCA, who suggested that the Department might wish to review its practice. The Department did so, and decided against any change. Only after Knechtl complained to the European Commission of Human Rights was a limited change in practice achieved (*Knechtl v. U.K.* 4115/69, Yearbook 13, p. 730). More fundamental reform, of course, has recently come about following the *Silver* case. It may well be that such apparent lack of effectiveness on the part of the PCA, coupled with an initially cautious approach to this task, has dampened enthusiasm for using him by prisoners as a channel for redress. He is unfortunately not empowered to undertake investigations on his own initiative, so that an important means of detecting maladministration is not open to him. The value of such independent inspection may be seen in the reorganisation of the Prisons Inspectorate following the report of the May Committee.

The Swedish Justitieombudsman (JO), the first "ombudsman" in the world, initially had a considerable impact on prison conditions, but has less scope for finding abuses now following substantial reforms. The functions of JO are carried out by four ombudsmen, one of whom deals with criminal justice, including prisons (al-Wahab, 1979). The duty of the JO, contained in s.1 Act of Instruction to the Parliamentary Ombudsmen 1975, is to "supervise the observance of laws and other statutes by those exercising public activity and that they in all respects properly fulfill their obligations." Section 3 stresses that "It is the particular duty of the ombudsmen to ensure that courts of law and administrative authorities observe the provisions of the Instrument of Government concerning objectivity and impartiality and that the fundamental rights and freedoms of citizens are not encroached upon in the processes of public administration." The supervision is carried out by examining complaints from the public and carrying out inspections which the JO regard as an important device for monitoring administration. Some inspections are part of a regular pattern of visits, while others are taken on the initiative of the JO when a possible abuse comes to light, for example, through the media.

It is interesting to compare the workload of the four JO, in a country of eight million people, with that of the PCA with about 50 million. From July 1, 1981, to June 30, 1982, the JO completed 3,427 cases, 286 concerning the KVS; 1,293 were dismissed without investigation, 41 of which were prison complaints; 424 cases resulted in admonition of the officials, or other criticism, of which 42 were prison cases. The average prison population was about 4,000. Thus about 12 percent of all cases resulted in some criticism, about 14 percent of prison cases (JO, 1982). It has been shown (Gwyn, 1982) that between 1976 and 1980, although the JO upheld the administration in 80 percent of all cases, as opposed to 60 percent in cases investigated by the PCA, about three times as many complainants were successful in Sweden because of the greater speed of investigation enabling more cases to be dealt with. It also seems that the JO in Sweden is a much more obvious institution to turn to for redress than the PCA.

However, the fact that the JO can take up complaints on his own initiative, or at the request of a third person, means that he has sometimes criticised the KVS for being too lenient with a prisoner, not too harsh. For example, (JO, 1979), a self-employed businessman was sentenced to four months' imprisonment. He had this postponed for eight months under a standard procedure allowing for deferment of sentence in case of special circumstances. When he finally served his sentence, he was allowed out each weekday to work in his business and went home each weekend. A person who read about this in a newspaper complained to the JO. The JO stressed that the relevant provision in the Act on Correctional Treatment in Institutions (s.11) is intended to prepare the prisoner for release by improving his social situation, training him for a job and building up his finances. The prisoner had had his sentence deferred in order to make arrangements for the continued functioning of his business. His readjustment to society would not be appreciably impaired through four months' imprisonment. The penalty of imprisonment had been watered down contrary to the intention of the legislator.

It is unclear whether the criticisms of the JO are always effective in producing a change in practice or policy. Historically, the JO's function was as a special prosecutor and before 1976, whenever an official was found at fault, the JO could institute legal proceedings against him. Now, prosecutions may only be brought for embezzlement, bribery, breach of the Act on Secrecy, or intentional or grossly negligent breach or neglect of duty. Although prosecutions were rare even before 1976, they were felt by the JO to have considerable deterrent value which has now possibly been diminished. For example, on a number of occasions, he has criticised the practice of automatically placing a prisoner in isolation pending a disciplinary hearing, yet it continues to happen (JO, 1979). Similarly, he has more than once had to criticise the imposition of collective punishments on prisoners as being incompatible with Swedish conceptions of justice (JO, 1978, 1981).

Prisoners may prefer to complain to the JO because no lawyer is necessary to help them present their complaint; because they might obtain media publicity, since the media may scrutinise and report complaints even before the JO sees them; because the JO is well-known and because his investigations are widely reported. On the other hand, he cannot order an official to alter a decision, but can only criticise, make recommendations, or very occasionally institute disciplinary or legal proceedings. However, prisoners seem to have faith in his independence and thoroughness and, just as is the case with the KR, the KVS may change its mind while the JO is investigating, so that the prisoner obtains his remedy.

The Danish Ombudsman provides a useful counter-balance in assessing the effectiveness of the Scandinavian model of ombudsman as a mechanism for dealing with prisoners' complaints. His duty is to "keep himself informed as to whether any person [within his jurisdiction] pursues unlawful ends, takes arbitrary or unreasonable decisions or otherwise commits mistakes or acts of negligence in the discharge of his or her duties" (Article 3, Directives for the Ombudsman adopted by the Parliament, 1962). He cannot investigate complaints which have not been aired internally, unlike the JO, and rejects 30 percent of complaints on this basis. He seems more cautious than the JO in criticising the merits of a decision. Whereas of Sweden it has sometimes been said that having four JO has resulted in a loss of public identification in the institution, it may be said on the other hand that having only one incumbent makes the choice of appointee all the more crucial. For example, in relation to Danish prisoners' complaints, the previous ombudsman to the present one had been the Director-General of the Prison and Probation Department and took a keen interest in prison affairs. The current ombudsman is regarded by prisoners as being much less sympathetic to them, although it is too soon to see if the number of complaints to him will drop as a result of this reputation. He does deal with far fewer cases than the Swedish JO. In the year July 1, 1981, to June 30, 1982, he received 1,518 complaints, of which 900 were dismissed without investigation; 32 were investigated concerning the Prison Department, of which three resulted in criticism or recommendations being made (Ombudsman, 1982). The average prison population was about 3,500.

As a checking mechanism it seems that ombudsmen can perform an important function in the prisons, if they are prepared to pursue their own inquiries and to question the merits of the exercise of discretion, as the Swedish JO seems prepared to do. The Danish Ombudsman and the British PCA seem to be too bound up in restrictions and too timid to be as effective, and certainly produce fewer complaints from prisoners. The greater role played by the JO may be due to the Swedish constitutional position, whereby ministers are not directly responsible to Parliament for the activities of administrative agencies, which are autonomous. Hence, the Minister of Justice is not responsible for the activities of the KVS. Political accountability may be achieved by subjecting bodies like the KVS to the penetrating and public scrutiny of the JO. In England and Denmark, on the other hand, this can be provided by Parliamentary questioning of the Minister concerned. All this is of little interest to the aggrieved prisoner, however, most particularly in Denmark, where we have seen that the courts have not yet been prepared to offer redress, and where, apart from the Ombudsman, there is no independent supervision of the prisons at all.

Conclusion

Advocates of prison reform have until recently concentrated on proposals that fewer offenders should be sent to prison, or that regimes offered to prisoners should be altered. At least in England and in the United States, increasing attention is now being paid to the issue of whether prisoners should have "rights." Such, attention may be a natural progression away from reformative ideals to a "just deserts" approach to penal measures. It has the effect of bringing into question how far prisoners are enabled to challenge what happens to them during their imprisonment, for unenforceable "rights" are not worth having. And even where significant progressive and liberal reform has occurred, as in Sweden and Denmark, prisoners still find plenty to complain about. This is no doubt inevitable, since the essence of imprisonment is the restriction on freedom of choice and action, which will lead to dissatisfaction. Yet complaints may reveal real unfairness, and it may be right that mechanisms exist to correct such unfairness.

In all three countries, however, existing mechanisms for dealing with complaints seem unsatisfactory. Internal mechanisms are not independent and so may not be regarded as fair by the aggrieved prisoner. They may be dealt with more from the standpoint of upholding authority than from achieving a fair result. Bureaucratic or peer-group concerns may take priority over the merits of the case.

External mechanisms may not be sufficiently accessible to prisoners, either through direct restriction, such as the requirement that internal remedies be pursued first, or limitations on the jurisdiction of the external body; or through indirect restriction, such as the expense of taking proceedings or difficulty in obtaining information on which to base an action. Even when procedures are utilised, the remedies available may be inappropriate or insufficient, such as an apology rather than monetary compensation or an unduly limited change in practice. Danish prisoners may be said to face direct restriction on complaining outside, since they must complain internally first before they can approach the Ombudsman, and the Supreme Court until very recently has regarded the prisons as beyond its jurisdiction. English prisoners face the indirect restriction of difficulty in obtaining information on which to bring their action. Ombudsmen of all three countries do not offer an individual prisoner a particularly apt remedy for his complaint in most instances.

However, the most important limitation on a prisoner obtaining redress is the reluctance of the external body to grant it, and such reluctance is apparent in all three countries; for example, it is seen in the extremely low success rate of prisoners' cases in the Swedish KR, and in the difficulty of invoking the courts' jurisdiction in England and Denmark. Behind such reluctance there seems to be the view that the prison authorities are experts whose decisions should not be upset by non-experts. Such a view historically may have been held because prisons were regarded as a world apart, separate from the rest of society. In recent times, it could have been justified on the basis that prisons were institutions designed to reform or cure people. Experts in reform needed a free hand to prescribe appropriate treatment to effect the cure. However, now that treatment is a much less significant aim of imprisonment such a rationale cannot be used. It is interesting that in areas where external bodies do feel that they have expertise, they have been prepared to intervene; for example, the English courts' control of adjudications by boards of visitors, or ombudsmen's recommendations on administrative practice.

The question of how prisoners' complaints should be handled depends on whether the view is taken that the authorities should be left alone to get on with the job entrusted to them, or whether it is felt that the weak position of prisoners is such that effective outside supervision must be available to correct possible unfairness. The fact that the three countries examined, having very different prison populations, regimes and social structures, all make some provision for such supervision, suggests that they do accept the latter view. They have failed so far, however, to provide adequate mechanisms to put the principle into practice.

Discussion Questions

1. To what extent do you believe prison inmates should have access to information and freedom of correspondence so that they can challenge prison conditions? Defend your position.
2. In your judgement, is it necessary to have procedures for addressing inmates' grievances? Why or why not?
3. How might the sociological context within which a prison system operates affect the system's procedures for dealing with inmates' grievances? Why are sociological factors important in accounting for differences in grievance procedures across nations' prison systems?
4. Compare and contrast the internal and external grievance mechanisms available to prisoners in the U.S. with the mechanisms available to prisoners in England, Sweden, and Denmark.

5. Douglas concludes his article by observing that, while England, Sweden, and Denmark seem to accept the idea that prison operations should be supervised for fairness, the countries have been slow to put this idea into practice. How can this discrepancy between principle and practice be explained?
6. How might the various limitations of the grievance procedures in the three countries, as discussed by Douglas, be improved? How could the countries do a better job of dealing with inmates' complaints?

References

Al-Wahab, I. (1979). *The Swedish Institution of Ombudsman: An Instrument of Human Rights.* Stockholm: Liberforlag.

Cohen, S. and Taylor, L. (1979). *Prison Secrets.* London: National Council for Civil Liberties and Radical Alternatives to Imprisonment.

Gwyn, W. B. (1982). "The Ombudsman in Britain: A Qualified Success in Government Reform." *Public Administration,* 60, 177.

Halsbury (1982). *Halsbury's Laws of England,* 4th edn. 1982, vol. 37. London: Butterworths.

Holm, N. (1975). "The Danish System of Open Files in Public Administration." *Scandinavian Studies in Law,* 153. Stockholm: Almqvist and Wiksell.

Holmberg, E. and Stjernquist, N. (1981). *Introduction to Constitutional Documents of Sweden.* Stockholm: The Swedish Riksdag.

Holmgren, K. (1974). "The new Swedish legislation on administrative jurisdiction." *Scandinavian Studies in Law,* 71. Stockholm: Almqvist and Wiksell.

House of Commons (1978). *The Reduction of Pressure on the Prison System,* 15th Report from the Expenditure Committee H.C. 662–1. London: H.M.S.O.

Jellicoe (1975). *Boards of Visitors of Penal Institutions.* Report of a Committee set up by JUSTICE, Howard League for Penal Reform and National Association for the Care and Resettlement of Offenders. Chichester and London: Barry Rose.

Justitieombudsman (1978, 1979, 1981, 1982). *The Swedish Parliamentary Ombudsmen Report.* (Summary in English). Stockholm: Norstedts Tryckeri.

Kriminalvardsstyrelsen (1980). *Measures of De-Institutionalisation.* Information paper for 6th United Nations Congress on the Prevention of Crime and the Treatment of Offenders, Norrköping: KVS.

Kühlhorn, E. (1981). *Imprisonment and the Criminal Justice System in Sweden.* Stockholm: National Swedish Council for Crime Prevention.

Martin, J. P. (1980). "Maintaining Standards: Who guards the guards?" in King R. D. and Morgan R. *The Future of the Prison System.* Farnborough: Gower.

Mathiesen, T. (1974). *The Politics of Abolition.* London: Martin Robertson.

May Committee (1979). *Committee of Inquiry into the United Kingdom Prison Services Report,* CMND 7673. London: H.M.S.O.

Ombudsman (1982). *Report from Folketingets Ombudsmand.* Copenhagen: Folketingets Ombudsmand.

Parliamentary Commissioner for Administration (1981). *Annual Report of the Parliamentary Commissioner for Administration* H. C. 258. London: H.M.S.O.

Parole Board (1979). *Annual Report* H.C. 651. London: H.M.S.O.

Prison Department (1981). *Annual Report of the Work of the Prison Department* CMND 8543. London: H.M.S.O.

Vestergaard, J. (1982). Lecture delivered at the Institute of Criminal Science University of Copenhagen, Sept. 22, 1982.

Wade, H. W. R. (1982). *Administrative Law,* 5th edn. Oxford: Clarendon Press.

Ward, D. A. (1979). "Sweden: the middle way to prison reform?" in Wolfgang, M. E. (ed.), *Prisons: Present and Possible.* Lexington, Mass.: Lexington Books.

Zellick, G. (1982a). "False and malicious allegations by prisoners." *British Journal of Criminology,* 22, 21–35.

Zellick, G. (1982b). "Who runs the prisons?" *Public Law,* 346–348.

Zellick, G. (1982c). "The Prison Rules and the Courts: A Postscript." *Criminal Law Review,* 575–579.

23. Through the Barricades: Prisoner Protest and Penal Policy in Scotland

Phil Scraton,* Joe Sim,** and Paula Skidmore*

In 1972 Stan Cohen and Laurie Taylor published *Psychological Survival.*[1] This book was the first critical account of long-term imprisonment in the United Kingdom. Since that time a number of other publications have taken up and developed some of the themes identified by Cohen and Taylor in their pioneering study. This body of work has included the analysis of the containment and control of long-term prisoners in England, Wales, and Scotland;[2] case studies of the Kafkaesque rules governing the lives of long-termers;[3] the politics of long-term imprisonment in Northern Ireland;[4] the differential impact of long-term imprisonment on women;[5] and the dynamics of life inside from the autobiographical perspective of the incarcerated.[6]

Academics involved in such work have been concerned to provide a voice for the confined and to shift the terrain on which the debate about long-term imprisonment has taken place. That terrain has been dominated by official discourse, with the imprisoned rarely given a chance to articulate their

---

*Centre for Studies in Crime and Social Policy, Edge Hill College of Higher Education, Ormskirk, Lancashire, England.
**Department of Combined Studies, Liverpool Polytechnic, C. F. Mott Campus, Prescot, Merseyside, England.

The authors were members of the Independent Committee of Inquiry into the Protests at Peterhead Prison. The full report *The Roof Comes Off* can be obtained from The Gateway Exchange, 3–5 Abbeymount, Edinburgh, Scotland (price £3.00 including postage).

1. S. Cohen and L. Taylor, *Psychological Survival* (1972).
2. M. Fitzgerald, *Prisoners in Revolt* (1977); D. MacDonald and J. Sim, *British Prisons* (1982).
3. I. Cameron, "Life in the Balance: The Case of Frank Marritt" in *Causes for Concern* (1984; eds. P. Scraton and P. Gordon).
4. B. Rolston and M. Tomlinson, "Long-Term Imprisonment in Northern Ireland: Psychological or Political Survival?" in *The Expansion of European Prison Systems* (1986; eds. B. Rolston and M. Tomlinson) European Group for the Study of Deviance and Social Control, Working Papers in European Criminology No. 7.
5. See various editions of *The Abolitionist: The Journal of Radical Alternatives to Prison;* A. Mandaraka-Sheppard, *The Dynamics of Aggression in Women's Prisons in England* (1986).
6. J. Boyle, *A Sense of Freedom* (1977); B. Sands, *One Day in My Life* (1983); P. Adams and S. Cooklin, *Knockback* (1984); P. Carlen et al., *Criminal Women* (1985); A. and E. Nic Giolla Easpaig, *Sisters in Cells* (1987).

views or express their feelings about existing inside what two prison researchers have called the "electronic coffins" of long-term maximum security institutions.[7] This academic work, which has been termed "criminology from below," has been a major and influential strand in the development of British criminology in the last twenty years.[8] Within the prison system it has been particularly relevant in a number of areas: providing a platform which has allowed prisoners to describe the pains of confinement;[9] challenging official explanations in the highly contentious area of deaths in custody;[10] and developing alternative explanations and accounts of the major disturbances which have occurred in the prisons of the United Kingdom over the last two decades.[11]

Between 1969 and 1983 there were ten such prison disturbances in England and Wales alone.[12] Government ministers and state spokespersons have explained the cause of the trouble in seemingly straightforward and simplistic terms. They argue that there are individual prisoners who, either alone or in small groups, manipulate the rest of the quiescent prison population into riot and demonstration. This "bad apple" theory of disorder has a long history in the United Kingdom and has become significant particularly in the state's repertoire of responses since the fundamental restructuring of the British prison system in the mid-1960s.[13] Since then structural questions—such as the increasing length of sentences, the chilling alienation of long-term prison regimes, and the institutionalised use of violence and drugs to maintain order—have been avoided and replaced with a positivistic emphasis on psychological irrationality and individual pathology. Given the well-established links between the media and the state,[14] these official explanations have found their way easily and quickly into the press, radio, and television and—although often challenged—nonetheless lay the foundations for the building of popular perceptions, fears, and fantasies about those who contest the authority of the prison regime.

One mechanism for generating alternative accounts—in the face of an increasingly corporately-owned, authoritarian, and centralised media network[15]—

7. R. King and K. Elliott, *Albany: Birth of a Prison—End of an Era* (1977), p. 3.
8. For a fuller account of this concept see J. Sim, P. Scraton, and P. Gordon, "Crime, the State and Critical Analysis" in *Law, Order and the Authoritarian State* (1987; ed. P. Scraton).
9. M. Fitzgerald, op. cit., n. 2.
10. P. Scraton and K. Chadwick, *In the Arms of the Law: Coroners' Inquests and Deaths in Custody* (1987).
11. M. Fitzgerald and J. Sim, op. cit., n. 2, chap. 4; J. Sim, "The Fire from Below: Prisons in Scotland" in (1987) 23 *The Abolitionist*, pp. 28–30.
12. Home Office, *Managing the Long-Term Prison System: The Report of the Control Review Committee* (1984).
13. M. Fitzgerald and J. Sim, op. cit., n. 2. It should be noted that this is the explanation for disturbances in *men's* prisons. Women prisoners react very differently to the pain of confinement. It is an area in which far more research needs to be conducted. See P. Carlen et al., op. cit., n. 6.
14. S. Chibnall, *Law and Order News* (1977); L. Curtis, *Ireland: The Propaganda War* (1984).
15. J. Pilger, *Heroes* (1987).

has been the establishment of independent inquiries. Academics working with civil libertarian and grass-roots organisations have been involved in a range of inquiries established by these groups over the last fifteen years to provide "a challenge to those whose voices are heard exclusively as part of government-backed official discourse."[16] "Criminology from below" has been geared to making interventions, exploiting the contradictions within state institutions, and establishing links with the "powerless."

It was in this academic and political context that the Gateway Exchange, a community-based organisation in Edinburgh, established an independent inquiry into the major disturbance and hostage-taking incident that occurred in November 1986 at Peterhead, Scotland's only maximum security prison. This was one of a series of prison demonstrations that took place at the time. Once again, government ministers and state spokespersons, with often uncritical help from the media, mobilised the image of pathological irrationality and marginalised the collective voice of the prisoners involved. The Gateway, through the inquiry, sought to establish an alternative account which would investigate the problems of the prison, not simply in terms of pathology but in relation to structural questions and issues. These issues—the condition of the prison, the violence of the regime, the length of sentences, the lack of constructive rehabilitative philosophy—formed the context in which the social action of the demonstration took place. As ever, it was this context which was virtually ignored by media commentators, government ministers, and state servants.

Penal Politics in Scotland

The initial impetus for the inquiry centered on the events surrounding the hostage-taking in November 1986. These events, however, were the culmination of a more general pattern of disturbances, overcrowding, and conflict which had gripped the prison system in Scotland in the mid-1980s. There are several dimensions to that crisis which are significant to a full understanding of the background to the Peterhead inquiry. First, the prison population in Scotland had been rising steadily throughout the previous ten years and by 1986 the average daily population had risen, in the words of the Scottish Home and Health Department, "to an unprecedented level." Indeed, the highest prison population ever recorded in Scotland was reached on 4 March 1986 when 5,797 women and men were incarcerated.[17] Statistics released by the Council of Europe in June 1987, covering twenty-three western European countries, indicated that Scotland was second only to Northern Ireland in the rate of imprisonment per 100,000 of its population.[18] Within this general category, the rise in the number of long-term prisoners as a proportion of the average daily population is crucial. Between 1985 and 1986 the number of those serving determinate sentences of three years or more rose from 982 to 1,116—an increase of nineteen percent.[19] The Chief Inspector of Prisons recently has developed a category known as very

16. J. Sim, P. Scraton, and P. Gordon, op. cit., n. 8, p. 34.
17. Scottish Home and Health Department, *Statistical Bulletin* (1987A).
18. Council of Europe, *Prison Information Bulletin* (1987), p. 23.
19. Scottish Home and Health Department, op. cit., n. I7, p. 4.

long-term prisoners (V.L.T.P.) which, in his 1986 report he argued, had "steadily increased and current views are that an upward trend is likely to continue."[20] This position has been compounded by the "knock-on" effect of sentences which have minimum recommendations attached to them. These numbered forty-six between 1965 and 1985 and were supported by the use of indeterminate sentences for crimes other than murder, of which there were twelve in the same period.[21]

At the other end of the penal spectrum, large numbers of individuals were sent to prison for non-payment of fines. 548 women and men were imprisoned in 1986 for having outstanding fines of less than £25, while 4,857 individuals were imprisoned for non-payment of fines of more than £25 but less than £100.[22] This expansion of prisoners has been paralleled by a concomitant rise in spending on the prisons. Total gross expenditure in the financial year ending 31 March 1986 was £48,743,000. As with the police, the majority of this expenditure went on staff costs (eighty percent), while a paltry proportion (three percent) was devoted to welfare considerations such as education, training, recreation, and assisted visits.[23]

These developments were underpinned by a wave of protests, demonstrations, conflicts, and hostage-takings in a number of prisons in the period between 1985 and 1987. In 1985 there were "dirty protests," nine reported fire-raising incidents, two rooftop incidents at Barlinnie prison, numerous hunger strikes lasting between one and twenty-five days, 143 assaults on staff, a hostage-taking incident in Dumfries prison, and another at Peterhead where seven members of staff were held at gunpoint.[24] In 1986 there were fires at Peterhead, Perth, Long-riggend, and Glenochil, "dirty protests" in Glenochil and Inverness, rooftop protests at Saughton and Barlinnie, and hostage-taking incidents at Saughton where a prison officer was held for five days. At Peterhead a similar event occurred and this became the subject of the Gateway Exchange inquiry.[25] In 1987 there were demonstrations, rooftop protests, and hunger strikes at Perth, Barlinnie, Saughton, and Peterhead and a further spate of hostage-taking incidents at Shotts, Perth, Barlinnie, and again at Peterhead. The latter incident lasted for five days and was ended by the intervention of a unit of the military elite Special Air Service.[26]

The state's response to these events has worked at two levels. First, at an ideological level spokespersons for the Scottish Home and Health Department, the Scottish Prison Officers' Association, and government ministers have continued to raise the spectre of the "depraved, violent individual" manipulating other passive prisoners into dangerous confrontations. Malcolm Rifkind M. P.,

20. Scottish Home and Health Department, *Her Majesty's Chief Inspector of Prisons for Scotland* (1987B).
21. J. Sim, "Repressing the Living Dead: Penal Policy and the Peterhead Demonstration" in (1987) 19 *Critical Social Policy*, p. 21.
22. Scottish Home and Health Department, op. cit., n. 20, p. 15.
23. Scottish Home and Health Department, *Prisons in Scotland: Report for 1986* (1987C), p. 28.
24. Scottish Council for Civil Liberties, *Facing Reality: The Scottish Prisons Crisis in the 1980s* (1987), p. 1.
25. Compiled from press reports during the year.
26. Ibid.

the Scottish Secretary of State, encapsulated these views in a television interview during the hostage-taking at Perth in October 1987:

> . . . I think the real point to make is that whatever the regime—be it harsh or liberal, be it in an old prison or a modern prison—there will always be a tiny number of individual prisoners who are violent, who are psychopaths, who are in prison precisely because of their dangerous proclivities and we shouldn't perhaps be too surprised that they do not cease to be violent from the moment they enter the prison gates. What we have to do is to minimize—indeed try and remove entirely—the threat they pose not only to the public and to the prison officers but very often to other prisoners as well.[27]

Second, the state has responded at a policy level by the introduction of measures designed to isolate and punish those individuals deemed to be responsible. The internal regime at Peterhead was rationalised in the wake of the disturbances. One prisoner wrote to a national newspaper in November 1987:

> Body-belt manacles, which secure hands directly at the stomach level, have been in use for years in Peterhead. Prisoners in segregation at Peterhead are escorted by up to six **warders** carrying baseball-bat-size clubs; have been for years. It's permanent policy. No one denies it.
>
> The lock-down system went into effect immediately after Peterhead's most recent incident. It is now a permanent segregation prison. Only sex offenders and a small number of short-termers—all of whom have recently been ghosted into service (clean and fetch) are not in permanent segregation 23 hours a day.
>
> There are cells in Peterhead which have sheets of steel welded box-steel frames covering the entire window area; small holes have been drilled to allow air in (there's no glass); but only barbed wire can be seen through a hole your finger couldn't pass through.[28]

The Scottish Council for Civil Liberties highlighted the existence of a linked series of maximum security units which contained:

> . . . the "Cardboard Cells" of A Hall where there is a mattress on the floor of the cell and cardboard furniture which is removed at night while the hall is patrolled by officers in groups of 12 or 14 carrying riot sticks, the "Ten Cell Unit" from which there has been total silence but which appears to be used for taking the most "difficult" prisoners out of the system long-term and which is thought to have a psychiatric control function, the infirmary, which, it is claimed, is used as an isolation unit, and the old punishment block which was refurbished several years ago. We now know of plans to turn B Hall into a Maximum Security Unit, while in the longer term work has begun on building a new high security prison within the existing perimeter.[29]

This "Chinese Box"[30] includes a silent cell which has been described as a "cube of concrete within another cube of concrete."[31] The cell has a bare con-

---

27. Newsnight, B.B.C.T.V., 6 October 1987.
28. *The Guardian,* 2 November 1987.
29. Scottish Council for Civil Liberties, *Some Documents and Observations on the Scottish Prison System: A Discussion Document Following a Hostage-Taking at Saughton and Peterhead* (1986), p. 9.
30. S. Cohen, "Prisons and the Future of Control Systems: From Concentration to Dispersal" in *Welfare in Action* (1977; eds. M. Fitzgerald et al.), p. 220.
31. *The Observer,* 16 November 1986.

crete floor and walls, there is a two-inch platform where the prisoner sleeps and there is no mattress provided. The only "furniture" is a plastic chamber pot.

These units have been supported by the introduction of a range of different tactics to deal specifically with sieges. They include: bartering for food; the management of information through temporary news black-outs; keeping reporters at a distance; the creation of special squads involving police and prison officers which draw on the expertise of Scotland Yard's Anti-Terrorist Squad; the drawing up of a new manual setting out siege tactics; the use of sophisticated electronic equipment for eavesdropping and, as indicated above, the use of the army's Special Air Services to end one of the demonstrations.[32] These changes are to be supported by the building of a new prison at Peterhead based on a range of ideas which are derived from the new generation of prisons in the United States of America, particularly around what the Scottish Home and Health Department euphemistically describes as "unobtrusive supervision."[33] These developments, then, provide a backcloth against which the Gateway Exchange inquiry was initiated. The independent committee of inquiry reported on 9 November 1987—exactly one year after the original disturbance.

Challenging State Power

As noted above, independent inquiries into the prison system and the criminal justice process in general has a well-established history in Britain. In recent times there have been a number of independent inquiries into prison disturbances,[34] racial violence,[35] police violence,[36] violence against women,[37] and the inner-city disturbances in the autumn of 1985.[38] It is important to recognise the contribution of such inquiries to the landscape of criminal justice in the United Kingdom. They provide a challenge to official, state-sponsored inquiries with their set agendas, their partial sifting of evidence, and the ideologies of their chairpersons and members which combine to close down issues rather than to provide critical scrutiny. Official inquiries themselves have a long tradition in Britain and tend to reinforce and legitimize state policies and practices.[39] The voices of the 'powerless' are heard rarely or they are marginalised through these processes in what Mark Lane, in another context, has described as a "rush to judgement."[40]

---

32. *The Independent*, 6 October 1987.
33. Scottish Home and Health Department, op. cit., n. 23, p. 14.
34. National Prisoners' Movement, *Don't Mark His Face* (1977).
35. National Council for Civil Liberties, *Southall* 23 April 1979 (1980).
36. Report of the Independent Inquiry Panel, *Leon Brittan's Visit to Manchester Students' Union 1st March 1985* (1985); Welsh Campaign for Civil and Political Liberties and National Union of Mineworkers (South Wales Area), *Striking Back* (1985); Sheffield Policewatch, *Taking Liberties: Policing During the Miners' Strike April–October 1984* (1984).
37. R. Hall, *Ask Any Woman* (1985); Manchester Police Monitoring Unit, *Breaking the Silence* (1987).
38. Report of the Review Panel, *A Different Reality* (1986); Report of the Independent Inquiry, *The Broadwater Farm Inquiry* (1986).
39. P. Corrigan and D. Sayer, *The Great Arch* (1985); J. Sim, "Watching the Wheels Grind: The 1984 Report of Her Majesty's Chief Inspector of Prisons" (1986) 21 *The Abolitionist*, pp. 21–3.
40. M. Lane, *Rush to Judgement* (1967).

At Peterhead official inquiries and inspections of the prison already had taken place, internally conducted by Her Majesty's Inspector of Prisons. In his report, published in June 1982, the inspector made a number of critical comments about the welfare, work, recreational, and dining facilities in the prison. He placed the responsibility for the outbreaks of violence at Peterhead "on a small number of inmates who are prepared to create serious trouble regardless of the consequences to themselves or to the remainder of the inmate population.[41] In March 1987, the chief inspector published the results of his confidential investigation into the 1986 disturbances at Saughton and Peterhead. Once more he re-affirmed the official line. While calling for a greater range of activities, in terms of work and recreation, and for a clear path of progression for prisoners through their sentence, he pointed towards those who:

> . . . will continue to kick against the system and show anti-authoritarian and disruptive behaviour. . . . In order to allow other prisoners to get on with their sentences constructively and to protect prison officers there seems little choice but to transfer such men to smaller units, where association is limited and the regime is tailored to suit the occupants.[42]

It was precisely this official philosophy and explanation—reductionist in its foundations—that the Gateway Exchange inquiry sought to challenge.

The Work of the Inquiry

Following the dramatic events in Scottish prisons during 1986—particularly the protests at Peterhead—the Secretary of State for Scotland ordered an internal inquiry to be carried out in camera by Her Majesty's Chief Inspector of Prisons. His remit was to investigate the "nature, extent, and validity of the general grievances voiced by the inmates . . . at the time of the hostage incident."[43] Many commentators, campaign groups, and lawyers considered an internal inquiry to be inappropriate. As recently as 1981, the prison inspectorate had conducted an inspection of Peterhead.[44] While the inspectorate had been critical of the available facilities for welfare, work, eating, and recreation, it endorsed without reservation the regime and the overall organisation of the prison. Furthermore, the inspectorate blamed the persistent conflict and disturbances on "the small number of inmates who are prepared to create serious trouble regardless of the consequences to themselves or to the remainder of the inmate population."[45] This conclusion drew criticism from a range of organisations closely involved with Peterhead.[46] Albert McQuarrie, the Conservative

41. H. M. Inspectorate of Prisons for Scotland, *Report on H. M. Prison Peterhead* (1982), p. 3.
42. H. M. Chief Inspector of Prisons (Scotland), *Report on an Inquiry into Prison Grievances at H. M. Prison Peterhead* (1987), p. 85.
43. B.B.C. Radio Four News, 18 November 1986.
44. H. M. Inspectorate of Prisons for Scotland, *Report on H. M. Prison Peterhead* (1981), p. 5.
45. Ibid.
46. These organisations were: Scottish Association for the Care and Resettlement of Offenders; Scottish Council for Civil Liberties; Scottish Churches Council; the district councils of Glasgow, Edinburgh, and Clackmannon; the regional councils of Tayside and Lothian.

M.P. for Banff and Buchan, called for "an independent, judicial panel to investigate allegations of brutality . . . not just an Inquiry by H. M. Chief Inspector of Prisons."[47]

The chief inspector's inquiry, however, went ahead amidst growing criticism of its lack of independence and impartiality. It was considered that his publicly expressed general satisfaction with the Peterhead regime demonstrated a reluctance to consider serious criticisms of the operational policies and practices within the prison. Further, the initiation of an internal inquiry would guarantee only selective publication of its methodology, priorities, and findings. Finally, the stated and much-publicised grievances of prisoners would be ignored by officials who had stated repeatedly their unequivocal position: that a 'hard-core' element of violent men made false accusations and intimidated others to do likewise.

On 4 December 1986, a public meeting to discuss Peterhead was held at the Gateway Exchange in Edinburgh. The Gateway Exchange is an independent, community-based organisation and drop-in centre whose work provides concrete opportunities for people living on Edinburgh's poorly-resourced housing schemes. It offers a facility where people meet together, organise, develop community arts projects, and participate in a range of creative work. Central to its campaigning initiatives have been the Gateway's direct interventions concerning drug use among young people, the monitoring of the excesses of the Scottish penal system,[48] and the provision of necessary support for prisoners and their families.[49] The Gateway meeting over Peterhead was chaired by Donald Macaulay Q.C. with speakers from all the main political parties. In the audience were ex-prisoners and their families, prison staff, prison visitors, community group representatives, and members of the public. The meeting expressed a general dissatisfaction with the limited and partisan internal inquiry and it was unanimous in its call for an independent public inquiry. Early in 1987 the Gateway Exchange established an independent inquiry team. In marked contrast to the internal inquiry, the independent inquiry prioritised the personal experiences of Peterhead prisoners,[50] the concerns of prisoners' families, and the considered statements of lawyers involved at the prison.

Surveying all prisoners who were at Peterhead during the 1986 protest was impossible. A significant number of prisoners had been moved after the protest and there was no means of gaining access to the names of prisoners in the prison. Because letters from outside have to be addressed personally to prisoners, the authorities only allowed questionnaires to be issued to those known to

47. *The Scotsman,* 14 November 1986.

48. This work has included assistance with complaints from within Scottish prisons, the provision of legal assistance, and in the case of suicides at the Glenochil Youth Detention Complex, the mounting of a full campaign. See P. Scraton, and K. Chadwick, "The Experiment That Went Wrong: the Crisis of Deaths in Custody at the Glenochil Youth Detention Complex" in B. Rolston and M. Tomlinson (eds.), op. cit., n. 4.

49. This work includes assistance with visiting, support for prisoners' families, and help on release.

50. A questionnaire was issued to all prisoners *known* to be at Peterhead. It took parliamentary pressure to persuade the authorities to release the questionnaires.

the inquiry. The Scottish Office was overtly hostile to the work of the inquiry team. In April 1987 the Deputy Director of the Scottish Prison Department, Mr. T. J. Kelly, wrote to the inquiry team in response to its complaints concerning the long delay in receiving replies to the questionnaire survey. He indicated that the work of the inquiry was less than credible, alleging that its investigation was "narrower in scope and less balanced in approach" than that of the chief inspector's internal inquiry. Eventually, nearly fifty questionnaires were returned.

The questionnaires not only provided a range of comparative quantitative data but were also designed to encourage respondents to write longer replies to open-ended questions. This produced extensive qualitative data on the experiences of each individual. Although prisoners were asked to comment freely, openly, and honestly, there was considerable evidence from the detailed replies that they were inhibited because their comments were scrutinised by their officers. Their concern ranged from intimidation and harassment to the real possibility, stated clearly by the authorities, of having charges brought for making "false" or "malicious" allegations. Despite the level of official hostility and the succession of restrictions imposed on the research, the prisoners' replies were extensive.

While the survey research, along with interviews with ex-prisoners and families, provided the main experiential evidence to the independent committee of inquiry, it was important also to draw on historical data to test official assumptions concerning the long-term causes of the protests. This involved a detailed examination of official and media records back to the conception of Peterhead in 1881. In contrast to recent official reports, the early Prisons in Scotland Reports provided considerable specific information. This included breakdowns and tables on the health of inmates, deaths in custody, offences, and punishments for each prison in Scotland. Although the range and specificity of information declined markedly after the 1950s, there are important conclusions to be drawn from the earlier reports.

A comparative analysis of the tables concerning "Punishments and Offences for which Inflicted" for the 1920s and 1950s shows that prisoners in Peterhead received more punishments per head of prison population than in other male prisons in Scotland. For the 1920s, on average per year one out of every four prisoners at Peterhead received punishment, whereas in other prisons an average of one prisoner in thirty received punishment. By the 1950s on average one in five prisoners at Peterhead received punishment, whereas the average for other male prisons was one prisoner in thirteen. This pattern obtained through to the 1960s when the annual average for other male prisons was one in thirteen prisoners being punished, whereas Peterhead's annual average was one in nine, rising to one in two by the end of the 1960s.

Significant conclusions also can be drawn from the types of punishments inflicted. From its opening in 1888 to the 1920s—in common with the annual average for other male Scottish prisons—the most used punishment in Peterhead was "reduction of diet," followed by "sleeping on a wooden guard bed." By the 1950s, however, there were marked differences in punishments inflicted at Peterhead. The most common punishment throughout this period was "forfeiture of **remission** or loss of grade" with "forfeiture of association or recreation" also featuring significantly. In contrast, the most common punishment inflicted in other male prisons was "sleeping on a wooden guard bed" followed by "forfeiture of earnings."

The offences committed by prisoners at Peterhead show considerable similarity to those committed in other prisons, with "disobedience and refusal to work" being the most common offence throughout all male prisons. A regular and generalised category, "other offences," was common throughout male prisons and is a clear indication of the discretion given to officers in bringing charges. Significantly, figures for "assault" offences in the 1950s showed Peterhead to be regularly *below* the ratio for other prisons. In 1952, for instance, one in eighty-seven offences in Peterhead was an assault, compared to an average of one in thirteen for other male prisons. The well-established official explanation—the cornerstone of the Scottish Office position—that prisoners in Peterhead were likely to be more violent, and therefore a danger to the wardens, is not borne out by their figures. On the contrary, they show that for the 1950s the ratio of assault to other offences was significantly higher in other male prisons than in Peterhead.

The official Scottish Office figures show that Peterhead prisoners consistently received more punishments per head of prison population than in other Scottish male prisons and that the most common punishment was loss of remission. This punishment is well-established as the most severe form because in effect it is an extended sentence. Offences committed in Peterhead are consistent with those in other male prisons but violence or assault by prisoners has been a less common offence in Peterhead than in other male prisons in Scotland. This analysis of the historical records concerning the development of the Peterhead regime contradicts the official claims that there is a long history of disruption at the prison based on a "hard-core" element of violent men.

However, from the historical evidence peculiarities of the Peterhead regime are as clear as they are brutal. A cutlass with scabbard was worn by every warder until 1939 and rifles were carried until 1959. In 1948 Peterhead was the only Scottish prison in which the "cat"—a multi-thong whip—remained available for use with a maximum of twenty-one lashes recommended as punishment. The evidence suggests that the regime was one in which arbitrary and excessive punishment was commonplace with the disproportionate use of loss of remission. There is no record of unusual or excessive levels of violence among prisoners. Yet the intimidatory nature of the prison officer's role at Peterhead became entrenched and it provided a background to the developments at the prison following the 1966 reorganisation of Scottish prisons.

This reorganisation classified prisoners into two groups: those who showed willingness and ability to benefit from trade training, and those who had no aptitude for a trade or "demonstrate an unwillingness to participate in training."[51]

51. Scottish Home and Health Department, *Prisons in Scotland Report for 1966* (1966; Cmnd. 3319), pp. 6–7.

Prisoners in this latter category, aged thirty-five years or under, were allocated to Peterhead. "Recalcitrant" or "subversive" prisoners, considered a "bad influence" on others, were to be sent to the segregation unit at Inverness Prison. If Peterhead was not the "end of the road," it led to it. With the well-established history of punishment at Peterhead, the new Peterhead/Inverness axis became central to the prisoners' protests and resistance which grew during the 1970s. The allocation of prisoners to thc solitary confinement unit at Peterhead and the segregation unit (the "cages") at Inverness failed to deal with the structural problems of long-term imprisonment in Scotland. By their very nature these procedures, and the incoherent philosophy which underpinned them, contributed directly to the worsening situation.

For the prisoners, classification brought its own contradictions, frustrations, and inevitable conflict. The punitive philosophy of the Peterhead/Inverness axis, the appalling conditions at Peterhead, the lack of accountability, and the length of sentences imposed by the courts together combined to create a rigidity and harshness which inevitably drew resistance and protest. In the six years following reorganisation there were several significant confrontations at Peterhead and Inverness with open conflict between staff and prisoners. Peterhead was consolidated in its position as Scotland's *gulag,* a prison of no hope. Its repressive use of segregation, its arbitrary classification of prisoners, and its regime of physical and psychological brutalisation were the foundations of violent confrontation. By 1969 a disproportionate number of prisoners at Peterhead (one fifth) were refusing to apply for parole.[52] The atmosphere of the early 1970s was volatile with containment-through-segregation the sole response from the authorities.[53] In 1971 a Home Office researcher commented on the relationships between staff and prisoners at Peterhead as follows:

> There is a wide gulf between staff and prisoners and it is rare for staff to get close to prisoners. Violence is endemic. A wall of silence separates staff and inmates and punishments are accepted without argument.[54]

Throughout the 1970s there were many serious incidents at Peterhead including fire-raising, hostage-taking, and rooftop demonstrations. Individual prisoners smuggled out statements to the press and made representations to the Scottish Council for Civil Liberties. The prisoners' accounts consistently emphasised that these incidents were not "mindless acts" of a few uncontrollable prisoners. Rather, they represented the sole means available to prisoners to protest about conditions at the prison.[55] With an independent prison researcher arguing that Peterhead should be "knocked down"[56] and reformist groups concerned with the "inhumanity" of the regime,[57] the Scottish Prisons Department an-

52. Scottish Home and Health Department, *Parole Board for Scotland Report for 1969* (1969), pp. 7–17.
53. J. Boyle, op. cit., n. 6.
54. J. McMillan, *Some Notes and Observations on the Prison Subculture* (1971; unpublished).
55. Scottish Council for Civil Liberties, interview at H. M. Prison, Peterhead, 4 April 1979.
56. Comments by Russell Dobash, University of Stirling in *Daily Record,* 22 August 1979.
57. Joint statement by Radical Alternatives to Prison, the National Prisoners' Movement, and the Newham Alternatives Project, in (1979) 4 *The Abolitionist,* pp. 17–9.

nounced the development of paramilitary riot training for prison officers to meet head-on the protests of prisoners. By the 1980s the authorities' clear intention to respond to protests through increased force consolidated the institutionalisation of confrontation. There followed a series of prosecutions against prisoners for their part in protests and regular allegations by prisoners concerning brutality. Sieges were ended with riot-equipped officers storming barricades and dirty protests spread through the prison. By mid-1986 reports from inside and by observers claimed that tensions at Peterhead were "unbearable."[58]

Yet, despite all the evidence to the contrary, in October 1986 the Scottish Office Industry and Home Affairs Minister, Ian Lang, stated that conditions and atmosphere at the prison were "extremely good."[59] He commended the "professionalism" of the staff. Within a month of his statement several Scottish prisons erupted in scenes of unprecedented anger and frustration. James Freeman, Home Affairs correspondent of the *Glasgow Herald,* wrote, "the last reaction anyone should display to the Peterhead hostage-taking is surprise."[60] The protest at Peterhead lasted four days and three prisoners received ten years each for mobbing, rioting, and hostage-taking.

Conscious and considered decisions by prisoners to riot, hold hostages, and occupy rooftops are not taken lightly. Given recent precedents at Hull[61] and Wormwood Scrubs,[62] prisoners who protest expect immediate retaliation through physical beatings and solitary confinement followed by heavy sentences. A key objective of the independent committee of inquiry was to establish the full extent of grievances held by the prisoners at Peterhead which, taken together, could give a real insight into the motivation and meaning behind the protests. The inquiry committee considered physical conditions, hygiene, food, medication, heating, sanitation, work, recreation, education, physical training, privacy, fear/safety, and time spent locked in cells as the categories which together comprise the overall "quality of life" experienced by prisoners. The survey affirmed fifteen years of critical comment from within the prison—that poor conditions and the harsh regime are key contributory factors to the unrest. Two more general statements reflect sharply the general concern:

> The conditions are inhumane and barbaric, dehumanising, counter-productive to the "imaginary" sphere of reform. Geared simply towards the cheapest possible confinement and maintenance and maximum industry.

and

> After all, the High Court Judge sentenced me to life imprisonment. I don't recall him saying anything about being kept in abject poverty in a filthy, condemned slum.

58. Glasgow Herald, 7 May 1986.
59. Statement reported in the *Glasgow Herald,* 15 October 1986.
60. "Battle to keep lid on simmering prison," *Glasgow Herald,* 15 October 1986.
61. See J. E. Thomas and R. Pooley, *The Exploding Prison* (1980).
62. See (1982) 11 *The Abolitionist* no. 2, and National Prisoners' Movement, *Wormwood Scrubs: Special Report* (1980).

What is clear from the survey is that prisoners at Peterhead endure appalling conditions in terms of all basic needs: poor food, bad sanitation, lack of hygiene, cold cells, meaningless work, and limited recreation, education, and physical training. A good deal of time is spent "banged up" in cells and most prisoners criticised the lack of privacy, cell searches, body searches, censorship of mail, electronic surveillance, and personal surveillance in the toilets and showers. Added to this minimal level of existence is the majority view that prisoners live in a persistent state of fear at Peterhead, a fear which comes to dominate their daily life. The picture drawn is that of a community riddled with fear, suspicion, and mistrust, in which a harsh regime and its low quality of life produce outbreaks of frustration and anger which draw a staff response based on the regular use of unreasonable force.

The evidence given to the independent committee of inquiry by former and serving prison officers, lawyers, prisoners' families, and prisoners was emphatic in demonstrating that brutality by staff has become institutionalised at Peterhead. Seventy-one percent of the respondents to the questionnaire survey stated that they had experienced brutality by prison staff and sixty-two percent stated that they had witnessed acts of brutality against other prisoners. Prison officers carry out such acts often in situations of isolation, such as solitary confinement, which makes allegations difficult to substantiate. Prisoners commented on the difficulties experienced in making official complaints against officers. If they fail to substantiate their allegations prisoners are charged, in turn, with making false or malicious allegations as well as having to face the officers concerned. With families often prevented from seeing prisoners who allege brutality, the picture which is drawn is one of isolation and injustice compounded by a lack of accountability. The survey produced a mass of serious allegations of brutality of which the following statement is typical in its frustration:

> The most recent was a man being kicked near to death and left in a cell for five hours before the authorities would call a doctor. The man was badly injured and had to undergo an emergency operation to save his life. I was a witness. I have complained to the Governor about assaults on me. At every turn I have been met with negative responses. I have given statements to the police. . . . Petitioned the Lord Advocate. . . . The authorities don't want to know and no action is ever taken.

Again, the survey showed that there was an overwhelming distrust of the complaints system. The report concluded that the complaints system at Peterhead is held in open contempt and that frustration with its lack of effectiveness was a major contributory factor to the escalation of violence in the prison. Certainly the inconsistency and ineffectiveness of the complaints system is the flip-side of the arbitrary use of prison rules to discipline prisoners who are considered to be awkward or who resist the regime. Again, prisoners wrote at length about victimisation through the use of disciplinary procedures. The Prison Rules give officers permissive discretionary powers to charge prisoners at will, and the regime has the power to administer internal punishments against accused prisoners who have no right of legal representation. Consequently, prisoners often lose remission, which is effectively the extension of a sentence.

One of the most sensitive issues for a prisoner whose sentence is for a fixed period over eighteen months is parole. A prisoner can apply for parole after serving a third of a sentence. The survey showed that it was a commonly-held assumption that Peterhead prisoners rarely received parole. Prisoners were unanimous in their opinion that recent changes in the parole system, introduced by former Home Secretary Leon Brittan, had resulted in feelings of bitterness and hopelessness and had removed any remaining incentive to cooperate with the regime. The following responses are as typical as they are instructive:

> Prisoners convicted of crimes of violence and those involving drugs realise that they will not be afforded an opportunity for early release, unlike other prisoners. Prison apartheid is how I would describe it.

and

> Now that some prisoners know that they have no chance of parole, violence has increased and the whole atmosphere has become markedly hostile.

Conclusion

The above comments on the work of the independent committee of inquiry provide a schematic account of the 140-page report and the many detailed quotes taken from the survey and from interviews. The report of the independent committee of inquiry also discussed at length the problems faced by prisoners' families and their frustrations over access, location, conditions for visiting, and personal hostility. Also considered were the lack of training given to prison officers and the poor procedures which govern their selection. The independent committee of inquiry concluded that inadequate training, inappropriate selection, poor administration, lack of clearly defined policies, and bad facilities for staff and prisoners further compound the tensions outlined above.

As the independent committee of inquiry was commissioned to examine specific issues, so it concluded its report with a series of specific recommendations. These focused on all aspects of conditions: food, hygiene and sanitation, heating and lighting, health and safety, work, education, recreation, medical care, visiting and outside contact, discipline, and complaints. Also it called for more rigorous recruitment and selection of prison officers and a major expansion of officer training. It recommended the abolition of the recently constructed parole policy and that parole should be instituted as a right rather than a privilege. The seventeen recommendations represented the concern of the independent committee of inquiry with Peterhead as it exists. It considered that their implementation would be geared to developing social skills, increasing personal responsibility and autonomy, breaking down the long-established barriers between staff and prisoners, and establishing accountability within and outside the prison for the regime's policies, priorities, and practices.

In a situation as entrenched and institutionalised as Peterhead, specific recommendations such as a "good, varied menu" or the provision of "proper washing, showering and toilet facilities" are no more than a move towards damage limitation through the provision of a basic level of humane containment. It is the intention of the Prison Department to build a new prison at

Peterhead on a site adjacent to the existing prison. The rationalė behind this decision hinges on three related strands of penal policy in Scotland. First, is the tacit acceptance that people who commit "serious" crimes should be given longer prison sentences and serve all or most of those sentences. Second, is the commitment to eighteenth-century penal philosophy—that long-term prisoners should be concentrated and contained in one high security prison. Third, is the acceptance of the criticism of British prisons as being out-of-date crumbling warehouses which offer appalling conditions and the move towards a North American model of high-technology security, control, segregation, surveillance, and isolation. The vision is one of clean, sanitary conditions in which all movement within the prison is controlled centrally through electronic surveillance. It is the panopticon for the twenty-first century.

The independent committee of inquiry rejected all three emphases. It quoted from the Home Office *Handbook for Courts:* "no realistic increase in prison terms would make a substantial impact on crime rates simply by virtue of locking up the particular offenders caught, convicted and sentenced."[63] This is supported by research into the programme of reduction of imprisonment in The Netherlands, where the policy of decarceration and markedly lesser sentences has had no significant effect on increased crime rates.[64] The committee of inquiry argued that the concentration of long-term prisoners on a single site had created penal apartheid. Certainly the use of modern technology to consolidate a clear commitment to personal isolation within the context of a policy of concentration could reinforce rather than challenge the structural relations of alienation, dislocation, and confrontation. It was for these reasons that the independent committee of inquiry called for the closure of Peterhead and for the abandonment of plans for the new prison. It emphasised a commitment to the relocation of prisoners to prisons close to their homes and to the extension of Barlinnie-type special units in which thorough programmes of care and rehabilitation could be pursued.

Violence in regimes such as Peterhead is not an irrational response to a peaceful and calm situation, nor is it an aberration within an otherwise smooth-running system. It is an inevitable and rational reaction of resistance to a violent and repressive regime. Statements from prisoners, their lawyers, and their families, reports from official sources and from campaign groups and, now, the report of the independent committee of inquiry provide unequivocal evidence that during the 1970s Peterhead developed institutionally as a prison regime of extreme brutalisation and alienation. At one end of its continuum is the daily routine of bullying and intimidation. At the other is the inhumane, torturous punishment of the "cages." Standing naked before prison officers in a "cage" nine feet by six feet, the prisoner endures a full body search three times each day. The solitary confinement and personal humiliation of the "cages" represent the ultimate loss of dignity for any prisoner. Prisoners' accounts underline the ease with which untrained prison officers can exploit their absolute discre-

63. Quoted in V. Stern, *Bricks of Shame* (1987), p. 73.
64. See D. Downes and P. Mitchell, "The Origins and Consequences of Dutch Penal Policy Since 1945" (1982) 22 *Brit. J. Criminology*, pp. 325–57.

tionary powers in such situations. At all levels the regime and its operation reflect and are dominated by the institutionalisation of physical and psychological violence supported by fear and intimidation. The effects on individuals who suffer this regime cannot be assessed exactly but they are clear to those inside:

> Peterhead isn't a prison—it's something other than a prison. I watch men drifting into insanity and no one helps them. . . . After years of this misery I can honestly say that the gates are opened and it's not human beings that walk out—it's "creations." No one in here receives help.

and

> Right now I am ready to blow like I've never blown before. Everything is just building up inside me. When I go, believe me I'll go. It may be a lost cause but I'll fight Peterhead to the death.

Discussion Questions

1. Are independent inquiries into prison conditions, of the type discussed by Scraton et al., necessary as a check on official power? Why or why not?
2. Would you say that the inmates or officials are most to blame for the problems at Peterhead prison? That is, do you agree or disagree with what the authors term the "bad apple" theory of prison disorder? Explain.
3. Should inmates be penalized for trying to air their protests peacefully? If peaceful protest is ignored or repressed, are inmates justified in resorting to disruptive behavior (e.g., taking hostages) so as to voice their complaints? Why or why not?
4. Explain why you agree or disagree with the recommendations of the independent committee of inquiry.
5. The authors point out that Scottish officials have shown interest in moving toward a North American model of penology. Explain why this move is wise or unwise.

24. Privatization of Corrections and the Constitutional Rights of Prisoners

Harold J. Sullivan, Associate Professor of Government
John Jay College of Criminal Justice,
The City University of New York

At a time when increasing the role of the private sector in general government operations has attracted broad support,[1] it should come as no surprise that pressure for "privatization" has been felt by the criminal justice system. Corrections, in particular, has attracted the attention of politicians and private entrepreneurs. Dissatisfaction with the correctional system and pressure for rapid expansion of facilities have stimulated proposals for private alternatives to both public prison construction and operation.[2]

In debating the merits of proposals for privatized corrections, many in the legal and corrections community have presumed that private correctional facilities will be held to the same constitutional standards as those directly administered by the state itself. Summarizing this view, Connie Mayer has argued: "There is no legal principal to support the premise that public agencies can

1. See: S. Butler, *Privatizing Federal Spending, a Strategy to Eliminate the Deficit* (Washington: The Heritage Foundation, 1985); Carroll, "Public Administration in the Third Century of the Constitution: Supply-Side Management, Privatization, or Public Investment?" vol. 47 *Public Administration Review* 106 (January/February 1987); R. DeHogg, *Contracting Out for Human Services* (Albany: State University of New York Press, 1984); Farrell, "Public Services in Private Hands." *Venture,* July 1984, at 34; Ferris and Graddy, "Contracting Out: For What? With Whom?" 46 *Public Administration Review* 332 (July/August 1986); Main, "When Public Services Go Private." *Fortune,* May 27, 1985, at 92; E. S. Savas, *Privatizing the Public Sector* (Chatham: Chatham House, 1982).
2. See: Brakel, " 'Privatization' in Corrections: Radical Prison Chic or Mainstream Americana?" 14 *New England Journal of Civil and Criminal Confinement* 1 (Winter 1988); C. Camp and G. Camp, *Private Sector Involvement in Prison Services and Operations* (Washington, DC: U.S. Department of Justice, National Institute of Corrections, 1984); J. Mullen et al., *The Privatization of Corrections* (U.S. Department of Justice, National Institute of Justice; U.S. Government Printing Office No. 027-000-01226-4, February 1985); Savas, "Privatization and Prisons." 40 *Vanderbilt Law Review* 889 (May 1987); Wollan, "Prisons: The Privatization Phenomenon." 46 *Public Administration Review* 678 (November/December 1986); Wooley, "Prisons for Profit: Policy Considerations for Government Officials." 90 *Dickinson Law Review* 307 (Winter 1985); *Comment,* "Private Prisons." 36 *Emory Law Journal* 253 (Winter 1987).

avoid or diminish their liability by contracting to a private operator."[3] Although the U.S. Supreme Court has not yet ruled on the constitutional status of privately run correctional facilities, the Court has in a wide variety of cases addressed the circumstances under which privately owned and operated agencies, which provide services to government, are subject to constitutional restraints. These cases provide reasons to doubt the emerging conventional wisdom that the recognized rights of those confined to public correctional institutions must in all instances be protected by private facilities. If this proves correct, privatization can be used by governments to evade constitutional protections.

In an attempt to contribute to the on-going debate concerning privatization of corrections, this article identifies circumstances under which arrangements between government and private corrections contractors could jeopardize the constitutional rights of inmates. No effort is made to identify all potential legal or policy concerns arising in the private corrections context; rather the sole intent of this essay is to highlight factors which could serve to diminish both government responsibility and constitutional protections.[4]

The State Action Doctrine

Generally rights guaranteed by the U.S. Constitution are protected only from government infringement. The 14th Amendment, for example, provides that "[n]o state shall deprive any person of life, liberty or property without due process of law." According to the U.S. Supreme Court, before one can challenge an alleged denial of due process rights, he or she must first show that the deprivation results from "state action."[5] Under the state action doctrine, anyone challenging an action of an ostensibly private institution on constitutional grounds must first satisfy the court that the action under challenge is "fairly attributable to the state."[6] It is not yet clear how the Supreme Court might apply this state action doctrine to private correctional facilities. Although there have been lower court decisions relating to privatized corrections,[7] no case has as yet received a full U.S. Supreme Court review.[8] In coming to their decisions concerning private corrections, the lower courts have, of course, sought guid-

3. Mayer, "Legal Issues Surrounding Private Operation of Prison." *Criminal Law Bulletin* (July–August 1986) at 321. See also: Johnson, "What Are the Legal Problems Involved in Privatization of State/Local Corrections." 17 *Corrections Digest* 1 (April 9, 1986); Kay, "The Implications of Prison Privatization on the Conduct of Prisoner Litigation Under 42 U.S.C. Section 1983." 40 *Vanderbilt Law Review* 813 (May 1987); Robbins, "Privatization of Corrections: Defining the Issues." 69 *Judicature* 325 (April–May 1986); Robbins, "Privatization of Corrections: Defining the Issues." 40 *Vanderbilt Law Review* 813 (May 1987); Wooley, *Id.;* "Private Prisons," *Id.*
4. For comprehensive discussion of some of the broader policy and legal issues concerning privatized corrections, see: Camp and Camp, *supra* note 2; Mayer, *Id.;* Mullen; Wooley, *Id.;* "Private Prisons," *Id.*, especially at 253–260.
5. Civil Rights Cases, 109 U.S. 3 (1883).
6. *Lugar v. Edmondson Oil Co.*, 457 U.S. 922, 937.
7. See *infra*, notes 29 through 36 and accompanying text.
8. In *West v. Atkins*, 56 LW 4664 (6–21–88) the Court did find "State Action" in the actions of a private physician who had contracted with the state to provide medical services to prisoners confined in a state owned and operated correctional facility. For a further discussion of the relevance of *West* see note 27 *infra.*

ance from prior decisions of the U.S. Supreme Court concerning the applicability of constitutional restraints to private conduct. Before assessing what the lower courts have done in the private corrections field, a brief review of some of the most relevant recent Supreme Court decisions is in order.

In a series of decisions during the 1970's and early 1980's, the Court made it increasingly clear that state funding and/or regulation of a private agency is insufficient to establish the necessary state action. Generally, only those private actions that are specifically "ordered" or "initiated" by the state or in which state officials have directly participated are subject to constitutional restraint.[9]

Two Court decisions, *Rendell-Baker v. Kohn* and *Blum v. Yaretsky*[10] in particular raised issues resembling those that could arise in litigation concerning privatized corrections. The cases involved constitutional challenges to decisions of privately owned facilities, one a school for maladjusted students and the other a nursing home. Both institutions were subject to extensive and detailed governmental regulations and both served a clientele whose expenses were borne almost entirely by government. Because both institutions were so heavily reliant on government funding, it is fair to say they owed their existence to government programs, the first to a Massachusetts program requiring the state to provide education for "special needs" students[11] and the second to Medicaid coverage for nursing home expenses of indigents.[12]

In these cases the Supreme Court identified the very limited circumstances under which constitutional guidelines would apply to actions of governmentally funded and extensively regulated private institutions. In effect the Court ruled that the level of funding or the degree of overall regulation does not determine the applicability of constitutional restraints to actions of privately owned and operated institutions. In *Blum,* for example, although the Court recognized that the decision to transfer categories of patients to a lower level of nursing home care was both publicly funded and mandated by detailed regulation, if the determination concerning which specific patients would be transferred were left in private hands, the state could not be held accountable for such decisions nor would the private decision makers be required to follow 5th and 14th Amendment due process guidelines in making those decisions.[13]

From these and other recent cases[14] it has become clear that unless government compels a private actor to make a specific decision in an individual case, only direct official participation in the implementation of a policy or in

---

9. *Moose Lodge No. 107 v. Irvis,* 407 U.S. 163 (1972); *Jackson v. Metropolitan Edison Co.,* 419 U.S. 345, 351 (1974) (1982); *Blum v. Yaretsky,* 457 U.S. 991 (1982); *Rendell-Baker v. Kohn,* 457 U.S. 830 (1982).
10. *Id.*
11. *Rendell-Baker, id.* at 832–33.
12. Blum, *id.* at 1011.
13. Phillips, "The Inevitable Incoherence of Modern State Action Doctrine." 28 *St. Louis University Law Journal* 683 (June 1984), especially at 715.
14. See: *Flagg Bros., Inc. v. Brooks,* 436 U.S. 149 (1978) [discussed *infra*] and *Lugar v. Edmondson Oil,* 457 U.S. 922 (1982).

determining individual eligibility for some government mandated section or benefit will trigger constitutional restraints applicable to government action.

The exceptions to these state "compulsion" or "participation" requirements are those activities covered by the so-called "public function" doctrine. When the state turns over to a private institution a function that has traditionally been performed "exclusively" by the state,[15] the private institution in question is held to the same constitutional standards as the state itself. To date the Court has only explicitly and unequivocally recognized two such traditional and exclusive public functions: the conduct of elections which determine "the uncontested choice of public officials" and a company town that "has taken on *all* the attributes of a town."[16] Although Justice Rehnquist in *Flagg* mentioned such "functions as education, fire and police protection, and tax collection" for possible inclusion in the exclusively public functions category, he explicitly withheld judgment concerning whether government "might be free to delegate to private parties the performance of such functions and thereby avoid the strictures of the Fourteenth Amendment."[17] In considering whether the Court might recognize these and other areas as exclusively governmental functions, one commentator has observed: "[a]s of late, the Supreme Court has demonstrated little inclination toward characterizing any function as traditionally the exclusive prerogative of the State."[18] As Justice Rehnquist, himself, stated in *Flagg*, "[w]hile many functions have been traditionally performed by government, very few have been 'exclusively reserved to the State.' "[19]

In essence, in the public functions area the Court asks whether the activity in question is one that the state has exercised alone or if it is one in which the private sector has shared. This requirement of state "exclusivity," however, is not purely a question to be determined through historical research. In *Flagg Bros. v. Brooks*, the Court opens the door for a private agency to exercise, free of constitutional restraints, what had been historically an exclusive public function as long as the state continues to provide *some* potential alternative channels for redress to those adversely affected by the private party's action.[20]

The issue in *Flagg* was whether 14th Amendment due process requirements applied to "a warehouseman's proposed sale of goods entrusted to him for storage, as permitted by the New York Uniform Commercial Code."[21] The U.S. Supreme Court rejected the finding of the U.S. Court of Appeals that "New York not only had delegated to the warehouseman a portion of its sovereign monopoly power over binding conflict resolution . . . , but also let him, by

15. Jackson, *supra* note 9, at 352–353.
16. *Flagg,* 436 U.S. 149, 158, citing *Terry v. Adams,* 345 U.S. 461 (1935) and *Marsh v. Alabama,* 326 U.S. 501, 502 (1946).
17. *Flagg, id.* at 163–64.
18. Hala Ayoub, "The State Action Doctrine in State and Federal Courts." 11 *Florida State University Law Review* 893 (Winter 1984), at 915.
19. *Flagg, supra* note 13, at 158.
20. *Id.,* at 160.
21. *Id.,* at 151.

selling the stored goods, execute a lien and thus perform a function which had traditionally been that of the sheriff."[22]

Although Justice Rehnquist's opinion argued that "the settlement of disputes between debtors and creditors is not an exclusive public function,"[23] it placed greatest emphasis on the fact that within the law there were options available to block the proposed sale. It was the availability of such options that appeared to dictate the Court's conclusion that the warehouseman in question had not been delegated an exclusive public function. He had, in effect, not been delegated "exclusive" control over this alleged governmental power. The state still retained some role. As the warehouseman exercised his "private" role, he would be free from constitutional restraint. Only the state would be subject to the 14th Amendment when, and if, it were called upon to intervene.

The dissenters on the Supreme Court in *Flagg* challenged the majority's notion of "exclusivity" on a number of grounds. Justice Stevens claimed that the Court's position was based ". . . on some vague, and highly inappropriate, notion that the respondents should not complain about this state statute if the State offers them a glimmer of hope of redeeming their possessions . . . through some other state action."[24] As Justice Marshall emphasized, the alternative available to one damaged by the private use of state power may in reality prove so burdensome to the party seeking redress as practically to leave them at the mercy of the private party arguably clothed with the authority of the state.[25] In the instant case Justice Marshall pointed out that the only legal remedy available to Flagg would have required her to put up money potentially greater than the value of the goods in dispute. While the remedy in question, "replevin," was technically available, "it is also true that, given adequate funds, respondent could have paid her rent and remained in her apartment, thereby avoiding . . . [the] eviction [which later led to] the seizure of her household goods by the warehouseman."[26]

As a result of *Flagg* the question for those claiming that a private agency is exercising a "traditional" public function becomes: has the state abdicated completely its power to a private entity? If yes, and if the activity in question has been "traditionally" an "exclusively" governmental prerogative, the private party now exercising state power is bound by the constitution as if it were the state. If, however, the state retains *some* continued role in the exercise of the power in question, the private party is free from constitutional restraints as it exercises its share of what had been a governmental power.

---

22. *Id.*, at 155, quoting from 533 F.2d, at 771.
23. *Id.*, at 161.
24. *Id.*, Stevens, J., dissenting, at 172, n.8.
25. *Id.*, Marshall, J., dissenting, at 166–67.
26. *Id.*, at 167.

Privatized Corrections Litigation

Although the Supreme Court has yet to rule on any case directly relating to privatized corrections,[27] commentators who have argued that privatized corrections facilities will be subject to the same constitutional restraints as those operated by the state have found support for their position in lower Federal courts. The limited litigation to date concerning privately operated detention and corrections facilities generally supports the continued applicability of constitutional protections. The only court decision that has directly addressed issues involving private correctional facilities[28] is *Medina v. O'Niell.*[29] *Medina* concerned the detention of stowaways in a private facility pursuant to an Immigration and Naturalization Service (INS) order. Plaintiffs challenged the failure of the INS to oversee their detention, contending that the conditions within the facilities within which they were detained amounted to "punishment" in violation of their fifth amendment due process rights.[30]

Without discussing whether there was historic precedent for private detention facilities and without citing any relevant U.S. Supreme Court precedent, the *Medina* Court asserted that "detention is a power reserved to government, and is an exclusive prerogative of the state."[31] Because Congress delegated its authority over immigration to the INS and because Congress authorized the INS to designate places of detention for excludable aliens, the Court concluded that both the INS and the private facilities in which it ordered the plaintiffs detained were bound by the fifth amendment due process standards.

The question for anyone considering this case is: do its findings control the issues of the constitutional status of private corrections? The answer is unclear. If, for example, the decision is based at least in part on the Court's conclusion that the statutes demonstrate that "Congress intended the agency to furnish suitable facilities which comply with minimum due process standards,"[32] then the evident failure of the INS and the private parties detaining the plaintiffs would amount to a failure to meet statutorily imposed legal obli-

---

27. Because in *West v. Atkins, supra* note 8, Dr. West ". . . was paid approximately $52,000 annually to operate two 'clinics' each week at Central Prison Hospital" *id.* at 4665, he was considered for constitutional purposes to be a state employee. "The fact that the State employed respondent pursuant to a contractual arrangement . . . does not alter the analysis." *Id.* at 4668. "[S]tate employment is generally sufficient to render the defendant a state actor." *Id.* at 4666 citing *Lugar,* 457 U.S. at 936, n. 18. The fact that West worked within a state prison leaves unresolved the status of private prisons.
28. *Wooley, supra* note 2, at 328.
29. 589 F. Supp. 1028 (1984).
30. *Id.*, at 1032.
31. *Id.*, at 1038. The only decision cited by the District Court, *Flagg Brothers,* 436 U.S. at 157 citing *Fuentes v. Shevin,* 407 U.S. 67, 84 (1972), in fact provides no support for the conclusion that "detention is a power reserved to government." On the contrary, the decision argues that *only deprivations* of property and, by implication, liberty *by the state "or private persons whose action may be fairly treated as that of the State itself"* may be subject to constitutional challenge (emphasis added). When, or if, action of private detention facilities, or persons employed by them "may fairly be treated as that of the State itself" is *not* addressed by the decision. In citing this section of *Medina* in support of its conclusion that private prison operations will be considered state action, "Private Prisons" simply compounds this error, at 275–276.
32. *Medina,* 589 F. Supp. 1028, 1040.

gations. The application of constitutional standards would then hinge on the specific statutorily imposed tripartite relationship between the INS, the private shipping concern, and the detainees. This could leave open the question of whether in instances in which statutory requirements were less clear, treatment of detainees in a private facility would be regulated by constitutional standards.

In *Milonas v. Williams,*[33] the Court of Appeals for the Tenth Circuit focused on the degree and nature of the interactions between government and private institutions. The Court's decision upheld a Section 1983 Civil Rights judgment against a private school for violating the rights of youths who were assigned to it by the state because of behavioral problems. The Court did not find explicitly that the school performed a "public function," rather it found against the school because some students ". . . [had] been involuntarily placed in the school by state officials who were aware of, and approved of, certain of the practices which the district court has enjoined."[34] The Court's decision, however, does not make clear whether the state placement of the youths alone would trigger constitutional protections or whether the state's "approval" of the challenged practices was the determining factor in finding state action. If the state's approval of the practices was the determining factor, then the result might be different were a state to decide to follow a less pervasive regulatory policy toward private institutions in which prisoners or detainees are confined.

In discussing the *Milonas* decision, Paul B. Johnson and Ira Robbins conclude that even in the absence of a court finding that private correctional institutions perform exclusively public functions, constitutional restraints will be applied to their operations as a result of such factors as "the involuntary nature of confinement, the detailed nature of contracts between the government and the private entities, the level of government funding, and the extent of state regulation of policies and programs."[35] In support of their conclusion that funding and regulation would trigger a finding of "state action," the authors cite U.S. Supreme Court decisions in *Blum v. Yaretsky* and *Rendell-Baker v. Kohn;* yet in both those cases the Court found that state action was *not* present despite almost complete reliance on government funding of the institutions in question. On the issue of regulation state action was also found to be absent in both cases cited because the government regulation did not dictate the specific decision under challenge.[36]

It is on the basis of cases such as these that commentators have concluded that privatization cannot be used to evade constitutional protections within pri-

33. 691 F.2d 931 (1982), U.S. cert. den. 460 U.S. 1069.
34. *Id.,* at 940.
35. Robbins (1986), *supra* note 3, at 328–39, Johnson, *supra* note 3, at 4; see also "Private Prisons," *supra* note 2, at 263.
36. The *Milonas* Court, itself, recognizing the apparent conflict between its decision and that of the U.S. Supreme Court in *Rendell-Baker,* argued that the cases can be distinguished. Although both cases concerned institutions in which the state had placed "special needs" youth, the issue in *Rendell-Baker* concerned the discharge of employees at the school while *Medina* concerns the treatment of students placed at the school. "The [U.S. Supreme] Court recognized that 'in contrast to the extensive regulation of the school generally, the various regulators showed relatively little interest in the schools personnel matters.'" 102 S. Ct. 2764, cited at 940.

vate correctional facilities. This conclusion in turn has led some to warn states that they must carefully supervise private correctional facilities if they are not subsequently to become liable for possible abuses which might follow from failure to carefully supervise.[37] These warnings combined with the reasoning supporting them, however, border on the tautological. On the one hand we are told that the Courts will find state action and thus both the state and the private prison contractors are liable for constitutional violations, *because the state so heavily and comprehensively regulates* private agencies which provide correctional services. On the other hand, we are warned that because the states will be held liable, the *states ought comprehensively to regulate* private correctional facilities in order to assure they will not have to pay for abuses not of their own making. The alternative argument, that commentators on "privatization" of corrections generally ignore, is the real possibility that the state can avoid liability precisely by limiting its role in the management of private corrections agencies.[38] The question that remains is how might this be accomplished?

State Action and Privatized Corrections

Much of the constitutional litigation in the corrections area focuses on 8th Amendment challenges to prison conditions which impose "cruel and unusual punishment" and 5th and 14th Amendment challenges to the imposition of discipline without due process. Because the state would certainly retain responsibility for conviction and sentencing, it would appear improbable that the state could evade its eighth amendment requirements for assuring that no punishment is "cruel and unusual."[39] Contracts between governments and private prison operators would, however, likely address such issues as "classification," security and the use of force, discipline and "good time."[40] On such questions, it is far less clear that privatization accompanied by loose regulation could not lead to the diminution of constitutional safeguards.

In assessing the impact of "privatization" on such issues, there is no need to outline in any detail the current status of due process requirements governing such issues. The issue here is not the precise nature or adequacy of those re-

37. See, e.g., Mayer, *supra* note 3, at 321–22; Wooley, *supra* note 2, at 327–330.
38. Although Kay has recognized that by limiting its supervisory role over the details of prison administration, the state might "effectively . . . shield the private contractor from civil rights liability," she argues, in so doing the state ". . . might increase its own liability on the theory that it did not comply sufficiently with its responsibility to assure the proper care of the prisoners placed in its custody." See Kay, *supra* note 3, at 872–74. As Kay, herself acknowledges, however, no such state liability has as yet ". . . been addressed by any court." *Id.* at 873.

    In the absence of direct participation by state officials in private prison operations, it is still possible that the courts might find that the initial conviction and placement in a private prison is sufficient to implicate the state in all that follows. Since the state incarcerates an individual in a private facility, the state assumes responsibility for all that happens within. Such an approach, however, would entail the Supreme Court's carving out an exception to its overall approach to the state action doctrine. As the discussion above demonstrates, state funding or regulation of an institution, however extensive, does not make every action of the institution the responsibility of the state.
39. See: *Estelle v. Gamble,* 429 U.S. 97 (1976) and *West v. Atkins,* 56 LW 4664 (1988).
40. *Id.,* Mayer, at 316–17; Wooley, at 320–23.

quirements, rather it is whether any requirements of due process apply in privatized correctional facilities.

The fate of constitutional protections within privatized correctional facilities hinges on two factors: first, on the precise nature of the contractual relationships between the state or Federal governments on the one hand and private corrections agencies on the other; and second, on whether or not all aspects of corrections will be deemed traditionally exclusive governmental functions.

Even if a state's contract with operators of private prisons specified in detail the conditions of incarceration, including, for example, specific procedures to be followed in administering discipline and/or providing security, there are reasons to doubt that the U.S. Supreme Court would find that the requirements of the state action doctrine had been met.

If, however, state officials or employees participate directly in disciplinary proceedings or in maintaining security within "private" correctional institutions, such participation would trigger constitutional restraints. When public and private officials or employees act in concert, the actions of both are considered by the Court to be subject to constitutional limitations.[41] When, on the other hand, private actors, such as private security personnel, act independently of the state, their actions have not been viewed as controlled by constitutional restraints.[42]

If the requirements of the state action doctrine are triggered by extensive government regulation of, and participation in, specific practices of private institutions, then the greater the discretion left to such institutions, the less the chance that they or governments will be held to constitutional standards. Were governments to leave significant discretion in the hands of private prison operators over security and disciplinary matters and leave implementation of such policies to private prison employees, then the applicability of constitutional restraints would likely depend on, first, whether the courts determine that the activity in question is traditionally an exclusive public function, and second, a continuing government role in the exercise of the public function.

Although decisions concerning what constitutes a criminal offense and who may be subject to a criminal sanction are clearly both traditionally and exclusively governmental functions,[43] there is historical precedent for privately owned and operated jails and places of detention. Indeed, Travis et al. argue

41. See, e.g., *Lugar v. Edmondson Oil*, 457 U.S. 922, especially at 937 and private security cases: *Lusby v. T. G. & Y Stores Inc.*, 749 F.2d 1423, *certiorari* granted and vacated *City of Lawton, Oklahoma v. Lusby*, 106 S. Ct. 40, 88 L. Ed. 2d 33, on remand 796 F.2d 1307, *certiorari* denied 107 S. Ct. 275, 93 L. Ed. 2d 241 (1984); *El Fundi v. Deroche*, 625 F.2d 195 (1980).
42. See, e.g., *Hurt v. G. C. Murphy Co.*, 624 F. Suppl. 512, affirmed 800 F.2d 260 (1986); *Granet v. Wallich Lumber*, 536 F. Supp. 479 (1983); *Gipson v. Supermarkets General Corporation*, 564 F. Supp. 50 (1983); *Davis v. Carson Pirie Scott & Co.*, 530 F. Supp. 799 (1982); *Klimzak v. City of Chicago*, 539 F. Supp. 221 (1982); *White v. Schrivner*, 595 F.2d 140 (1979); *Hurt v. G. C. Murphy Co.*, 624 F. Supp. 512.
43. Mayer, *supra* note 2, at 320.

that the development of publicly run institutions was a response to the record of abuses in private facilities.[44]

Even before the current drive for privatized corrections gained momentum, there was extensive private involvement in providing juvenile facilities, halfway houses, and drug and alcohol rehabilitation centers.[45] For the courts to conclude that corrections is an "exclusive" public function, therefore, they will have to disregard both historical precedent and current practice. The fact of private corrections in the past means simply that corrections cannot be viewed as a function that has been traditionally "exclusively" performed by the state. Additionally the *Flagg* decision appears to permit private actors participating in the execution of even a traditional and exclusive public function to disregard constitutional restraints as long as the state provides those adversely affected by the private action some possible alternative governmental channels for protecting their interests.

Within the corrections context, if the state provided guidelines for private correctional officials in applying discipline and crediting "good time," but left actual implementation to the private prison operators, the private agents could avoid the procedural due process requirements demanded of public prisons as long as the state provided prisoners some means of appeal or some alternative channel to challenge abuse of the state guidelines. As both Justice Marshall and Stevens made clear in their *Flagg* dissents, however, alternative channels might well prove burdensome to those who must rely on them—so burdensome as to make their routine use impractical. Under such conditions the initial decisions of the private prison operators on matters of discipline and security might stand unchallenged even though those decisions were arrived at without due process.

Finally, even the need for such appeals mechanisms might be avoided if placement in a private correctional facility rather than a public one were an option selected by a convicted felon. If the state were to provide for both public and private correctional facilities, prisoners could be given a choice. The state might offer such inducements as possible early release or more rehabilitation options as an inducement to prisoners to elect the private facilities. Under such circumstances because the state has not completely abandoned the corrections field to private contractors, both the contractors and the state might be freed from liability for any alleged denial of constitutional rights within private corrections facilities.

Conclusion

At least until the U.S. Supreme Court rules definitively in a case concerning actions of private correctional institutions, we cannot assume that such institu-

44. Lawrence F. Travis et al., "Private Enterprise and Institutional Corrections: A Call for Caution." XLIX *Federal Probation* 11 (December 1985); also for a discussion of the role of the private sector in the 19th century, see generally Cody, "The Privatization of Correctional Institutions: The Tennessee Experience." 40 *Vanderbilt Law Review* 829 (May 1987); also see Mayer, *supra* note 2, at 311; Savas, *id.*, at 898; and "Private Prisons," *id.*, at 253–254. None of these authors, however, discuss the implications of the historical role of private corrections under the Supreme Court's "public function" doctrine.
45. See Camp and Camp and Mullen, *supra*, note 2.

tions must follow the same constitutional standards as those operated by the state itself. The Court's approach to the state action doctrine in recent years has raised the threshold of state involvement that is required before constitutional restraints apply to ostensibly private conduct. This shift has been led by now Chief Justice Rehnquist; it has been supported by the Court's emerging conservative majority. There is no reason to expect that this inclination to insulate actions of private institutions which provide services to the state, or in the place of the state, from constitutional constraints will not continue.

If private correctional facilities are freed from many of the constitutional constraints placed on public institutions, then both they and their government sponsors will be freed from the constant threat of Section 1983 civil rights suits from inmates. Neither they nor government would be subject to liability for denying civil rights to inmates. Because most observers have assumed that private prisons will be held to the same constitutional standards as public ones, however, many have counseled governments to regulate and control virtually every aspect of private prison operations. Such regulations have often been recommended as a means of assuring that governments will only be held liable for conditions of their own making. It is, however, possible that these regulations designed to protect governments from liability may, themselves, prove to be the mechanisms for assuring government liability. Such continued government participation in prison operations may implicate government as much or more than it may protect government.

Neither advocates nor opponents of privatization can safely assume that privatized corrections will be held to the same constitutional standards as those operated by the state itself. All must consider the real possibility that a privatized correctional institution may be free to accord inmates less rights and legal protections than a public facility. If corrections officials or political decision makers elect tightly to regulate and control the operations of private correctional facilities, they should do so because they want to assure that those confined within continue to benefit from the procedural protections afforded by the Constitution of the United States. In the absence of such continued direct government involvement, much of the limited progress made to date in assuring prisoner rights may be lost. In drawing up contracts for private correctional facilities, public officials must recognize the dangers of allowing private operators discretion over matters of such fundamental public concern. Advocates of prisoners' rights, however, should be alert to the possibility that governments will deliberately use privatization effectively to evade constitutional restraints.

Discussion Questions

1. What do you think has led to the recent privatization movement in U.S. corrections? What has been the driving force behind the movement?
2. Define the meanings of the state action doctrine and the public function doctrine. Of what relevance are these doctrines to the arguments advanced by Sullivan?
3. (a) Do you agree with Sullivan that there is *potential* for governments to evade constitutional protection of prisoners' rights through privatization? Why or why not? (b) Assuming that there *is* potential for governments to use privatization to avoid constitutional liability for prisoners' claims, is it your opinion that governments would deliberately do so? Explain.
4. How might the fears expressed by Sullivan best be put to rest?

GLOSSARY

Board of Visitors: A Board of Visitors has two primary functions. First, the Board acts as a hearing body for more serious infractions of prison rules allegedly committed by prisoners. Second, as a citizen group, the Board provides a "watchdog" function for prison administration in an effort to identify and propose solutions to prison problems.

Bunt: As used in this context, the term refers to a protest clash between inmates and officials.

Dispersal Prisons: These prisons hold inmates who have been convicted of committing a variety of felonies and who may be serving any length of sentence (i.e., from short-term to life). Dispersal prisons are distinct from institutions which hold *only* persons serving long- *or* short-term sentences.

Gaol: This is another spelling for the word "jail" and is pronounced exactly the same way.

Governor/Prison Governor: A governor is the chief administrator (warden or superintendent) of a prison.

Industrial Officer: Industrial officers are trade instructors in such areas as mechanics and carpentry.

Kapos: The term refers to concentration camp inmates who worked for the Nazi Germans so as to stay alive, at least for a short time longer.

Kasha: *Kasha* is a whole grain dish.

Mandatory Supervision: This procedure is akin to a mandatory release arrangement in the U.S., under which a prisoner is released at the expiration of the maximum term minus good time credits and then supervised in the community (ordinarily by a parole officer) for a period roughly equal to the amount of good time.

Prison Officers' Award: This refers to an industrial agreement or labor contract.

Remand: This refers to the detention of an alleged but unconvicted offender pending further court processing.

Remission: To remit a sentence is to lessen its severity in some fashion (e.g., good time or release on parole), because of good behavior and/or in accordance with the provisions of law.

RSFSR: This is the acronym for the Russian Republic of the U.S.S.R.

Samizdat: The term refers to various underground publications that are not condoned by the Soviet State.

Warders: Warders are prison guards or correctional officers.

Welfare Officers: Welfare officers deal with matters pertaining to the welfare of inmates and their relatives. While their activities are similar to those of social workers, welfare officers do not hold university degrees and are often former prison officers.

Zek: A *zek* is a political inmate, as distinct from a criminal prisoner.